FROM CHRISTIAN HEBRAISM
TO JEWISH STUDIES

STUDIES IN THE HISTORY
OF
CHRISTIAN THOUGHT

EDITED BY

HEIKO A. OBERMAN, Tucson, Arizona

IN COOPERATION WITH
HENRY CHADWICK, Cambridge
JAROSLAV PELIKAN, New Haven, Connecticut
BRIAN TIERNEY, Ithaca, New York
ARJO VANDERJAGT, Groningen

VOLUME LXVIII

STEPHEN G. BURNETT

FROM CHRISTIAN HEBRAISM
TO JEWISH STUDIES

Portrait of Johannes Buxtorf, detail from the engraved title page of
his *Lexicon Chaldaicum Talmudicum et Rabbinicum* of 1639

FROM CHRISTIAN HEBRAISM TO JEWISH STUDIES

JOHANNES BUXTORF (1564–1629) AND HEBREW
LEARNING IN THE SEVENTEENTH CENTURY

BY

STEPHEN G. BURNETT

The Frank S. and Elizabeth D. Brewer
Prize Essay for 1994
The American Society for Church History

E.J. BRILL
LEIDEN · NEW YORK · KÖLN
1996

The paper in this book meets the guidelines for permanence and durability of the Committee on Production Guidelines for Book Longevity of the Council on Library Resources.

Library of Congress Cataloging-in-Publication Data

PJ
4534
.B89
B87
1996

Burnett, Stephen G.
  From Christian Hebraism to Jewish studies : Johannes Buxtorf (1564-1629) and Hebrew learning in the seventeenth century / by Stephen G. Burnett.
      p.   cm. — (Studies in the history of Christian thought, ISSN 0081-8607 ; v. 68)
  Includes bibliographical references and index.
  ISBN 9004103465 (cloth)
  1. Buxtorf, Johann, 1564-1629. 2. Hebraists, Christian--Switzerland—Biography. 3. Hebrew language—Study and teaching (Higher)—History—17th century. 4. Bible. O.T.—Criticism, Interpretation, etc.—History—17th century. I. Title.
II. Series.
PJ4534.B89B87   1996
492.4'092—dc20
[B]   96-16632
                                                                        CIP

Die Deutsche Bibliothek - CIP-Einheitsaufnahme

Burnett, Stephen G.:
From Christian Hebraism to Jewish Studies : Johannes Buxtorf (1564 – 1629) and Hebrew learning in the seventeenth century / by Stephen G. Burnett. – Leiden ; New York ; Köln : Brill, 1996
  (Studies in the history of Christian thought ; Vol. 68)
  ISBN 90–04–10346–5
NE: GT

                    ISSN   0081-8607
                    ISBN   90 04 10346 5

uxori carissimae

CONTENTS

CONTENTS

ACKNOWLEDGMENTS

Reformation era Christian Hebraism can be a rather forbidding field of research since it touches on humanism, the history of printing, historical theology, biblical studies, and Jewish history. Without the judicious advice of individuals and the financial assistance of institutions I would not have been able to complete this book. The original research for this book was supported in part by a German Academic Exchange Service grant, a Swiss Government Grant, and a Charlotte W. Newcombe Dissertation Fellowship. A timely Research Assistance Grant from the American Academy of Religion enabled me to clear up some thorny questions I had about early modern anti-Jewish polemical writing generally. Professional support from the Norman and Bernice Harris Center for Judaic Studies at the University of Nebraska-Lincoln made it possible for me to present my research to a wider scholarly audience. I would particularly like to thank the Brewer Prize Committee of the American Society of Church History, who awarded this book the Brewer Prize in 1994.

While working on Johannes Buxtorf I have benefited constantly from the advice and encouragement of scholars from a number of fields. Dr. Joseph Freedman helped me to begin archival research in the arcane world of seventeenth century university history. Professor Hans R. Guggisberg, Dr. Martin Steinmann, director of the Basel UB manuscript department, and Dr. Andreas Staehelin, former director of the Basel Staatsarchiv, all gave generously of their time and advice. Professor Peter T. Van Rooden and his wife graciously invited me to stay with them in Leiden for a week as I examined manuscript materials in Leiden, Amsterdam and Leeuwarden, at the same time giving me the opportunity to discuss Dutch Christian Hebraism with him. M. Bernard Turrettini of Geneva had photocopies made of several Buxtorf letters that are preserved in the Turrettini Family Archive. Dr. F. Seck of Tübingen UB kindly gave permission for me to quote from his unpublished four volume collection of Wilhelm Schickhard's correspondence. Professor Thomas Willi of Greifswald University and Dr. Abraham David of the Jewish National and University Library in Jerusalem have aided me by examining manuscripts I was unable to see personally and by arranging for me to obtain copies of them. Terrance Dinovo, curator of the Lutheran Brotherhood Foundation Reformation Research Library, acquired a number of rare books on microfilm and made them available to me through Interlibrary Loan. Professor Robert Kingdon read an earlier draft of this work with scrupulous care and his comments on it were most helpful. By suggesting that I study Johannes Buxtorf, Professor Norman Roth started me on the path which had ended with this book. I have appreciated his sage advice and his willingness to help with the numerous conceptual and bibliographic problems I have encountered while writing it. I would especially like to thank Professor Heiko A. Oberman for accepting this book in the series Studies in the History of Christian Thought.

Finally, this list of acknowledgments would not be complete without mentioning my wife Amy, a friend and colleague, paleographer and linguist extraordinaire. Without her encouragement and help this book would not have been possible.

Stephen G. Burnett
Lincoln, Nebraska, USA
April 17, 1996

ABBREVIATIONS

BT   Babylonian Talmud

FFM   Fuks, L. and Fuks-Mansfeld, R. G. *Hebrew Typography in the Northern Netherlands 1585-1815: Historical Evaluations and Descriptive Bibliography.* Vol. 1: *Leiden (-1793); Franeker (-1742); and Amsterdam (1605-1655).* Leiden: E. J. Brill, 1984.

MPL   J. P. Migne, ed. *Patrologiae Latina.* 221 Vols. Paris: Siron; Vrayet, 1844-1864.

Prijs   Prijs, Joseph. *Die Basler Hebräischen Drucke (1492-1866).* Ed. Bernhard Prijs. Olten and Freiburg i. Br.: Urs Graf, 1964.

StCB   Steinschneider, Moritz. *Catalogus Librorum Hebraeorum in Bibliotheca Bodleiana.* Berlin: Ad. Friedlaender, 1852-60; reprint ed., Hildesheim: Georg Olms, 1964.

StBH   _____. *Bibliographisches Handbuch über die theoretische und praktische Literatur für hebräische Sprachkunde. Mit Zusätzen und Berichtigungen von A. Freimann, M. Grunwald, E. Nestle, N. Porges, M. Steinschneider.* Hildesheim: Georg Olms Verlag, 1976.

Voet   Voet, Leon and Voet-Grisolle, Jenny. *The Plantin Press (1555-1589): A Bibliography of the Works Printed and Published by Christopher Plantin at Antwerp and Leiden.* 6 Vols. Amsterdam: Van Hoeve, 1980-1983.

WA   *D. Martin Luthers Werke. Kritische Gesamtausgabe.* Weimar: Hermann Böhlau, 1883ff.

The following abbreviations have been used to shorten foot note references, particularly to manuscripts.

FB   Forschungsbibliothek
HAB   Herzog August Bibliothek, Wolfenbüttel.
HUC   Hebrew Union College, Cinncinati, OH.
SA   Staatsarchiv
SB   Staatsbibliothek
StA   Stadtarchiv
StB   Stadtbibliothek
UB   Universitätsbibliothek or Universiteitsbibliotheek
WLB   Württembergische Landesbibliothek, Stuttgart
ZB   Zentralbibliothek

INTRODUCTION

Young Goethe was fascinated by the Jews of his native Frankfurt. He frequently visited the walled Judengasse (Jewish quarter) with its strange sights, smells, and sounds. He was curious about their religion and way of life, and he frequently took walks there on the Sabbath. Goethe was hospitably received and well entertained by residents of the Judengasse, and was invited to a circumcision and a wedding.[1] Had Goethe merely wished to learn more about the Jews, however, he could have done so without visiting the Judengasse at all. He could have read his father's copy of Johann Jacob Schudt's *Die Jüdische Merckwürdigkeiten*, a massive four-volume work on Jewish history and life in Frankfurt.[2] Goethe could also have read the Mishnah and other important Jewish books in Latin translation. Had he wished, he could even have studied rabbinical Hebrew and Talmudic Aramaic (in addition to the biblical Hebrew which he had learned in school) with the help of textbooks written by Christian Hebraists specifically to help Christian students read the Jewish classics in their original languages.[3] In Goethe's day it was possible for non-Jews to study the Hebrew language, Jewish literature, and even Judaism without Jewish help.

Christian Hebraism was an offshoot of Renaissance humanism, and its devotees—Biblical scholars, theologians, lawyers, physicians, astronomers, philosophers, and teachers in Latin schools—borrowed and adapted ideas and literary forms from post-biblical Hebrew literature to meet Christian cultural and religious needs.[4]

---

[1] R. Po-chia Hsia, "Christian Ethnographies of Jews in Early Modern Germany," 223-235, in: *The Expulsion of the Jews: 1492 and After*, ed. Raymond B. Waddington and Arthur H. Williamson, Garland Studies in the Renaissance, vol. 2 (New York: Garland, 1994), 223. Cf. Johann Wolfgang von Goethe, *Dichtung und Wahrheit*, part 1, book 4 in: *Goethes Werke*, ed. Erich Trunz, 17 vols. (Hamburg: Christian Wegner Verlag, 1967), 9: 149-150.

[2] Ibid., 9: 667, n. 149, 31.

[3] Ibid., 9: 124.

[4] Aaron L. Katchen, *Christian Hebraists and Dutch Rabbis: Seventeenth Century Apologetics and the Study of Maimonides' Mishneh Torah*, Harvard Judaic Texts and Studies, no. 3 (Cambridge: Harvard Univ. Press, 1984), ix-x. Johannes Buxtorf the younger boasted that many kinds of scholars would benefit

Generations of Christian Hebrew scholars had created an array of
linguistic helps for Hebrew learning and had translated a number
of Jewish classics, making them accessible to a broader reading
public. They pioneered a new academic discipline, Jewish studies,
albeit in a form which catered to the needs of Christians. By making Jewish learning more accessible to the educated public these
Christian Hebraists had a profound impact upon western culture
out of all proportion to their numbers. By the same token, these
scholars created a "knowledge" of Jews, their religion, and way of
life without regard for the effects that it might have upon Jews and
Jewish communities. Christian Hebraists had, in effect, appropri-
ated Jewish literature from its rightful custodians, an exercise in
what R. Po-chia Hsia called "the dialectic of Christian power."[5]

Christian Hebraism drew its strength not only from the devotion of individual Hebraists to their discipline, but also from the
active support of schools and universities, as well as the governments and churches which funded them. What began in the late
fifteenth and early sixteenth centuries as the hobby of a few
learned churchmen and gentlemen scholars such as Cardinal Giles
of Viterbo or Johannes Reuchlin or the vocation of informal
groups of pastors and professors such as those identified with the
"Rhineland School of Biblical Exegesis" had become a recognized
academic subdiscipline a century later, linked to theology but distinct from it.[6] The rapid progress of Hebrew learning, which during this period included both the Hebrew Bible and post-biblical
Jewish literature, is all the more astonishing since it took place in

---

from his father's talmudic lexicon. "Sunt in eo multa Juridica, Medica, Physica,
Ethica, Politica, Astronomica, & aliarum scientiarum praeclara documenta, quae
istius gentis & temporis historiam mirifice commedant." Buxtorf II to the Rulers
of the States of Groningen, Basel, February, 1639, *Lexicon Chaldaicum
Talmudicum et Rabbinicum*, ed. Johannes Buxtorf II (Basel: Ludwig König,
1639; reprint ed., Hildesheim: Georg Olms, 1977), f. (*)3r.

[5] Hsia, "Ethnographies of Jews," 224.

[6] On Viterbo's patronage of Hebrew learning, see Gérard E. Weil, *Élie
Lévita. Humaniste et Massorête (1469-1549)*, Studia Post-Biblica, vol. 7
(Leiden: E. J. Brill, 1963), 81-90. Jerome Friedman discussed Reuchlin's life-
long enthusiasm for Kabbalistic learning in *The Most Ancient Testimony:
Christian Hebraica in the Age of Renaissance Nostalgia* (Athens, OH: Ohio Univ.
Press, 1983), 71-98. See also Bernard Roussel, "Un "École Rhénane
d'Exégèse" (ca. 1525-1540)," in: *Le Temps des Réformes et la Bible,* ed. Guy
Bedouelle and Bernard Roussel, Bible de Tous les Temps, no. 5 (Paris:
Beasuchesne, 1989), 215-240.

an age which witnessed the splintering of the western church into mutually hostile confessional churches. At a time when Christians pursued vicious polemical vendettas against adherents of other Christian confessions and against the Jews, the study of post-biblical Jewish literature was not only tolerated but even encouraged both by universities which championed particular confessional positions and by the interconfessional Republic of Letters. Hans Joachim Schoeps noted that during the seventeenth century, Lutheran scholars studied rabbinical literature more intensively than any other group of non-Jews before or since.[7] How did this transformation of Hebrew studies from the hobby of a few to a recognized academic pursuit take place? Which kinds of Jewish literature did Christian scholars consider most valuable for their own work, and how did they reconcile their intellectual pursuits with their moral and legal obligations to remain loyal to the official confession of their state? The career and works of Johannes Buxtorf the elder illustrate the ways in which he thought that Christian theologians could benefit from a healthy dose of Jewish education, and the extent to which his ideals were shared by other educators.

Johannes Buxtorf the elder was in many ways responsible for establishing Hebrew studies as a recognized academic discipline within early modern schools and universities. He composed a long series of grammars, dictionaries, and manuals which set a new standard for Hebrew knowledge among Christians, single-handedly replacing nearly every comparable book written by Christian Hebraists during the previous century. While Buxtorf focused his attention upon the needs of biblical scholars, his works also served to open up the wider world of post-biblical Jewish literature to Christian study. Even some of Buxtorf's Jewish comtemporaries were familiar with some of his works. R. Jacob Roman was so impressed by Buxtorf's *Bibliotheca rabbinica* that he considered translating it into Hebrew so that Jews too might benefit from it.[8] Buxtorf's critique of Judaism, *Juden Schul*, was read by Leon Modena and a number of other contemporary Jewish apologists because it was the most influential Christian interpretation of Judaism

---

[7] Hans Joachim Schoeps, *Philosemitismus im Barock: Religions- und geistesgeschichtliche Untersuchungen* (Tübingen: J. C. B. Mohr, 1952), 134.

[8] Prijs, *Drucke*, 371.

and Jewish life, and therefore the standard by which their books would be judged. By the time of his death Buxtorf had gained an academic reputation bordering upon legend.

Unfortunately the existing scholarly literature on Buxtorf has largely failed to penetrate the fog of his formidable reputation. Scholars have long recognized Buxtorf's significance for the history of theology, biblical studies, and Jewish studies, but they have usually examined only his theological works, *Juden Schul* and *Tiberias*, without relating them to his other works or to his career. They have also largely ignored his vast correspondence, study notes, unpublished works, and enormous personal collection of Hebrew books and manuscripts preserved at Basel University Library.[9] The strengths and limitations of Buxtorf's works cannot be fully explained unless they are interpreted as products of their early modern confessional university setting. Forced by economic need to seek outside employment, Buxtorf was able to hone his academic skills through his involvement in the Hebrew book trade. He censored Hebrew books for the city of Basel, corresponded in Hebrew with prospective Jewish clients, and prepared Hebrew books and manuscripts for the press. Buxtorf's activity within two distinctly different social spheres form a coherent background against which his works must be interpreted.

Buxtorf's works can be divided into three categories: pedagogical, philological, and theological. His pedagogical works—grammars, dictionaries, manuals of Hebrew poetry and letter-writing, and a guide to Hebrew bibliography—represent a fusion of Hebrew and Latin forms, appropriately packaged for use in Latin schools and universities. In substance these books consisted mostly of information mined from "the Jews' own books" so that Christians might profit from them without having to read the Hebrew origi-

---

9   The works of Peter T. Van Rooden, *Theology, Biblical Scholarship and Rabbinical Studies in the Seventeenth Century: Constantijn L'Empereur (1591-1648) Professor of Hebrew and Theology at Leiden*, trans. J. C. Grayson, Studies in the History of Leiden University, vol. 6 (Leiden: E. J. Brill, 1989), François Laplanche, *L'Écriture, Le Sacré et L'Histoire: Érudits et Politiques Protestants devant la Bible en France au XVIIe siècle*. Studies of the Institute of Intellectual Relations Between the West-European Countries in the Seventeenth Century, vol. 12 (Amsterdam: APA-Holland Univ. Press, 1986), and Emil Kautzsch, *Johannes Buxtorf der Ältere* (Basel: C. Detloff, 1879) are honorable exceptions to this rule.

nals. Buxtorf's chief philological works, his edition of the Bomberg *Biblia rabbinica* and Isaac Nathan's Hebrew Concordance, are important not only in their own right as contributions to biblical philology, but they also attest to the close links between his philological work and his theological agenda. While Buxtorf was aware of textual variations within the Hebrew Bible and understood some of the principles of textual criticism, he refused to employ them in his study of the Bible for what he considered good and sufficient reasons. The close relationship between biblical philology and theology is even more apparent in his two theological works, *Juden Schul* and *Tiberias*. Although they embodied different literary forms, the former an ethnography of the Jews and the latter a philological treatise, both works were clearly informed by the emerging high orthodox doctrine of Scripture as defined by Buxtorf's colleague Amandus Polanus and can be best understood as theological books in other guise. *Juden Schul* is a particularly fascinating work since it provides a recognizable, if unsympathetic, portrayal of contemporary German Jewish life.

Buxtorf's works together represent a milestone in the progress of Hebrew learning, and they shaped biblical studies and Jewish studies for over a century after their composition. Their importance for promoting Christian Hebraism in early modern Europe was profound, since they made Jewish learning possible without any assistance from Jews. When Reuchlin, Pico, Cardinal Viterbo and other prominent Christian Hebraists of the Renaissance wished to learn Hebrew they did so by finding Jews to tutor them; by the early seventeenth century it was possible for John Lightfoot to teach himself not only Hebrew but also talmudic Aramaic by using textbooks.[10] Buxtorf laid a philological foundation upon which the next two generations of Christian Hebraists would build. Amazingly, many of Buxtorf's books continued to be used by both Christian and Jewish scholars long after the demise of confessional academies and the emergence of both modern biblical studies and Jewish studies during the nineteenth century. Solving the riddle of Buxtorf's influence upon scholars active during the Confessional age, the Enlightenment, and the nineteenth century clarifies not

---

[10] Chaim E. Schertz, "Christian Hebraism in Seventeenth Century England as Reflected in the Works of John Lightfoot," (Ph.D. diss., New York University, 1977), 19-20.

only the impact his works had upon them and their academic disciplines, but also the uses to which Christians put the information they found in "the Jews' own books."

CHAPTER ONE

THE CAREER PATH OF A CHRISTIAN HEBRAIST

Johannes Buxtorf's contributions to Hebrew studies were shaped by his activities in two distinctly different social spheres, the university of Basel, and the Hebrew book trade. The university was an institution dedicated to serving Basel and other Reformed territories by educating religiously loyal school teachers, clergymen, physicians, and lawyers. Its professors were obligated by oath, conscience, and law to uphold the Reformed confession. The Hebrew book trade, by contrast, was a business almost entirely devoted to preserving and encouraging the cultural and religious viability of Judaism. Jewish sponsors paid for the printing of books and handled their distribution to Jewish communities throughout Europe. Non-Jews were involved only in censoring individual books before they were printed, printing them, and in overseeing the Hebrew book market to ensure that no book containing blasphemy or sedition could be purchased. To measure Buxtorf's achievements in biblical studies and Jewish studies it is first necessary to understand how his experiences in these two distinctively different societies informed his academic work. This chapter will examine how Buxtorf fit into the academic world of the seventeenth century, shaped by the confessional school and the supraconfessional Republic of Letters.

The German border territory of Westphalia was a bubbling cauldron of political, social, and religious conflicts during the late sixteenth century. These disputes became even more charged when territorial princes—whether Catholic, Lutheran, or Reformed—attempted to impose religious conformity upon their often unwilling subjects.[1] In addition to the religious diversity among the

---

[1] Heinz Schilling, "Confessionalization in the Empire: Religious and Societal Change in Germany between 1555 and 1620," in: idem, *Religion, Political Culture and the Emergence of Early Modern Europe. Essays in German and Dutch History*, trans. Stephen G. Burnett, Studies in Medieval and Reformation Thought, no. 50 (Leiden: E. J. Brill, 1992), 216-222.

Germans themselves there were also ethnic and religious minorities in various Westphalian towns, including Dutch Calvinists, Mennonites, and Jews.[2] Westphalia proved to be a particularly fertile recruiting ground for adherents of the Reformed confession and when the Reformation finally reached the town of Kamen it was in a Calvinist form.

Johannes Buxtorf was born into a leading family of the social elite of Kamen, a territorial town in the County of Mark (Westphalia) on December 25, 1564.[3] His grandfather Joachim Buxtorf had served as burgomaster of Kamen for thirty years, and his uncle Joachim was a councillor to the Count of Waldeck.[4] Buxtorf's father Johannes was a pastor in Kamen from 1556 until his death in 1581/2, and played an important role in the introduction of Protestantism there between 1562 and 1567.[5] He married Maria Volmar in 1563 and Johannes was probably their only child.[6]

All that is known of Buxtorf's childhood are the bare outlines of his education. He first attended the Latin school in Hamm (Westphalia) where he also received his first Hebrew instruction, and then he studied at the *Archigymnasium* in Dortmund where he was a student of Friedrich Beurhusius, a famous Ramist philosopher. He left Dortmund and returned to Kamen briefly after his father's death in 1581/2.[7] According to his eulogist Tossanus,

---

[2] R. Po-chia Hsia, *Society and Religion in Münster, 1535-1618*, Yale Historical Publications, Miscellany, no. 131 (New Haven: Yale Univ. Press, 1984), 199.

[3] Heinz Schilling provides a social definition of elite status in Westphalian cities during this period in "The Rise of Early Modern Burgher Elites during the Sixteenth and Seventeenth Centuries," in: idem, *Religion*, 142-144.

[4] Hermann Steinmetz, "Waldeckischen Beamten vom Mittelalter bis zur Zeit der Befreiungskriege (Fortsetzung)," *Geschichtsblätter für Waldeck* 56 (1964): 81-2, and Joachim Buxtorf to Leo Curio, Korbach, October 31, 1592, Basel UB Ms G I 66: 52-53. This letter was translated into German by Karl Buxtorf-Falkeisen in *Johannes Buxtorf Vater, Prof. ling. hebr., 1564-1629, erkannt aus seinem Briefwechsel* (Basel: Bahnmaier's Buchhandlung (C. Detloff), 1860), 1-3.

[5] Friedrich Buschmann, "Geschichte der Stadt Camen," *Zeitschrift für vaterländische Geschichte und Altertumskunde* (Münster) 4 (1841): 231-232.

[6] Friedrich Wilhelm Bauks, *Die evangelischen Pfarrer in Westfalen von der Reformationszeit bis 1945*, Beiträge zur Westfälischen Kirchengeschichte, Bd. 4 (Bielefeld: Luther-Verlag, 1980), 73.

[7] Johannes Buxtorf, *Praeceptiones de Grammaticae Lingua Hebraea* (Basel: Conrad Waldkirch, 1605), ff. (:)2v-(:)3r. Buxtorf dedicated this book to the City

Buxtorf began his university studies at the University of Marburg before enrolling at the *Gymnasium Illustre* at Herborn.[8]

Herborn was located in the County of Nassau-Dillenberg and its ruler, Count John VI, was a recent convert to Calvinism. He was determined to impose the Reformed confession upon his subjects and he founded the Herborn Academy to further his religious and political goals by providing his domain and neighboring territories with a steady stream of clergymen, physicians and civil servants who had received a thorough Calvinist education.[9] In Buxtorf's day it was a composite school, consisting of a *Paedagogium* or secondary school with six grade levels and a university-level institution with philosophy and theology faculties.[10] Herborn could offer "university level" instruction, but was not a recognized university and it could not grant officially recognized degrees because only the emperor and the pope had the legal right to charter universities within the territories of the German Empire. They were by no means prepared to offer a charter to Herborn since they were bitterly opposed to Calvinism which they perceived as a threat to both imperial authority and to the Catholic church.[11] The lack of accreditation was not a professional barrier for law and medical graduates of Reformed academies, but presented problems for

---

Council of Hamm/Westfalen, and mentioned Guido Fabricius, his school master and first Hebrew teacher. Daniel Tossanus, *Johannis Buxtorfii, Senioris, Linguae Sanctae in Academia Basileensi Professoris Publici, Vita et Mors, Quam Oratione Parentali, in frequenti Theologorum Auditorio, Basil, d. 22. Octobr. Anno M. DC. XXIX* (Basel: Ludwig König, 1630), 6.

[8] Ibid. Buxtorf did not matriculate at Marburg, and apart from Tossanus' oration there is no evidence that he studied there. Cf. *Catalogus studiosorum scholae Marpurgensis*, ed. Julius Caesar, 23 fascicles (Marburg: Elwert, 1872-1913), 7: 4-16 for the matriculation lists of 1581-4.

[9] On the use of schools and universities to further confessional politics in Germany, see Heinz Schilling, "The Second Reformation—Problems and Issues," in: idem, *Religion*, 255-256 and n. 18.

[10] Joseph S. Freedman described the different types of institutions of of higher learning during this period in "Philosophy Instruction within the Institutional Framework of Central European Schools and Universities During the Reformation Era," *History of Universities* 5 (1985): 118-122. The term "composite school" is his (121).

[11] Gerhard Menk, *Die Hohe Schule Herborn in ihrer Frühzeit (1584-1660): Ein Beitrag zum Hochschulwesen des deutschen Kalvinismus im Zeitalter der Gegenreformation*, Veröffentlichungen der Historischen Kommission für Nassau, no. 30 (Wiesbaden: Historischen Kommission für Nassau, 1981), 124-125.

theology and philosophy graduates. These students either had to attend an officially chartered university in order to receive a recognized degree, or work in a city or country where Calvinism was the state confession.[12]

Buxtorf arrived in Herborn some time in 1585, the second year of the school's existence, and remained there until late March of 1588.[13] He studied theology and his course of study can be reconstructed with some confidence.[14] In 1585 lecture courses were offered in Hebrew, taught from the Psalms and the "books of Solomon;" theology from the Old Testament Prophets, the Gospels, and Epistles; and systematic theology taught from Calvin's *Institutes*. In addition to attending lectures, theology students were required to deliver orations and sermons periodically, and they also responded to disputations delivered by professors or older students. Wednesdays and Saturdays were devoted to these activities

---

12 Ibid., 126-128.

13 Gottfried Zedler and Hans Sommer, *Die Matrikel der Hohenschule und des Paedagogiums zu Herborn*, Veröffentlichungen der historischen Kommission für Nassau, Nr. 5 (Wiesbaden: J. E. Bergmann, 1908), 7, no. 22. The earliest indication of when Buxtorf arrived in Herborn is the first entry in his *Album Amicorum*, Basel UB Ms AN VI 26z (no foliation) by Paul Olevianus in Herborn on October 3, 1585. An *Album Amicorum* (*Stammbuch*) was a souvenir book often kept by students of Buxtorf's time. Students would ask friends, fellow students who were of the nobility, professors, and famous men to sign their autographs in these books. See Erich Trunz, "Der deutsche Späthumanismus als Standeskultur," in: *Deutsche Barockforschung. Dokumentation einer Epoche*, ed. Richard Alewyn, Neue wissenschaftliche Bibliothek (Cologne: Kiepenheuer & Witsch, [1966]), 169-170. Johannes Piscator wrote a letter of introduction for Buxtorf and Robert Howie to Johann Jacob Grynaeus, Professor of Theology at the University of Basel on the 25th of March, 1588, Basel UB Ms G II 9: 943-944. Buxtorf probably left Herborn shortly afterwards, because he was in Worms on April 2 according to an entry in his *Album Amicorum*.

14 Buxtorf's name appears on a list of students who requested permission to practice preaching which was enclosed with a letter from the rector Johannes Piscator to Johann the Elder, Count of Nassau, Herborn, April 19, 1587, Wiesbaden SA Abt. 171R 1334b: 215r. I have reconstructed Buxtorf's course of study from a course list for 1585 which was printed in *Leges Scholae Herbornensis: Quam nuper Illustris Ac Generosis Dominus Iohannes Comes A Nassovv Catzenelnbogen, Dietz, Vianden: Dominus in Bielstein & c. in oppido Herborna feliciter aperuit* ([Neustadt a. d. Weinstraße: Matthaeus Harnisch], 1585), ff. A4r-B1r (Leiden UB 515 C 8 no. 3); and an unpublished faculty report, *Consilia und bedencken des Schulraths, und Professorum zue Herborn ... 1587*, Wiesbaden SA Abt. 171H 322C. Johann Herman Steubing, *Geschichte der hohen Schule Herborn* (Hadamer: Gelehrten Buchhandlung, 1823), 38-39, claimed that it was written on February 1, 1587, without providing evidence for his dating.

although, according to Steubing, not all of these exercises were performed on any given day. For example, every month two of the theology students were to respond during public disputations.[15]

Buxtorf had the opportunity to study theology with Caspar Olevian (1536-1587) and Johannes Piscator (1546-1625) during his time at Herborn. Olevian had taught theology at the University of Heidelberg from 1560 until 1576, when he was forced to leave Heidelberg because of a Lutheran purge of the university faculty. He was best known for co-authoring the Heidelberg Catechism with Zacharias Ursinus in 1562, a work of pivotal importance for the spread of Calvinism in Germany.[16] Olevian was probably responsible for most of the systematic theology and New Testament lectures given at Herborn until his death on March 10, 1587. He published textbooks on the Gospels, the Epistles to the Romans, Philippians and Colossians, an epitome of Calvin's *Institutes*, and an explanation of the apostles' creed and articles of faith, in addition to numerous volumes of sermons.[17]

Johannes Piscator was not as well known as Olevian when he began teaching at Herborn, but subsequently became a prolific writer who developed a reputation that drew students from all parts of Europe to the school.[18] Piscator's responsibilities during Buxtorf's time included teaching logic, Hebrew language, and other unspecified theology courses; he also served as the school's rector from 1584-1590.[19] Hebrew language instruction was not Piscator's major interest in teaching or research, but he wrote an introductory Hebrew grammar, probably to support his own classroom in-

---

[15] Steubing, *Herborn*, 111.

[16] See Gerhard Menk, "Caspar Olevian während der Berleburger und Herborner Zeit (1577-1587). Ein Beitrag zum Selbstverständnis des frühen deutschen Kalvinismus," *Monatshefte für Evangelische Kirchengeschichte des Rheinlandes* 37/38 (1988-1989): 139-204.

[17] Hermann Steubing, "Lebensnachrichten von den Herborner Theologen. Aus dem literarischen Nachlasse des D. Johann Hermann Steubing. Erste Lieferung. Caspar Olevian und Johannes Piscator," *Zeitschrift für historische Theologie* (Leipzig) 11/3 (1841): 95-97.

[18] Ibid., 104-105. For discussions of Piscator's life and works see Steubing, "Lebensnachrichten," Frans Lukas Bos, *Johannes Piscator; ein Beitrag zur Geschichte der reformierte Theologie* (Kampen: Kok, [1932]) and Menk, *Herborn*, passim.

[19] H. Steubing, "Lebensnachrichten," 104-106 and n. 7.

struction.[20] He recognized, however, that Hebrew instruction be-
yond an introduction to biblical Hebrew might be desirable. Five
years after Buxtorf's departure Piscator solicited the gift of a
Babylonian Talmud for Herborn from Count Wilhelm Ludwig,
Stadholder of the Dutch province of Friesland and eldest son of
Count Johann VI of Nassau-Dillenberg.[21]

The place of Hebrew language instruction in the curriculum at
Herborn was spelled out in the *Concilia* of 1587. The professors
apparently undecided about what role Hebrew literature should
play in curriculum.

> Concerning the Hebrew language, however, there are two opinions: some
> think that it is necessary only for theology, while others think that books of
> such learning and skill have been written in the Hebrew language that their
> equal has never appeared in Greek or Latin. Thus both parties hold the
> Hebrew language in great honor. One can see from this indeed that it is not
> desirable to exclude these three great languages—Latin, Greek and
> Hebrew—from a good school. However, because the Hebrew authors in
> the arts and philosophy are unknown at this time, we will continue with the
> practice of considering it a theological language.[22]

The admission by some of the faculty that Hebrew works in the
Liberal Arts and philosophy could rival works in Greek and Latin
is striking. Their refusal to encourage more advanced Hebrew
training was practical and not an indication of theological bias.[23]

---

[20] *Rudimenta linguae Hebraicae* (Leiden: Officina Plantiniana, Apud
Franciscum Raphelengium, 1588) in 4° (HAB call no. Alv Kf 128). Steubing
and Steinschneider wrongly gave the city of publication as Frankfurt am Main.
See Steubing, "Lebensnachrichten," 137 and StBH, no. 1573.

[21] Johannes Piscator to Johann Eulner, Herborn, March 30, 1593, Wiesbaden
SA, Abt. 171Z 1931: 7. On Count Wilhelm Ludwig see Menk, *Herborn*, 33, 58-
59.

[22] "Uber der hebraischen Sprachen ist aber zweirleÿ mainungk, dem etlich
halten dafur, sie sei nuhr zur Theologia nöttig, andere aber meinen, das auch in
hebraischen Sprachen buchern noch von weltlichen weisheit, verfassen sein,
solchen lehre und kunste, das sie so gut nochniemals weder in grigisch noch in
lateinisch sprach sein kohnen, halten beide Partheÿen, die hebraische sprach in
grossen ehren. Hieraus siehet man wol, das diese drei sprachen, lateinisch,
Grichisch, hebraisch, bei einer gueten schulen nicht mögen vnderlassen werden,
weil aber die hebraischen authores artium und Philosophia noch zur zeit un-
bekandt, bleibts auch noch bei den gebrauch, das man solche sprach zu Theologia
sprach." *Concilia*, Wiesbaden SA 171H 322C, f. 28v.

[23] The abysmal state of Hebrew bibliography during this period did not encourage schoolmen to incorporate further Hebraica into the curriculum. See below, chap. 5.

Johannes Buxtorf was to devote himself in the course of his scholarly career to making these Hebrew authors known, and to providing the philological tools necessary for Christian scholars to use them. He might have become interested in the problem because of the concern expressed by Piscator and other professors at Herborn.

Buxtorf's ongoing relationship with Piscator after he left Herborn illustrates how far he had progressed beyond the instruction that he received there. Piscator sent a copy of his *Rudimentis Linguae Hebraicae* to Buxtorf in 1606 or 1607 to have it printed in Basel by Conrad Waldkirch. Buxtorf sent the work back to him for correction, because it contained no discussion of the Qal Passive Participle. Buxtorf offered to take responsibility for its publication should Piscator resubmit it, but he apparently never sent it back since it was never published in Basel and does not appear in Steubing's bibliography.[24] While the two men remained on friendly terms, Piscator was not shy to admit that his former student had surpassed him as an Hebraist.[25]

Buxtorf's educational plans after his studies at Herborn are a matter of dispute. Tossanus claimed that Buxtorf wished to study at Heidelberg, but the presence of invading Spanish troops in the area convinced him to move on to Switzerland. While there he planned to study with Johann Jacob Grynaeus at Basel, Heinrich Bullinger and Hospinian at Zürich, and Theodore Beza in Geneva.[26] Fortunately a few surviving letters of introduction and Buxtorf's *Album Amicorum* (*Stammbuch*) make it possible to reconstruct Buxtorf's journey to Basel, and his possible motivations for staying there.

Buxtorf's uncle Joachim, an alumnus of Basel University, suggested that he travel to Switzerland in order to further his theolog-

---

[24] Kautzsch suggested (*Buxtorf*, 13) that Piscator sollicited Buxtorf's help in his Bible translation work, but there is no evidence for this in Buxtorf's surviving correspondence with Piscator where Buxtorf only briefly mentioned the translation. See Johannes Buxtorf to Johannes Piscator, n. p. September 10, 1607, Gotha FB Ms. Chart. A 130, f. 134, printed in Earnst Salomon Cyprian, *Clarorum virorum epistolae CXVII e Bibliothecae Gothanae Autographis* (Leipzig: Jo. Frider. Gleditsch & Filium, 1714), 154-155. For Piscator's bibliography see H. Steubing, "Lebensnachrichten," 125-138.

[25] Tossanus, *Buxtorfii*, 7.

[26] Ibid. Both Bullinger and Hospinian were dead by this time. Kautzsch, *Buxtorf*, 13.

ical studies.[27] Before Buxtorf left Herborn, he and his fellow student Robert Howie asked Johannes Piscator to write them a letter of introduction to Johann Jacob Grynaeus. In this letter, dated March 25, 1588, Piscator explained that the two students planned to further their theological studies at Zürich after their three years of study at Herborn.[28] This letter suggests that Buxtorf had no plans to study at the University of Heidelberg. Kautzsch plausibly suggested that Buxtorf's trip to Switzerland was probably planned as an *iter litterarium*.[29] Travelling to other universities was an accepted part of a student's education during this period and an *iter litterarium* provided the opportunity to meet famous scholars and make future professional contacts.[30]

Buxtorf's *Album Amicorum* provides a detailed chronology of the actual journey to Basel and his travels afterward during 1589.[31] Buxtorf and Howie left Herborn around March 26, 1588 and travelled to Heidelberg, after first stopping in Worms to see another former Herborn student, Albertus Hankrot.[32] The two students probably stayed no longer than a week in Heidelberg. Howie visited his old friend and countryman John Johnston, who provided him with a second letter of introduction to Johann Jacob Grynaeus.[33] While there Buxtorf had the chance to meet Franciscus Junius, Georg Sohn, and Daniel Tossanus, all professors of theology at the University of Heidelberg.[34] Buxtorf and Howie were in

---

[27]   Joachim Buxtorf to Leo Curio, Korbach, October 31, 1592, Basel UB Ms G I 66: 52-3, translated in Buxtorf-Falkeisen, *Buxtorf*, 1. Cf. Wackernagel, *Matrikel*, 2: 243.

[28]   Johannes Piscator to Johann Jacob Grynaeus, Herborn, March 25, 1588, Basel UB Ms. G II 9: 943-4. On Robert Howie, see James K. Cameron, ed., *Letters of John Johnston c. 1565-1611 and Robert Howie c. 1565-c.1645* (Edinburgh and London: Oliver & Boyd, 1963).

[29]   Kautzsch, *Buxtorf*, 13.

[30]   Trunz, "Späthumanismus," 162-164.

[31]   *Stammbuch Johannes Buxtorfs (Vater)*, Basel UB Ms AN VI 26z (no foliation).

[32]   Ibid., and Hankrot on April 2, 1588.

[33]   John Johnston to Johann Jacob Grynaeus, Heidelberg, April 17, 1588, Basel UB Ms G II 6: 123-4, printed in Cameron, *Letters*, 4-6. Apparently Howie was not positive that he wished to study in Zürich and wanted to make provision for himself in Basel as well.

[34]   Buxtorf definitely spent at least five days in Heidelberg. The *Album* entries begin on April 12 with Ludovicus Hofius and Junius, continue on April 15 with Sohn and Tossanus and end on April 17 with John Johnston. If Buxtorf studied

Basel by April 28, because on that date he met Johann Jacob Grynaeus.[35] Buxtorf travelled on to Zürich, but probably did not spend more than a week there.[36] He returned to Basel and registered as a student at the University in either May or June of 1588, Howie having matriculated there in April.[37]

The University of Basel enjoyed a period of great popularity between 1570 and 1620.[38] The medical and law faculties benefited from Basel University's unique status as a Protestant university with a titular Catholic Chancellor, the Bishop of Basel.[39] Graduates in these fields were able to work in both Catholic and Protestant areas thanks to this unusual arrangement.[40] The theology faculty was also a factor in drawing foreign students to Basel, chiefly because of Johann Jacob Grynaeus. Grynaeus who had gained an international reputation thanks to his short tenure at the University of Heidelberg. Count Johann Casimir of the Palatinate had asked Grynaeus in 1584 to accept a professorship at Heidelberg in order to help restore the theological faculty and student body to a Reformed confessional standard. Grynaeus taught at Heidelberg for two years and returned to Basel in 1586 to accept the position of *Antistes*, chief pastor of Basel, and to become the Professor of New Testament, the top position on the theological faculty.[41]

---

at Marburg, as Tossanus asserted, he may have met Sohn there since he was professor of Hebrew and Old Testament at Marburg before his call to Heidelberg.

[35] *Stammbuch* (no foliation).

[36] Buxtorf met Johann Stucki, Prof. of Theology on May 4, Heinrich Wolf, deacon at the Grossmünster church on May 5, and with Johann Rudolf Stumph, the chief pastor (*Antistes*) of Zürich on May 8.

[37] Wackernagel, *Matrikel*, 2: 363 (Buxtorf) and 2: 361 (Howie). According to his *Stammbuch*, Buxtorf did not travel to Geneva until the summer of 1589.

[38] Andreas Staehelin, *Geschichte der Universität Basel 1632-1818*, Studien zur Geschichte der Wissenschaften in Basel, vols. IV-V, 2 vols. (Basel: Helbing & Lichtenhahn, 1957), 93.

[39] Ibid., 21-22. The Bishop of Basel remained the Chancellor of Basel University even after the Reformation, although he had little or nothing to do with the governance of the university.

[40] Andreas Staehelin, "Die Universität Basel und Ihre Deutschen Besucher von 1580 bis 1620," in: Ulrich Im Hof and Suzanne Stehelin, eds. *Das Reich und die Eidgenossenschaft 1580-1650*, 1982, 7. Kolloquium der Schweizerischen Geisteswissenschaftlichen Gesellschaft (Freiburg/U: Universitätsverlag, 1986), 14.

[41] Johann Jacob Grynaeus is an important, but little studied, figure in the history of Basel University. See Johann W. Herzog, *Athenae Rauricae sive Catalogus Professorum Academicae Basileensis ab anno MCCCCLX ad annum MDCCLXXVIII*, 2 vols. (Basel: Car. Aug. Serini, 1778-1780), 1: 29-34, and

How long Buxtorf originally planned to study in Basel is unknown; his stay there could have been simply one more stop on his
iter litterarium. Grynaeus, however, was able to convince Buxtorf
to stay in Basel. He recognized Buxtorf's potential as a scholar and
his personal qualities and recommended him to his friend Leo
Curio as a tutor for his children. Buxtorf accepted the offer and
lived with the Curio family for the next six years.[42]

Grynaeus asked Buxtorf to accept a professorship of Hebrew on
the Arts faculty in late summer of 1588, even though he had not
yet received a Master of Arts degree.[43] Before tendering the offer,
however, Grynaeus also almost certainly examined Buxtorf's theological credentials. In his role as *Antistes*, Grynaeus was in the
midst of a struggle to steer the Basel church and university away
from the less dogmatic stance they had had under Simon Sulzer's
tenure as *Antistes* into a more thorough-going form of Reformed
orthodoxy. In 1590, the year that Buxtorf became a regular professor of Hebrew, Grynaeus promulgated a new church ordinance
for Basel and the countryside under its jurisdiction which required
that all pastors undergo a theological examination to prove their
doctrinal soundness.[44] Herborn-trained Buxtorf was apparently
comfortable with Basel's confessional stance and agreed to serve as
acting professor of Hebrew, but was unwilling to accept a perma-
nent appointment. Whether he did not accept the regular professorship out of sheer modesty, as Tossanus maintained, or because he

---

Fritz Buri, "Johann Jacob Grynaeus," in: *Der Reformation Verpflichtet: Gestalten
und Gestalter in Stadt und Landschaft Basel aus fünf Jahrhunderten* (Basel:
Christoph Merian, 1979), 55-58.
   [42] "Lustratis feliciter praedictis urbibus, & cum nihil minus in animo haberet,
quam hic pedem figere, tantum apud ipsum valuit D. Johannis Jacobi Grynaei
beatissimae m. authoritas, ut illius consilio & suasionibus morem geret. Cum
enim sanctissimus ille vir singularem, pro suâ agchinoia, animadverteret in nostro
Buxtorffio judicii acrimoniam, indefessum studium, morum probitatem, non
tantum singulari amore ipsum complexus est, sed etiam omnibus modis, ut hîc
retineretur allaboravit. Quod quo facilius idipsum obtineret, de honestâ conditione
ipsi prospexit apud D. Leonem Curionem, Magni illius Caelii Secundi Curionis
filium, de quo plura mox erunt dicenda." Tossanus, *Buxtorfii*, 7-8. See also
Joachim Buxtorf to Leo Curio, Korbach, October 31, 1592, Basel UB Ms G I
66: 52-53.
   [43] Buxtorf's predecessor, Israel Ritter, died on February 14, 1588. *Athenae
Rauricae*, 444.
   [44] Max Geiger, *Die Basler Kirche und Theologie im Zeitalter der
Hochorthodoxie* (Zürich: Evangelischer Verlag, 1952), 41-49.

did not wish to stay in Basel is not clear.[45] According to his colleague Wolleb, Buxtorf had not planned to stay in Basel permanently even after he accepted a regular professorship.[46]

Whether Buxtorf attended classes at the University of Basel during his student years there, in addition to teaching Hebrew, is also unknown. He participated as a respondent in one theological disputation under the direction of Johann Jacob Grynaeus on June 20, 1588.[47] The only other extant records of Buxtorf's student activities are a poster announcing his public disputation, the final requirement for graduation, on August 6, 1590 and a broadsheet of poems written by his friends to honor the occasion on August 8, 1590.[48] Buxtorf's disputation was not a Hebrew-related topic, but a philosophical one: "Whether or not animals are wholly without reason." Kautzsch wryly noted that no record of Buxtorf's position on this truly debatable question exists since the disputation itself was not preserved.[49]

While Buxtorf had come to Basel to study theology, he took his degree as a Master of Arts. Theology students were not absolutely

[45] Kautzsch, *Buxtorf*, 14, and Johannes Wollebius, *Leichen Predigt über Johannes Buxtorf, den 14. September 1629*, in: *Christliche Leich=und Trost-Predigten Darinn allerhand außerlesene Text heiliger Schrifft/ auß dem Alten und Newen Testament/ grundlich erkläret/ nutzlich appliciert, auff läidige Trawr=und Todes-fähl gerichtet/ beneben auch Christlicher Ehren-leuthen seliges Absterben beschreiben wird* (Basel: Georg Decker, 1657), 860. (Basel SA Sig. Bibl. LB 1) Buxtorf's temporary appointment does not appear in the University records, but record keeping by the academic Senate at the University of Basel was somewhat casual during the sixteenth and seventeenth centuries, and such events as the appointment of an acting professor could easily have gone unrecorded. See Staehelin, *Geschichte*, 19. Buxtorf's appointment was recorded in the list of professors of Hebrew recorded in Basel UB Ms Ki Ar 56, f. 83r, and in a handwritten note in Basel UB Ms VB O 11b, vol. 3, p. 11.

[46] "Als er aber widerumb härkommen, und eben damalen die hebraische Profession vacierte, hat er in dem Jahr Christi 1591 sich in gedachter Profession angefangen brauchen zu lassen, nicht so vast auß Vorhaben, allhier zu verbleiben, und sich um solche zu bewerben, als sich selbst zu üben, und sein zeit, die er hie zu verbleiben gesinnet war, wol anzulegen." Wolleb, *Buxtorf*, in *Predigten*, 859.

[47] *ANASKEUE Opinionis a Petro de Aliaco, Cardinale Cameracensi, de Coena Dominica olim repetite: de qua in publica Disputatione 20. Iunij, Preside Iohanne Iacobo Grynaeo, respondebit Iohan. Bvxdorfivs, Westphalvs* (Basel: Oporinus, 1588). (Basel UB Ki Ar H III 34, no. 20).

[48] The official announcement poster is preserved in Basel UB Ms VB 11b, p. 77 and his friends' poster in Basel UB Ms EL I f. 191r.

[49] *Utrum bestiae rationis sint omnino expertes necne?* Kautzsch, *Buxtorf*, 14.

obligated to complete a MA degree before studying theology, but
to earn a theology degree they had to meet a rigorous set of requirements, including the completion of a specific number of disputations, declamations and other exercises. Seven years of
theological study at Basel and other schools were usually required
in order to receive a theological degree.[50] Presumably Buxtorf
studied toward a MA degree from Basel, in order to regularize his
previous education at Herborn, and perhaps also to earn a degree
that would qualify him to be a regular professor at the University
of Basel itself.

Buxtorf completed the remainder of his *iter litterarium*, as described by Tossanus, during August of 1589 when he visited Bern,
Geneva, and Lausanne. Buxtorf began his journey during late July
or early August and travelled first to Bern where he met Abraham
Musculus, a prominent theologian and pastor.[51] Then he travelled
to Geneva where he met Theodore Beza, Calvin's successor as head
pastor of the Genevan church.[52] Afterward he visited Lausanne,
where he met Cornelius Bonaventura Bertram, who was professor
of Hebrew at the Lausanne academy. Buxtorf's acquaintanceship
with Bertram was one of the few that he had with Christian
Hebraists before he himself became a regular professor at Basel
University.[53] Buxtorf was back in Basel again by September 4.[54]

Buxtorf made a number of close friends during his student days
in Basel. His two earliest extant letters are addressed to Jacob
Zwinger, then a medical student at Padua, the son of famous Basel
humanist Theodore Zwinger.[55] Buxtorf's daughter Magdalena later

---

[50] Staehelin, *Geschichte*, 101, 179.
[51] Buxtorf was still in Basel on July 29 (*Stammbuch* entry for Tobias
Engelman), and met Musculus on August 9 (*Stammbuch*).
[52] Buxtorf met Beza on August 13. Ibid.
[53] Another acquaintanceship which he made during this period was with
Johannes Pistorius of Basel. The only evidence for this is a Hebrew manuscript
(undated) in the Basel library which contains six Hebrew biblical texts set to mu-
sic (Basel UB Ms A XII 16), written in honor of J. Buxtorf. Presumably Buxtorf
met Pistorius in 1588, before Pistorius' conversion to Catholicism. See *Religion
in Geschichte und Gegenwart*, 3d ed., s. v. "3. Pistorius, Johann."
[54] *Stammbuch* entry for Edward Jordan in Basel, Basel UB Ms AN VI 26z
(no foliation).
[55] Johannes Buxtorf to Jacob Zwinger, Basel, January 18, 1593, Basel UB
Ms Fr Gr II 8: 257. and idem to idem, Basel. August 4, 1593, Basel UB Ms Fr
Gr II 9: 89. The latter is printed and translated in Carl Roth and Th. Schmidt,
Handschriftsproben zur Basler Geistesgeschichte (Basel: R. Geering, 1926), no.

married Jacob Zwinger's son Theodore II.[56] He also became a close friend of another medical student, Pascalis Gallus (Le Coq). As a parting gift Gallus gave Buxtorf a copy of David de Pomi's Hebrew lexicon *Semah David*.[57] In 1611 when Robert Boyd, rector of the French Protestant academy at Saumur, tried to persuade Buxtorf to accept an academic call there, Gallus also wrote to Buxtorf as a part of the effort.[58] Kaspar Waser, later Antistes of Zürich and professor of Hebrew at its academy, became a lifelong friend of Buxtorf while they studied together at Basel. While only seven letters from Waser to Buxtorf are extant, the 54 surviving letters from Buxtorf to Waser reflect a close friendship which ended only with Waser's death in 1625.[59] The most enduring "friendship" Buxtorf made during his student days, however, was with Margaretha Curio, one of the children he tutored.[60]

Margaretha's father Leo Curio was a prominent citizen of Basel, the son of Coelius Secundus Curio, a famous humanist and professor at Basel university.[61] He had been a diplomat in the Polish service and then served as an officer in the French Huguenot army until his capture by the Guise faction.[62] Curio knew six languages and was so interested in the study of Hebrew that Johann

---

30. On the lives of Jacob and Theodore Zwinger see *Historisch-Bibliographisches Lexikon der Schweiz*, 8 Vols. (Neuchâtel: Adminstration des Historisch-Biographischen Lexicons, 1921-34), s. v. "Zwinger," and on Jacob, Wackernagel, *Matrikel*, 2: 311.

56 Kautzsch, *Buxtorf*, 18, n. 1.

57 Wackernagel, *Matrikel*, 2: 363. In an unusually revealing letter Buxtorf told J. Zwinger about Gallus' parting gift and how much he valued Gallus' friendship. Buxtorf to Zwinger, Basel, August 4, 1593, Basel UB Ms Fr Gr II 9: 89. Basel UB FA IV 23 is Buxtorf's copy of צמח דוד (Venice: di Gara, 1587).

58 Pascalis Gallus to Johannes Buxtorf, Saumur, August 6, 1611, Basel UB Ms G I 62: 104-105.

59 Wackernagel, *Matrikel*, 2: 349. Although many of Buxtorf's letters have been preserved, the family apparently did not save many others, especially Buxtorf's personal letters, or did not include them in the sale of the family library in 1705.

60 Kautzsch noted that although his friends did encourage Buxtorf's attraction to Margaretha Curio there is no evidence of an "arranged match" between the two (as Johann Herzog argued in *Athenae Rauricae*, 445) to tie him more firmly to Basel. Kautzsch, *Buxtorf*, 15.

61 See Markus Kutter, *Celio Secondo Curione: Sein Leben und Werk (1503-1569)*, Basler Beiträge zur Geisteswissenschaft, Bd. 54 (Basel & Stuttgart: Helbing & Lichtenhahn, 1955) and Carl Roth, "Stammtafeln einiger ausgestorbener Basler Gelehrtenfamilien," *Basler Zeitschrift* 16 (1917): 402-403.

62 Kutter, *Curio*, 268.

Jacob Grynaeus gave him a Hebrew Bible.[63] While he apparently was favorable to a marriage between his daughter and the young professor of Hebrew he needed more information about Buxtorf's family and personal fortune before agreeing to the match. Buxtorf asked his uncle Joachim to write a letter on his behalf, which is the most reliable source of information on Buxtorf's family.[64] Buxtorf and Margaretha Curio were officially engaged on January 14, 1593 and married on February 18 of the same year.[65]

Johannes Buxtorf and Margaretha Curio were married for nearly thirty seven years and had eleven children. Of these children only four daughters and two sons survived childhood. His daughters Maria, Magdalena, and Judith married pastors and Lucia married the Hebrew printer Johann Ludwig König.[66] Hieronymus Buxtorf (1607-1650) studied for a while at Basel University, and

---

[63] Tossanus said of Curio, "Quâ quidem in provinciâ ita se gessit, ut omnibus, qui judicare de ingeniis, aliquod poterant, jucundus esset: Vivebat cum Domino Grynaeo colebatur a Brandmüllero (professor of Old Testament at Basel University when Buxtorf was a student) amabatur a quibusvis. Quia vero Hebraeas litteras avide arripiebat quasi diuturnam sitim explere cupiens, idem Grynaeus editionem Venetam Hebraeorum Bibliorum elegantissimis typis excusam ei dono dedit. Tossanus, *Buxtorfii*, 8. See also Kutter, *Curio*, 268.

[64] Joachim Buxtorf to Leo Curio, Korbach, October 31, 1592, Basel UB Ms G I 66: 52-53. The author of the Gernler family history, the *Gernler'schen Stammbuch*, wrote that Curio had suffered much and lost most of his property during his imprisonment by the Guise faction (Basel UB Ms VB Q 73, p. 191). Kautzsch suggested that the question of Buxtorf's personal fortune could have been more important than usual not only because of Curio's own financial standing after his losses in the French religious wars, but also because the professors of the University of Basel received proverbially low wages. Kautzsch, *Buxtorf*, 17.

[65] For the date of the engagement see Buxtorf to Jacob Zwinger, Basel, January 18, 1593, Basel UB Ms Fr Gr II 9: 89 and for the wedding date see Johann Jacob Leucht, *Geistlicher Kauffmann/ Christliche Leich-predigt anzeigend/ Welches das edelste Perle und wahrhaftes Keinot seye der Kinderen Gottes ... Bey Christlicher Leich-Bestattung der Ehren=und Tugendreichen Frawen/ Margaretha Curionin ....* (Basel: Georg Decker, 1659), 26. (Basel UB Ki Ar G X 15 no. 8).

[66] Kautzsch, *Buxtorf*, 18, n. 1 and Carl Roth, "Buxtorf," in W. R. Staehelin, ed. *Wappenbuch der Stadt Basel*, 1. Teil, 1. Folge (Basel: [Historische und Antiquarische Gesellschaft], 1918). Maria married Samuel Grynaeus, the pastor of St Leonhard's church, and Magdalena married Theodor Zwinger II, who later became the chief pastor of Basel, both members of prominent Basel families.

then left the city to become a mercenary soldier, ultimately dying in Poland.[67]

Johannes Buxtorf II was to become as famous a Hebrew scholar as his father. The younger Buxtorf was born on August 13, 1599, and it was said that by the age of four he could read and speak Latin, Greek, and Hebrew, as well as German. He enjoyed the benefits of a well-educated father who made sure that his son began learning foreign languages as early in life as possible.[68] Buxtorf II began his university studies at Basel when he was twelve years old and graduated at age sixteen, his father presiding over the final disputation.[69] Then he studied theology at Heidelberg for about a year where he lived in the house of Georg Michael Lingelsheim, a councillor of the electoral court and a leading humanist.[70] Buxtorf II travelled to Holland in 1619 in order to observe the Synod of Dordrecht, and afterwards he travelled through Holland, England, and France with Wolfgang Meyer and Sebastian Beck, two theology professors from Basel University.[71] After completing his grand tour, Buxtorf II returned to Basel to continue his theological studies. During 1623 he studied briefly at the Academy in Geneva in order to improve his French.[72] After returning to Basel Buxtorf II was ordained a deacon in the Basel church.

Before his father's death in 1629 Buxtorf II considered leaving Basel on two occasions in order to begin an academic career. In 1624 he was offered a professorship of Logic at the Lausanne academy, which he turned down. Then he was recommended by his father for the vacant chair of Hebrew at Leiden university in 1626. Buxtorf II was passed over for the appointment at Leiden in favor of Constantijn L'Empereur.[73] He succeeded his father as professor

---

[67] Kautzsch, *Buxtorf*, 18-19 and Wackernagel, *Matrikel*, 3: 248 (March, 1622).

[68] Herzog, *Athenae Rauricae*, 45 and Kautzsch, *Buxtorf*, 18.

[69] Wackernagel, *Matrikel*, 3: 130.

[70] Ibid.

[71] Herzog, *Athenae Rauricae*, 45 and Sebastian Beck to the Rector and Professors of Basel University, The Hague, April 4, 1619, Basel SA, Universitätsarchiv VIII 5, 1.

[72] Johannes Buxtorf I to Peter Cunaeus, Basel, June 24, 1625, Leiden UB Ms Cun 2: 89, printed in Peter Cunaeus, *Petri Cunaei & Doctorum Virorum ad Eumdem Epistolae. Quibus accedit Oratio in obitum Bonaventurae Vulcanii*, ed. Pieter Burmann, (Leiden: Peter Vander Aa, 1725), 145-147.

[73] Van Rooden, *Theology*, 83-84.

of Hebrew at the University of Basel and held the post until his
death on August 16, 1664.[74] The younger Buxtorf is perhaps best
remembered for his controversy with Louis Cappel over the age of
the Hebrew vowel points and for translating two Jewish classics
into Latin, Maimonides' *Guide to the Perplexed* (1629) and Judah
ha-Levi's *Kuzari* (1660).[75] Buxtorf II became as famous an
Hebraist as his father, and was the subject of the proverb, "The two
Buxtorfs are as much alike as two eggs."[76]

Buxtorf II was an important Hebrew scholar in his own right,
but he was also his father's most important co-worker in later
years. He was responsible for reprinting both *Thesaurus
Grammaticus* (1629) and *Institutio Epistolaris* (1629).[77] He also
worked with his father on the *Concordantiae Bibliorum Hebraicae*,
finished the work and saw it through press in 1632.[78] The *Lexicon
Chaldaicum, Talmudicum et Rabbinicum* was the product of twenty
years of work by Buxtorf I and a further ten years of labor by
Buxtorf II. Had it not been for Buxtorf I's devoted and equally talented son this milestone work would never have been published.

It was the combination of a learned and experienced editor and
corrector in Buxtorf II and a thriving Hebrew printing business
under Ludwig König, his brother-in-law, that ensured Buxtorf the
elder's lasting scholarly influence in a practical sense.[79] During the
seventeenth century very few printers had the Hebrew type,
punches, and matrices or learned personnel necessary for producing Hebrew books. The scarcity of learned compositors, proofreaders, and editors who could work with Hebrew and other oriental languages was particularly difficult to overcome. Frans and
Joost Raphelengius of Leiden were able to print their father's mas-

---

[74] Staehelin, *Geschichte*, 546. From 1642 until his death Buxtorf II also
served as a professor on the Theology faculty, first as a professor of Common
Places and Controversial Theology and then as Professor of Old Testament.

[75] See Richard A. Muller, "The debate over the vowel points and the crisis in
orthodox hermeneutics," *Journal of Renaissance Studies* 10 (1980): 53-72.
Buxtorf II's role in this dispute is discussed below in chap. 7.

[76] "Non ovum ovo similius, quam Buxtorfius pater et filius." Kautzsch,
Buxtorf, 18, n. 3.

[77] Prijs nos. 229, 230. See Buxtorf II to Peter Cunaeus, Basel, March 20,
1629, Leiden UB Ms Cun 2: 102, printed in Cunaeus, *Epistolae*, 164-5.

[78] Prijs no. 235.

[79] After 1658 Buxtorf II published some of his father's books himself. Prijs,
Drucke, 375.

sive Arabic-Latin lexicon in 1611, but had to leave the Arabic printing business in 1614 when their most valuable employee died, the only compositor who could set Arabic type.[80] The König press with its experienced Hebrew compositors and established channels of distribution, and the younger Buxtorf's expert knowledge and printing experience made it possible for König and his successors to reprint the elder Buxtorf's works frequently which, in turn, served to perpetuate his intellectual legacy.

Johannes Buxtorf I served as regular professor of Hebrew language at the University of Basel from 1590 until his death in 1629. The professor of Hebrew at Basel University was a member of the Arts faculty and was obliged to teach both the rudiments of Hebrew to beginners and to lecture on biblical books.[81] Buxtorf's grammar lectures were probably given on an elementary level, since the Basel *Gymnasium* apparently did not offer Hebrew instruction during most of his teaching career.[82] Any Basel students wishing to study theology had to learn all of their Hebrew at the University. The content of Buxtorf's classroom grammar instruction should probably be sought in his *Praeceptiones de Grammaticae Lingua Hebraea* (1605) and its revision *Epitome Grammaticae Hebraeae* (1613, 1617, 1620, 1629, etc.) rather than in his *Thesaurus Grammaticus*, which was a reference grammar.

Buxtorf's other teaching responsibility was to lecture on biblical books. Several manuscript fragments of his lectures have been pre-

---

[80] Alastair Hamilton, *William Bedwell the Arabist 1563-1632*, Publications of the Thomas Browne Institute, Leiden, n. s., no. 5 (Leiden: E. J. Brill, 1985), 39, 46.

[81] See Basel SA Universitätsarchiv R 3, 1, f. 131 (July 1589), Basel SA Universitätsarchiv B 1, ff. 137r-v (1617). See also the broadsides of course listings dating from 1612-1615, and from November 28, 1619 (Basel UB Ms VB O 11g, ff. 89, 175), quoted by Eberhard Vischer, "Die Lehrstühle und der Unterricht an der theologischen Fakultät Basels seit der Reformation," in *Festschrift zur Feier des 450 Jährigen Bestehens der Universität Basel*, eds. Rektor und Regenz der Universität (Basel: Helbing & Lichtenhahn, 1910), 139, 144.

[82] One incidental reference in Buxtorf's correspondence, however, indicates that Hebrew was offered in the Basel Gymnasium for a while. "Edideram ante biennium Epitomen brevissimam Grammaticae Hebraeae, maxime pro usu Gymnasii nostri Basileensis. Ea praeter spem sic excepta est, ut et Herbornae, et aliquot Scholis in Palatinatu nostraque Helvetia publice discenda proponatur." Johannes Buxtorf to Konrad Vorstius, Basel June 8, 1608, Bibliotheca Rosenthaliana (Amsterdam UB) Brieven-collectie, no. 110.

served, including lectures on Hebrew proverbs collected by
Johannes Drusius (1594), an introduction to Obadiah (1600) and
lectures on Proverbs chapters 1-5, and 8-10.[83] His lectures on
Hebrew proverbs were not confined to the book of Proverbs, but
took in proverbs and other figures of speech from other books of
the Hebrew Bible, based on a selection published by Johannes
Drusius, an important Dutch Hebraist.[84] Buxtorf's introduction to
Obadiah contains a brief discussion of the peculiarities of medieval
Hebrew which he hoped would enable his students to use rabbinical
commentaries in their studies. He promised to use both them and
the Targum in his verse-by-verse explanation of the book. The
lectures on the biblical book of Proverbs are the most complete example of Buxtorf's classroom lectures. These lectures contain a
verse by verse explanation of the text. Buxtorf made periodic use
of the commentaries of Levi b. Gerson, Rashi, Ibn Ezra and
"Kabhvenaki" (David ibn Yahya's commentary *Qab venaqi*) to
clarify interpretive problems.[85]

Buxtorf's Hebrew lectures were not well attended. He com-
plained to Waser in 1608 that few students studied Hebrew at all.[86]
In 1617 the academic Senate felt compelled to require attendance at
Buxtorf's classes for students studying for Master of Arts and for
Theology degrees.[87] Perhaps this lack of students allowed Buxtorf
to study and write more than he otherwise might have done.

---

[83] See Basel UB Ms Fr Gr III 22b (Drusius' Proverbs) and Basel UB Ms A
XII 7 (Obadiah) and Ms. Fr Gr III 22a (Book of Proverbs), described in Stephen
G. Burnett, "Buxtorf Family Papers," in: Joseph Prijs, *Die Handschriften der
Universität Basel: Die hebräische Handschriften*, ed. Bernhard and David Prijs
(Basel: Verlag der Universitätsbibliothek, 1994), 79, 83.

[84] The colophon of Ms Fr Gr III 2b reads "Proverbia quaedam hebraica ex
Johanne Drusio collecta." The source for these lectures was *Proverbiorum
Classes duae, in quibus explicatur proverbia sacra, & ex sacris litteris orta: Item
Sententiae Salomonis et allegoriae, & etc.* (Franeker: Aegidius Radaeus, 1590).
4° [FFM no. 89].

[85] The Proverbs commentaries of Levi b. Gerson and Ibn Ezra (actually writ-
ten by Moses Kimhi according to J. Prijs, *Drucke*, 334) are found in the second
Bomberg Rabbinical Bible of 1525 (StCB p. 11, no. 52), and קב ונקי in the first
Bomberg Rabbincal Bible of 1517 (StCB p. 6, no. 28).

[86] "Rari hic sunt studiosi hujus linguae." Buxtorf to Waser, February 7,
1608, Zürich ZB Ms S-160: 45.

[87] Basel SA, Universitätsarchiv B1, ff. 138r-v, and Wilhelm Schulze-
Marmeling, "Johannes Buxtorf der Ältere: Ein Leben für die Wissenschaft," in:
100 Jahre Stätische Höhere Lehranstalt Kamen: Festschrift, ed. Theo Simon

Buxtorf's professorship at Basel provided him with a source of income, but not with a livelihood. In an era when universities paid notoriously low salaries the University of Basel had the dubious distinction of paying the lowest wages of any German university.[88] In 1589 the *Deputaten* of the University raised the salaries of Arts faculty professors (of the third class, including the professor of Hebrew) to 37 Pounds, 10 Shillings, and 3 *Viernzel* of grain per quarter.[89] Buxtorf's salary remained at this level until 1626. Only Buxtorf's academic calling to Leiden in 1626 persuaded the university authorities to give him a raise.[90] His income was increased to 53 Pounds, 2 Shillings, 6 pence per quarter, with 16 *Viernzel* of grain instead of the previous 12 *Viernzel*.[91] Buxtorf's additional income was not, however, added to the base salary of his position as professor of Hebrew; it was paid to him personally as a bonus and was so noted in the records.[92] This arrangement made him the highest paid member of the arts faculty, though he still received less than the professors of theology.

Professors of the Arts faculty in Basel normally had few opportunities to supplement their meager salaries. Faculty members could work as administrators and receive some remuneration for

(Hemer=Sundwig: Schälter, [1958]), 105. (Münster SA library, call no. WF 965).

[88] Philip Scherb of Basel, an older contemporary of Buxtorf's, when he received a call to leave the University of Altdorf and become a professor of medicine at Basel turned down the offer with the comment that it was better to live in exile than to die of hunger in his native land. Staehelin, *Geschichte*, 71.

[89] Basel SA Universtiätsarchiv C1, Archivum Academicum I: 1459-1634, ff. 181r-v. Professors' salaries were recorded in Basel SA Universitätsarchiv C 6, Ausgabenbuch, and the records of grain payments are noted in Basel SA Klosterarchiv 001 Domstift: Domprobstei Rechnungen. Rudolf Thommen, *Geschichte der Universität Basel, 1532-1632* (Basel: C. Detloff, 1889), 51-52 explains the academic (and pay) structure of the Arts faculty at Basel. Basel's official currency was the Pound, which divided into 20 Shillings, each of these worth 12 Pennies. Other commonly used currencies were the *Thaler*, or *Reichstaler*, worth roughly two Pounds and the Guilder, worth 1 Pound, 5 Shillings. Guilders were divided into 15 Batzen (1 Batzen = 60 Kreuzer). Staehelin, *Geschichte*, XVIII-XIX.

[90] Copies of the city council discussions of Buxtorf's calling from June 22, 1625 and July 16, 1625 are kept in Basel SA Erziehungsakten CC 8, and the University Regenz discussions of June 21, 1625 in Basel SA Universitätsarchiv B 1, f. 157r.

[91] The *Viernzel*, about 298 Liters, was the standard measure of dry volume in Basel. Staehelin, *Geschichte*, XIX.

[92] Ibid., 74.

their work. Buxtorf's first position was administrator of the *Obere Kollegium* where professors met and ate together in 1594.[93] He served as *Dekan* (dean) of the Arts faculty in 1596, 1602-1603, 1606-1607, 1611-1613, 1617-1618, 1622, and 1626-1627, and he was Rector in 1614-1615.[94] Buxtorf also supervised many disputations. The university paid small fees to professors serving in these capacities.[95] In addition to these official duties, Buxtorf also gave private instruction from time to time. Who he tutored and how often he gave private classes are difficult to determine, since the subject matter taught and the costs were agreed upon privately by the professor and individual pupil.[96]

Since Buxtorf was an employee of the city of Basel he sometimes had to perform other duties which were not directly related to teaching. He received some remuneration for some of these tasks, but much of his labor probably went unrewarded. Buxtorf's appointment as a visitor for the Gymnasium is a good example of this.[97] The rector and senate of the University were responsible for overseeing the curriculum and personnel of the Basel Gymnasium. They in turn appointed visitors to perform these tasks and created special committees to perform other tasks as necessary. Buxtorf served on the committee that worked to revise its curriculum in 1618, and later served as a Gymnasium visitor.[98] In 1625 he was paid 12 Basel Pounds per year for his work as a visitor.[99]

---

[93] Ibid., 383-384, and Basel SA Universitätsarchiv B 1/I, f. 84 for August 21, 1594. Buxtorf received 60 pounds per year for this responsibility. He was also appointed acting professor of Greek at this same meeting, but no mention of remuneration is given.

[94] Rudolf Bernoulli, *Basler Akademiker Katalog*, s. v. "Buxtorf, Johannes I." The BAK is a card catalogue kept in the Basel UB manuscript department, containing file card index to records of the official activities of Basel University professors.

[95] Thommen, *Geschichte*, 61-62.

[96] See Staehelin, *Geschichte*, 130 on private instruction. According to Tossanus, *Buxtorfii*, 14 Buxtorf gave private instruction to Johannes Svaningius (Hans Jens Svaning), a famous Danish scholar (Wackernagel, *Matrikel*, 3: 316).

[97] Another important example, his work as the municipal Hebrew censor, is discussed below in chap. 2.

[98] Thommen, *Geschichte*, 41-44, 331 (para. 19).

[99] Basel SA Erziehungsakten CC 8. For Buxtorf's activities see Daniel A. Fechter, *Geschichte des Schulwesens in Basel vom Jahr 1585-1733: Einladungsschrift zur Promotionsfeier des Gymnasiums und der Realschule* (Basel: Schweighauser'schen Buchdruckerei, n. d.), 10-12. (Basel UB call no. Hagb. 2114 N° 3), Wolleb, "Leichpredigt," 861, and Kautzsch, *Buxtorf*, 29.

Late Renaissance humanist studies were nurtured not only by schools and universities which existed to uphold the existing political and religious order of particular states, but also by a supranational, interconfessional network of scholars, the Republic of Letters.[100] The international academic community of Buxtorf's day had an informal, but rigid hierarchical structure of patrons and clients. It was important for ambitious young scholars to seek recognition from an established scholar who could, in turn, lend his prestige and support to the aspirant.[101] Buxtorf became known as an outstanding Hebraist even before any of his works appeared in print. He first attracted the attention of a recognized scholar when he sent a Hebrew letter to Johannes Drusius, professor of Hebrew at Franeker in the Netherlands. Drusius wrote back enthusiastically that Buxtorf could have written anything "more learned or elegant," and published his response in a collection of his letters on scholarly topics.[102] Both the elder Drusius and his talented son Johannes continued to correspond with Buxtorf in Hebrew as well as in Latin.[103] After this promising start, Buxtorf's first publications served to confirm his correspondents' good opinion of him.

The appearance of *Juden Schul* and *Syvula Epistolarum* in 1603 marked Buxtorf as an expert on both Judaism and the Hebrew language, and brought him to the attention of Joseph Scaliger, one of the leading intellectual lights of Europe. Scaliger invited Buxtorf to begin corresponding with him through Jacob Amport, a former

---

[100] Van Rooden noted the paradoxical tensions experienced by scholars caught between the particularist demands of confessional schools and the determined internationalism and non-confessional character of the Republic of Letters during this period in *Theology*, 199-209.

[101] See Trunz, "Späthumanismus," 161-162 and van Rooden, *Theology*, 109-110, 203-205. Isaac Casaubon regarded Joseph Scaliger as the "author of his fame." Mark Pattison, *Isaac Casaubon: 1599-1614* (Oxford: Clarendon, 1892; reprint ed., Geneva: Slatkine, 1970), 65.

[102] "Legi epistolam tuam, quam Ebraice scriptam ad me Basilea misisti. Quaeris quid sentiam? nihil ea doctius, nihil elegantius." Johannes Drusius to Johannes Buxtorf, n. p., n. d. (before 1595); the original letter has not been preserved, but it was printed in Johannes Drusius, *De Quaesitis per Epistolam* (Franeker: Aegidium Radaeum, 1595), 153.

[103] L. Fuks, "Het Hebreeuwse Brievenboek van Johannes Drusius Jr. Hebreeuws en Hebraisten in Nederland Rondom 1600," *Studia Rosenthaliana* 3 (1969): 1-52.

student of Buxtorf's, an invitation that he accepted with alacrity.[104] In his first letter to Buxtorf Scaliger praised *Juden Schul* and his abilities as a writer of Hebrew, urging him to compose a handbook for Hebrew epistolary.[105] Scaliger's admiration for Buxtorf's attainments was unfeigned and was expressed privately as well as publicly. Since Scaliger was best known for his acerbic criticism of fellow scholars his praise for Buxtorf is all the more remarkable.[106] Scaliger's recognition was a great honor for Buxtorf and was crucial in establishing his reputation. By invoking Scaliger's name and reputation, and by petitioning Scaliger's friends within Dutch academic and court circles, Buxtorf was able to appeal to the Estates General for financial support with some hope of a positive response. Since Leiden university was an important "node" within the scholarly communication network of the late sixteenth and seventeenth centuries Buxtorf's fame quickly spread. By 1610, the year that he published his *Institutio Epistolaris*, Buxtorf's reputation as a Hebraist was established.

Once Buxtorf achieved recognition he was able to set much more ambitious scholarly goals, but also suffered from some of the drawbacks of being a celebrity. Buxtorf's monumental projects such as the rabbinical Bible of 1618-19 and Hebrew Bible concordance were feasible in part because he was editor-in-chief. He produced specimens of both works as advertisements for prospective buyers and he also sent them to his correspondents in order to assure his publisher that there was a market for these works and to attract financial support from outside of Basel.[107] By the same to-

---

[104] "Inter alia scribit (Jacob Amport), T. M. perhonorifice de me in privato coloquio locutum esse, ac laudabiles in lingua Hebraea profectus mihi ascripsisse." Johannes Buxtorf to Joseph Scaliger, Basel, April 3, 1606, Utrecht UB Ms 987: 237-238; printed in: Pieter Burman, *Sylloges epistolarum a viris illustribus scriptarum*, 5 Vols. (Leiden: S. Luchtmans, 1727), 2: 362.

[105] Joseph J. Scaliger to Johannes Buxtorf, Leiden, June 1, 1606, Basel UB Ms G I 59: 363; printed in Scaliger, *Epistolae omnes quae reperiri, potuerunt, nunc primum collectae ac editae*, ed. Daniel Heinsius (Leiden: B. & A. Elzevir, 1627), 521-524.

[106] Joseph J. Scaliger, *Scaligerana* (Cologne: Gerbrandum Scagen, 1667), 39-40. On Scaliger's witty and often acerbic criticism of other scholars, see Anthony Grafton, "Close Encounters of the Learned Kind. Joseph Scaliger's Table Talk," *The American Scholar* 57 (1988): 584-586.

[107] Walter Keuchen mentioned a sample printing of the Basel rabbinical Bible in his letter to Buxtorf, n. p., January 19, 1618, Basel UB Ms G I 60: 320r. On the sample printings of the *Concordantiae*, see below, chap. 6.

ken his reputation as an expert on Judaism made him an obvious candidate to edit and print Raymond Martini's *Pugio fidei* in the mind of Philippe du Plessis de Mornay, the "pope" of the French Huguenots. While Mornay's commission was a great honor for Buxtorf he considered the work itself to be a low priority and did not live to complete it.[108]

Three of the most tangible forms of scholarly recognition during Buxtorf's lifetime were the acceptance of his dedications by wealthy or influential patrons, offers of promotion at one's own university, and academic callings to other universities, usually with a substantially higher salary. Monetary gifts from important patrons were an important form of financial support for struggling authors in early modern Europe.[109] Buxtorf dedicated nearly all of his books to important individuals or the ruling bodies of cities or nations, including the city councils of Hamm and Bremen, Counts Adolph, Arnold Justus, and Wilhelm Heinrich of Bentheim in Westphalia (whom he knew from his student days in Herborn), and Philippe du Plessis de Mornay. He also dedicated books to famous scholars such as Johannes Drusius, Joseph Scaliger, and Daniel Heinsius, and even to two of his students, Johann Gosvini Bosman of Dordrecht and Jakob Guilhelmi Hooft of Amsterdam.[110] Buxtorf is known to have received monetary rewards in only two cases, for his *Thesaurus Grammaticus* in 1609 and for *Tiberias* in 1620.[111] The Estates General of the Dutch republic awarded him 300 Dutch

---

[108] See below, chap. 3.

[109] Leon Voet discussed the importance of dedications to sixteenth and seventeenth century authors in *The Golden Compasses: A History and Evaluation of the Printing and Publishing Activities of the Officina Plantiniana at Antwerp*, vol. 2: *The Management of a Printing and Publishing House in Renaissance and Baroque* (Amsterdam: P Vangendt & Co., 1972), 283-290.

[110] Bosman was a former student of Lubbertus at Franeker. See G. P. Itterzon, "Nog Twintig Brieven van Gomarus," *Nederlands Archief voor Kerkgeschiedenis* 56 (1975-76):416-417, 430-431. Bosman and Hooft matriculated at Basel University on July 8, 1611 and October 7, 1611 respectively. Wackernagel, *Matrikel*, 3: 120, 127.

[111] The Buxtorf II's dedications of his father's two postumously published works were similarly well rewarded. He received 600 Dutch Guilders from the Estates General of the Dutch republic for the *Concordantiae* and 300 Reichstalers (= 750 Dutch Guilders) for the *Lexicon Chaldaicum Talmudicum et Rabbinicum* from the Estates of Groningen. See Franciscus Gomarus to Johannes Buxtorf II, Groningen, December 28, 1639, Basel UB Ms G I 59: 4, printed in Itterzon, "Gomarus," 446-447.

Guilders for the former and 200 Guilders for the latter book as tokens of thanks.[112] Buxtorf told Johannes Uytenborgard in a letter
that 300 Dutch Guilders was worth 173 Basel Pounds. Accordingly
these two gifts were worth more than a year's salary and nine
month's salary (115 Pounds, 6 Shillings) respectively.[113] Less
wealthy recipients of dedications, such as Drusius, acknowledged
them by giving copies of their own books.[114]

Another indication of Buxtorf's reputation as a scholar and professor was the promotion offered him by the University of Basel.
When the Professor of Old Testament on the Theology faculty,
Amandus Polanus, died of plague in 1610, Buxtorf was offered his
chair. Although the position carried both higher status and higher
pay he turned the offer down. While Tossanus reported that he did
this out of sheer modesty, Kautzsch suggested, more plausibly, that
Buxtorf wished to remain an Hebraist.[115]

Buxtorf received academic callings to three different institutions
during his professional career. The first, in 1611, was to the theological academy at Saumur. The Rector, Robert Boyd, wrote to
him, urging that he consider coming to Saumur.[116] Buxtorf wrote

112 For the *Thesaurus Grammaticus* see the record for November 23, 1609 in
H. H. P. Rijperman, ed., *Resolutiën der Staten-Generaal van 1576 tot 1609*, vol.
4: *1607-1609*, Rijks Geschiedkundige Publicatiën, vol. 131 ('s-Gravanhage:
Martinus Nijhoff, 1970), 914. *Tiberias* was recognized by the Estates General on
June 6, 1620. See J. G. Smit and J. Roelovink, eds., *Resolutiën der Staten-
Generaal, 1610-1670*, vol. 4: *1619-1620*, Rijks Geschiedkundige Publicatiën,
vol. 176 ('s-Gravenhage: Martinus Nijhoff, 1981), 490 and n. 3388b.
113 Johannes Buxtorf to Johannes Uytenbogard, Basel, March 15, 1610,
Leiden UB Ms Pap 2; the letter is printed in *Praestantium ac Eruditorum virorum
Epistolae Ecclesiasticae et Theologicae* (Amsterdam: Henricum Dendrinum,
1660), 938-940, and is partially translated in Buxtorf-Falkeisen, *Buxtorf*, 15-16.
Between November 1592 and November 1609 the Estates General awarded sums
of money to the authors of 77 different works. Only nine received 300 Guilders
or more and only three of these received more than Buxtorf himself did.
114 Johannes Drusius told Buxtorf that in his experience authors normally received fifty complementary copies of their books from printers. Johannes Drusius
to Johannes Buxtorf, n. p., February 21, 1605, Basel UB G I 59: 257.
Author's copies were a small but helpful addition to their income, particularly
since they could be used as gifts, to sell or to trade for other books. See Voet,
The Golden Compasses, 2: 284-288.
115 Kautzsch, *Buxtorf*, 21.
116 Kaspar Waser wrote, possibly reflecting Buxtorf's opinion, that Saumur
wanted him to use his academic talents to oppose Catholic disputants of various
kinds, including the Jesuits. "Nam capiunt Scholas illas, quae ecclesiarum sunt
plantatia (sic), quam optime constitutas & dotatas contra Jesuitarum & aliorum

back to him and gently turned down the offer. He had a wife and six children to consider in any decision to leave Basel, not to speak of the danger and expense of the move.[117] While he did not seriously consider accepting the call, he tried unsuccessfully to use it as a bargaining tool for a pay raise.[118] His next offer was from the University of Heidelberg. The younger Buxtorf lived for a time in the house of Georg Michael Lingelsheim, a professor at the University and councillor to the Elector of the Palatinate, while he was a student at Heidelberg. In one of Lingelsheim's letters to Buxtorf he told of the son's progress and mentioned that Heidelberg University was interested in hiring him as professor of Hebrew. Buxtorf-Falkeisen suggested that Buxtorf may have had another reason for leaving Basel at this time, the infamous circumcision incident involving Abraham Braunschweig.[119] Unfortunately Elector Friedrich, the ill-fated Winter King of Bohemia, was at war in the east and the university could not hire a new professor.[120] Lingelsheim's hopes of hiring Buxtorf soon came to naught, for Elector Friedrich was defeated in his attempt to rule Bohemia at the Battle of White Mountain, and Heidelberg itself was sacked in 1622.

The final institution which tried to hire Buxtorf away from Basel was the University of Leiden. This calling to the premier Protestant university in Europe was in itself a great honor and the university authorities also offered him a generous salary. Buxtorf

---

Pontificiorum machinas perpetuas." Kaspar Waser to W. Zündelin, Zürich, August 23, 1611, Zürich SA E II 383: 197, quoted by Menk, *Herborn*, 200, n. 12.

[117] Robert Boyd to Johannes Buxtorf, Saumur, August 6, 1611, Basel UB Ms G I 62: 102-3, and Johannes Buxtorf to Robert Boyd, Basel, August 17, 1611. Both letters are printed in Johannes Buxtorf, ספר קבוצים *sive Catalecta Philologico-Theologica* (Basel: Johann Ludwig König, 1707), 452-461, and are translated by Buxtorf Falkeisen, *Buxtorf*, 17-22.

[118] Johannes Buxtorf to Kaspar Waser, Basel, September 8, 1611, Zürich ZB Ms S-162: 47.

[119] Georg M. Lingelsheim to Johannes Buxtorf, Heidelberg, November 1, 1619, Basel UB G I 60: 11-12, and Buxtorf-Falkeisen, *Buxtorf*, 31-2. See also Stephen G. Burnett, "Johannes Buxtorf I and the Circumcision Incident of 1619," *Basler Zeitschrift für Geschichte und Altertumskunde* 89 (1989): 135-144.

[120] Georg Michael Lingelsheim to Johannes Buxtorf, Heidelberg, November 1, 1619, Basel UB Ms G I 60: 11-12, translated in Buxtorf Falkeisen, *Buxtorf*, 31.

would receive between 600 and 700 Dutch Guilders per year and a
further 80 *Reichstaler* for moving costs.[121] The starting salary for
Leiden professors on the arts faculty was usually 600 Dutch
Guilders and so Buxtorf would have received something of a pre-
mium, reflecting his reputation as a Hebraist.[122] However, Buxtorf
had other factors to consider besides money and prestige. He was
61 years old, and owned a house in Basel. He also had financial
obligations to meet, most notably a loan in 1622 for 1000 Guilders
(1250 Basel Pounds).[123] Although Buxtorf ultimately turned down
Leiden's offer, it did serve to encourage Basel University to raise
his salary to 212 Pounds, 10 Shillings per year.[124]

Buxtorf's death was mourned by scholars all over Europe. Half
of Tossanus' book on his life and achievements was devoted to
poems in Greek, Latin, Hebrew and Aramaic written in his
honor.[125] Poems were sent by professors and scholars from

---

[121] Peter Cunaeus to Johannes Buxtorf I, Leiden, June 4, 1625, Basel UB
Ms G I 59: 265-6. This letter is printed in Cunaeus, *Epistolae*, 143-4 and translated in Buxtorf-Falkeisen, *Buxtorf*, 37-39. The resolution of May 12, 1625,
made by the Curatoren of Leiden University to offer Buxtorf the position is
printed in P. C. Molhuysen, ed., *Bronnen tot de Geschiedenis der Leidsche
Universiteit*, Rijks Geschiedkundige Publicatien, no. 29, 7 vols. ('S-
Gravenhage: Martinus Nijhoff, 1916), 2: 121.

[122] Thomas Erpenius received 600 Guilders a year when he became regular
professor of Arabic in 1618, and Constantijn L'Empereur received the same
when he was hired as a professor of Hebrew in 1627. See Wilhelmina M. C.
Juyboll, "Zeventiende-eeuwsche Boenfenaars van het Arabisch in Nederland"
(Universiteit Utrecht, Ph. D. diss., 1931), 95-96 and Van Rooden, *Theology*,
92, n. 35.

[123] From at least 1610 until his death Buxtorf lived at Bäumligasse 9. See
Felix Platter, *Beschreibung der Stadt Basel 1610 und Pestbericht 1610/1611*, ed.
Valentin Lötscher, Basler Chroniken, Band 11 (Basel and Stuttgart: Schwabe
Verlag, 1987), 432. Buxtorf took out the loan on July 15/25, 1622. Basel SA
Urk n° 3791 (A), printed in *Urkundenbuch der Stadt Basel*, Bd. 11: 1602-1797,
ed. Historischen und Antiquarischen Gesellschaft zu Basel (Basel: Helbing &
Lichtenhahn, 1910), 343, #138. The guilders that circulated in Basel were worth
1.25 Basel Pounds. Staehelin, *Geschichte*, 1: XVIII.

[124] Buxtorf wrote to Cunaeus on July 8, July 22 and September 15, 1625
about the proposed calling to Leiden University. Leiden UB Ms Cun 2: 90, 92,
93, printed in Cunaeus, *Epistolae*, 147-8, 150-2. What these figures do not con-
vey, however, is the comparative cost of living in Basel and Leiden. From his
correspondence with Erpenius, Buxtorf knew that Leiden professors had great
difficulty living on their salaries. See Thomas Erpenius to Johann Buxtorf,
Leiden, April 10, 1614, Basel UB G I 59: 273; translated by Buxtorf-Falkeisen,
Buxtorf, 27-28.

[125] Tossanus, *Buxtorfii*, 21-48. Prijs no. 232.

Leiden, Bremen, Rostock, Silesia, and Bohemia as well as Switzerland. Buxtorf II also received numerous letters of condolence, including several touching ones written by Dutch scholars. Louis de Dieu, a young pastor in Leiden who would himself become a famous Semiticist, wrote "With your father has departed knowledge of the Hebrew language; (he was) a father to me who offered me daily nourishment." Daniel Heinsius, Leiden University librarian and a leading member of the Republic of Letters wrote, "Your father had no greater admirer than me, and my longing for him grows when I consider what he could still have accomplished. For years all scholars have waited impatiently for his highly important rabbinical Lexicon."[126] Sixtius Amama, professor of Hebrew at the Reformed academy of Franeker in northern Netherlands, wrote to a colleague in Leiden, "I had not previously heard that the illustrious Buxtorf had died. I mourn the loss to the Academy and to the Republic of Letters."[127]

Buxtorf's professional career illustrates how much his contemporaries valued his work. Even before he received his MA degree he received his first offer to teach Hebrew. He was offered academic promotion at Basel and received several flattering offers of professorships at other universities. His calling to Leiden, one of the premier universities of Europe, was the culmination of recognition for his academic achievements. Institutional recognition for Buxtorf came much later than the acclaim of his peers as a survey of his works will demonstrate. His teaching career and writings had enhanced the status of Hebrew language and literature within schools and universities in a way that no scholar had done since Sebastian Münster. His constant use of Jewish sources in his work, whether in grammar, lexicography, or biblical interpretation, bibliography or Hebrew composition, demonstrated their value to

---

[126] L. de Dieu to Johannes Buxtorf II, Leiden, October 26, 1629, Basel UB G I 59: 307, and Daniel Heinsius to Johannes Buxtorf II, Leiden, October 29, 1629, Basel UB G I 59: 250, the latter printed in *Catalecta*, 470-471. These letters were partially translated in Buxtorf-Falkeisen, *Buxtorf*, 43-44.

[127] "De obitu cl. D. Buxtorfii nihil antea inaudivisam. Doleo vicem Acad. et Reip. literaria." Sixtinus Amama to J. Polyander, October 16, 1629, Oxford: Bodleian Library, MS. Rawlinson letters 76 (b), f. 91r, quoted by J. E. Platt, "Sixtinus Amama (1593-1629): Franeker professor and citizen of the Republic of Letters," in: *Universiteit te Franeker: 1585-1811. Bijdragen tot de geschiedenis von de Friese hogeschool*, eds. G. Th. Jensma, F. R. H. Smit and F. Westra (Leeuworden: Fryske Akademy, 1985), 246, n. 23.

Christian scholars who had mastered only biblical Hebrew, and encouraged them to follow his example. His numerous books, written both for experts and beginning students, gave them the means to do so.

Most strikingly, however, Buxtorf's tremendous achievements in Hebrew learning took place during one of the most intense periods of political and religious conflict in European history, the period immediately prior to the Thirty Years War and the during the first years of that conflict. Despite the propensity for scholarly adherents of all three confessions to quarrel bitterly, casting even philological issues in a theological light, no one ever questioned the legitimacy of Buxtorf's study of post-biblical Jewish literature.[128] This type of Hebrew learning, like the study of biblical Hebrew, was obviously considered by all three confessions to be beneficial for theological study. Buxtorf's career is ample testimony to the curious fact that at least some kinds of Jewish learning were thought to be useful and worthy of financial and institutional support during an age of bitter interconfessional conflict among Christians.

---

[128] According to Tossanus, *Buxtorfii*, 13, Buxtorf had received Jesuit visitors in Basel who came to pay their respects. J. C. H. Lebram described a philological argument that turned into an interconfessional quarrel between Scaliger and Drusius and the Jesuit Nikolaus Serarius in "De Hasidaeis: Over Joodse studiën in het oude Leiden," *Voordrachten Faculteitendag 1980* (Leiden, 1981): 21-31. I am indebted to Prof. Lebram for sending me with a copy of the article.

CHAPTER TWO

CENSORSHIP AND THE HEBREW BOOK TRADE

Hebrew printing and the Jewish book trade encouraged the spread of Hebrew learning among Christians by providing them not only with Hebrew Bibles, textbooks, and post-biblical Jewish works, but also with a socially acceptable forum where they could make contacts with Jews who could explain the contents of these works.[1] Johannes Buxtorf was active in almost every aspect of the manufacture and sale of Hebrew books for most of his adult life. His work as a censor, editor, corrector, and business representative first for Conrad Waldkirch and then for Ludwig König enabled him to hone his knowledge of Hebrew and of Jewish literature to a fine edge and provided him with both a printer for his own works and a network of Jewish contacts who were willing to help him build a remarkable Judaica library and to inform him about their literature and culture.[2] Buxtorf's second job also gave him a way to augment his meager university salary, money he desperately needed to support his large family.[3]

Hebrew printing was a complicated and costly business venture in early modern Germany for a variety of reasons. Like all forms of printing, Jewish printing was heavily regulated by imperial authorities. Printers had to purchase massive quantities of expensive

---

[1] See Friedman, *Most Ancient Testimony*, 36-48 and Frank Manuel, *The Broken Staff. Judaism through Christian Eyes* (Cambridge, MA: Harvard Univ. Press, 1992), 36.

[2] Conrad Waldkirch took over Peter Perna's press in Basel during 1582. After a brief stay in Schaffhausen during 1591/2, he returned to Basel in 1593 and remained there until his death in 1615/1616. See Karl Schmuki, "Wann wurde in Schaffhausen die erste Druckerei eingerichtet? Zur Niederlassung des Buchdruckers Hans Conrad von Waldkirch in Schaffhausen," *Schaffhauser Beiträge zur Geschichte* 61 (1984): 30, 40. Ludwig König II worked as press manager for Waldkirch and eventually succeeded him as owner. See Josef Benzing, "Die Deutsche Verleger des 16. und 17. Jahrhunderts. Eine Neubearbeitung," *Archiv für Geschichte des Buchwesens* 18 (1977): col. 1191.

[3] Buxtorf complained to Wolfgang Ratich, "...ich durch den segen Gottes siben kinder hab, und des wegen zwei mal grossere sumptibus in der haushaltung brauche, als mein stipendium professionis eintragt...." Buxtorf to Ratich, Basel, January 31, 1617, Magdeburg SA, Abt. Kothen C 18 30: 181v.

Hebrew type to produce anything more complicated than a prayer book. They also had to find and hire skilled compositors and editors, often Jews, who could command higher wages than their fellow workmen. Jewish printing also required close cooperation between Christian owners of presses and Jewish authors, financiers, and printers at a time when local magistrates sought to regulate closely contact between Jew and Christian. Despite all of these restrictions, however, Jewish printing was profitable and both Waldkirch and König found ways to deal with these problems.

The manufacture and sale of Hebrew books was a licit but dubious activity in the eyes of local and imperial officials in early modern Germany. Imperial law required that all Jewish printing take place in cities where competent censors were available, so that each book could be examined before publication.[4] Failure to comply with these laws could result in the confiscation of the printer's presses and every copy of the book in question, as occurred in Thannhausen during 1592.[5] Books which were not officially censored could not legally be sold within the Holy Roman Empire. Border controls and imperial officials at the Frankfurt book fair and elsewhere sought to ensure that only licit books were available for sale.[6] Practically speaking, however, pre-publication censorship was the only way for German imperial, princely, or municipal authorities to control what was published in Hebrew. While officials could inspect books in Latin, German or other languages either in transit or at the point of sale, they could not maintain the same level of surveillance for Hebrew books, since only experts could read and evaluate them.[7] Although Basel was not a part of the

---

[4] The initial soul-searching of the Hanau magistrate over whether they should allow Jewish printing in the city and the often drastic steps which they took to ensure that no Jewish book printed there contained blasphemous or seditious statements illustrates how politically sensitive a matter Jewish printing was within Germany during Buxtorf's day. See Stephen G. Burnett, "Hebrew Censorship in Hanau: A Mirror of Jewish-Christian Coexistence in Seventeenth Century Germany," in: *The Expulsion of the Jews*, 203-208.

[5] Moshe N. Rosenfeld, "The Development of Hebrew Printing in the Sixteenth and Seventeenth Centuries," in: *A Sign and a Witness: 2,000 Years of Hebrew Books and Illuminated Manuscripts*, ed. Leonard Singer Gold (New York: Oxford Univ. Press, 1988), 97.

[6] Guido Kisch, "Die Zensur jüdischer Bücher in Böhmen. Beiträge zu ihrer Geschichte," in: idem, *Forschungen zur Rechts-, Wirtschafts-, und Sozialgeschichte der Juden* (Sigmaringen: Jan Thorbeck, 1979), 328.

German Empire, its printers too had to comply with imperial law in order to market their wares in Frankfurt, home to Germany's largest Jewish community and also the site of an important book fair.[8]

Johannes Buxtorf played an official role in the oversight of Jewish printing, since he served as Basel's Hebrew censor. According to the Basel censorship ordinance of February 23, 1558, the deans of the four university faculties were responsible for appointing censors from among their professors to examine works in their respective fields.[9] The censor would read the manuscript (or revised edition of a previous book) and submit a report to the city government approving or rejecting the work.[10] He would receive six pence for reading each quire (*Bogen*) and a copy of the printed work as payment. Presumably he was then obliged to report on the book, either orally or in writing, to the council or a representative from it. The Basel city council may have reserved for itself the right to approve or disapprove each and every Hebrew title, since it refused to allow at least two Hebrew books to be printed.[11] It was also quite insistent that no "blasphemies" or slurs against Christians

---

[7] Early modern Germany never had the same degree of oversight for the Hebrew book trade or even for private libraries as the secular and papal states of Italy did. See William Popper, *The Censorship of Hebrew Books* (New York: The Knickerbocker Press, 1899).

[8] Carl Roth, "Die Bücherzensur im alten Basel," *Zentralblatt für Bibliothekswesen* 31 (1914): 50-51.

[9] Ibid., 52; Roth printed the entire ordinance on pp. 62-64. The original is preserved in the Basel SA Ratsbücher A 6 ("Schwarzesbuch"), f. 178; it was renewed on August 20, 1610. Unfortunately the reports of censors on individual books have not been preserved in the city censorship records (Basel SA, Handel und Gewerbe, JJJ 4: Zensur 1524-1833, and Universitätsarchiv, VII: Zensur 1558-1804). For an example of the standards and practices of a contemporary German Hebrew censor, see Burnett, "Hebrew Censorship in Hanau," 206-210.

[10] The city council relied upon stiff fines to ensure that the printers themselves did not print anything other than what the censor had approved. Roth, "Zensur," 52.

[11] Basel SA Protokolle, Kleiner Rat, Bd. 9, f. 71r (August 27, 1604) and Bd. 15, f. 16r (February 21, 1616), printed in Achilles Nordmann, "Geschichte der Juden in Basel seit dem Ende der zweiten Gemeinde bis zur Einführung der Glaubens und Gewissensfreihiet. 1375-1875," *Basler Zeitschrift für Geschichte und Altertumskunde* 13 (1914): 27, n. 1. The Hanau magistrates approved each Jewish book before it could go to press on the basis of a written censor's report. See Burnett, "Hebrew Censorship in Hanau," 206.

or Christianity appear in any book printed in Basel.[12] Buxtorf's expertise in Hebrew language and literature made him the obvious candidate for the position of Hebrew censor, and university regulations obliged him to accept the responsibility.

Buxtorf's personal library and papers contain mute evidence of his work as a censor. His library contains numerous copies of Basel Hebrew imprints, which were probably part of what he was paid to censor them.[13] He compiled extensive notes on Jewish prayer books printed in Germany, Italy, and Poland, noting where objectionable phrases appeared. This kind of information would have been useful to someone who was obliged to censor fourteen different prayer books between 1598 and 1603.[14] He was also familiar with euphemisms which Jewish printers used in place of more objectionable phrases, and with the practice of leaving a space where a word or phrase was deleted, so that it could be supplied later.[15]

---

[12] Buxtorf II, recalling the rabbinical Bible project in 1618-19, told James Ussher, "Deinde quod illa quae contra Christianos faciunt non fuerint restituta, factum esse, partim mandato et voluntate magistratus nostri qui ea lege permisit editionem illam, ut ne quid vel in Christum blasphemi, vel in Christianos et Christianam religionem maledici et contumeliosi in iis relinqueretur. Et qui novit persecutiones et odia gravissima, quae occasione Bibliorum istorum in hac ipsa urbe contra se excitavit pater meus, non mirabitur, ipsum sibi ab istius modi Judaeorum cavillis exprimendis cavisse." Johannes Buxtorf II to James Ussher, Basel, August 26, 1633, printed in *The Whole Works of the Most Rev. James Ussher, D. D., Lord Archbishop of Armagh, and Primate of All Ireland*, 17 vols. (Dublin: Hodges, Smith, 1864), 17: 566.

[13] The Buxtorf family library contains Prijs nos. 158, 159, 163a-b, 164-166, 174-177, 179, 187, 191-192, 194, 201, 206. See Appendix 4.

[14] Prijs, nos. 148-151, 153a-b, 157, 163a-b, 167, 169-170a-b, 181. Basel UB Ms A XII 20: 254-264. Unfortunately none of his reports on particular Hebrew books have been preserved. Buxtorf's editorial work on the medieval Jewish Bible commentaries printed in his *Biblia rabbinica* of 1618-1619 also reflect a censor's mentality and skills. See chap. 6. Similar lists of objectionable passages were compiled by Catholic censors in Italy during the sixteenth and seventeenth centuries. See Gustave Sacerdote, "Deux Index Expurgatoires de Livres Hébreux," *Revue des études juives* 30 (1895): 257-283; N. Porges, "Der hebräische Index expurgatorius qwqyzh rps," in: *Festschrift zum Siebzigsten Geburtstage A. Berliner's*, ed. A. Freimann and M. Hildesheimer, 2 vols. (Frankfurt a. M.: J. Kauffmann, 1903), 2, part 2: 273-295.

[15] Johannes Buxtorf, *Juden Schul* (Basel: Henric-Petri, 1603), 227-228. Jewish printers began to leave spaces where material was left out already in Antonius Margaritha's day. See Hans-Martin Kirn, *Das Bild vom Juden im Deutschland des frühen 16. Jahrhunderts dargestellt an den Schriften Johannes Pfefferkorns*, Texts and Studies in Medieval and Early Modern Judaism, no. 3 (Tübingen: J. C. B. Mohr (Paul Siebeck), 1989), 45, n. 134.

The printing of Hebrew books, whether for Jews or for Christian readers, was also difficult for technical reasons. Conrad Waldkirch and Ludwig König were able to produce Hebrew books only after they had acquired enough Hebrew type for the works they wished to print, including not only square script of various sizes, but also fonts for Rashi script and for *Weiberteutsch*, a typeface used for printing Yiddish books.[16] More practically, Jewish printers were indispensable for producing high quality books. Christian compositors could be trained to set type which they were not able to read, but the editing and proofreading had to be done by someone who knew Hebrew well, usually a Jew.[17]

Buxtorf's own involvement in the printing process was limited to evaluating manuscripts, preparing them to be typeset, and correcting newly typeset proofs.[18] One of Buxtorf's responsibilities was to serve as a kind of general editor for books written by Christian Hebraists. He was instrumental in printing Hugh Broughton's *An Epistle of An Ebrew Willinge to Learne Christianity,* first transcribing Abraham Ruben's letter into square Hebrew script so that the compositors could work from a clearer copy,[19] and then seeing it through press.[20] He carefully kept Kaspar

---

[16] Waldkirch probably bought most of his type from Ambrosius Froben. See Prijs' discussion of the types used by Waldkirch and König in *Drucke*, 245. On the use of a special typeface for Yiddish, see Herbert C. Zafren, "Variety in the Typography of Yiddish: 1535-1635," *Hebrew Union College Annual* 53 (1983): 137-163.

[17] Leon Voet described the responsibilities of editors and correctors in *The Golden Compasses*, vol. 2, 174-193, 286-290.

[18] Johannes Buxtorf to Kaspar Waser, January 28, 1595, Zürich ZB Ms S-150: 96, and idem to idem, December 15, 1596, Zürich ZB Ms S-151: 64, and idem to idem, Basel, December 15, 1596, Zürich ZB Ms S-151: 64.

[19] Two years later Elijah Loanz was similarly forced to transcribe his own manuscript of שַׁעֲרֵי דּוּרָא (Prijs 164), which was written in Ashkenazic script, into Italian or Spanish square script in order to simplify the work of the Christian compositors who were illiterate in Hebrew. Prijs, *Drucke*, 268.

[20] "...humanissime praestitit operam D. Boxdorphius ut transcriberet pro typographo." Hugh Broughton to the Basel Senate, n. p., n. d., printed in Hugh Broughton, *The Works of the Great Albionean Divine*, 4 vols. (London: Nathan Ekins, 1642), 3: 780. Prijs (and many of Broughton's contemporaries) have assumed that Broughton himself wrote Abraham Ruben's letter, concocting a hoax to raise money for his various projects. See Prijs, *Drucke*, 253-254, and John Strype, *The Life and Acts of John Whitgift, D. D. The Third and Last Lord Archbishop of Canterbury in the Reign of Queen Elizabeth*, 3 vols. (Oxford: Clarendon, 1822), 2: 406-415. Broughton always angrily denied these charges, and the fact that Buxtorf had to transcribe the original letter before it could be

Waser informed of the progress of his *Archetypus Grammaticae Hebraeae* between 1599 and 1600.[21] In 1607, Buxtorf sent back Johannes Drusius Jr.'s revision of Elias Levita's *Nomenclator* because Waldkirch would not be able to print it in the immediate future.[22] Buxtorf rejected Piscator's Hebrew grammar that same year as unready for publication, sending the manuscript back for revision, even though Waldkirch was willing to print it.[23] Buxtorf may also have been commissioned by Waldkirch or others to edit books written by Jewish authors for reprint, most notably Elias Levita's *Tishbi* and *Masoret ha-Masoret.*[24]

Buxtorf also helped in the manufacture of the actual Hebrew books themselves. He explicitly stated that he corrected proofs for books during 1596,[25] 1600, 1608,[26] and 1618-1619 (for the rabbinical Bible). He was presumably the anonymous gentile responsible for correcting galley proofs on Saturdays, the Jewish Sabbath, whose work was routinely criticized by the regular Jewish correc-

---

typeset may lend credence to these denials. Moreover, it is possible that Broughton was himself the victim of a hoax rather than its originator. See Cecil Roth, "The Strange Case of Hector Mendes Bravo," *Hebrew Union College Annual* 18 (1944): 223-224.

[21] Prijs 168. Buxtorf informed Waser that the book was accepted for printing in his letter of October 16, 1599 (Zürich ZB Ms S-154: 76) and informed him that work was completed on August 6, 1600 (Zürich ZB Ms S-155: 39). He also sent a stream of letters to Waser reassuring him that his book had not been forgotten by the printers. (Zürich ZB Ms S-154: 113; Ms S-155: 8b; 14,1; 14,3; 38).

[22] Drusius Sr. submitted the book for his son with his letter of February 21, 1605, Basel UB Ms G I 59: 257; Buxtorf's rejection and the reasons he gave for it are reflected in Drusius' letter of August 17, 1607, Basel UB Ms G I 59: 259.

[23] Johannes Buxtorf to Johannes Piscator, n. p., September 10, 1607, Gotha FB Ms Chart. A 130: 134; printed in: Cyprian, *Clarorum virorum epistolae*, 154-155.

[24] Prijs nos. 172, 188.

[25] "Addere debuo superioribus causis labores typographicos quibus detineor rarsus. Alterium cuium tractatum Talmudicum excudendum suscepit Waldkirchius cui artb abb nomen huic corrigendo operam do." Buxtorf to Waser, Basel, December 15, 1596, Zürich ZB Ms S-151: 64. Prijs did not mention this imprint in *Drucke*; the earliest known Jewish books printed by Waldkirch appeared in 1598 (nos. 148-153).

[26] "Editionem Bibliorum hebraicorum molimur, et habes hic examplar ex quo de forma utcuique judicare poteris. Correctura mecum praeerit aliquis doctus judaeus, ut et inter ipsos tanto melius distrahi possint." Buxtorf to Waser, Basel, February 7, 1608, Zürich ZB S-160: 45. Presumably this Bible edition is Prijs no. 207, which was completed in January 26, 1612 and was edited by Mordecai b. Joseph Judah Wahl of Frankfurt.

tors.[27] Buxtorf probably corrected his own books as well, an arrangement that would have enabled him to ensure that they were accurately printed and given him the chance to earn a little more money or a few extra copies of his works to sell, trade, or give as gifts.[28]

The most intractable problem faced by Waldkirch and König when trying to run a profitable Hebrew press was where they could house their Jewish workers. Since 1397 no Jews had been allowed to live in Basel itself except for a few who worked for the Hebrew printers.[29] Jewish merchants were allowed to enter the city only once a month.[30] Basel's northerly neighbors—the Austrian-ruled Breisgau, Baden-Durlach, and a sprinkling of smaller principalities—had for the most part expelled their Jewish residents before 1590.[31] Fortunately the Bishops of Basel were less restrictive in their Jewish residence policies than other neighboring countries, making Hebrew printing possible in Basel.[32]

---

[27] Isaac Eckendorf, Elijah Loanz, and Abraham Braunschweig all complained about gentile correctors on the Sabbath. See Abraham Yaari, "Complaints of Proofreaders about Printing by Gentiles on the Sabbath (Hebrew)," in *Studies in Hebrew Booklore* (Jerusalem: Mossad Harav Kook, 1958), 174-175.

[28] Voet, *Golden Compasses*, 2: 300-301.

[29] See Nordmann, "Geschichte," 28, and Burnett, "Circumcision Incident," 136-137.

[30] This policy, first established in 1552, is recorded in the Basel SA, Basel Stadt, Ratsbücher, A 6 (Schwarzes Buch), f. 87a, and is printed in Nordmann, "Geschichte," 15, n. 2. The *Oberstknecht* was responsible for supervising the master of the watch, the paymaster and the city messengers. He reported directly to the city council. Rudolf Wackernagel, *Geschichte der Stadt Basel*, vol. 2, part 1 (Basel: Helbing & Lichtenhahn, 1911), 233.

[31] See Georges Weill, Recherches sur la Démographie des Juifs d'Alsace du XVIe au XVIIIe Siècle," *Revue des études Juives* 130 (1971): 60-61, and Werner Baumann, *Ernst Friedrich von Baden-Durlach: Die Bedeutung der Religion für Leben und Politik eines süddeutschen Fürsten im Zeitalter der Gegenreformation*, Veröffentlichungen der Kommission für geschichtliche Landeskunde in Baden-Württemberg, Reihe B: Forschungen, Band 20 (Stuttgart: W. Kohlhammer, 1962), 15. Franz Hundsnurscher and Gerhard Taddey relate the history of Jewish communities within the smaller principalities in *Die jüdischen Gemeinden in Baden. Denkmale, Geschichte, Schicksale*, Veröffentlichungen der Staatliche Archivverwaltung Baden-Württemberg, Bd. 19 (Stuttgart: Kohlhammer, 1968).

[32] The only other place in Switzerland which allowed Jewish residence at this time were the villages of Lengnau and Endingen in the County of Baden and the domain of Rheintal in the *Gemeine Herrschaften*. See Karl Heinz Burmeister, "Die jüdische Landgemeinde in Rheineck im 17. Jahrhundert," and Thomas Armbruster, "Die jüdische Dörfer von Lengnau und Endingen," in:

The Catholic Bishops of Basel allowed individual Jews to live for fixed periods of time within the territories where they had secular jurisdiction.[33] Although there was no official Jewish community within the prince bishopric, a Jewish cemetery was maintained in Zwingen throughout this period.[34] Allschwil was the only village in the prince bishopric that had a substantial number of Jewish inhabitants during Buxtorf's lifetime.[35] When the town was opened to Jewish settlement in 1567, a handful of other Jews were allowed to reside there, the most prominent of them a physician named Joseph who managed to establish a thriving practice that included many Baslers, thus "provoking" the Basel city council to complain to the bishop.[36] Dr. Joseph lived in Allschwil until his death in 1610. After 1612/1613 there are no more entries in the Jewish tax records for Allschwil, suggesting that there were no more Jewish inhabitants.[37]

The Jewish residence policies of Basel and the dearth of Jewish communities anywhere near it meant that Basel's Hebrew printers were constantly forced to seek out skilled Jewish printers from abroad and to look for business from Jewish clients in other lands. Both Conrad Waldkirch and Ludwig König were general printers who produced Jewish books when commissioned by Jewish clients.

Landjudentum im Süddeutschen- und Bodenseeraum. Wissenschaftliche Tagung zur Eröffnung des Jüdischen Museums Hohenems vom 9. bis 11. April 1991, Forschungen zur Geschichte Vorarlbergs, vol. 11 (Dornbirn: Vorarlberger Verlagsanstalt, 1992), 22-37, 38-86.

[33] This was a fairly common practice during the sixteenth and seventeenth centuries. See Hedwig Heider, "Die Rechtsgeschichte des Deutschen Judentums bis zum Ausgang des Absolutismus und die Judenordnungen in den Rheinischen Territorialstaaten," (Doctor of Legal Sciences, Universität Bielefeld, 1973), 85. Hans Berner discussed the Jewish policy of the bishops of Basel during this period in *"Die Gute Correspondence." Die Politik der Stadt Basel gegenüber dem Fürstbistum Basel in den Jahren 1525-1585*, Basler Beiträge zur Geschichtswissenschaft, no. 158, (Basel: Helbing & Lichtenhahn, 1989), 132, 139-140, 150.

[34] Achilles Nordmann, "Über den Judenfriedhof in Zwingen und Judenniederlassungen im Fürstbistum Basel," *Basler Zeitschrift für Geschichte und Altertumskunde* 6 (1907): 120-151.

[35] There may also have been Jews living in Aesch. See Nordmann, "Zwingen," 145. Buxtorf owned a copy of a Jewish marriage contract written in Aesch on June 3, 1591 (Basel UB Ms R III 7).

[36] See Felix Platter, *Tagebuch (Lebensbeschreibung) 1536-1567*, ed. Valentin Lötscher, Basler Chroniken, no. 10 (Basel: Schwabe, 1976), 337-338, and Berner, "Gute Correspondenz," 139-140.

[37] Nordmann, "Zwingen," 145.

They also printed Hebrew books for Christian authors, such as Buxtorf himself and his friend Kaspar Waser of Zürich. Whether dealing with Christian Hebraists or with Jews, Waldkirch and König needed a competent correspondence secretary and representative who was literate in Hebrew, someone like Buxtorf himself.

Buxtorf first mentioned Waldkirch's printing business in his correspondence during 1596, yet within four years he had become a well-known figure in the Hebrew book trade.[38] In 1599 he told Kaspar Waser, "I receive numerous letters from Jews in various places, even Poland, but the Waldkirch printing firm is the reason. [It is for] the same [reason] that they repeatedly send works to be printed."[39] Incidental references to Jewish financiers, authors, and print shop workers from Lithuania, Poland, Bohemia, and Germany in the books that Waldkirch printed lend credence to Buxtorf's claims.[40] In other letters Buxtorf told his correspondents of contacts he had made with Jews in Vienna, Cracow, Prague, and Constantinople.[41] In 1610 he boasted to Isaac Casaubon that he wrote Hebrew so well that many of his Jewish correspondents assumed that he was a Jewish convert "because they think that it is impossible for a Christian to achieve my level of stylistic profi-

---

[38] The first book printed by Waldkirch which contained Hebrew characters was a disputation which appeared in 1593 (Prijs no. 146*), indicating that he owned at least some Hebrew type even at that early date.

[39] "A judiais crebras literas accipio ex variis locis, etiam ipsa Polonias sed typographia Waldkirchii causam illis praebet, id quam suabinde scripta excudem demittunt." Buxtorf to Waser, n. p., ca. February 6-July 23, 1599, Zürich ZB Ms S-154: 40. This undated letter served as a letter of introduction for Johann Philipp Pareus, a student of Buxtorf's who had just received his Master of Arts (=Doctor of Philosophy) degree at Basel and was about to begin his *iter litterarium*. Pareus graduated on February 6, 1599 and enrolled as a student at the Academy in Geneva on July 23, 1599. Pareus' journey ended on May 1, 1600 when he registered as a student again at the University in Heidelberg, his home city. See Wackernagel, *Matrikel*, 2: 468.

[40] Lithuania: Jacob Menahem b. Judah Eliezer (Menkes) of Brest Litowsk (Prijs 198) and Jacob b. Abraham Pollock Buchhändler (Prijs nos. 153, 159, 167, 169, 174, 185); Poland: Sabbatai b. Mordecai Gumplin (Prijs no. 158) and his son Mordecai b. Sabbatai (Prijs nos. 182, 205-206, 219?) of Poznan; Bohemia: Haim b. Simha Ashkenazi of Leipa (Prijs no. 197); Germany: Elia Loanz (Prijs nos. 163-166), Isaiah Anaw (Prijs no. 201), and Mordecai Wahl (Prijs no. 207), all of Frankfurt.

[41] See his letters to Kaspar Waser, May 1, 1599, Zürich ZB Ms S-150: 32, and to Joseph Scaliger, Basel, April 3, 1606, Utrecht UB Ms 987: 237-238; printed in: Burman, *Sylloges*, 2: 362-364, and to Isaac Casaubon, September, 1610, London: British Library, Burney Ms 363: 130.

ciency."[42] Unfortunately very little of his business correspondence with Jews survives.[43]

Buxtorf also travelled frequently to book fairs to represent the Basel Hebrew printers.[44] These contacts were particularly important to Conrad Waldkirch because he probably worked only as a manufacturer of Jewish books. Waldkirch produced twenty six Hebrew and Yiddish books intended primarily for Jewish buyers between 1599-1603, but he did not advertise any of them in the Leipzig book fair sales catalogues; he did advertise Hebraica books intended for Christian buyers. When Waldkirch printed *Iggeret Shelomim*, a collection of Hebrew letters in 1603, the version intended for Christians appeared in the Leipzig catalogue, but the Jewish version did not. When Buxtorf mentioned the book in *Institutio Epistolaris Hebraica* (1610), his own introduction to Hebrew letter-writing, he referred to the book as "printed in Basel," but "available for purchase from the Jews in Frankfurt."[45] Waldkirch's Jewish clients probably paid for the production of Jewish books and were then responsible for selling them.[46] Buxtorf

---

[42] "...plera judaeorum pars putant me esse judaeum baptizatum, quod incredibile putarunt Christianum ad tantum linguae peritiam pervenire posse, qualem ex stilo meo dijudicarunt." Johannes Buxtorf to Isaac Casaubon, Basel, September 1610, London: British Library, Burney Ms 363: 130.

[43] The Günzburg collection of the Russian State Library, Moscow, Ms 1213, ff. 5b-6a, 8b-13a (copy held by the Institute of Microfilmed Hebrew Manuscripts, Jewish National and University Library, Jerusalem) contains correspondence from Abraham Braunschweig, Isaac Eckendorf, and Mordecai Gumplin to Buxtorf I. The collection of letters was described by Eliakim Carmoly in "Varietes Critiques et Litteraires. IV. Sefer ha-Maaloth," *Revue orientale* (Brussels) 1 (1841): 345-348.

[44] For example, in late 1596 Buxtorf made arrangements to offer copies of Johannes Drusius's *De Quaesitis per Epistolam* (Franeker: Aegidium Radaeum, 1595) for sale in Strasbourg. See Johannes Buxtorf to Kaspar Waser, January 28, 1595, Zürich ZB Ms S-150: 96, and idem to idem, December 15, 1596, Zürich ZB Ms S-151: 64.

[45] *Catalogus universalis pro Nundinis Frankfurtensibus Autumnalibus de Anno 1603...Mit vermehrung anderer Bücher/so in der Leipziger Michels Mess aussgehen* (Leipzig: Abraham Lamberg, [1603]), f. C 2r. Buxtorf wrote, "Alter *Iggeret Shelomim*, qui hic Basileae ante paucos annos recusus, apud Judaeos Francofurti venditur." *Institutio Epistolaris Hebraica sive De conscribendis Epistolis Liber, Cum Eipstolarum Hebraicaurm Centuria*, ed. Johannes Buxtorf II (Basel: König, 1629), 76. For a description of the two printings see Prijs no. 185A-B.

[46] E. g., Simon Levi Günzburg was financial sponsor of the Basel Talmud and also planned to sell it; Froben was only responsible for overseeing its printing. See Ernst Staehelin, "Des Basler Buchdruckers Ambrosius Forben

would have had ample opportunity to meet with Jewish book dealers personally when he attended the spring and autumn Frankfurt book fairs.[47] His visits to Frankfurt and perhaps to Hanau would have given Buxtorf some opportunity to observe Jewish community life at first hand.[48]

Buxtorf's efforts to find new business for Waldkirch were relatively successful. During two periods, from 1598-1603 and 1606-1612, Waldkirch produced forty nine books specifically intended for a Jewish reading public. During the first period thirty four books were printed, including fourteen prayer books, an important staple in the Jewish book trade, and six Yiddish books, five of them printed in 1602.[49] The lull in printing between 1604-1605 may have been a result of new restrictions which a rabbinical synod in Frankfurt placed upon Jewish printing in 1603, renewing a regulation passed in 1582.[50] It stated that

> No Jew in our province shall be permitted to publish any book, old or new, at Basel or any other city in Germany, without the permission of the "central courts" (*Batai Aboth Beth Din*). If anyone transgresses this law and publishes the books without permission, no man shall purchase the books under punishment of the ban.[51]

Talmudausgabe und Handel mit Rom," *Basler Zeitschrift für Geschichte und Altertumskunde* 30 (1931): 7-37.

[47] See Johannes Buxtorf to Kaspar Waser, September 1, 1599, Zürich ZB Ms S-154: 56 and idem to Wilhelm Schickhard, Basel, August 12, 1627, WLB Cod. hist. 2to 563. Buxtorf once complained to Waser, "Judaei non libenter mecum amplius libros communicant, nec aliunde quam Francofurto comparandi occasionem habeo." Buxtorf to Kaspar Waser, Basel, July 14, 1609, Zürich SA Ms E II 383: 853-4.

[48] In *Juden Schul* Buxtorf mentioned that he heard a homily on circumcision (124) and had seen a cantor at work (232-233).

[49] Moshe Rosenfeld noted that as a "mass-produced item" prayer book printing was the "daily bread" of early modern Jewish printing. See idem, "Jüdischer Buchdruck am Beispiel der Sulzbacher Druckerei," in: *Geschichte und Kultur der Juden in Bayern. Aufsätze*, eds. Manfred Treml, Josef Kirmeier, and Evamaria Brockhoff, Veröffentlichungen zur Bayerischen Geschichte und Kultur, Nr. 17/88 (München: Haus der Bayerischen Geschichte, 1988), 238.

[50] The Basel magistrate may also have temporarily refused to allow Jewish printing during 1604-1605, since it refused to give permission for one Jewish book to be printed in August of 1604. See Basel SA Protokolle, Kleiner Rat, Bd. 9, f. 71r (August 27, 1604), printed in Nordmann, "Geschichte," 27, n. 1.

[51] Eric Zimmer, *Jewish Synods in Germany during the Late Middle Ages (1268-1603)* (New York: Yeshiva Univ. Press, 1978), 83. On the possible

Not long afterwards, in 1607, the Council of the Four Lands in
Poland decreed that "learned men" (*Medakdekim*) were to examine
newly published prayer books from Basel or Moravia, a regulation
which served to control the spread of subversive ideas (such as
aristotelianism) and to defend local Polish printers against foreign
competition at the same time.[52] Although rabbinical regulations
may have hindered Jews from having their books printed in Basel,
in the end it was the foundation of a Jewish press staffed by Jewish
workers in the principality of Hanau that effectively put an end to
Jewish printing in Basel. Apart from the Rabbinical Bible of 1618-
1619, the only other time after 1612 that Basel's Hebrew printers
sought permission to print a Jewish book was in 1616, a year when
the Hanau press was experiencing financial difficulties.[53]

After 1612 the Basel Hebrew printers were able to continue in
their specialty business largely because Christian Hebraists, particularly Buxtorf, took the place of their Jewish clients. Buxtorf himself edited and helped produce two monumental works, the *Biblia
rabbinica* and Hebrew Bible Concordance, in addition to a number
of shorter works. By allowing Jewish printing in the city, the Basel
magistrate had in effect made it possible for Waldkirch, and later
König to assemble a skilled work force and the necessary type to
produce Buxtorf's works.[54] They were also able to produce more
ephemeral works such as collections of occasional poetry and
printed disputations with Hebrew phrases and quotations, thanks to
the investments they had first made to meet the needs of their
Jewish clients.[55] During these years Hebrew printing became an

---

effectiveness of these regulations, see Burnett, "Hebrew Censorship in Hanau,"
201-203.

[52] Zimmer, *Jewish Synods*, 85.

[53] Gustav Könnecke, *Hessisches Buchdruckerbuch enthaltend Nachweis aller
bisher bekannt gewordenen Buchdruckereien des jetzigen Regierungsbezirks
Cassel und des Kreises Biedenkopf* (Marburg: N. G. Elwert, 1894), 138. On the
attempt to restart Jewish printing in Basel during 1616, see Basel SA Protokolle,
Kleiner Rat, Bd. 15, f. 16r (February 21, 1616), printed in Nordmann,
"Geschichte," 27, n. 1.

[54] Van Rooden discussed the problems that Christian Hebraist Constantijn
L'Empereur had in finding a printer willing to print his books in *Theology*, 131-
132.

[55] Buxtorf contributed a Hebrew occasional poem to *Carmina Gratulatoria ab
amicis scripta, in Honorem Ornatiss. Viri D. M. Balthasiris Crosnievvicii, Lituani
cum ei in Illustri Academic Basiliensi Gradus Docturae Theologicae 8. Septembr.
conferretur à Clariß. & excellentiß. viro, Dn. Amando Polano à Polansdorf, SS.*

important part of Basel's overall book production, constituting 10% of all books printed there between 1600-1625.[56]

Buxtorf made many useful contacts through the printing business who helped him to build an impressive personal library of Hebraica and to find particular books for his friends and correspondents.[57] Before 1620 Buxtorf probably directed most of his requests to Walter Keuchen, the Hebrew censor of Hanau, to his friends in the Netherlands, most notably Thomas Erpenius of Leiden, and to several German and Polish Jewish booksellers, including Abraham Braunschweig and Mordecai Gumplin.[58] Paul Ferry, a Reformed pastor in Metz, also served as a purchasing agent for Buxtorf.[59]

Buxtorf's purchasing agents and representatives may have simplified his task of finding copies of rare and unusual Hebrew books, but he was still obliged to pay for what they found. Unfortunately he left no record of when he bought each of his books or how much they cost him, but he must have spent a considerable part of his annual income on building up his library. According to one account Buxtorf paid 200 Reichstaler to purchase a complete set of the Basel Talmud, about 3 years of his annual

---

Theo. D. & Professore, Decano Facultatis Theologicae (Basel: Conrad Waldkirch, 1601). [Gdansk: Polish Academy of Sciences library, call no. Cf 816 8° [Pol.XVI w] adl. 20]. For examples of disputations containing Hebrew words or phrases, see see Prijs, nos. 146+, 168*, 245, 247-249, passim.

[56] Hans R. Guggisberg, "Reformierter Stadtstaat und Zentrum der Spätrenaissance: Basel in der zweiten Hälfte des 16. Jahrhunderts, in: *Renaissance/Reformation: Gegensätze und Gemeinsamkeiten*, ed. August Buck, Wolfenbütteler Abhandlung zur Renaissanceforschung, no. 5 (Wiesbaden: O. Harrassowitz, 1984), 214.

[57] Joseph Scaliger and Johannes Drusius both requested that he purchase books for them. See Johannes Buxtorf to Joseph Scaliger, Basel, April 3, 1606, Utrecht UB Ms 987: 237-238, printed in *Sylloges*, 2: 363, and Johannes Drusius to Johannes Buxtorf, n. p., August 10, 1607, Basel UB Ms G I 59: 259.

[58] See, for example, Keuchen to Buxtorf, Frankfurt am Main, April 10, 1615, Basel UB Ms G I 60: 322; Erpenius to Buxtorf, Leiden, April 10, 1614, Basel UB Ms G I 59: 273, and Abraham Braunschweig to Johannes Buxtorf, n. p., October 7, 1615, (Hebrew); printed in M. Kayserling, "Richelieu, Buxtorf Pére et Fils, Jacob Roman. Documents pour servir à l'histoire du commerce de la librairie juive au XVIIe siècle," *Revue des études juives* 8 (1884): 84.

[59] Ferry to Buxtorf, Metz, March 5, 1623, Basel UB Ms G I 62: 131. On Ferry see *Religion in Geschichte und Gegenwart*, 3d ed., s. v. "Ferry, Paul." by J. Moltmann.

salary.[60] Apart from paying cash for books Buxtorf was sometimes able to trade copies of his own books for Hebrew books.[61] Through purchase, trading, and censor's copies Buxtorf was able to amass a large collection of Hebrew and Yiddish books, one which in a real sense served as the foundation upon which the first Hebrew bibliography would be based.[62]

Buxtorf's involvement with Hebrew printing and the Jewish book trade also gave him unusual opportunities to become acquainted with Jews and to question them about academic matters, their culture, and their religion. The two Jewish scholars Buxtorf probably knew best were Jacob Buchhändler and Abraham Braunschweig, both of whom worked for the Basel Hebrew printers. Jacob was an important figure in the early Waldkirch press and was responsible for editing numerous works, both Hebrew and Yiddish between 1598 and 1603. Abraham Braunschweig served as the principal editor of Buxtorf's edition of the Venice rabbinical Bible of 1618-1620.[63] Other Jews who worked for Waldkirch included R. Elijah Loanz of Frankfurt and Isaac Eckendorf, who

---

[60] J. F. A. de le Roi, *Die evangelische Christenheit und die Juden in der Zeit der Herrschaft christlicher Lebensanschauungen unter den Völkern*, vol. 1: *Von der Reformation bis zur Mitte des 18. Jahrhunderts* (Karlsruhe und Leipzig: H. Reuther, 1884; reprint: Leipzig: Zentralantiquariat der Deutschen Demokratischen Republik, 1974), 137. Buxtorf's salary was only 150 Basel Pounds annually and the price was about 400 Basel Pounds. See Staehelin, *Geschichte*, XVIII for a conversion table.

[61] Although Erasmus was not paid for his publishing a century earlier he did a brisk business in selling complementary copies of his books, a practice followed by other authors. See Voet, *Golden Compasses*, 2: 284.

[62] See below, chap 5, and Appendix 4.

[63] Jacob b. Abraham of Meseritz (=Miendzyrzercz) in Lithuania, known as Jacob Buchhändler, served as editor or corrector for Prijs nos. 153a-b, 157, 159, 167, 169, 170a-b, 174, 178, and 185 a-b. Buxtorf mentions Abraham of Klingnau ("Abraham judaeum Klingovensem") in his letter to Waser, Basel July 14, 1609, Zürich SA Ms E II 383: 853-4. Augusta Weldler-Steinberg, *Geschichte der Juden in der Schweiz vom 16. Jahrhundert bis nach der Emanzipation*, ed. Florence Guggenheim-Grünberg, 2 vols. (Goldach: Schweizerischen Israelitischen Gemeindebund, 1966-1970), 1: 61 noted that Abraham Braunschweig lived in Lengnau (a town in the same area as Klingnau) after his period of residence in Basel. The earliest reference to Braunschwieg's professional relationship with Buxtorf is his letter of October 7, 1615, printed in Kayserling, "Richelieu," 84. He served as printer in both Basel and in Hanau. See StCB nos. 383 (1610) and 413 (1617), and Burnett, "Circumcision Incident," 136-143.

edited R. Nathan's *Aruk*.[64] These scholarly workmen were probably the Jews whom Buxtorf would periodically invite to eat at his home in order to discuss his questions about Jewish beliefs and practices.[65] Buxtorf also went to Allschwil several times to question Jews about their beliefs and practices, and he drew upon several of these conversations when writing *Juden Schul*.[66] Buxtorf's conversations with his Jewish informants probably took place in German, although he claimed that he could also speak Hebrew when necessary.[67] The fact that they took place at all reflects the trust that Buxtorf's Jewish acquaintances had in him as a person, since they skirted close to the boundaries of Jewish law by having such a close relationship with a Christian and explaining their religion to him.[68] One of the printers even told him about a Jewish

---

[64] Elijah b. Moses Loanz of Frankfurt worked on Prijs nos. 163a-b, 164, 165, 166. 1599-1600 (see StCB pp. 942-3) and Isaac b. Moses Eckendorf (Eggendorf?)/Austria served as editor and corrector for Nathan b. Yehiel's rps °wr[(Prijs no. 158. 1599).

[65] "Judaeorum etiam conversationem adhibuit, qua factum est, ut propriis sumptibus saepe per aliquot menses Judaeos in aedibus aleret, & ab iis quicquid secretioris & reconditioris doctrine quicquid rituum & Ceremoniarum Judaicarum est rimaretur successu plane admirabili ut ipsius libri, quos exegitaere perenniores documenta suggerunt ad omnem memoriam illustrissima." Tossanus, *Johannis Buxtorfii, Senioris*, 10. Tossanus might, however, be alluding to July and August of 1619 when Buxtorf (and also Ludwig König) was obliged to take Jewish printers into his home until the completion of the Basel rabbinical Bible. Unfortunately neither Buxtorf nor his biographer indicated whether he made special arrangements (such as serving them kosher food) to accomodate Jewish boarders in his home.

[66] Basel UB Ms A XII 20, pp. 282 (May 29, 1600), 287 (May 10, 1600). See Buxtorf, *Juden Schul*, 40, 412, 521, 585, 311-312. Buxtorf might also have learned of regional variations in Jewish customs from his Jewish informants, although some of this information was available in print through books of Jewish customs (*Minhagim*). Cf. *Juden Schul*, 412, 462, 466, 468, 489-491, 498, 517, 525, 581

[67] Yiddish had become the dominent vernacular language of northern European Jews by the sixteenth century, and so Buxtorf would have had a common language with both Polish and German Jews. Simon Dubnov, *History of the Jews*, vol. 3: *From the Later Middle Ages to the Renaissance*, trans. Moshe Spiegel (South Brunswick: Thomas Yoseloff, 1969), 836 (and n. 1). Buxtorf once met two Jewish converts from Italy and spoke some Hebrew with them. "Cum alternito tantum illex loqui potui, et quidem hebraea lingua quantum necesse fuit." Buxtorf to Caspar Waser, Basel, September 1, 1599, Zürich ZB Ms 154: 56.

[68] Jacob Katz, *Exclusiveness and Tolerance: Studies in Jewish-Gentile Relations in Medieval and Modern Times*, Scripta Judaica, no. 3 (Oxford: Oxford University, 1961), 37-39. A number of rabbis addressed the question of what

convert who had returned to Judaism, an extremely sensitive topic.[69] Had Buxtorf been rabidly anti-Jewish they would hardly have eaten with him, much less discussed their religion.

It was Buxtorf's close relationship with a Jewish co-worker which brought about the best-known incident of his life: the circumcision incident of 1619.[70] When Abraham Braunschweig's wife bore him a son he invited Buxtorf, Ludwig König the Younger and several others to attend the circumcision together with some Jewish guests from outside of Basel. Inviting Buxtorf and the other Christians to witness the circumcision must have been a unique gesture of friendship by Abraham Braunschweig. The ceremony itself took place on June 2, 1619, without any problems, although Buxtorf told Waser that he took the opportunity to admonish Braunschweig and the other Jewish guests to avail themselves of the true circumcision of the heart and convert to Christianity.[71]

Official reaction to the circumcision was both swift and harsh. One of the city's pastors submitted a written complaint about the incident on June 5 to the city council. The council ordered that the Jews be arrested and decided to investigate the entire incident.[72] Buxtorf feared the worst from the council's deliberations. He wrote to Waser on June 15 that he had become an object of hatred for all, not only because he had witnessed the circumcision, but because he had sponsored the publication of a Jewish book.[73] He fully expected that the three Jewish correctors would be expelled from

---

Jewish teachers could appropriately teach their Christian Hebrew students during the sixteenth century. See Eric Zimmer, "Jewish and Christian Collaboration in Sixteenth Century Germany," *Jewish Quarterly Review* 71 (1980): 70-71, n. 5.

[69] "Es ist zu Seltz ... ein Jud welchen die andere Juden uberaus rhümen von grosser geschicklichkeit und wissenschafft, und wie er die Christen an vielen Orten mit disputieren überwunden hab ... Daher mir von meinem Judischen mit Corrector alhie, in ein Ohr vertrauwet worden als wenn man denselben im argwohn halte, es seye der, welcher sich bei euch (i. e. in Zürich) hat tauffen lassen." Buxtorf to Kaspar Waser, Basel, February 3, 1619, Zürich ZB Ms F-169: 46r.

[70] I have discussed the incident in considerable detail in "Circumcision Incident," 135-144.

[71] Ibid., 140-141.

[72] Basel SA, Basel Stadt, Protokolle, Kleiner Rat, Bd. 16, f. 154r (June 5, 1619), and Buxtorf to Waser, Basel, June 15, 1619, Zürich ZB Ms F 167: 47, printed in Burnett, "Circumcision Incident," 143-144.

[73] "Non tantum ob spectata circumcisionem, sed et propter librum judaicum, cujus impressionis ego sim author." Burnett, "Circumcision Incident," 143.

the city and that the rabbinical Bible edition would have to be abandoned although it was nearly finished. There was even talk that Buxtorf himself should be expelled from the city.[74]

In the end, Ludwig König the elder was able to persuade the city council to relent and allow his Jewish workers to finish the rabbinical Bible edition in time for the autumn book fair at Frankfurt. The council ruled that the Jews would be allowed to remain in Basel until their work was completed, but they were ordered to stay in the houses of König and Buxtorf, who would also pay for their keep. Once the Bible edition was completed, the Jews were to be expelled from the city. Abraham Braunschweig was sentenced to pay a fine of 400 *Reichstaler*, an enormous sum, because he was responsible for the whole incident; Buxtorf and König were each fined 100 Reichstaler for their role in the affair. For Buxtorf the fine was higher than his entire annual salary as a university professor.[75]

The circumcision incident illustrates the social and religious barriers separating Jew and Christian in the Germanic world. Braunschweig and his family were allowed to live in Basel only under exceptional circumstances, and even though they had sought permission for the circumcision they were punished all the same, as was the *Oberstknecht*, Georg Martin Gläser, for exceeding his authority and allowing the ceremony to take place at all. While Jewish printing and the Jewish book trade afforded Christians and Jews greater opportunities for social and intellectual exchanges, there were certain limits which could not be transgressed without incurring the wrath of civil and ecclesiastical authorities.

Whatever Buxtorf actually did say to Abraham Braunschweig at the circumcision did not end their relationship. Johannes Buxtorf II continued to buy books from Braunschweig after his father's death.[76] For his part Abraham Braunschweig remained friendly to Christians and was willing to indulge their curiosity. In 1645 he invited Johann Heinrich Hottinger's father to a Purim celebration.[77]

---

[74] "Sunt qui dicant, et me cum libro ejici debere." Ibid.

[75] Buxtorf's salary was only 150 Basel Pounds annually and the fine was about 200 Basel Pounds. Staehelin, *Geschichte*, XVIII.

[76] Kayserling, "Richelieu," 79.

[77] "Invitat Parentem ad festum Purim." Johann Heinrich Hottinger added this note to a letter written by Abraham Braunschweig to him on February 5, 1645, n. p., Zürich ZB Ms F 85: 550.

Buxtorf's dealings with his Jewish acquaintances reveal that he was quite approachable and could discuss even such potentially divisive issues as the differences between Judaism and Christianity without alienating them. The Jews employed by Waldkirch and König were willing to talk with him about their religion and customs. Abraham Braunschweig was even willing to invite Buxtorf to witness the circumcision of his son. It is clear from Buxtorf's dealings with the Jews that whatever his thoughts were toward their religion he had few difficulties relating to them on either a personal or professional level. While this familiarity hardly excludes his harboring anti-Semitic attitudes against the Jews, it is none the less a significant factor in understanding the background of Buxtorf's works on the Jews.

Buxtorf's involvement in the Hebrew book trade provided him not only with an additional source of income, but also with a variety of useful professional skills and a network of Jewish contacts. He was able to perfect his Hebrew composition skills through regular business correspondence with Jewish clients, and he learned to edit and correct proofs for Hebrew books, skills which he put to good use when he began to produce his own books. By helping to build up Waldkirch's Hebrew printing business, he also created a channel for publication of his own books, which gave him a decided advantage over many other Christian Hebraists. However, the greatest professional advantage which Buxtorf gained through his work in the book trade was not the technical skills and experience he acquired, but the Jewish acquaintances he made through the business.

The impact that Buxtorf's personal and professional contacts with Jews had upon his works is hard to assess fully, but it was probably quite important. He sought their advice on his study of the Hebrew language, the rabbinical Bible, post-biblical Jewish literature. They were also probably unwitting informants for *Juden Schul*. When Buxtorf discussed Judaism he was referring not merely to a theological abstraction derived from the biblical text and anti-Jewish polemics, but also in part to a living religion he himself had observed and discussed with his Jewish contemporaries. Through them he was also able to build his personal library of Hebraica, which he used to enrich both his teaching and writing. Through his teaching at Basel university, his private study of

Hebrew, and his involvement in the Hebrew book trade Buxtorf became uniquely qualified among his Christian contemporaries to adapt Jewish learning for use in the Christian academy.

CHAPTER THREE

THEOLOGICAL POLEMICS AND BUXTORF'S
ETHNOGRAPHY OF THE JEWS

Johannes Buxtorf was considered by his contemporaries to be the greatest Christian authority on Jews and Judaism. His only published work on the subject, *Juden Schul* (*Jewish Synagogue*), helped establish his reputation as a Hebraist and remained a standard work on Judaism until well into the eighteenth century. Buxtorf's two unpublished works, *Aus was Ursachen die Juden andere völker alzeit gehasst unnd veracht haben* (*The Reasons Why Jews have Always Hated and Despised Other Peoples*) and a new edition of Raymond Martini's *Pugio fidei*, attest both to his theological opposition to Judaism and to his familiarity with post-biblical Jewish literature. While Buxtorf's polemical tone in each of these works is apparent, his reasons for composing them have remained obscure, as have his opinions concerning the Jews, Judaism, and Jewry as a social order within the German empire. Addressing these problems clarifies not only the place of Buxtorf's works within the history of anti-Jewish discourse, but also tests his reliability as a witness to early modern Jewish life.

Buxtorf was uniquely qualified among his Christian contemporaries to understand and explain Judaism. He was unusually well-read in post-biblical Jewish literature, and he had extensive personal contacts with Jews in the area around Basel and in centers of Jewish life such as Frankfurt which he had made through the printing business. He was not, however, a neutral observer of Jewish culture. Buxtorf had been trained in Reformed theology at Herborn and functioned as a member of the theology faculty in Basel. Buxtorf's anti-Jewish writings were a relatively small part of his entire corpus, but they mirror his theological concerns, his professional activities as a censor, and his personal and professional relationships with Jews. How these different factors affected Buxtorf's understanding of Jews and Judaism can be seen most clearly in his only published book on Judaism, *Juden Schul*.

Juden Schul can justly be considered an "ethnography of the Jews," since Buxtorf devoted almost 500 pages to a narrative description of Jewish life from cradle to grave, quoting copiously from Jewish books throughout.[1] Buxtorf himself was able to confirm and elaborate upon some of the customs and practices he described by referring to conversations he had had with Jews or to phenomena he himself had seen.[2] To characterize the book solely as a kind of anthropological treatise, however, would be to misunderstand it in a fundamental way. Buxtorf wrote *Juden Schul* as a theological examination of Judaism, using ethnography as his literary vehicle. He was not the first author to employ ethnographic description in the service of theology, and his book drew upon previous works by Jewish converts for its underlying theology, its structure, and some of its contents.

Antonius Margaritha's book *Der Gantz Jüdisch Glaub* (1530) was the literary model that Buxtorf followed when composing *Juden Schul. Der Gantz Jüdisch Glaub* in many ways epitomizes the use of ethnography in anti-Jewish polemics. Margaritha set out to prove that the Jews were not true followers of the Old Testament law but instead followed laws of their own making, illustrating his contentions by contrasting observant Jewish life with the dictates of the Scriptures. He hoped that by demonstrating that the Jews had forsaken the Bible for the teachings of the rabbis he could convince them to abandon their ancestral faith and convert to Christianity as he had done. Christians who read his book were not to despise the Jews for their ignorance and blindness, but rather they should look to themselves lest they suffer a similar fate.[3] Margaritha's book consisted of two major sections, an ethnographic description and a translation of the prayer book into German, as well as several several smaller parts including one which treated Jewish messianic expectations.

The underlying theology of *Juden Schul* is strikingly similar to what Margaritha spelled out in his *Gantz Jüdisch Glaub*. In the in-

---

[1] Hsia, "Ethnographies of Jews," 230-231.

[2] Buxtorf, *Juden Schul*, 40, 124, 158, 232-233, 412, 469, 521.

[3] Victor of Carben, Johann Pfefferkorn, Antonius Margaritha, and Ernst Ferdinand Hess all espoused much the same underlying theological program in their "ethnographies of the Jews." See Stephen G. Burnett, "Distorted Mirrors: Antonius Margaritha, Johann Buxtorf and Christian Ethnographies of the Jews," *Sixteenth Century Journal* 25 (1994): 277.

troduction to *Juden Schul* Buxtorf reiterated the common theme that the Jews were obedient not to the laws of Moses but to traditions, interpretations, and ordinances invented by the rabbis.

> I have provided a basic and truthful explanation of the Jewish faith and religion for all, derived from their own books, including their fables as the apostle said (Titus 1:14), together with the entire Jewish life and conduct so that we Germans might also have a clear understanding of whether the Jews indeed lead a holy life and so zealously observe the law of Moses and whether they are actually the only wise, holy, pure, and righteous people of God as their outward observance might suggest and as they present themselves.[4]

Buxtorf hoped that his exposé of how the Jews had abandoned the revelation of God would lead Christians to humility rather than scorn. They were thankfully to acknowledge God's goodness and compassion in saving them from their sins, lest they too lose the light of revealed divine truth.[5] He also hoped that Jews would recognize that Judaism was actually a form of unbelief and that they would convert to Christianity.[6]

If Buxtorf's underlying theology of Judaism was fairly traditional, his theological critique in the first chapter was cast in a distinctively Reformed Protestant mold. By examining the Jews' con-

---

[4] "Damit aber nun uns Teutschen auch ein mal kund unnd wissend seyn möchte, ob die Jüden ein so heiligen Wandel führen, unnd auff das Gesetz Mosis so stark unnd eifferig halten, unnd das allein verstendig, heilig, rein unnd gerecht Volck Gottes seyn, wie sie ein eusserlichen Schein führen, unnd dessein ein Rhum haben wollen. So hab ich jedermenniglichen ihrem Glauben unnd Religion, mit Jüdischen Fabeln, wie die Heiligen Aposteln geredt, wol durch spicket, mit sampt dem gantzen jüdischen Leben und Wandel, auß ihren eigenen Büchern, gründlich und wahrhafftig erkläret, und jederman für augen stellen wöllen." Buxtorf, *Juden Schul*, ff.):(6r-v.

[5] "Solches aber erstlich und fürnemlich darumb, dz wir durch den grossen unglauben, verstockung und verhartung der Jüden, uns den erschrocklichen zorn und ernst Gottes an jnen zu gemüt führen, und dardurch zur betrachtung der grossen güte und barmherzigkeit Gottes an uns, und zu schuldiger danckbarkeit für dieselbe, ernstlich bewegt werden, damit nit auch uns das Liecht der erkandten Warheit umb unser undanckbarkeit willen genommen/ und widerumb in die finsternuss gesetzt wurden/ wie wir gesessen sind, eh uns Gott genediglich zu den heilsammen Erkandtnuss seines Wortes berüfen hat." Ibid., f.):(6v.

[6] "Zum andern auch darumb, dass die verstockten und verblendten Jüden in sich selbst gehen, ihren schweren unglauben lernen erkennen . . . . Es wölle aber der Barmhertzig Gott sich jhren gnediglich erbarmen, und sie bekehren . . . ." Ibid., ff.):(6v-7v. All three of these themes were common in anti-Jewish polemics written by Jewish converts during the sixteenth century. See Burnett, "Distorted Mirrors," 277.

fession of faith and their source of religious authority Buxtorf sought to create a theological lens through which the reader could critically examine Jewish beliefs and practices in the ethnographic part of his book. He began his discussion by examining the Jewish "creed," Maimonides' Thirteen Principles.[7] Creedal statements were a natural place for seventeenth-century theologians to begin analyzing the theological views of rival churches, since creeds served as theological rallying points for adherents of particular confessional churches; they also constituted a religious rationale for political alliances throughout Europe, particularly within the Holy Roman Empire.[8] Buxtorf's choice of the Thirteen Principles as his point of departure was reasonable, since they had been popularly accepted by German Jews as a creedal statement since the early fifteenth century and were frequently printed in prayer books.[9] Buxtorf first translated the "creed" together with a summary of Maimonides' gloss on each article,[10] and then he gave a biting critique of them, claiming that Maimonides had written them in response to Christianity in order to deny its tenets and to make it hateful to the Jews.[11] Buxtorf claimed that since the Jews had lost

---

[7] On the role of creeds within Judaism see Menachem Kellner, *Dogma in Medieval Jewish Thought from Maimonides to Abravanel* (Oxford: Oxford University Press, 1986).

[8] On the political and theological importance of creeds and catechisms during the period of confessionalization, see Wolfgang Reinhard, "Konfession und Konfessionalizierung in Europe," in: *Bekenntnis und Geschichte. Die Confessio Augustana im historischen Zusammenhang*, ed. Wolfgang Reinhard, Schriften der Philosophischen Fakultäten der Universität Augsburg, no. 20 (München: Ernst Vögel, 1981), 165-189.

[9] Buxtorf, *Juden Schul*, 3. On the acceptance of the Thirteen Principles by German Jews, see Sidney Steiman, *Custom and Survival. A Study of the Life and Work of Rabbi Jacob Molin (Moelln) known as Maharil (c. 1360 -1427) and his influence in establishing the Ashkenazic Minhag (customs of German Jewry)* (New York: Bloch, 1963), 106.

[10] Buxtorf, *Juden Schul*, 3-20. Buxtorf drew the text and gloss from Judah al-Harizi's Hebrew translation in the first Bomberg rabbinical Bible of 1517. Moshe Goshen-Gottstein reprinted both the text and gloss in his "The Thirteen Principles of Rambam according to al-Harizi's Translation," (Hebrew) *Tarbiz* 26 (1957): 188-196.

[11] "Wenn man aber diese Artikel fleissig auss ihren Bücheren betrachtet, so wird man leuchtlich spüren und erfinden, dass der Rambam, alss er sie also geordnet, und bey verlust des Jüdischen nammens und seines heils, jedermenniglichen sich darauff zu bekennen, ernstlich befohlen, anderswo hin nicht geschen, dann dass er den Christlichen Glauben damit bey den Jüden

all faith in the true God because of their hardness of heart and
blindness, they were not capable of believing anything with a "true
and mature faith," as each article stated. Although the Jews claimed
to believe in all that Moses and the Prophets had taught them
(articles 6-7), Buxtorf argued that they actually were far more
concerned with what the rabbis taught about the Bible and with the
traditions, interpretations, and ordinances of the "elders," meaning
the talmudic sages. The Jews believed this body of doctrine and law
to be not a supplement to the written law, but rather an integral
part of the law itself, given orally to Moses himself on Mount Sinai
(article 8).[12] Buxtorf, by contrast, asserted that the Oral Torah, as
preserved in the Talmud, had actually superseded the Bible as the
Jews' final religious authority, while Christians (at least
Protestants) remained faithful to the teachings of Scripture. The
most profound difference between Christianity and Judaism lay not
in creedal differences, but in their differing sources of divine revelation.[13]

Buxtorf devoted the remainder of his first chapter to sacral
history, a discussion of how and why he believed that the Jews
abandoned the Bible in favor of the Talmud. In the introduction to
Juden Schul, Buxtorf used his own version of the "chain of tradition" to trace Jewish apostasy from the biblical period to his own
day.[14] He linked contemporary rabbis to the unfaithful Israelites
whom Moses and the prophets opposed, the Pharisees, and the authors of the Talmud in an unbroken chain, because all of these

---

umstossete, falsch und verhasset machete, und die Jüden von demselbigen
abgehalten wurden." Buxtorf, *Juden Schul*, 20- 21.

[12] "Dann erstlich glauben sie nicht allein wahr zu seyn alles, was in Moses
und der Propheten Bücher geschrieben ist, sonder auch der Chachamim unnd
hochweisen Rabbiner Ausslegungen uber das Gesatz unnd Gottes wort, ja dass
mahr auff dieselbige zuhalten sey, denn auff Mosis worte. Demnach halten sie die
Traditiones, Auffsetze und Ordinantzen ihrer Voreltern, nicht für Tosephos oder
Zusetze des Gesatzes, sonder für das Gesatz selbst, das Moses mündlich von
Gott empfangen habe, auch mündlich andere gelehrt unnd nicht Schrifftlich
verfasset . . . ." Ibid., 26.

[13] Pace Peter T. Van Rooden who suggested that Buxtorf thought that the
Jews derived their "religious ceremonies, customs, and rituals" from their articles
of faith, in "Conceptions of Judaism as a Religion in the Seventeenth Century
Dutch Republic," *Studies in Church History* 29 (1992): 302.

[14] On the chain of tradition, see Gerson D. Cohen, introduction to *The Book
of Tradition (Sefer Ha-Qabbalah)*, by Abraham Ibn Daud (London: Routledge &
Kegan Paul, 1967), XXVIII-LXII.

scholars and leaders preferred their own human "wisdom" to God's truth as revealed in the Bible.[15] When discussing the origins of the Talmud in chap. 1 Buxtorf again picked up on this theme. He discussed the 613 commandments which had been derived from the Bible, stating that the Jews believed they maintained their covenant with God through scrupulous obedience to the commandments. Since strict observance of the law required precise instructions and guidelines, the rabbis and their predecessors obligingly formulated far more detailed laws than those given in the Bible.[16] Buxtorf argued that this kind of obedience amounted to a kind of performance or display of skill rather than an inward commitment to godliness.[17] The body of law, doctrine, and tradition against which Moses and the Prophets railed and which Christ opposed was eventually codified in the Babylonian Talmud, the true locus of religious authority among the Jews.[18]

The problem of religious authority among the Jews was not settled, however, with the codification of the Talmud. Buxtorf asserted that the devil, in his opinion the ultimate inspirer of the Talmud, incited the Jews to take one final step: since rabbis wrote the Talmud and Jews were obligated to believe and obey what they had written, Buxtorf erroneously assumed that his Jewish contemporaries were also obligated to obey the teachings of their rabbis with the same sort of respect.[19] To demonstrate his point, Buxtorf

---

[15] Buxtorf, *Juden Schul*, ff.):(5r-v.

[16] Ibid., 56-58.

[17] "Sind also allzeit auff ihrer meinung verblieben, und auff den eusserlichen Bund, auff das bloss unnd eusserlich Gesatz nach dem schlechten Buchstaben, auff die eusserlichen Wercke, Ceremonien und Ubungen des Gesatzes, der opffer, etc. starck gehalten, und damit Gott und alle seine Propheten getrotzet, und sich nicht bekümmern lassen, ob die rechte erkandtniss, forcht, und ehre Gottes in ihren hertzen stecke oder nicht, also dass Gott endlich einen grossen unwillen wider sie gefasset . . . . Ibid., 51.

[18] Ibid., 65-70.

[19] "Wie nun der Teuffel, ein Vatter aller lügen, inn massen vermeldet, mit den Jüden umb das Göttlich wort gewürfflet, unnd den ersten anwurff ihnen glücklich abgewonnen, ist er weiter im Spiel fortgefahren, unnd ihnen diese gantz liebliche unnd annemliche Consequentz eingeblasen, nemlich: Dieweil der Talmud das recht Fundament, unnd die gewisse Richtschnur ist, nach welcher das Geschrieben Gesatz soll abgemessen, gehoblet, behawen, gerichtet und zerlegt werden, so müsse auch aller Rabbiner Lehr, in ausslegung des Göttlichen Worts, nach dieser Schnur gerichtet seyn: und wie der Talmud wahr ist unnd nicht fehlen kan, also müsse auch alles wahr seyn, was die Rabbiner nach der

quoted several exhortations from the Talmud and from printed collections of sermons.[20] R. Isaac Aboab, for example, asserted that anything "our rabbis" (i. e., the talmudic sages) said in any genre was binding on the conscience.

> Everything that our Rabbis have taught and said in their preaching and mystical or allegorical interpretations we are obliged to believe, just as surely as the law of Moses. And if something can be found within them which seems to us hyperbolic or contrary to nature and too high for our understanding, then we should ascribe it to our weak and faulty understanding, not however to their words.[21]

Buxtorf, who thought that Aboab's statement referred to all post-talmudic rabbis as well, felt that pretensions to this kind of authority were outrageous and he often referred sarcastically to the "most wise" rabbis, especially when relating what he thought were ridiculous aggadic explanations for specific laws and practices.[22] In fact most of the abuse that Buxtorf hurled in *Juden Schul* was directed not at Jews generally, but at the rabbis, the theologians of Judaism.[23]

Buxtorf believed that the demarcation between Christianity (at least in its Protestant form) and Judaism was clear: one held the Bible to be the locus of divine revelation and authority, and the

---

richtschnur des Talmuds schrieben, reden und lehren." Buxtorf, *Juden Schul*, 80-81.

20 Buxtorf quoted similar admonitions from Moses b. Enoch Altschuler, ברנט שפיגל (Basel: Conrad Waldkirch, 1602), ff. 182a-183a (chap. 48), and BT Gittin, ff. 23a-b. Cf. Buxtorf, *Juden Schul*, 83-85, 90-91.

21 "Alles was unsere Rabbiner in jhren Predigen und Mystischen oder Allegorischen ausslegungen, gelehrt unnd geredt haben, sind wir schuldig zu glauben, eben so wol und vest, alss das Gesatz Mosis. Und wenn schon etwas darinn gefunden wird, das uns dunckt hyperbolisch oder gar der Natur zuwider unnd unserm Verstand zu hoch seyn, so sollen wir die schuld unserm bresthafften und mangelbaren Verstand, nicht aber jhren worten, zuschreiben." Ibid., 81-82. Cf. Isaac Aboab, מנורת המאור (Warsaw and Kiev: B. Kopchinskii Medovai, 1883), 124.

22 Buxtorf, *Juden Schul*, 2, 18, 26, 41, 43-45, 47, 81, 90, 96, 103, 119, 170-171, 263, passim. Buxtorf greatly overestimated the nature and extent of the rabbis' authority, even in religious matters, over ordinary Jews. See Kenneth R. Stow, *Alienated Minority: The Jews of Medieval Latin Europe* (Cambridge: Harvard Univ. Press, 1992), 164-71, 183-91.

23 Burnett, "Distorted Mirrors," 281. Blaming rabbis for the unbelief of ordinary Jews was a stock polemical charge dating back to the times of the church fathers. Justin Martyr warned Trypho not to trust the sages who led both themselves and their followers into error. *Dialogue with Trypho*, chap. 52.

other gave precedence to the Talmud, a work containing "nothing but pure error, misinterpretation and falsification of God's word, hypocrisy, superstition, external pomp and 'eye-service'."[24] By building upon the wrong revelatory foundation, nothing the Jews did would ultimately please God. This charge was not particularly original—theologians had been making it since the Disputation of Paris in 1240, and Johannes Pfefferkorn had made it forcefully in his book, *Handspiegel* (1511).[25] When considered in light of seventeenth- century Reformed theology, however, the contrasting claims of the Bible and the Talmud as loci of divine revelation assume a new importance.

The role of the Bible in shaping theology and church life and in settling controversies was one of the chief points of contention between Protestant and Catholic polemicists during the Reformation and the Confessional age that followed it. Most Protestants argued that the Bible alone was the sole source of divine truth, while Catholics believed that the Bible did not contain enough information and was not clear enough to provide guidance in all things. The official position of the Catholic Church as promulgated at the Council of Trent was that both the Bible and Church tradition were sources of revelation.[26] Beginning with Calvin, Reformed theologians stressed the importance of Scripture, declaring God and his word to be the two *principia* of true religion.[27] Buxtorf's colleague Amandus Polanus, professor of Old

---

[24] "Also hab ich bissher . . . anzeigen, wie die Jüden von Gottes wort abgewichen , und in den Labyrinth und Irrgarten aller Lügen, den Talmud, gehraten, und jemerlich dadurch verfüret worden sind, also dass keine reine Lehr von ihrer Seeligkeit, nicht mehr bey ihnen zufinden, sonder dass eitel irrthumm, verkehrung und verfelschung Göttlicher Lehre, heucheley, Aberglauben, eusserlicher Pracht und Augendienst . . . bey ihnen im schwang geht." Buxtorf, *Juden Schul*, 92-93.

[25] See Jeremy Cohen, *The Friars and the Jews: The Evolution of Medieval Anti-Judaism* (Ithaca: Cornell University Press, 1982), 68-69, and Hans Martin Kirn, *Das Bild vom Juden im Deutschland des frühen 16. Jahrhunderts dargestellt an den Schriften Johannes Pfefferkorns*, Texts and Studies in Medieval and Early Modern Judaism, no. 3 (Tübingen: J. C. B. Mohr (Paul Siebeck), 1989), 140-141.

[26] George H. Tavard, *Holy Writ or Holy Church? The Crisis of the Protestant Reformation* (New York: Harper, 1959), 89-93, 108-110, 195-209.

[27] Cf. Jean Calvin, *Institutes of the Christian Religion*, ed. J. T. McNeill, trans. Ford Lewis Battles, Library of Christian Classics, vols. 20-21 (Philadelphia: Westminster, 1960), I. vi. 1- 3; IV. viii. 1-10.

Testament at Basel, played an important role in developing and
promulgating this theological position. He believed that the Bible
was not only fundamental to true religion, but that it was the efficient cause of both religion and theology. Shortly before his death
in 1610 Polanus wrote,

> The immediate and proximate efficient cause of our theology is the Word of
> God, which, consequently is the foundation (principium) of our theology.
> The first principle, indeed, into which all theological doctrines are resolved
> is, "Thus said the Lord" or "God said." This foundation is one or whole
> and necessarily so, both because all the Prophets and Apostles call us back
> to this alone, as is witnessed by all of Scripture; and because God cannot be
> understood except through himself.[28]

In the fifty or more years since the Council of Trent this dispute
over Scripture and Church tradition had become a standard feature
of Protestant polemics, and it is scarcely surprising that Buxtorf
used tools developed to address this controversy in his critique of
Judaism. Although the argument that Jewish law contradicted the
Bible originated in the medieval Latin Church, early modern
Catholic polemicists had to be far more circumspect in using it in
their theological polemics against the Jews than Protestants, since
the argument could easily be turned against them.[29]

Buxtorf repeatedly used the metaphor of a foundation in *Juden
Schul* to describe Judaism and its basis of religious authority, the
Talmud, arguing that Judaism was built upon a foundation of human wisdom, which is to say the "false and baseless commandments
and fables of their rabbis."[30] While he drew no explicit comparison
between the Catholic understanding of Church tradition and the
Jewish Oral Torah as examples of human wisdom masquerading as
divine revelation, it was a parallel that would have readily occurred to Protestant readers.[31] Theologically speaking, Judaism

[28] Amandus Polanus, *Syntagma Theologiae Christianae* (Geneva: Jacob
Stoër, 1617), I. xiv, quoted by Richard A. Muller, *Post-Reformation Reformed
Dogmatics*, vol. 1: *Prolegommena to Theology* (Grand Rapids: Baker, 1987),
304.

[29] Mark R. Cohen pointed out this element of Buxtorf's argument in "Leone
da Modena's *Riti*: a Seventeenth Century Plea for Social Toleration of the Jews,"
Jewish Social Studies 34 (1972): 306-307.

[30] Buxtorf, *Juden Schul*, 662-663. Buxtorf also used the "foundation"
metaphor on pp. 72-73, 80, 94-95, 559-560.

[31] For example, the second chapter of the Second Helvetian Confession
(1566) drew an explicit comparison between the Catholic doctrine of tradition

was completely beyond the pale of true religion because the Talmud was its efficient cause. Reconciliation with God was possible only if the Jews recognized how far they had strayed from biblical truth. Buxtorf sought to make the contrast between biblical revelation and talmudic precept as clear as possible in *Juden Schul.*

After Buxtorf's harsh, uncompromising theological critique of Judaism in chap. 1, his narrative tone throughout the remainder of *Juden Schul* is deceptively mild. Detached, almost clinical, descriptions of Jewish rites and beliefs alternate with page after page of direct quotations from Jewish authorities. However, Buxtorf's milder rhetoric does not reflect a change of heart but rather a shift in tactics. He sought to illustrate his contention that Judaism was based upon adherence to the Talmud rather than faithfulness to the Scriptures by examining specific Jewish customs, rituals and beliefs and linking them whenever possible to talmudic precept. To evaluate Buxtorf's portrayal of Judaism in the second part of *Juden Schul*, it is necessary to examine the Jewish sources he consulted, the narrative strategy he employed, and to evaluate the ways that his theological bias colored his treatment of Jewish life.

On the title page of *Juden Schul* Buxtorf stated that he had written it using "the Jews' own books," and even a cursory reading of the book confirms his boast. At least 60% of the 570 pages of ethnographic description and theological discussion in chaps. 2-36 are either direct quotations or summaries of passages in Jewish sources.[32] To some degree, however, Buxtorf's welter of quotations from endless Jewish authorities overstates the number of books he routinely consulted when preparing *Juden Schul*. Buxtorf

---

with pharisaic reliance upon tradition in the Gospels. See *Reformed Confessions of the 16th Century*, ed. Arthur C. Cochrane (Philadelphia: Westminster Press, 1966), 227.

[32] The following are rough estimatates of the proportion of pages which consist entirely or mostly of quotations (including biblical quotations) to the total number of pages, broken down by chapter, beginning with chap. 2. **2**: 20/45; **3**: 4/16; **4**: 27/39; **5**: 33/39; **6**: 15/17; **7**: 15/24; **8**: 7/10; **9**: 10/17; **10**: 35/37; **11**: 37/47; **12**: 20/20; **13**: 9/29; **14**: 11/11; **15**: 7/7; **16**: 19/21; **17**: 9/9; **18**: 9/16; **19**: 4/8; **20**: 9/17; **21**: 6/11; **22**: 1/6; **23**: 1/3; **24**: 5/5; **25**: 3/11; **26**: 4/6; **27**: 3/9; **28**: 3/13; **29**: 3/3; **30**: 2/3; **31**: 2/3; **32**: 0/3; **33**: 0/2; **34**: 3/4; **35**: 7/13; **36**: 32/47. Buxtorf's discussion of Tabernacles (see below), however, suggests that these figures may understate the actual proportions in some cases; only a close reading of each chapter would reveal the actual proportion of quotations to the text as a whole.

actually based most of his book upon only a few Jewish sources as
he revealed to a colleague in 1606. For each topic he would first
read Simon Levi Günzburg's *Minhagim,* a Yiddish language halakic summary.[33] Then he would consult the relevant paragraphs of
Joseph Karo's *Shulhan Aruk,* which gave an overview of "their entire law—civil and canon," and finally he read relevant portions of
the Talmud. After collating his findings he reread *Minhagim.*[34]
Buxtorf's description of his method for studying Judaism is reflected in both the structure and content of *Juden Schul.* The heart
of the book, chaps 3-25 (pp. 159-550) treats Jewish customs and
practices performed daily, weekly, or during the liturgical year,
arranged according to the order of *Orah Hayyim* in Joseph Karo's
Shulhan Aruk. Buxtorf frequently used *Minhagim* as the basis of
his description of Jewish customs, and at times he cited the two
works together at the beginning of chapters or sections.[35] In keeping with his goal of linking Jewish practice to the Talmud, Buxtorf
referred to the Talmud no less than 94 times in *Juden Schul,* often
providing extended quotations in translation. These three works
served as the conceptual foundation upon which Buxtorf built his
book, using material drawn from both Jewish sources and from the
works of Jewish converts.

To flesh out his discussion of Jewish beliefs and practices
Buxtorf drew upon works of popular piety written in Yiddish, academic books written in Hebrew, and prayer books in both lan-

---

[33] Morris Epstein discussed the particular *Minhagim* book used by Buxtorf in
"Simon Levi Ginzburg's Illustrated Custumal (Minhagim-Book) of Venice,
1593, and its Travels," *Proceedings of the Fifth World Congress of Jewish
Studies, Jerusalem, 3-11, August 1969,* 4: 197-218. Although the book was
originally written in Hebrew by Isaac Tyrnau, it is usually attributed to
Günzburg, its Yiddish translator.

[34] "Quaeris praeterea, quomodo Fabulas illas judaicas congesserim.
Respondeo ipsos Judaeos mihi suggessisse. Primo & principaliter oblato libro
Rituum, cui *Minhagim* nomen. Et qui hebraeo germanice editus est. Eum si cupis
tibi dono mittam. Deinde intellexi totum illorum jus, civile & canonicum & quae
praeterea habeat, *dinim* quasi Aphorismis comprehensum in libro, cui *Shulhan
Aruk* nomen. Hunc etiam opera Judaeorum accepi. Postea Talmud ipsum & eos,
quos praeterea cito, assecuus sum, in hos animi gratia excurri, & quicquid reperi,
ad Minhagim retuli." Johannes Buxtorf I to Matthias Martinius, Basel, September
4, 1606, printed in Johann Buxtorf, "Epistola Johannis Buxtorfii, P. ad Matthiam
Martinium," *Bibliotheca historico-philologico-theologica* classis 4, fascicle 3
(1721): 601.

[35] Buxtorf, *Juden Schul,* 176, 280, 322, 349, 354-355, 434.

guages. Since Basel was a center of Yiddish printing in the early seventeenth century Buxtorf was obliged to censor, and possibly to help print, a number of these works. His familiarity with this corpus is reflected in the pages of *Juden Schul* since he frequently quoted from Basel Yiddish imprints such as Moses b. Enoch Altschuler's sermon collection entitled *Brantspiegel*, Joseph b. Eliezer Halfan's *Orah Hayyim*, Benjamin Slonik's discussion of women's commandments, *Ein Schön Frauenbüchlein*, and the first edition of the *Maasebuch*, which billed itself as the "Yiddish Gemara."[36] These books had either been composed in Yiddish or translated into that language in order to encourage piety among women and "men who are like women in not having much knowledge," to quote Moses b. Enoch Altschuler.[37] They served not only to instruct ordinary Jews in their religious duties, but often sought to provide a talmudic basis for the commandments and customs.[38] Coincidentally, they also provided Buxtorf with a source of talmudic references and an introduction to central European Jewish life, written in a vernacular similar to his own.

In addition to Yiddish sources, Buxtorf used a number of Hebrew books printed in Basel or elsewhere, including Isaac Tyrnau's *Minhagim*, Elias Levita's *Tishbi*, and Isaac Alfasi's *Halakot*.[39] Since Buxtorf sought to contrast Jewish with Christian interpretations of specific biblical passages he frequently quoted Jewish commentators such as Rashi, David Kimhi, Abraham Ibn Ezra, Nahmanides and Bahya ben Asher, as well as midrashic collections such as *Midrash Rabba*, *Pirke de Rabbi Eliezer* and *Tanhuma*.[40] Academic books written in Hebrew were intended for a more educated Jewish reading audience, and Buxtorf used them not only to explain individual Jewish commandments and practices, but also to clarify some of their theological underpinnings.

Buxtorf's use of Jewish prayer books is particularly important for understanding both *Juden Schul* and *Aus was Ursachen*. He had

---

[36] Prijs nos. 173, 175-178. Cf. Chava Weissler, "The Religion of Traditional Ashkenazic Women: Some Methodological Issues," *AJS Review* 12 (1987): 82.

[37] Quoted by Weissler, "Religion," 78.

[38] Herman Pollack, "An Historical Explanation of the Origin and Development of Jewish Books of Customs (*Sifre Minhagim*): 1100-1300," *Jewish Social Studies* 49 (1987): 207.

[39] Prijs, nos. 152, 172, 182.

[40] Cohen, "Leone da Modena's *Riti*," 295.

been obliged to read and censor fourteen different prayer books
between 1597 and 1603, and to simplify his task he compiled a
textual commentary containing notes on the prayers he considered
most objectionable. A number of passages in *Juden Schul* reflect
these notes.[41] Following earlier anti-Jewish polemicists, Buxtorf
felt that anti-Christian statements within Jewish liturgical prayers
were especially egregious since they were spoken by all Jews during worship services, and that they reflected what Jews "really
thought" of Christians and Christendom.[42] Since a censor's task
was to review books for objectionable material, Buxtorf's approach
to "Jewish blasphemy" in *Juden Schul* reflects his five years service
as Basel's Hebrew censor.

Buxtorf did not rely solely on the works of practicing Jews for
his descriptions and explanations of Jewish practices; he also used
Jewish convert literature. He made most frequent reference in
Juden Schul to Margaritha's *Gantz Jüdisch Glaub* but also made
heavy, largely unattributed, use of Ernst F. Hess's *Juden-Geissel*.[43]
He acknowledged quoting Hess only once in *Juden Schul*, when discussing how the Jews celebrate the birth of a daughter. In fact
Buxtorf shamelessly copied numerous details from Hess's description both of the circumcision ceremony itself and even of the circumcision eve party, although he himself had once attended one
and could presumably have spoken from his own experience.[44]

---

[41] E. g., Basel UB Ms A XII 20, f. 255 (=*Juden Schul*, 227-228) on the
Alenu prayer; both mention that a space was left where some words were left out
in an Augsburg imprint (Basel UB call no. FA VIII 57, no foliation). Cf. also Ms
A XII 20, f. 259r (= *Juden Schul*, 260). Presumably Buxtorf's collation reflects
not only books from his own library, but also other books submitted to
Waldkirch for publication.

[42] Burnett, "Distorted Mirrors," 284.

[43] Antonius Margaritha, *Der Gantz Judisch Glaub* (Augsburg: Heynrich
Steyer, 1530); and Ernst Friedrich Hess, *Flagellum Iudaeorum. Juden Geissel*
(Erfurt: Martin Wittel, 1599). I consulted microfilms of Margaritha's book pro-
vided by HUC, and of Hess's work provided by the HAB (C 215 Helmst. 8°).
Buxtorf made explicit reference to Margaritha in *Juden Schul*, 294-298, 361,
398, 510, 573, 599, 614; and to Hess on p. 127.

[44] Buxtorf, *Juden Schul*, 127. Cf Hess, *Juden Geissel*, f. h 8v. On circumcision: ibid., pp. 98 (=*Juden Geissel*, f. h 4v), 105 (=ibid, f. h 5r), 106 (=ibid, f.
h 5r-v), 107 (=ibid, f. h 6r), 108 (ibid, f. h 6r), 110 (ibid, f. h 6r), 114 (ibid, f.
h 7r), 115 (=ibid, f. h 7r), and 116 (ibid, f. h 7v). Buxtorf's only comment about
the circumcision eve party which he attended was "Auff ein mahl hab ich bey
ihnen ein Predig am Beschneidung Maal gehört uber diese Worte Solomonis
[Prov. 8: 18] . . . ." Buxtorf, *Juden Schul*, 124.

Buxtorf was also forced to rely upon convert literature when discussing more public aspects of Jewish life such as the ways that Jewish communities dealt with beggars and criminals.[45] More generally, Buxtorf echoed some charges leveled by Margaritha and Hess regarding the Jews' hatred for Christians as reflected in their prayers and in other ways.[46] He privately professed some skepticism as to the reliability of convert literature, however, and he checked his findings whenever possible with works written by practicing Jews.[47]

Buxtorf's professional activities as a Hebrew bookseller and printer also gave him opportunities to discuss some Jewish customs directly with Jewish informants. For example, his personal study notebook contains an account of an interview he had with a Jew on May 10, 1600, about the ritual cutting of fingernails before the Sabbath, a practice which he mentions in *Juden Schul*.[48] If Daniel Tossanus, Buxtorf's contemporary biographer, was correct, Buxtorf often invited Jews to eat with him in order to learn more about their way of life. During these dinners he would have had ample opportunity to pose clarifying questions about Jewish practices and to inquire about regional variations.[49] The importance of these conversations should not, however, be overestimated. No amount of discussion with the few Jews who lived near Basel, or occasional visits to the Jewish community in Frankfurt, could have overcome Buxtorf's lack of first-hand exposure to Jewish communal life. This lack of contact could not fail to hinder his understanding of how Jews actually lived their lives since he had no

---

[45] Buxtorf, *Juden Schul*, 595-597, 600-603.

[46] See Burnett, "Distorted Mirrors," 282-3.

[47] In describing his tract *Aus was Ursachen* (written at roughly the same time as *Juden Schul*), Buxtorf explained what he thought of convert writings: "Is continebit Causas odii Judaeorum in omnes gentes ... non quidem illa ex scriptis baptizatorum Judaeorum *quibus non semper fides habenda* (italics mine); sed ex ipsissimis libris circumcisorum Judaeorum...." Buxtorf, "Epistola Johannis Buxtorfii," 601.

[48] Cf. Basel UB Ms A XII 20, f. 287 and Buxtorf, *Juden Schul*, 311-312.

[49] Tossanus, *Vitae*, 10. Buxtorf mentioned several common German Jewish customs in *Juden Schul*, 517, 489-491, one specific to Worms on pp. 525, and one French custom ("Welschen") on p. 489. Several other customs from unspecified areas are mentioned on pp. 412, 466, 468, 596, 601-603. He may have learned of some regional variations from Minhagim or other written sources. Cf. Günzburg, מנהגים, f. 76b (Polish), 89b (Worms) and Buxtorf, *Juden Schul*, 462, 581.

living pattern with which to compare what he had learned about
Judaism through reading. Even when Buxtorf witnessed a specific
custom or practice his description in *Juden Schul* does not
necessarily reflect only what he himself saw; instead he drew upon
other sources to clarify and round out his account in much the
same way that later writers such as Lancelot Addison used *Juden
Schul* to supplement their ethnographic observations.[50]

Buxtorf's use of an enormous number of Hebrew quotations
does not indicate how he utilized Jewish sources or how well he
understood them in his effort to analyze Judaism. Buxtorf's admission that he based his portrait of Jewish life upon Günzburg's
Minhagim and the *Shulhan Aruk*, together with the mass of material he quoted from other Yiddish books, indicates that his portrayal of Judaism grew out of a relatively unsophisticated understanding of Jewish beliefs and practices. Yiddish books of piety
were intended to edify women and under-educated Jewish men and
to teach them the rudiments of Jewish observance. They did not
contain instructions for refined halakic practice or, during
Buxtorf's day, much esoteric teaching.[51] With the best will in the
world, Buxtorf could not have communicated what he himself had
not learned first. Although Buxtorf was satisfied with the depth and
detail of his portrayal of Jewish beliefs and practices, it was a portrait which contemporary rabbis would have criticized both for its
distortions and omissions.[52]

Beneath the welter of quotations of Jewish books, *Juden Schul*
was intended first and foremost to be a theological work. Buxtorf's
implicit narrative strategy in the ethnographic part of the book was
intended to prove the point that he had made explicitly in chap. 1:
that Judaism was based upon the Talmud, not the Bible. Buxtorf's
treatment of the Feast of Tabernacles illustrates how he sought to

---

[50] For example, Elliott Horowitz in "The Eve of the Circumcision: a chapter in
the History of Jewish Night Life," *Journal of Social History* 23 (1989): 47 mentioned Buxtorf's description of a pre-circumcision celebration (*Juden Schul*, 105-
107) as an account of given by an "unfriendly outsider," but Buxtorf actually
took much of it (without attribution) from an account given by Ernst F. Hess in
Juden Geissel, ff. h5r-v. Horowitz pointed out how Addison used Buxtorf's
Juden Schul to supplement his own experience when writing an ethnography of
the Jews in "'A Different Mode of Civility': Lancelot Addison on the Jews of
Barbary," *Studies in Church History* 29 (1992): 319-323.

[51] Weissler, "Religion," 77-80.

[52] For Leon Modena's response to *Juden Schul*, see below.

contrast the practice of rabbinic Judaism with what he considered to be biblical teaching.

Buxtorf's portrayal of the Feast of Tabernacles (*Succot*) illustrates how he sought to prove his theological point using an ethnographic narrative as his literary vehicle. He began the chapter by setting forth the biblical laws governing Tabernacles, quoting from Deut. 16, Lev. 23:40 and Neh. 8: 15. The Jews, he argued, had distorted what the Scripture taught by separating the injunction to build booths and to live in them for a week from the command that they should collect leafy tree boughs of whatever sort to build the booths. Instead of using the tree branches to build the booths, these bundles of branches together with a citron (ethrog), collectively called the Lulav, were brought to the synagogue by worshipers and used in public worship. Buxtorf felt that this rabbinic innovation was a violation of both the letter and spirit of the biblical feast of Tabernacles. The Jews "superstitiously" devoted their attention to setting standards for building proper booths and for proper use of the Lulav, multiplying regulations while ignoring the biblical basis of the feast and undercutting its true meaning.[53]

> They have written a large tractate in the Talmud concerning this festival, how one should correctly celebrate it, how huts should be constructed, how the various forms should be observed. [They] argue very subtly, as is their custom, of the outward ceremonies, but do not worry very much about how they ought to turn their hearts to God.[54]

Then Buxtorf discussed, in turn, public worship during the festival (456-465), life in the booths (465-468), and the Lulav (468-470).[55] In order to drive home the contrast between the Jewish and Christian understanding of Tabernacles, Buxtorf closed the chapter

---

[53] Buxtorf, *Juden Schul*, 455, 468. Curiously Buxtorf did not refer to BT Sukka at all in his discussion of Tabernacles, suggesting that his Talmudic knowledge was not as extensive as his many Talmud quotations elsewhere in the book might suggest.

[54] "Sie haben im Talmud ein grossen Traktat geschrieben von diesem Fest wie man es recht Feyren und halten soll, wie die Hütten gemacht, wie die viererley gattungen gebraucht werden sollen, disputieren sehr subtil, nach jhrem brauch, von den eusserlichen Ceremonien, kümmeren sich nicht sehr, wie sie das Hertz zu Gott richten sollen." Ibid., 455. Buxtorf echoes Margaritha's criticism of Succot at this point. Cf. Margaritha, *Ganz Judisch Glaub*, f. F3r.

[55] On the composition and use of the Lulav, see Cecil Roth and Geoffrey Wigoder, eds. *Encyclopaedia Judaica* (Jerusalem: Macmillan, 1971-1972), s. v. "Sukkot," by Louis Jacobs and Abram Kanof.

by quoting a midrash from BT *Aboda Zara* which expressed the
Jewish view that God loved them and hated the Gentiles, and also
Ezech. 20: 10, a passage where the prophet gave a scathing assessment of the spiritual state of his Jewish contemporaries.[56] By placing these two quotations side by side Buxtorf used the biblical
quotations to undermine the message of the talmudic midrash,
implicitly suggesting that the Jews loved their own wisdom more
than God's revealed word.

Apart from the introduction and conclusion of the chapter, the
heart of Buxtorf's discussion of Tabernacles consists of a dense
network of interlocking quotations from Jewish sources. He gave a
narrative description of Jewish practice in which he tried to reflect
how contemporary Jews celebrated the feast based upon descriptions written by observant Jews.[57] In a few places Buxtorf employed direct quotes of particular Jewish authors, often giving page
or paragraph numbers to the books he consulted.[58] Most of
Buxtorf's description, however, amounts to a paraphrase of
Günzburg's *Minhagim*. In some instances he virtually quoted it
word for word, as he did in the interpretation of shadow omens on
the eve of Hoshana Rabba, the final day of Tabernacles.[59] For the
most part, however, he summarized what Günzburg said, incorpo-
rating many smaller quotations into his text. His treatment of how
booths were to be constructed, for example, bristles with embedded
quotations. The Jews were commanded to build booths in a place

---

[56] Buxtorf, *Juden Schul*, 470-473.

[57] While Buxtorf may have witnessed first-hand how Jews celebrated
Tabernacles, the only statement he made to this effect in his book was that Jewish
pedlars charged exorbitant prices for citrons; in the fall of 1602 an ethrog cost
four Gulden. Ibid., 469.

[58] In his description of Tabernacles Buxtorf quoted BT Avoda Zara, 3a-b
(*Juden Schul*, 471-472), a Mahzor printed in Cracow (p. 460), and Bahya b.
Asher, כד הקמח; I have used the text printed in:כתבי רבינו בחיי, ed. Haim Dov
Shevel (Jerusalem: Mossad ha-Rav Kook, 1970), 289, 236.

[59] Buxtorf: ". . . mangelt ihm ein finger, so wird im ein guter freund sterben,
mangelt im die rechte hand/so wird ihm ein sohn sterben: die linke, so wird ihm
ein Tochter mit todt abgehen . . . ." *Juden Schul*, 463. Günzburg: "Mangelt im
eyn vinger da gilt es zeyni kerovim (neighbors). Mangelt im der shaten von der
recht hant za iz es eyn siman (sign) zu zeyni zoyn has veshalom ("God forbid").
Un' die link hand iz eyn siman zu zeyn toychter has veshalom." מנהגים, 76a. To
facilitate textual comparisons between *Minhagim* and *Juden Schul* I have transliterated the Yiddish text according to the transliteration guide of the *Encyclopedia
Judaica*, vol. 1, p. 91.

that "did not stink," and they were to be built under open sky, not under a passage way or a roof.[60]

The following table illustrates how frequently Buxtorf referred to Jewish sources (direct quotations are starred).

PageSource

457-8	*Minhagim*, ff. 72b-73b, 76b
458-9	*Bahya b. Asher, *Kad ha-Qemah*, 289
460	*Mahzor Prayer Book
461	*Minhagim*, ff. 73a-74a, 75b
	Shulhan Aruk, Orah Hayyim, para 664
462	*Minhagim*, f. 76b
462-3	Ibid., f. 76a-b
464-5	Ibid., ff. 77a-78a
465	*Shulhan Aruk, Orah Hayyim*, para 667 (Isserles)
465-8	*Minhagim*, ff. 68b-69b
469-70	Ibid., f. 70a
470	*Bahya, *Kad ha-Qemah.*, 236
470-2	*BT *Avoda Zara*, 3a-b

Nearly thirteen of the twenty-two pages Buxtorf devoted to Tabernacles are little more than direct quotations or summaries taken from *Minhagim*. These quotations were, in general, accurately translated and aptly cited.

Despite his fidelity to *Minhagim*, Buxtorf's text is still much shorter than the original because his concern was not to provide every last detail of the halakah, but to summarize it and then to make his theological points. Günzburg's treatment of Tabernacles in *Minhagim* included instructions on how the normal synagogue liturgy should be modified for Tabernacles, including the times when the Lulav was to be used. Buxtorf, by contrast provided only a bare description of the synagogue services associated with the

---

[60] Buxtorf: "Es sollen aber diese Laubhutten nicht gemacht werden an einer ort da es unlustig ist, oder stinkt . . . ." *Juden Schul*, 466; Günzburg: Man zol di sukka nit makken vo es stinkt oder vo es unlustig iz." מנהגים, f. 68b. Buxtorf: "Soll under dem blossen und offnen himmel seyn, nicht under einem Gang oder Tach." *Juden Schul*, 466-467. Günzburg: "Di succa zol unter dem himil zeyn un' nit unter eynem gang oder tak." מנהגים, f. 68b.

feast.[61] His discussion focused instead on the booths themselves, the use and symbolic meaning of the Lulav, and the eschatological significance of Tabernacles as a season when the Jews looked ahead to God's judgement of the nations. All of these topics were linked to the interpretation of particular biblical texts and presented Buxtorf with the opportunity to contrast his understanding of these passages with traditional Jewish interpretations.

Buxtorf's treatment of Tabernacles also illustrates his desire to let the Jews "speak for themselves" in order to better critique their religion. When he wished to explain the implications of particular Jewish beliefs and practices he quoted from liturgical prayers, sermons, or aggadic literature, since they expressed Jewish "theology" in a form more accessible to Christians than technical halakic treatments did. When discussing the traditional procession around the chancel which Jews performed with Lulav in hand each day during Tabernacles (ha-Kafot), Buxtorf quoted from a sermon of Bahya b. Asher to explain its significance. The procession was intended to commemorate the march around Jericho, but "the circuit we make nowadays is thus a sign and an allusion in the future that the wall of Edom (i. e. Christianity) will fall and will be completely obliterated from the world."[62] Both the ritual itself and the words spoken by the worshipers indicated that they were living in hope against the day when God would judge Christendom and, in Buxtorf's opinion, they were a kind of ritual curse. Some of the most polemical portions of *Juden Schul* are places where Buxtorf commented on Jewish prayers, often by glossing names such as "Esau" and "Edom" which Jews had traditionally used as code words for Christendom.[63]

If Buxtorf's descriptions of Jewish life in *Juden Schul* have an "objective" character it is not because he respected Jews and Judaism, but because he employed Jewish works in such a way as to reflect Jewish opinion, preserving the tone of his sources in the process. Had Buxtorf cast his discussion of Succot in the form of a

---

[61] Cf. Günzburg, מנהגים, ff. 70b-78b with Buxtorf, *Juden Schul*, 456-462.

[62] Bahya b. Asher, כד הקמח *Encyclopedia of Torah Thoughts*, ed. and trans. Charles B. Chavel (New York: Shilo, 1980), 461 = idem, כד הקמח, 289. Other eschatological references include the liturgical reading of Ezk 38 on Gog and Magog, feasting on Leviathan at the Messianic banquet, and the midrash from Avoda Zara. Buxtorf, *Juden Schul*, 461, 465, 471-472.

[63] Buxtorf, *Juden Schul*, 213, 222.

dialogue between a Jew and a Christian respondent, his editorial strategy would have been more apparent, since most of what he wrote was a report of what Jews did to observe the festival and why they did so. Apart from obvious editorial remarks at the beginning and end of chapters, glossing code words, and using biblical quotations as foils to Jewish practice, Buxtorf most often indicated his disagreement through short, snide comments rather than through conscious distortion or parody.[64] For example, after reporting that the Jews thought the devil could be scared away by shaking the branches of the Lulav, Buxtorf remarked in a printed marginal note, "O you faint-hearted devil."[65] Buxtorf's relatively subtle editorial criticisms contribute to the misleading impression that he was "objectively" relating how Jews lived their lives.[66]

Buxtorf's portrayal of Jewish life could not fail to be skewed by his theological objective of seeking to portray Judaism as religiously invalid. Not only was Buxtorf's reporting selective and occasionally misleading, but his biases shaped and colored his characterization of Jews and Judaism in other ways as well. These prejudices are reflected not only in the topics Buxtorf chose to address but, more subtly, in his attitudes toward Jews and Jewry as a social order within the German empire.[67] The topics Buxtorf glossed over are not always readily apparent, given the overwhelming welter of detail he provides on early modern Jewish life. Three major themes in Jewish life which Buxtorf did not discuss were Jewish communal life, corporate religious obligations, and the religious concerns and practices of the rabbinical elite. His depiction of the public spaces of Jewish life were abstract and lifeless. His Jews were rather like stick men who spoke ritual words and performed various acts inside the home, the synagogue, the ritual bath, and elsewhere, but the places in which they were performed re-

---

[64] Ibid., 29, 58, 140, 241-242, 466 (scilicet); 184-185 (probatum est); 18-19, 47, 165, 223, 233, 285 (ironic/sarcastic remarks).

[65] "O du forchtsamer Teufel," Ibid., 458.

[66] In a public lecture Rudolf Hallo went so far as to assert that Buxtorf's descriptions were made both accurately and respectfully. "(*Juden Schul*) schildert in systematischer Vollständigkeit und exakter Breite die Sitten und Gebräuche der zeitgenössischen Juden, und zwar durchgängig mit bester Vertrautheit, mit stauneswerter Gelehrsamkeit und mit völliger Achtung." Hallo, "Die Christliche Wissenschaft vom Judentum," *Der Morgen/Monatschrift der Deutschen Juden* 10 (Sept./Oct. 1934): 290.

[67] Ibid.," 294-301.

mained, for the most part, shadowy and ill-defined.[68] Buxtorf's Jews were never at work and seldom on the streets, and so they almost never interacted with Christians. The responsibilities of communal officials such as the sexton (*Schulklopfer*) and the cantor were mentioned only in passing.[69] To some degree these omissions may be attributable to the nature of Buxtorf's sources. His discussion of Jewish beliefs and practices was drawn mainly from works focusing upon the lives of individual Jews, and he did not use books which would have given a better idea of the dynamics of community life such as *Hoshen Mishpat* in the *Shulhan Aruk* or collections of responsa. For example, his discussion of the punishment of malefactors, drawn largely from Margaritha's *Gantz Jüdisch Glaub,* was more fanciful and far less detailed than his account of how Jews were to prepare for the Sabbath.[70] By describing primarily the religious life and obligations of Jewish households, Buxtorf arbitrarily eliminated much of Jewish life from consideration.

Buxtorf's focus upon the lives of individual Jews also distorts his account of corporate religious practices and obligations. While Jewish observance is centered upon the household, individual Jews, especially heads of households, had other opportunities for public religious expression through the synagogue, rabbinical court, kabbalistic circle, halakic study groups, and confraternities.[71] There

---

[68] Buxtorf, *Juden Schul*, 199-237 (Synagogue), 594-5 (ritual bath).

[69] Ibid., 280, 537-539.

[70] Ibid., 600-603. Rabbi Benjamin Aaron Slonik, for example, discussed means of maintaining communal discipline in his responsa. See Nisson Shulman, *Authority and Community: Polish Jewry in the Sixteenth Century* (Hoboken, NJ and New York: KTAV Publishing House/Yeshiva Univ. Press, 1986), 55-57. Buxtorf's Jewish informants may also have been reluctant to discuss the inner workings of Jewish communities with an outsider, since German authorities considered any exercise of authority by Jews to be a provocation. See Volker Press, "Kaiser Rudolf II und die Zusammenschluss der deutschen Judenheit. Die sogenannte Frankfurter Rabbinerverschwörung von 1603 und ihre Folgen," in: *Zur Geschichte der Juden im Deutschland des späten Mittelalters und der frühen Neuzeit,* ed. Alfred Haverkamp, Monographien zur Geschichte des Mittelalters, no. 24 (Stuttgart: Anton Hiersemann, 1981), 243-293. Buxtorf's list of punishments was taken from Margaritha, *Ganz Judisch Glaub,* K3v-4r.

[71] See Weissler, "Religion," 74, Jacob Katz, *Tradition and Crisis: Jewish Society at the End of the Middle Ages,* trans. and ed. Bernard Dov Cooperman (New York: New York Univ. Press, 1993), 132-140, and Jacob R. Marcus, *Communal Sick Care in the German Ghetto* (Cincinnati: Hebrew Union College Press, 1947), 68-70, 95-145.

was less of a distinction between the sacred and secular spheres of life in Jewish communities than in Christian society, not only because of their obligations under talmudic law, but also because the Jews were both an ethnic and religious minority who suffered heavily from legal and social disabilities and were obliged by majority society to live within self-contained social communities. Buxtorf's focus upon the religious duties of individual Jews obscured their corporate obligations.

Juden Schul was also written to reflect how ordinary Jews were to live their lives without considering the religious concerns and practices of the rabbinical elite. While most educated Jews could aspire to a certain level of halakic knowledge, authoritative knowledge of the halakah was the province of only a small minority of rabbinic experts who played a pivotal role in Jewish community life.[72] Mirroring his sources, Buxtorf's descriptions of Jewish practice were drawn from a mixture of halakic manuals, sermon collections, kabbalistic works, and minhagim books.[73] What he failed to communicate to his readers was that not all of these forms of religious "guidance" were equally authoritative, and rabbis frequently fought over how the differences between them should be resolved.[74] There was no single halakic standard for all of Europe during Buxtorf's day, as long-running disputes over issues such as kosher slaughtering and levirate marriage illustrate.[75] Buxtorf never once mentioned the vast responsa literature in *Juden Schul*, although he quoted hundreds of times from other Jewish sources.[76] More importantly, Buxtorf showed no understanding of how the rabbis "updated" talmudic legislation by using *pilpul* interpreta-

---

[72] Katz, *Tradition and Crisis*, 143.

[73] Cohen, "Leone da Modena's *Riti*," 299-301.

[74] See Marvin Fox, "Nahmanides on the Status of Aggadot: Perspectives on the Disputation at Barcelona," *Journal of Jewish Studies* 40 (1989): 98-101.

[75] See Howard Adelman, "Rabbis and Reality: Public Activities of Jewish Women in Italy during the Renaissance and Catholic Restoration," *Jewish History* 5 (1991): 27-40, and idem, "Custom, Law, and Gender: Levirate Union among Ashkenazim and Sephardim in Italy after the Expulsion from Spain," in: *The Expulsion of the Jews*, 107-125.

[76] Even ten years later, Buxtorf remained relatively unfamiliar with responsa literature. He mentioned only eleven responsa collections in his rabbinical bibliography. Buxtorf, *De Abbreviaturis Hebraicis liber novus & copiosus* (Basel: Konrad Waldkirch, 1613), 324-325.

tion.[77] By overlooking the opinions and concerns of the Jewish re-
ligious elite in favor of a few works on popular Jewish piety,
Buxtorf gave a truncated portrait of the religious dynamics of
Judaism in his day.

By downplaying the role that Jewish communal life, corporate
religious participation, and the religious concerns and practices of
the rabbinical elite played in Jewish life, Buxtorf presented a distorted picture of Judaism in *Juden Schul*. Corporate religious life,
the relationship of the religious and civic communities, and theological controversy were, of course, important features of early
modern Protestantism as well, but were less significant for the religious lives of individual Christians than the corresponding features of Judaism were for Jews. Buxtorf stressed what he considered to be the essence of Judaism in order to facilitate his critique
of it, but the portrait of Judaism was distorted in important ways.
While he was philologically "accurate" in reporting what he had
read in "the Jews' own books," he misrepresented the conceptual
framework within which they functioned. Buxtorf subtly "rede-
fined" Judaism by identifying the Talmud as the principium
(Fundament) and thus efficient cause of Judaism, mirroring
Polanus' doctrine as Scripture as the principium and "effective
cause" of Christianity.[78] In Buxtorf's opinion, the Jews had rejected
the one true source of divine revelation and their rejection of God
was clearly reflected in their feverish attempts to live according to
the Talmud.

Buxtorf's anti-Jewish biases manifested themselves not only in
the way that he portrayed Judaism, but also in his implicit characterization of Jews and of German Jewry as an order in the German
empire. Buxtorf was convinced that Jews hated both Christians and
Christianity. Jews cursed Christians to their face and in private,
and cheated them in business deals.[79] Jews refused to have social
dealings with Christians, never inviting them to weddings or to the

---

[77] Johann Andreas Eisenmenger also misunderstood this aspect of talmudic
interpretation. See Jacob Katz, "The Sources of Modern Anti-Semitism—
Eisenmenger's Method of Presenting Evidence from Talmudic Sources,"
(Hebrew), in: *Proceedings of the Fifth World Congress of Jewish Studies,*
Jerusalem, 3-11 August, 1969, vol. 2 (Jerusalem: World Union of Jewish
Studies, 1969), 210-216; English summary, 227-228.

[78] Hsia, "Ethnographies of Jews," 224, 232.

[79] Buxtorf, *Juden Schul*, 159, 547, 585.

Passover meal.[80] They also blasphemed against Christ and cursed Christians in their prayers, violating both German imperial law and local ordinances.[81]   For the most part, however, the blasphemies they mouthed were implied rather than explicitly stated. Censorship by Christian authorities had eliminated most of the explicitly blasphemous prayers from the Jewish liturgy.[82]

To stress Buxtorf's latent implicit assumptions in *Juden Schul* that Jews hated Christians, however, would be to distort the thrust of the book. Even when Buxtorf reported on what he considered reprehensible Jewish attitudes he seldom departed from a detached narrative tone. Apparently he believed that the Jews condemned themselves by their own words, and he usually did not add any inflammatory comments of his own.[83] Buxtorf never mentioned usury or the Blood Libel, accusations which still aroused the passions of his contemporaries and were used to incite mobs to anti-Jewish violence.[84] Had Buxtorf wished to stir up social resentment against the Jews he could have done so without devoting so much obvious effort to describing the smallest, most unobjectionable details of Jewish life. His quarrel in *Juden Schul* was primarily with the rabbis and Jewish theology.

In another reflection of his anti-Jewish bias, Buxtorf asserted that the Jews were a superstitious people since they had rejected the word of God in favor of their rabbinical tradition. They had lost all sense of spiritual proportion and devoted inordinate attention to trivial practices, such as maintaining a kosher household or building a proper booth for Tabernacles.[85] This lack of proportion also revealed itself in their childish understanding of spiritual realities, particularly in their view of the devil. The Jews thought that they could protect themselves from the devil and evil spirits by making loud noises to scare them away, by saying the *Shema* frequently each day, or by wearing a *talit*, a prayer shawl with tassels, sug-

---

[80] Ibid., 427, 584

[81] Ibid., 91, 203-207, 219-220, 223-227, 249, 460, 477-479.

[82] There was always room for improvement, however. Buxtorf considered the Polish authorities to be especially lax. Ibid., 219-220.

[83] Kalir, "Jewish Service," 58.

[84] On Blood Libel accusations see R. Po-chia Hsia, *The Myth of Ritual Murder. Jews and Magic in Reformation Germany* (New Haven: Yale University Press, 1988).

[85] Buxtorf, *Juden Schul*, 455, 563.

gestions which Buxtorf greeted with ironic derision.[86] In Buxtorf's opinion the Jews lived in a spiritual fantasy world and he believed that "Judaism and superstition were almost synonymous."[87]

The ethnographic part of *Juden Schul*, like the first chapter, was composed as a critique of Judaism. Buxtorf discussed which commandments Jews were obliged to keep throughout their lives and why they were to observe them according to halakic literature.[88] He provided a vivid narrative description of how the Jews went about observing the 613 commandments and then sought to link these laws with specific talmudic passages in order to prove his contention that Judaism was based not upon the Bible, but upon the Talmud. Frequently his sources, particularly the *Shulhan Aruk* and *Brantspiegel*, made the link for him;[89] at other times he was obliged to use far less precise formulations such as "Gemara says" when he was unable to locate the talmudic reference himself.[90] At a time when almost no Jewish books were available in German or Latin translation, Buxtorf's display of learning was calculated to impress as well as to instruct his readers.[91] He clearly sought to provide a definitive interpretation and theological critique of Judaism. But he never let his virtuosity lead him astray from his theological purpose, which was to link Jewish beliefs and practices to their faulty source of revelation, the Talmud, and to contrast these with what the Bible taught.

Buxtorf's intended reading public for *Juden Schul* was the clergy rather than rulers and magistrates, or the educated reading public. He may actually have intended it for Lutheran clergy since his introduction contained a two-page quotation from Luther's *On*

---

[86] Ibid., 184-185, 215, 458. Cf. Günzburg, מנהגים, ff. 73a, 4b.

[87] Cohen, "Leone da Modena's *Riti*," 298.

[88] I believe that Cohen was incorrect in postulating that Buxtorf sought to dissuade "philosemitic Protestants" from idealizing the Jews for their "strict adherence to the Bible" in "Leone da Modena's *Riti*," 293. Victor of Carben, Pfefferkorn, Margaritha, and Hess all sought to persuade their audiences that the Jews were not "strict adherents" of the Bible, making this remark almost a theological commonplace in anti-Jewish polemics. Burnett, "Distorted Mirrors," 277.

[89] E.g., Buxtorf, *Juden Schul*, 176-185 (cf. Altschuler, ברנט שפיטל, ff. 181a-183a), 611.

[90] Buxtorf, *Juden Schul*, 197, 273, 463.

[91] The first Latin translation of the entire Mishnah appeared in print only in 1698. See David S. Katz, "The Abendana Brothers and the Christian Hebraists of Seventeenth Century England," *Journal of Ecclesiastical History* 40 (1989): 41.

the Jews and their Lies.[92] Buxtorf sought to provide clergymen with a thorough description and analysis of what the Jews actually believed and practiced in order to help them write better missionary books and sermons. His translations from Jewish books of piety provided ready-made sermon illustrations, particularly since he wrote the book in German rather than Latin.[93] The only power that Protestant clergymen had over the Jews of early seventeenth-century Germany was the power of persuasion, and Buxtorf conscientiously tried to reflect Jewish opinion accurately so that other scholars could forge effective counter-arguments.[94] Buxtorf's thesis that the fundamental difference between Judaism and Christianity was their differing sources of revelation would have been accepted and understood by Protestant clergymen, and it was a strategy they could employ when debating with Jews. As a further help for ministers Buxtorf translated John Calvin's tract

---

[92] Cf. Martin Luther, *Von den Juden und ihren Lügen,WA* 53, 480.30-481.22. It is difficult to overstate the volume and vituperative tone of Lutheran-Calvinist theological polemics between 1580 and 1620. I believe that Buxtorf's decision to quote Luther on the title page and to hide Calvin's contribution at the end was deliberate. See Schilling, "Confessionalization," in: *Religion*, 226-230.

[93] Whether *Jewish Synagogue* can be considered a missionary work itself remains open to question. It contained no positive argument for the truth of Christianity, a condition which Robert Chazan considered essential for a true missionary book in his *Daggers of Faith: Thirteenth Century Christian Missionizing and Jewish Response*, (Berkeley: Univ. of California Press, 1989), 14-16. Yet seventeenth-century Protestants often felt that they had fulfilled their obligation to persuade Jews to repent by demonstrating to their own satisfaction that Judaism was unbiblical. If God opened the eyes of individual Jews then they would repent and believe. See Martin Friedrich, *Zwischen Abwehr und Bekehrung. Die Stellung der deutschen evangelischen Theologie zum Judentum im 17. Jahrhundert*, Beiträge zur historischen Theologie, no. 72 (Tübingen: J. C. B. Mohr (Paul Siebeck), 1988), 51-52.

[94] In general by 1600 the Jewish policies of those German states and cities which had Jewish populations were shaped primarily by "reasons of state" and commercial considerations. The clergy could offer theological advice to their political masters and could, on their own initiative, seek to proselytize individual Jews, but otherwise they had little to say about the political and social conditions of Jewish life. See J. Friedrich Battenberg, "Reformation, Judentum und Landesherrliche Gesetzgebung. Ein Beitrag zum Verhältnis des protestantischen Landeskirchentums zu den Juden," in: *Reformatio et Reformationes. Festschrift für Lothar Graf zu Dohna zum 65. Geburtstag*, ed. Andreas Mehl und Wolfgang Christian Schneider (Darmstadt: Lehrdruckerei der Technische Hochschule Darmstadt, 1989), 315-346, Jonathan I. Israel, *European Jewry in the Age of Mercantilism 1550-1750* (Oxford: Clarendon Press, 1985), 64-68, and Friedrich, *Zwischen Abwehr und Bekehrung*, 50-54.

Response to questions and objections of a certain Jew and included it as an appendix to the book.[95] Curiously, *Juden Schul* does not contain a positive argument for the truth of Christianity, suggesting that while Buxtorf hoped that Jews would read the book it was not intended primarily for them.

Paradoxically, Buxtorf's detailed criticism of Jews and Judaism in *Juden Schul* may have had the effect of putting Christian minds at ease concerning the social and religious dangers that Jewish communities might pose for Protestant cities and territories. Buxtorf thought that although Jews blasphemed in their prayers, it was possible to suppress overt blasphemy by properly censoring their prayer books.[96] While Jews were superstitious, they were hurting only themselves, not Christians, by practicing their religion. Most of the practices that Buxtorf related in *Juden Schul* were, in fact, completely harmless theologically, involving neither blasphemy nor sedition. He was even willing to allow that some Jewish prayers contained excellent expressions of piety, although they were vitiated by the theological framework of Judaism.[97] His only explicit criticism of Christian governments concerned their willingness to allow Christians to work for Jews on the Sabbath, giving Jews the chance to exercise authority over Christians.[98] While Christian authorities traditionally had allowed the Jews to practice their religion and way of life without knowing much about Judaism, Buxtorf came to his conclusions on the basis of a first-

---

[95] Buxtorf, *Juden Schul*, 665-730. On the tract itself, see Stephen G. Burnett, "Calvin's Jewish Interlocutor: Christian Hebraism and Anti-Jewish Polemics during the Reformation," *Bibliothèque d'Humanisme et Renaissance* 55 (1993): 113-123.

[96] When Jewish books had been properly censored the right of Jews to own and use them was, of course, beyond question. The Jews of Windecken, a village in the German principality of Hanau-Münzenberg, took this argument one step further when on August 18, 1597, they appealed to their prince for permission to reopen their synagogue and to again allow them to worship there. They argued that since they used prayerbooks that had been printed in Germany, Basel and Venice (and censored there) that "surely" they could not contain any blasphemous statements and hence their worship would not cause offense. *Quellen zur Geschichte der Juden im Hessischen Staatsarchiv Marburg 1267-1600*, ed. Uta Löwenstein, 3 vols., Quellen zur Geschichte der Juden in Hessischen Archiven, no. 1 (Wiesbaden: Kommission für die Geschichte der Juden in Hessen, 1989), 3:97 (document #3463).

[97] Buxtorf, *Juden Schul*, 202, 272.

[98] Ibid., 391.

hand examination of Jewish religious literature. By approaching Judaism in this way, Buxtorf was able to distinguish between what he considered theologically intolerable practices such as blasphemy, which could bring God's judgement upon society as a whole and therefore had to be suppressed, and the vast majority of Jewish rituals and beliefs which did not in any way threaten Christian society. *Juden Schul* exudes a quiet confidence that the "Jews and their lies" posed no real danger to Christians and the Christian political order, a sense of security altogether lacking in Reformation era anti-Jewish polemics.[99]

Buxtorf's approach to Judaism had clear implications for social policy toward the Jews, since it offered rulers a clear set of criteria with which to judge the propriety of Jewish settlement within their lands and their conduct as subjects. *Juden Schul* was written at a time when Protestant theologians in both Germany and the Netherlands were obliged to address such questions. While it is possible to dismiss attempts to justify Jewish settlement on theological grounds as religious rationalizations for an economically beneficial arrangement, such a view overlooks how religious confessions functioned in early modern states. State control of confessional churches served to consolidate and legitimize the power of rulers over their subjects, and a common confession helped to unite society.[100] For the ruling authorities in a city or territory to allow Jewish settlement without first demonstrating that the Jews' presence would not be spiritually detrimental to society was to undercut their own legitimacy as rulers and to invite confessionally-based resistance to their plans. Thus the city fathers of Hamburg found it politic to seek advice from the Lutheran theological faculties of Jena and Frankfurt an der Oder before allowing Jewish settlement in their city.[101] While not all rulers were as scrupulous as

---

[99] Luther, for example, feared that Jewish "lies," denials of true religion, constituted the greatest danger that the Jews could pose to Christian society. See Heiko A. Oberman, *The Roots of Anti-Semitism in the Age of Renaissance and Reformation*, trans. James I. Porter (Philadelphia: Fortress Press, 1984), 121.

[100] See Heinz Schilling, "Religion and Society in the Northern Netherlands," in: *Religion*, 376-379, 409-410.

[101] See Joachim Whaley, *Religious Toleration and Social Change in Hamburg, 1529-1819* (Cambridge: Cambridge University Press, 1985), 74-75 and n. 20, and Schilling, "The Second Reformation," in: *Religion*, 266-271. On the political function of confessions in the process of state-building, see Reinhard, "Konfession und Konfessionalizierung," 174-189.

Hamburg's leaders, this city was by no means the only place in Germany where citizens quarreled with their rulers over the theological propriety of allowing Jewish settlement.[102] Although it is not possible at this time to determine how significant Buxtorf's book was for shaping social policies toward the Jews during the seventeenth century, his approach toward Judaism may have influenced Jewish policy in at least one German city less than a decade after *Juden Schul* was published. When the rulers of Hanau decided to allow a Jewish press to open for business in 1609, the censorship policy they imposed focused upon the presence of overt rather than implied blasphemy and was enforced by a former student of Buxtorf named Walter Keuchen.[103]

Assessing Buxtorf's place within the history of anti-Jewish polemics is rather difficult, if only because many of his basic theological positions differed little from those held by many patristic and medieval writers. Buxtorf's understanding of the religious status of the Jews, his opinions about the Talmud, and his belief that the Jews were an object lesson to Christians were all well-established ideas in theology.[104] The literary vehicle which Buxtorf employed, an ethnography of the Jews, had also been used a number of times before he wrote *Juden Schul*.[105] Even the Christian use of Jewish sources in anti-Jewish polemics was a medieval practice, as an array of late medieval Spanish anti-Jewish polemics attest.[106] Buxtorf's distinctive contribution to Christian discussions of Judaism grew out of his focus upon the practice of Judaism and the theological consequences which he drew from it.

---

[102]   See Rotraud Reis, "Zum Zusammenhang von Reformation und Judenvertreibung: Das Beispiel Braunschweig," in: *Civitatum Communitas. Studien zum europäischen Städtewesen. Festschrift Hans Stoob zum 65. Geburtstag*, eds. Helmut Jäger, Franz Petri, and Heinz Quirin, part 2 (Köln: Böhlau, 1984), 630-654.

[103]   Burnett, "Hebrew Censorship in Hanau," 207-8.

[104]   See Heinz Schreckenberg, *Die christlichen Adversus-Judaeos-Texte und ihr literarisches und historisches Umfeld (1.-11. Jh.)*, Europäische Hochschulschriften, ser. 23: Theologie, vol. 172, 2d rev. ed. (Frankfurt a. M.: Peter Lang, 1990) and Cohen, *The Friars and the Jews*.

[105]   Burnett, "Distorted Mirrors," 277.

[106]   Steven J. McMichael, *Was Jesus of Nazareth the Messiah? Alphonso de Espina's Argument against the Jews in the Fortalitium Fidei (c. 1464)*, South Florida Studies in the History of Judaism, vol. 96 (Atlanta: Scholars Press, 1994), 64-106.

Juden Schul broke new theological ground for Christian interpretations of Judaism in three important ways. When discussing the
role of the Talmud within Judaism, Buxtorf described it with a
theological vocabulary developed in the debate between Protestants
and Catholics over Scripture and Tradition. Although theologians
had questioned the legitimacy of the Talmud as a religious authority as early as the thirteenth century, its claim to be a source of
revelation assumed new importance in *Juden Schul*, reflecting confessional polemics over the problem of religious authority.
Buxtorf's focus upon the halakah as a visible expression of the
Jews' disobedience to God's word was also a new theological insight. While Buxtorf was not above deriding what he considered to
be ridiculous aggadic stories or egregious examples of Jewish misinterpretation of Scripture, he devoted relatively little space to
them.[107] His chief concern was to demonstrate that the Talmud, not
the Scriptures, was the efficient cause of Judaism. Finally Buxtorf
was able to provide a new critical assessment of Judaism which
demonstrated that most Jewish practices and beliefs were inoffen-
sive to Christians. As long as the clergy and magistrate were well-
informed and alert to the potential risks of blasphemy and sedition
posed by Judaism, Jews and Judaism posed no real danger to
church and state. By focusing on the actual practice of Judaism in
Juden Schul, Buxtorf also set a standard for Christian knowledge of
Judaism which would endure for over a century after his death.

Whatever the weaknesses of *Juden Schul* as a description of
Jewish faith and life, the book established Buxtorf's reputation as
an expert on Judaism and would ultimately help to shape Christian
perceptions of Jews and Judaism throughout the early modern period.[108] The publication of *Juden Schul* in 1603 marked a milestone
in Buxtorf's career, because it brought him to the attention of
Joseph Scaliger. When Scaliger read *Juden Schul* and Buxtorf's
book *Sylvula epistolarum*, a manual on writing Hebrew letters, he
was impressed enough with Buxtorf to become his academic pa-
tron, a favor Buxtorf never forgot. Scaliger once privately told
some of his students: "I must have a German copy of *Synagoga*

---

[107] Buxtorf, *Juden Schul*, 124, 514. Buxtorf made a special point of ridicul-
ing aggadic portrayals of the future messianic feast. Ibid., 97, 465, 647-651. Cf.
Van Rooden, *Theology*, 91, n. 133.

[108] Hsia, "Ethnographies of Jews," 230.

Iudaica since it is a good book. Buxtorf is uniquely learned in Hebrew. Today we do not have a greater man in Hebrew than him." This was high praise indeed from a man who normally made other scholars the butt of acerbic witticisms.[109]

Curiously, *Juden Schul* also gave Buxtorf a wholly undeserved reputation as a fervent missionary to the Jews.[110] Buxtorf clearly felt that the Jewish mission was important and corresponded at one time or another with Johannes Molther, Hugh Broughton, Christoph Helwig, Christian Gerson, and Philippe du Plessis Mornay, some of its most prominent advocates.[111] Molther, a strong proponent of the Jewish mission, praised the book unstintingly, stating that Buxtorf's proficiency in Jewish sources would be instrumental in building up the church and tearing down the synagogue.[112] Buxtorf's personal involvement in proselytism, however, was very limited. There are only two recorded instances when he spoke with a Jew about the Christian faith, and neither man ultimately converted.[113] Buxtorf apparently felt that his primary task as a professor of Hebrew was to build up the church by training ministers and writing books rather than to argue with Jews.

In addition to furthering Buxtorf's career, *Juden Schul* became a standard source for Christian knowledge of Judaism. Within one year of its publication an acquaintance of Buxtorf's named Hermann Germberg translated it into Latin, without first asking

---

[109] "Il faut que j'aye *Synagoga Iudaica* en Aleman, c'est un bon livre. Buxtorfius unicus doctus est Hebraice. Aujourd'huy nous n'avons que lui de grand homme en Hebreu." Joseph Scaliger, *Scaligerana*, 39-40. The *Scaligerana* are witticisms and comments recorded by several students. See also Joseph Scaliger to Johannes Buxtorf I, Leiden, June 1, 1606, Basel UB Ms G I 59: 363, printed in: Scaliger, *Epistolae*, 521.

[110] Cf. Nicolaus C. Heutger, "Johannes Buxtorf in Basel: Hebraist und Vater der Judenmission," *Judaica* 24 (1968): 69-81.

[111] Buxtorf was acquainted only with Broughton before 1603; he corresponded with the others after he had published *Juden Schul*. On the role of these men in the "Jewish mission," see Friedrich, *Zwischen Abwehr und Bekehrung*, 20-23, 34, 43-46, 174.

[112] "Hunc igitur tuum in Hebraismo profectum ex animo tibi gratulor: atque ut in hoc stadio decurrendo sedulo pergas, et Judaeorum perfidiam magis magisque detegas, et subinde aliquid proferas, unde Ecclesia filij Dei aedificari et ornari Judaeorum autem Sÿnagoga destrui possit, etiam atque etiam hortor." Johannes Molther to Johannes Buxtorf I, Friedberg, September 30, 1603. Basel UB Ms G I 60: 214r. On Molther, see Friedrich, *Zwischen Abwehr und Bekehrung*, 33-35.

[113] See Burnett, "Circumcision Incident," 142.

Buxtorf's permission.[114] Between 1603 and 1750 *Juden Schul* was reprinted five times in German, and was translated into Latin (twice), Dutch and English, appearing in print 19 times.[115] Thanks to its dual character as a theological work in ethnographic form, *Juden Schul* left its mark upon both anti-Jewish polemics and ethnographic studies on the Jews.

Theologians of all stripes found *Juden Schul* helpful as a source of information about Judaism. One of the first to use the book was Abraham Costerus, a Dutch minister who translated large parts of it and Margaritha's *Gantz Jüdisch Glaub* into Dutch and published them as a book under his own name in 1608.[116] Over 50 years later, Johannes Leusden, a professor of Hebrew at the University of Utrecht, conducted three academic disputations which addressed questions about the Talmud. One of the issues he raised was whether the Talmud legitimately could be used by present-day Jews as a foundation for their theology, a theme echoing Buxtorf's thesis in *Juden Schul*.[117] Surprisingly, Jewish converts also made considerable use of the book when writing their own exposés of Judaism.[118] Buxtorf's direct influence upon theological discourse through *Juden Schul* was, however, not as important in the long run as the impact that the book had upon ethnographic descriptions of Jewish life.

Juden Schul helped shape ethnographic discussions of Jewish life throughout the seventeenth and eighteenth centuries, serving as a source of explanations for Jewish customs and occasionally as a substitute for first-hand observation. Some writers excerpted entire passages from *Juden Schul* when describing their "experiences" with Jews in foreign lands. Thomas Platter the Younger, for example, took much of his description of Jewish life in Avignon directly from *Juden Schul*.[119] Lancelot Addison also made extensive

---

[114] Prijs, *Drucke*, 372.
[115] See below, Appendix 1, nos. 52-74.
[116] Van Rooden, "Conceptions of Judaism," 301-302.
[117] Ibid., 304. See Johannes Leusden, *Philologus Hebraeo-Mixtus* (Utrecht: Franciscus Halma, 1682), 91-97 (Dissertatio 13).
[118] Kalir, "Jewish Service," 55, n. 26 and Benjamin Ravid, "*Contra Judaeos* in Seventeenth Century Italy: Two Responses to the *Discorso* of Simone Luzzatto by Melchiore Palontrotti and Giulio Morosini," *Association for Jewish Studies Review* 7-8 (1982-1983): 339.
[119] Thomas Platter der Jüngere, *Beschreibung der Reisen durch Frankreich, Spanien, England und die Niederlande 1595-1600*, ed. Rut Keiser, Basler

use of *Juden Schul* in his book *The Present State of the Jews: More
Particularly Relating to those in Barbary* (1675).[120] These works,
and probably other Christian accounts of Jewish life as well, must
be used with care since their authors frequently interpreted what
they saw through the lens of Buxtorf's book.

   Juden Schul also played a more constructive role as a reference
source on Judaism for later authors. By writing a manual of
Judaism, Buxtorf helped make possible the monumental works of
Johann Jacob Schudt, Jacques Basnage, and Johann Caspar Ulrich,
all of whom used *Juden Schul* as a reference book.[121] Like *Juden
Schul* itself, these works contain much valuable information about
early modern Jewish life and still repay systematic study.
Christians, however, were not the only readers of *Juden Schul*.
Jewish responses to the characterization of themselves and their re-
ligion provide revealing insights into the book's significance.

   The importance of *Juden Schul* as a shaper of Christian opinion
on Judaism is best demonstrated by the only contemporary Jewish
response written to it—Leon Modena's *Historia de' riti hebraici*
(1637). Modena was a rabbi in the city of Venice who maintained
close relations with a number of Christian scholars. He wrote this
work around 1616 at the request of an English "nobleman," perhaps the ambassador Sir Henry Wotton.[122] He confided to Vincent
Noghera, a Catholic theologian friend, his purpose in composing
the work.

> The judgment made by you on my work about our *Rites* is most correct in-
> sofar as I had indeed the intention of refuting entirely that work of Buxtorf
> and of giving a true account of the fundamentals [i. e. of Judaism], leaving

---

Chroniken no. 9, 2 vols. (Basel and Stuttgart: Schwabe Verlag, 1968), 294, 300-
302, 304, passim. Cf. *Juden Schul*, 595, 458, 561, 572-573, 600-603, 616-617
for the corresponding quotations.

   [120] Horowitz, "'A Different Mode of Civility'," 319-323.

   [121] See Mariam Silvera, "Contribution à l'examin des sources de *L'Histoire
des Juifs* de Jacques Basnage: *Las Excelencias de los Hebreos* de Ysaac
Cardoso," *Studia Rosenthaliana* 25 (1991): 50, n. 36, Lothar Rothschild, *Johann
Caspar Ulrich von Zürich und seine "Sammlung jüdischer Geschichten in der
Schweiz* (Zürich: Dissertations- druckerei A. -G. Gebr. Leemann, 1933), 141-
143. and Hsia, "Christian Ethnographies," 230

   [122] Cohen, "Leone da Modena's *Riti*," 289 and n. 14. I have consulted the
first English translation of the *Riti* for my discussion: Leon Modena, *The History
of the Rites, Customes and Manner of Life, of the Present Jews, throughout the
World*, trans. Edmund Chilmead (London: John Martin and John Ridley, 1650).

out those items which have been considered by our own people (by the intelligent men among them) as superstitious.[123]

Modena's task was complicated by a need for discretion: he could not afford to attack Christianity in any way if he were to win Christians over to the cause of Jewish tolerance, particularly if he ever hoped to publish his work.[124] Modena sought to persuade his readers of the "essential rationality and morality of Judaism and the Jewish people" in an attempt to convince Catholic authorities in Italy that Jews were a virtuous people who deserved greater social toleration and acceptance.[125]

Although Modena employed a variety of rhetorical strategies to discredit *Juden Schul* and to build the ethos of Judaism and the Jewish people, one of the most effective was to undermine Buxtorf's portrayal of Judaism by implying that it was too simplistic. Modena discussed a number of factors which governed halakic practice, sharply distinguishing between halakic requirements that all Jews were obliged to observe from local customs (*minhagim*) which only certain Jews obeyed. He suggested that simple Jews practiced some customs which were rejected by their more learned brethren, and that some rituals reported by Buxtorf were no longer practiced at all. When discussing Jewish rituals and customs Modena sought to put them in the best possible light, attributing their practice to concerns for modesty, good manners, health and other laudable motives. When Modena had no effective counter argument at his disposal he often sidestepped topics, such as the Jewish liturgy. He also tended to avoid talmudic references, but quoted frequently from the Bible to buttress his explanations, leaving his readers with the impression that Judaism too was a biblical religion.[126]

Modena's discussion of the Feast of Tabernacles illustrates how he sought to refute Buxtorf and to reshape his Christian readers' attitudes toward Judaism. Modena stressed the biblical roots of Tabernacles by quoting twice from Lev. 23 and explaining how the

---

[123] Cohen, "Leone da Modena's *Riti*," 293.
[124] Salman Zvi Hirsch faced the same sort of dilemma when he wrote his apologetic work *Yudischer Theriak* in 1615. Burnett, "Hebrew Censorship in Hanau," 208-209.
[125] Cohen, "Leone da Modena's *Riti*," 298.
[126] Ibid., 298-301, 303-305.

Jews sought to obey God by building the booths and by using the
Lulav in worship "as they used to do in the Temple." He also emphasized the biblical content of their worship by relating that they
recited Psalms 29 and 113-119 during synagogue services.[127] While
he acknowledged that there were a number of rabbinic ordinances
governing the construction of a booth, he omitted all discussion of
them. Where Buxtorf charged the Jews with praying and acting out
ritual curses against Christendom, Modena emphasized that Jews
prayed that God would bless (Christian) princes during the festival.
Where Buxtorf made a point of discussing the eighth day of
Tabernacles, *Simhat Torah*, in a separate chapter of *Juden Schul*
since it was a rabbinical innovation, Modena referred to it simply
and unobjectionably as an "ancient custom."[128] In his discussion of
Tabernacles Modena stressed that Judaism was a biblical religion
and that the Jews sought to follow both the letter and spirit of
Scripture.

Modena's most pronounced departure from the agenda set by
Buxtorf was in his explanations of Jewish public activities. Where
Buxtorf left the interior of the synagogue and the activities of its
functionaries undefined, Modena provided detailed descriptions.[129]
He also discussed Jewish business ethics and usury, Jewish philan-
thropy, and public morality. By taking advantage of Buxtorf's
omissions in *Juden Schul* Modena was able to emphasize those elements of Jewish public life he felt best suited his apologetic purpose
without fear of contradiction.

Leon Modena's *Riti* was a literary tour de force and assumed an
important role in shaping educated Christian opinion concerning
Judaism during both the seventeenth and eighteenth centuries. Even
Buxtorf II used it as a source when he revised *Juden Schul* in
1661.[130] Despite the warm reception that Modena's book received,
however, it did not supersede *Juden Schul*. Indeed Modena's friend
Jacques Gaffarel, who arranged for the book to be published in
Paris, found it to be somewhat disappointing. In his letter of intro-

---

[127] Modena, *History of the Rites*, 148-151.
[128] Ibid., 149-150.
[129] Cohen, "Leone da Modena's *Riti*," 297, 310-313.
[130] Ibid., 318-319. See also Arthur Hertzberg, *The French Enlightenment and the Jews* (New York and Philadelphia: Columbia Univ. Press/Jewish Publication Society, 1968), 41.

duction Gaffarel mentioned a number of "hidden and mysterious points" of Judaism which he felt ought to have been covered in the *Riti* but were not. Gaffarel clearly referred to *Juden Schul* in at least two places in his letter, and may have alluded to it in eight others.[131] While Modena could seek to reshape his reader's opinions concerning Jews and Judaism he could not entirely undo the damage that Buxtorf had done. By providing so much information about the smallest details of the halakah in *Juden Schul*, Buxtorf had set the standard by which all later works would be judged.

In contrast to Modena's thoughtful, calculated response to *Juden Schul*, German Jews largely ignored the book when it appeared, despite its polemical purpose. Benedict de Castro, a Sephardic resident of Hamburg, probably spoke for many German Jews when he wrote, "The Jews are concerned with naught else but devoting themselves to their own religion, to calling upon immortal God, and never do they devise anything against Christianity, it matters not what Buxtorf may say."[132] Jewish leaders, however, apparently felt that *Juden Schul* posed no danger to their communities, since they were both willing and able to respond to those books they considered threatening. When some of Luther's anti-Jewish writings were reprinted in Dortmund during 1590, Jewish leaders complained vigorously to the emperor, seeking to have the works suppressed.[133] A decade after *Juden Schul* appeared several Jewish communities apparently cooperated in sponsoring Solomon Zvi Hirsch's *Yudischer Theriak* (*Jewish Antidote*) (1615), a response to Samuel Friedrich Brenz's defamatory *Judischer Abgestreiffter*

---

[131] The two clear citations are Jacques Gaffarel to Leon Modena, Paris, March 31, 1637, *History*, ff B3r, B6v. Cf. Buxtorf, *Juden Schul*, 294-295 (Vespesian's three ships), 600-603 (punishment of malefactors). Gaffarel may also have alluded to *Juden Schul*, 98-103 (Lillith), 169-170 (lavatory use), 176-196 (*Zizit* and *Tephillim*), 288 (beds arranged north-south), 311-312 (cutting nails to prepare for Sabbath), 364-366 (souls of damned rest on Sabbath), 510-516 (*Capporah*), and 606-607 (arrangement of dead man's hands).

[132] Benedict de Castro, *Flagellum Calumniatium seu Apologia* (Amsterdam: n. p., 1631), quoted by Harry Friedenwald, "Apologetic Works of Jewish Physicians," in idem, *The Jews and Medicine: Essays*, vol, 1 (Baltimore: The Johns Hopkins Press, 1944), 59.

[133] R. Po-chia Hsia, "Printing, Censorship and Antisemitism in Reformation Germany," in: *The Process of Change in Early Modern Europe: Essays in Honor of Miriam Usher Chrisman*, eds. Sherrin Marshall and Philip N. Bebb (Athens, OH: Ohio Univ. Press, 1988), 136-143.

Schlangenbalg (*Jewish Brood of Snakes Revealed*).[134] By contrast,
Jewish leaders made no attempt to respond publicly to *Juden Schul*.
Hirsch even quoted from it once in his book to parry an accusation
made by Brenz.[135] While German Jews probably found Buxtorf's
portrayal of Judaism unflattering, *Juden Schul* itself—a long, ab-
struse, recognizable portrayal of Jewish life as viewed by a
Christian theologian—was apparently no cause for alarm.[136]

More curiously still, the appearance of *Juden Schul* apparently
did not affect Buxtorf's business dealings with Jews. Between 1603
and 1620 he continued to work closely with Jewish print shop
workers, booksellers, and financiers. In 1617 Buxtorf was able to
hire two of Hanau's best Jewish printers to help him print a rabbinical Bible in Basel, even though a Latin translation of *Juden
Schul* had been printed twice in Hanau, a town near Frankfurt
which had both a Jewish community and Jewish press.[137] Since
Jewish businessmen paid for the printing of Jewish books in Basel
and then handled their distribution, it would have been important
both for Buxtorf and for his employers to maintain civil relations
with them. To some extent Buxtorf was dependent upon the good
will and patronage of Jews to earn a living and would probably
have thought twice before publishing a book that would have de-
stroyed his livelihood. By the same token, the Jewish businessmen
and printers who patronized the Basel printers probably would
have been willing to put up with occasional theological discussions
with Buxtorf and Waldkirch's other employees, since they too
wanted to stay in business and Basel was the closest Hebrew press
to Frankfurt. It is difficult to assess how offensively a Christian
could behave in early seventeenth century Germany—or how offensive a book on Judaism he could write—before he permanently
alienated a Jewish business associate or customer, but apparently
the sentiments Buxtorf expressed in *Juden Schul* were not outra-

---

134 Burnett, "Hebrew Censorship in Hanau," 209.
135 Idem, "Distorted Mirrors," 285 n. 61.
136 While it is possible that the lull in Hebrew printing experienced by
Waldkirch's press during 1604-1605 reflected a negative response to Buxtorf's
work among Waldkirch's Jewish clients, it may also have been either a Jewish
response to the Frankfurt rabbinical synod ordinance of 1603, or a change in
policy by the Basel magistrate forbidding further Jewish printing. See above,
chap. 2.
137 See Burnett, "Distorted Mirrors," 285.

geous enough to provoke a break in relations with his Jewish acquaintances.[138] Buxtorf's other book on Judaism, had it ever been published, would probably not have elicited the same response.

Between 1603 and 1606 Buxtorf wrote a second book on the Jews and Judaism entitled *Aus was Ursachen die Juden andere völker alzeit gehasst unnd veracht haben* (*The Reasons Why Jews have Always Hated and Despised Other Peoples*).[139] He stopped writing it part way through the sixth chapter and never composed an introduction or conclusion. Enough of the book was written, however, to indicate its overall structure, argument, and affinities with *Juden Schul*. In a sense the book's title obscures Buxtorf's evident purpose in composing it; Buxtorf wished to explain why the Jews hated Christ and Christians in particular, not gentiles in general.[140] The book consists of six chapters which can be divided into three parts. In the first part Buxtorf asserted that the Jews hated all other peoples on earth because they thought themselves superior to them. They enjoyed superior worth and holiness as descendents of Abraham (chap. 1), they were set apart as God's covenant people by the mark of circumcision (chap. 2), and God had revealed his Law to them on Mount Sinai, and had given them the land of Israel, the city of Jerusalem and the Temple as further tokens of his favor (chap. 3). The nations of the earth, by contrast, were the object of God's contempt and derision.[141] The second reason that Jews hated all other peoples, as Buxtorf explained it, was that they sought to apply God's command that the Israelites separate themselves from the seven nations of Canaan (Deut 7: 1-6) to their dealings with non-Jews (chap. 4). The third part explains why Buxtorf believed that Jews hated Christ and Christians with undying hatred (chaps. 5-6).

---

[138] I have related two cases where the line of social and religious controversy can be drawn with some confidence in "Hebrew Printing in Hanau," 210-11 and in "Circumcision Incident," 135-144.

[139] *Aus was Ursachen die Juden andere völker alzeit gehasst unnd veracht haben*, Basel UB Ms A XII 78.

[140] Dr. Martin Steinmann, curator of manuscripts, noted in an unpublished Basel UB finding aid that the title was supplied from "der ursprünglichen, jetzt gestrichenen Überschrift zu cap. 1." Buxtorf himself may not have found what he considered an acceptable title for it.

[141] Ibid., ff. 9r, 13v, 21v, 38r. Buxtorf had already made this argument in an abbreviated form in *Juden Schul*, 50-51.

Buxtorf used Jewish authorities wherever possible to prove his
theological contentions in *Aus was Ursachen*, but he related Jewish
opinion far more bluntly in it than he had in *Juden Schul*. Instead
of using halakic manuals, he quoted most often from biblical commentaries, sermon collections, prayer books, and midrashic material from the Talmud and from ancient collections such as *Midrash
Rabba*, *Tanhuma*, and *Pirke de Rabbi Eliezer*. Buxtorf's treatment
of circumcision in both books illustrates his differing purposes for
writing them.[142] While Buxtorf's discussion of circumcision in
Juden Schul was straightforward and devoid of commentary, his
portrayal of it in *Aus was Ursachen* was venomous in tone since he
focused upon its spiritual implications. Using quotations from
liturgical prayers, a number of sermons and midrashim to buttress
his point, he sought to prove that the Jews were at once smugly
complacent about their spiritual standing with God and that they
felt contempt for non-Jews. For example, he argued that Bahya b.
Asher's statement, "The power of the commandment of circumcision is great, for one who is circumcised does not descend to
Gehenna [for final destruction]," implied that Gehenna would be
the fate of non-Jews.[143] Buxtorf then sought to contrast this Jewish
"theology" with his understanding of biblical doctrine, and again he
used biblical citations from both the Old and New Testaments as
foils to his quotations from Jewish sources, indicating that the Jews
had abandoned the Bible in favor of their own wisdom.[144]

Buxtorf's biting polemical argument derives not only from his
personal response to the Jewish authors he quoted, but also from
his literary and theological model for the book, Martin Luther's
On the Jews and their Lies (1543). In the opening section of his
book Luther asserted that the Jews were blinded to the truth of the
Gospel by their belief in their own personal worthiness and holiness, the value they assigned to the rite of circumcision, and their
belief that God had singularly honored them by giving them the
Law on Mount Sinai, the land of Israel, the city of Jerusalem, and
the temple.[145] Buxtorf used not only Luther's pattern of organization to attack what he considered to be false Jewish theology, but

---

[142] Buxtorf, *Juden Schul*, 107-123 and *Aus was Ursachen*, ff. 13v-21v.
[143] Bahya b. Asher, *Encyclopedia*, 391 = כד הקמח, 248.
[144] *Aus was Ursachen*, ff. 15v-19v.
[145] Martin Luther, *Von den Juden und Ihren Lügen*, WA 53: 419-448.

also many of the same arguments. When discussing circumcision, for example, he repeated Luther's arguments when he remarked that many ancient peoples such as the Egyptians, Moabites, and Ammonites had also circumcised children, and circumcision did not inevitably bring divine favor upon even some of Abraham's descendents such as Esau.[146] Buxtorf's fourth chapter also contains a number of arguments drawn from Luther to substantiate the charge that the Jews had always hated the gentiles and had done them harm in whatever way they could. Like Luther, Buxtorf believed that Jews hated Christians, and although they no longer had the physical means to persecute Christians in Europe, they expressed their hatred in other ways. Both likewise believed that Jewish hatred for Christians was a direct outgrowth of their theology.

According to Buxtorf, Jewish hatred for Christ and Christians grew out of their fixation upon the outward forms of their covenant with God, to the detriment of true worship and obedience. While they believed that their descent from Abraham and circumcision marked them as the true people of God, Buxtorf argued that Moses, the prophets and Christ repeatedly warned the Jews not to trust in these outward expressions of piety alone. Similarly, Jeremiah had warned his contemporaries that God would not prevent Jerusalem from being captured simply to protect his temple there (Jer. 7:4).

After explaining in the first four chapters why Jews hated gentiles in general, Buxtorf devoted his final two chapters to exploring why Christ and Christians in particular became the particular target of Jewish anger. These chapters differ from the previous ones in that they focus upon the Gospel accounts and Christ's role in salvation history. When Christ came he inflamed the Jewish leaders of his day because he systematically attacked their outward forms of piety, which they in their disobedience and blindness had established. Buxtorf wrote,

> The reason for the great blindness, lack of attentiveness and complacency of the Jews, because of which they had not thought about their king and messiah for so long, was that they had falsified, obscured, corrupted, and systematically misinterpreted the law of Moses and teaching of the prophets. Sound and pure doctrine could no longer be found among them.

---

[146] Ibid., 429.15-37 and 431. 32-36. Cf. *Aus*, ff. 14v, 17v.

> Instead [there were] errors and superstition, sects and parties which es-
> poused false doctrines, divisions, and in general [pursued] a thoroughly
> obnoxious and sinful way of life, both among the clergy and the common
> people as the Gospels amply demonstrate.[147]

Rather than repenting from their sinful ways many Jews rejected
Christ and remained faithful to the traditions of the elders. They
continued, however, to nurse a grudge against Christ, blasphemed
against him, and cursed his followers both in their public and private prayers.[148]

While Buxtorf's tone and message in *Aus was Ursachen* seem to
differ from what he employed in *Juden Schul*, he had not changed
his position on Jews and Judaism in the least and the two books
share many similarities. In both books he stressed the Jews' focus
upon the external requirements of the law, echoing Luther's
"doctrine of the veil." He believed that the Jews consistently misin-
terpreted and misunderstood the Bible, and used their twisted interpretations to support their own beliefs and practices.[149] Buxtorf
also mentioned Jewish hatred for Christ and Christians in both
books, primarily expressed through cursing and blasphemy, especially in their liturgy.[150] When discussing the Thirteen Principles
in *Juden Schul*, Buxtorf argued that Maimonides had written them
deliberately so as to make Christianity hateful to Jews.[151] Buxtorf's
tone in *Aus was Ursachen* was sharper not because he had become
more anti-Jewish, but because he focused more sharply upon the
competing claims of Judaism and Christianity to be the one true
religion. Buxtorf sought to contrast Jewish fables with the true

---

[147] "Die ursach aber dieser grossen blindheit unachtsamkeit und sicherheit der
Juden, darin sie dieses ihres königs und Messias so lange zeit nicht geachtet ist
gewesen, dass Mosis gesatz und aller propheten lehr, damals gantz iemarlich bei
ihnen verfalschet, verfinstert, verderbet, und gäntzlich in einen anderen sinn und
meinung verkehret, und gerissen gewesen, also dass keine gesunde und reine
lehr mehr bei ihnen gefunden worden, sonder eital irthumb, grosse superstition
und aberglauben verfuhrliche Secten, widerwertige Spaltungen und uneinigkeit
und durchauss ein argerliche und sundliches leben, so wol unter dem geistlichen
stand alss dem gemeinen volck, wie die gantze Evangelische historien gnuchsam
aussweiset." *Aus*, f. 48v.

[148] Ibid., ff. 55r-v.

[149] Cf Buxtorf, *Juden Schul*, 514, and *Aus*, ff. 15v, 40r, 49r. On Luther's
"doctrine of the veil," see *Von den Juden*, WA 53: 444. 31-445. 5.

[150] Cf. Buxtorf, *Juden Schul*, 202-228, passim, and *Aus*, ff. 9v, 16r, 35r,
46v.

[151] Buxtorf, *Juden Schul*, 21.

words of Scripture in *Aus was Ursachen* just as he had in *Juden Schul*.

Buxtorf had written most of *Aus was Ursachen* by 1606, but he never finished the book.[152] His reasons for leaving the work unfinished and in manuscript can only be inferred, since he mentioned it only once after 1603. Buxtorf discussed the book in a letter to Matthaeus Martinius and offered to make a copy of the work, but urged his colleague to keep the book's existence a secret.[153] While he clearly stood by what he wrote, Buxtorf was worried that it might not please some of his readers. Since his argument was wholly orthodox, if rather mild when compared with Luther's *On the Jews and their Lies*, he probably did not fear that he would be castigated by Christians for the book. Instead, he worried that the book might upset his professional relationships with Jews. Buxtorf's rather dilatory efforts to publish Raymond Martini's *Pugio fidei* later in his career also suggest that he was reluctant to become visibly involved in anti-Jewish polemics.

Philippe du Plessis Mornay (1549-1623) first had the idea that Buxtorf should prepare an edition of *Pugio fidei* for publication.[154] Mornay, a prominent leader of the French reformed church and professor of Theology at the Saumur theological academy, owned a manuscript copy of the *Pugio*. He himself had written an anti-Jewish polemical work entitled *l'Advertissement sur la venue du Messie* (1607) and maintained a lively interest in the conversion of the Jews.[155] He told Buxtorf in a letter that he was uniquely quali-

---

[152] Buxtorf II published a Latin summary of the work in the introduction to the authorized Latin translation of *Juden Schul*. See *Synagoga Iudaica* (Basel: L. König, 1640), ff.):():(2r-):():(6v.

[153] "Sed alium librum eadem opera ante sex annos conceptum ac prope absolutum, adhuc supprimo. Is continebit Caussas odii Judaeorum in omnes gentes ac mundi populos, omnium autem maxime in Christianos: initium, progressum, continuationem, blasphemias duras, convitia in Christum, Christianorum Magistratum, Christianos omnes, imprecationes & illis similia .... Spem huius facio in aliquo loco Scholae Judaicae. Placet habere exemplum? Dabo, sed secretum esse cupio." Buxtorf, "Epistola Johannis Buxtorfii," 601-602.

[154] See F. Secret, "Notes pour une histoire du Pugio Fidei a la Renaissance," *Sefarad* 20 (1960): 401-407.

[155] Friedrich, *Zwischen Abwehr und Bekehrung*, 34, and François Laplanche, *L'Evidence du Dieu Chrétien. Religion, culture et société dans l'apologétique protestante de la France classique (1576-1670)* (Strasbourg:

fied to edit the work because of his profound knowledge of Jewish literature. He had revealed the Jews' hidden truths for the ridiculous fables that they were, and seemed destined to live "for the instruction and conversion of the Jews."[156] To Mornay's delight Buxtorf agreed to take on the task, probably in 1615.[157]

The later history of Mornay's *Pugio* manuscript from the time he sent it to Buxtorf until Buxtorf II had it returned to Saumur is exceptionally well documented. A Dutch theological student named Johannes Cloppenburg took the manuscript from Saumur to Basel, arriving before October 7, 1615.[158] Buxtorf and several of his students divided the manuscript up and each copied portions of it.[159] The project, however, did not progress any further during Buxtorf's lifetime. The death of Waldkirch forced a temporary suspension of Hebrew printing in Basel from 1615 until 1617 when Ludwig König formally took over the business. Buxtorf then felt it

---

Associon des Publications de la Faculté de Théologie Protestante de Strasbourg, 1983), 20, 177-183.

[156] "In has causâ (Judaeorum conversionem intelligens) quod potui, praestiti lubens, non tam utique operae pretium facturus, quam hoc tantum signo dato opem operámque Doctiorum, tuam inprimis ad tam necessarium opus excitaturus, nempe qui in eorum seu adyta seu abdita penitissimè ingressus nosceris: quique ridicula eorundem commenta unus omnium optimè nudaveris, everteris, unus maximè ad ipsorum institutionem, conversionem natus datúsque videaris." Philippe du Plessis de Mornay to Johannes Buxtorf I, n. p., n. d; The original letter has not been preserved but this fragment, probably written before the other extant Mornay letter to Buxtorf, dated July 23, 1615, was printed in Tossanus, *Vita*, 11 and translated in Buxtorf-Falkeisen, *Buxtorf*, 26.

[157] Mornay mentions in his letter of July 23, 1615, that he would have the manuscript sent to him as quickly as possible. Philippe du Plessis-Mornay to Johannes Buxtorf, Saumur, July 23, 1615, Basel UB Ms G I 62: 98, printed in Buxtorf, *Catalecta*, 473-474 and translated in Buxtorf-Falkeisen, *Buxtorf*, 23.

[158] "Accepi, Vir Clarissime idemque Doctissime, literas tuas ad me 7. Octob. scriptas…. Communicavi, quae ad me scripsisti cum Dn. Plessaeo, ut certior fieret, quàm tutò ad Te tandem delatus esset Raymundi Pugio." Louis Cappel to Johannes Buxtorf I, Saumur, January 18, 1616, Basel UB Ms G I 62: 106, printed in Buxtorf, *Catalecta*, 474-476 and Buxtorf-Falkeisen, *Buxtorf*, 24-25, and Louis Cappel to Johannes Buxtorf II, Saumur, November, 1627, Basel UB Ms G I 62: 115, printed in Buxtorf, *Catalecta*, 480-483 and Buxtorf-Falkeisen, *Buxtorf*, 25.

[159] Buxtorf's *Pugio* manuscript (Basel UB Ms A XII 9-11) consists of three quarto bound volumes. While the chapter numbers in the first and third parts differ slightly from Joseph de Voisin's first edition (Paris: Mathurinum, 1651), a close comparison of the two versions reveals that each contains the same number of sections with nearly identical titles. For a description of the manuscript, see Burnett, "Buxtorf Family Papers," in: Prijs, *Die Handschriften*, 80-81.

more appropriate that the new press should print a Hebrew Bible as its first work rather than *Pugio*.[160] These two delays prevented any further work on the project until 1620. Afterwards, the length of Buxtorf's work list delayed its publication still further. Buxtorf II later recalled that his father was very busy during these years, first revising the second edition of his *Thesaurus Grammaticus* in 1615, then working on the rabbinical Bible edition from 1617-1619, and finally beginning work on the Bible concordance and talmudic lexicon.[161] While Buxtorf had not given up all hope of printing the *Pugio*, his schedule did not allow him to work on it.[162] In 1627 Cappel wrote to Buxtorf II, thinking that the elder Buxtorf had died, and urged him either to assume responsibility for the *Pugio* edition himself or to return Mornay's manuscript to Saumur. The elder Buxtorf responded to the letter, assuring him that he had not given up on the project.[163] After Buxtorf I's death Cappel again demanded the return of the *Pugio* manuscript, which the younger Buxtorf eventually arranged.[164]

The *Pugio* project reveals a great deal about Buxtorf's scholarly and publishing priorities. He felt it far more important to encourage biblical studies through his publications than either to write further on Judaism or to promote Jewish missions. In an earlier letter he told Mornay that his scholarly work was largely directed

---

[160] "Sed cum ruinam tum passa fuisset Typographia vestra Hebraica Waldkirchiana, eamque instaure pararet L. König, nec primum ejus foetum vellet esse Pugionem, sed ipsa S. Biblia, scribebat Parens tuus, se coactum fuisse consilium illud suum de Pugione edendo differre." Cappel to Buxtorf II, Saumur, November, 1627, Basel UB Ms G I 62: 115, printed in *Catalecta*, 481.

[161] Johannes Buxtorf II to Johann Heinrich Hottinger, n. p., December 7, 1642, Zürich ZB Ms F 51: 82v.

[162] "De Martino Raymundo ... jam dudum forte intellexisti, illum quoque penes nos esse. Ederetur, si tempora essent magis tranquilla." Johannes Buxtorf II to Peter Cunaeus, Basel, November 1, 1626, Leiden UB Ms Cun 2:97, printed in Cunaeus, *Epistolae*, 157-158.

[163] "Gaudeo Te non abjecisse consilium edendi Pugionis, & sanè hac in parte deesse tibi non debet Typographus tuus." Louis Cappel to Johannes Buxtorf I, Saumur, June 27, 1628, Basel UB Ms G I 62: 116, printed in Buxtorf, *Catalecta*, 484-486, and partially translated in Buxtorf-Falkeisen, *Buxtorf*, 26.

[164] In 1643 Buxtorf II received another offer, this time through French Catholic correspondents, to prepare the *Pugio* for publication. He accepted the offer but for unknown reasons the project was never begun. For an account of this second attempt to publish the *Pugio* in Basel see Carlos Gilly, *Spanien und der Basler Buchdruck bis 1600*, Basler Beiträge zur Geschichtswissenschaft, no. 151 (Basel: Helbing & Lichtenhahn, 1985), 99.

toward promoting the study of the Hebrew Bible. Even his collections of Hebrew letters and book on Hebrew abbreviations were written to promote the reading of medieval Hebrew Bible commentaries.[165] While he was sympathetic to the cause of Jewish proselytism he was not willing to abandon biblical studies in order to promote it by publishing *Pugio fidei*.

Buxtorf may also have felt that publishing *Pugio fidei* could interfere with his stated priorities in another way. He required the cooperation of Jewish workers to print many of his works and he wished both to do business with Jewish book sellers and, perhaps, to consult Jewish scholars on technical points of his work. Without Jewish assistance projects such as the Basel rabbinical Bible edition would have been impossible to complete. Buxtorf apparently felt that he could not afford to express publicly some of his opinions about Judaism if he was to maintain personal and professional links with Jews.

Buxtorf's works on the Jews offer no new vision of them, their culture, or their religion. He argued in both *Juden Schul* and *Aus was Ursachen* that the Jews were slavishly obedient to the dictates of the rabbis and deaf to the words of Scripture. They focused their attention upon outward conformity to the letter of the Law rather seeking to please God. They felt assured that they were the apple of God's eye and that God hated every other people on earth besides them. Their hope was for an earthly Messiah who would conquer the world and subdue the gentiles rather than one who would redeem them from their sins. By interpreting Judaism in these terms Buxtorf spelled out a theological position wholly in accord with both Lutheran and Reformed orthodoxy of his day.[166] Indeed, it was not an uncommon position among scholars and the-

---

[165] "Edidi librum epistolarum Hebraicarum, in quo modum loquendi et scribendi Rabbinicum familiariter explico, et ad lectionem commentariorum Rabbinicorum studiosos invito. In his quia abbreviaturae frequentes quae remotae sunt et offendicula ingrata legentibus, illis nunc remedium affero" Johannes Buxtorf I to Philippe du Plessis-Mornay, Basel, September 8, 1613, Basel UB Ms Autogr. Slg. Geigy Hgb, no. 736.

[166] See Friedrich, *Zwischen Abwehr und Bekehrung*, 145-149, and Van Rooden, "Conceptions of Judaism," 302-304.

ologians of the Enlightenment; both Richard Simon and Phillip Limborch would have agreed with Buxtorf.[167]

If Buxtorf's theological evaluation of Judaism is difficult to distinguish from those held by earlier polemicists, his narrative description of how Jews lived their lives differed markedly from any previous work written for a Christian audience. *Juden Schul* set a new standard for Christian discussions of Jews and Judaism which was reflected in many later "ethnographies of the Jews," even in Leon Modena's *Riti*. The book represented an important milestone on the road leading to both Johann Jacob Schudt's *Jüdische Merckwürdigkeiten* (1714-1717) and Johann Andreas Eisenmenger's *Entdecktes Judenthum* (1700). For better or for worse, *Juden Schul* constituted an important part of what educated Christians "knew" about Jews and Judaism for over a century after it first appeared.

If *Juden Schul* set a new standard for Christian knowledge of Judaism, its characterization of Jews and their religion was by no means wholly pernicious. Although Buxtorf probably did not seek this end, his searching critique of Judaism revealed that Jews did not pose a major threat to Christian society. According to Buxtorf, Jews indulged on occasion in both blasphemy and sedition, particularly in their public prayers, but proper censorship of prayer books and appropriately vigilant ministers and state officials could control this problem. Taking Buxtorf's findings it could be argued that a policy of tolerating Jewish residence in German cities and territories was religiously as well as legally defensible. This kind of Christian "toleration" was grudging and ungracious, but it was a workable policy for Christian rulers to pursue at a time when religious conformity was a major component of state policy and issues such as Jewish residence could spark opposition to rulers. While Buxtorf himself did not advocate greater toleration of the Jews, Ettinger may have been correct in asserting that ethnographies of the Jews such as *Juden Schul* played an important role in

---

[167] See Miriam Yardeni, "The View of Jews and Judaism in the Works of Richard Simon," in: *Anti-Jewish Mentalities in Early Modern Europe*, by Myriam Yardeni, Studies in Judaism (Lanham, MD: University Press of America, 1990), 179-203, and P. T. van Rooden and J. W. Wesselius, "The Early Enlightenment and Judaism: The "Civil Dispute" between Philippus van Limborch and Isaac Orobio de Castro (1687)," *Studia Rosenthaliana* 21 (1987): 140-153.

creating an intellectual climate which ultimately allowed for greater toleration of the Jews.[168]

Buxtorf's anti-Jewish books reflect his study of Jewish literature both as a theology professor and as a censor. As a theologian and a teacher of theological students Buxtorf was responsible for teaching both the rudiments of biblical Hebrew and for lecturing on specific biblical books at Basel university. Buxtorf encouraged his students to learn enough post-biblical Hebrew to read Jewish commentators for themselves in order to benefit from the rich philological and interpretive insights which they had to offer. As he later pointed out in his edition of the rabbinical Bible, however, the commentators contained both "honey and poison" and students had to be aware that not all of what Jewish commentators said was true and edifying.[169] Buxtorf's routine pedagogical use of medieval Jewish Bible commentaries would have reminded him frequently of the religious conflict between Christianity and Judaism over who rightly understood the Hebrew Bible. Although he himself did not teach systematic theology, he was aware of what his colleague Polanus taught and agreed with him that the Bible was the efficient cause of all true religion, a view Buxtorf expounded implicitly and explicitly throughout *Juden Schul*.

Buxtorf's responsibilities as municipal censor of Basel also brought him frequently into contact with the religious claims of Judaism. In the line of duty Buxtorf read prayer books, halakic manuals, and Yiddish books of piety, all of which assumed that Judaism was the one true religion and that the Jewish covenant with God remained unbroken. Judging by his comments in *Juden Schul* and *Aus was Ursachen*, Buxtorf found Jewish prayer books to be

---

168 S. Ettinger, "The Beginnings of the Change in the Attitude of European Society Towards the Jews," *Scripta Hierosolymitana* 7 (1961): 203-208.

169 "Est in iis mel, est in iis fel. Melleum, quod ad linguae Hebraicae proprietatem melius explicandam, quodque ad literalem Grammaticumque Scripturae sensum genuine illustrandum facit commodumque est, suscipimus, quod & omnes alii viri docti, quotquot accuratiorem & perfectiorem linguae Hebraicae cognitionem inter Christianos assecuti sunt, hactenus fecerunt. Felleum, quod in rerum tractatione perversa aut falsa occurit, & maxime in iis locis qui de promisso Messia, ejusque persona & officio agunt, id totum ipsis relinquimus, ut sit contra eos loco testis perpetui, ut Moses loquitur Deut. 31: 26, quod cecitate percussi sint, ut idem praedixerat Deut 28: 28." Johann Buxtorf, introduction to the *Biblia rabbinica*, (Basel: Ludwig König, 1618-1619), vol. 1, f. (1)v.

particularly galling reading since they contained what he considered both implicit blasphemy and theological lies. Since Buxtorf was obliged to ferret out all explicit blasphemy and sedition he became quite familiar not only with different textual traditions of Jewish liturgy, but also with ways that Jews had been able to communicate objectionable messages while at the same time evading the attention of censors. Buxtorf may have written *Juden Schul* not only as a statement of theological principle, but also, perhaps, as a personal response to the materials he had censored.

Buxtorf's anti-Jewish books reflect very little of his extensive first-hand experience with Jews through the book trade. *Juden Schul* in particular represents an anthology of Jewish texts which Buxtorf set within a Christian theological framework and which he contrasted with biblical teaching rather than a first-hand testimony about early modern German life. Buxtorf's target was Judaism rather than Jews and Jewry, and his opponents were paper Jews rather than real ones. Buxtorf's Jewish customers and clients and German Jewish leaders apparently understood this and considered *Juden Schul* to be a relatively harmless piece of Christian theologizing. Their tolerance had its limits, however, and Buxtorf ultimately decided not to publish *Aus was Ursachen* and *Pugio fidei* not only because he had other more important business to attend to, but also probably because publishing them might have affected his ability to do business with Jews.

Buxtorf employed a plethora of post-biblical Jewish sources when writing *Juden Schul*, and his display of learning represented a new departure for Christian Hebraism. Rather than focusing upon the Talmud, biblical commentaries, and prayer books, he had read and analyzed a wide cross-section of Jewish literature written in Yiddish and Hebrew while composing *Juden Schul*. Where earlier Christian Hebraists had focused upon the use of Jewish tradition for biblical interpretation and kabbalistic studies, Buxtorf felt that it was his task as a pedagogue to make Jewish learning available to Christian scholars for use not only in the "Jewish mission," but also for theological studies, biblical studies, and profane scholarship. His entire scholarly career involved making "the Jews' own books" accessible to Christians, and his works were of fundamental importance for bringing these books into the confessional schools and

universities of early modern Europe since they made Jewish
learning possible without Jewish assistance.

CHAPTER FOUR

THE DEVELOPMENT OF HEBREW GRAMMAR AND LEXICOGRAPHY

The Christian scholarly ideal of fluency in Latin, Greek and Hebrew began with Jerome, but received official recognition as an educational goal only in 1312, through the eleventh canon of the Council of Vienne.[1] This canon directed that five universities—Paris, Oxford, Bologna, Salamanca and Rome—should each appoint two lecturers capable of teaching Greek, Hebrew, Arabic and Syriac.[2] The framers' intention was that the decree should promote missions by supporting instruction in oriental languages. Both a lack of funds in these institutions and the lukewarm commitment of the Church hierarchy to promoting oriental studies ensured that the injunction was ignored by the universities.[3] Later Christian Hebraists, however, regarded the Vienne decree as a legal and ideological reference point, reminding their patrons that the church had long been committed to Hebrew education.[4]

Renaissance humanism provided the ideological motivation that finally induced rulers to create teaching positions for Hebrew at many universities. The first trilingual college was founded in Spain at Alcalá in 1508. In 1520 another trilingual college was founded in Louvain, and it served as a model for other institutions such as the *Collège de France* in Paris, the Jesuit Gymnasium of Cologne,

---

[1] Jerome described himself as "philosophus, rhetor, grammaticus, dialecticus, Hebraeus, Graecus, Latinus, trilinguis." *Apologia adversus libros Rufini*, III, 6, *MPL* vol. 3, 483A.

[2] This decision was reaffirmed at the council of Basel on September 7, 1434. See Berthold Altaner, "Raymundus Lullus und der Sprachenkanon (can. 11) des Konzils von Vienne (1312)," *Historisches Jahrbuch* 53 (1933): 216-17.

[3] G. Lloyd Jones, *The Discovery of Hebrew in Tudor England: A Third Language* (Manchester: Manchester University Press, 1983), 19.

[4] Johannes Buxtorf referred to the Vienne decree in the dedicatory letters for three of his books. See Buxtorf to the the the Estates General of Holland, Basel, March, 1609, in *Thesaurus Grammaticus Linguae Sanctae Hebraeae* (Basel: Haered. Ludwig König, 1651; reprint ed., Hildesheim: Georg Olms, 1981), f.):(4r, to the Magistrates of Bremen, March 15, 1615, in *Grammaticae Chaldaicae et Syriacae Libri III* (Basel: Konrad Waldkirch, 1615), f.):(3r, and to the Estates General of the Netherlands, Basel, April 1, 1620, *Tiberias*, fol., ***3r.

and the Protestant University of Leiden.[5] The *Regius* professorships of Hebrew, endowed by King Henry VIII for Oxford and
Cambridge in 1536, and the chair of Hebrew endowed by King
Francis I at the *Collège de France* in Paris gave further institutional support to the furtherance of Hebrew study.[6] The remarkable succession of Hebraists who taught at the *Collège de France*,
including Guillaume Postel, Jean Mercier and Gilbert Génébrard,
was particularly important for the promotion of Hebrew learning.[7]

If humanism provided the initial impetus to endow professorships of Hebrew, the ideals of the Protestant Reformation motivated many students and educators alike to pursue Hebrew learning. The Protestant belief that doctrinal certainty could be attained
only through study of the Bible in its original languages compelled
universities and even secondary schools in Protestant areas to offer
instruction in Hebrew.[8] This prompted Catholics to respond in
kind; Jesuit schools also required their students to learn Hebrew.[9]
Finding qualified Hebrew teachers to fill these positions was, however, a constant challenge.[10] But a little knowledge is a dangerous
thing, and unfortunately that was the extent of many Reformation
era scholars' acquaintance with Hebrew. The situation was not
much better when Buxtorf began his professional career. In 1602

[5] Lloyd Jones, *Discovery*, 98-100 and J. C. H. Lebram, "Hebräische Studien
zwischen Ideal und Wirklichkeit an der Universität Leiden in den Jahren 1575-
1619," *Nederlandsch Archief voor Kerkgeschiedenis* 56 (1975-76): 317.

[6] Lloyd Jones, *Discovery*, 191-2, 207-208, and Lebram, "Hebräische
Studien," 317.

[7] Van Rooden, *Theology*, 113, n. 73, and Abel Lefranc, *Histoire du Collège
de France dupuis ses Origines Jusqu'a la Fin du Premier Empire* (Paris: Hachette,
1893), 381.

[8] The question of how many German schools and universities offered Hebrew
instruction during the sixteenth century (and what level of instruction they offered) has never been sytematically studied, but the trend toward greater opportunities for students to learn Hebrew is unmistakable. For a preliminary treatment
of the question see Ludwig Geiger, *Das Studium der Hebräischen Sprache in
Deutschland vom Ende des XV. bis zur Mitte des XVI. Jahrhunderts* (Breslau:
Schletter'sche Buchhandlung, 1870), 88-129.

[9] Karl Hengst, *Jesuiten an Universitäten und Jesuitenuniversitäten. Zur
Geschichte der Universitäten in der Oberdeutschen und Rheinischen Provinz der
Gesellschaft Jesu im Zeitalter der konfessionellen Auseinandersetzung*, Quellen
und Forschungen aus dem Gebiet der Geschichte, n. s., vol. 7 (Paderborn:
Ferdinand Schöningh, 1981), 64, 70-71.

[10] Leiden, Louvain and Wittenberg all had difficulties at one time or another
during the sixteenth century finding Hebraists. See Lebram, "Hebräische
Studien," 319-321, 326-330, and Friedman, *Most Ancient Testimony*, 33-35.

Joseph Scaliger complained to a friend that few contemporary scholars knew Hebrew even moderately well.[11]

Scaliger's contemporary and correspondent Johannes Buxtorf did more than any other Christian Hebraist to raise the standards of Hebrew learning among Christians through his teaching and especially through his composition of grammars and lexicons. Even during his lifetime he was recognized at one of the most important authorities on Hebrew education. In 1628 the theology professors of Strasbourg declared him to be the greatest Hebraist of the century and praised his works for giving brief, clear explanations for many "dark and difficult" aspects of Hebrew left unexplained by his predecessors.[12] Christian Hebraists of later generations were scarcely less laudatory. The accomplishments and shortcomings of Christian Hebraists throughout the seventeenth century cannot be understood properly without reference to Johannes Buxtorf's grammatical and lexicographical works.

By the end of the sixteenth century the study of Hebrew grammar among Christians had reached a plateau in terms of content. Grammarians had made thorough use of David Kimhi's *Miklol* and the works of Elias Levita as a starting point for their studies.[13] The grammatical works of Ibn Ezra were virtually unknown, as were the Arabic language grammatical studies of Ibn Janah and others. Arabic language works would have benefited few among Christian Hebraists in any case as so few could read them.[14] Differences in

---

[11] "O mi Casaubone, rari sunt inter nos, qui mediocriter Hebraice sciant, quum tamen rari sint, qui omnino nesciant Hebraice." Joseph J. Scaliger to Isaac Casaubon, Leiden, April 22, 1602, printed in Scaliger, *Epistolae*, 220.

[12] "Caeterum, uti omnes qui Hebraea vel à limine salutarunt, nominis tui famam maximi faciunt, teque facile Primatem atque Antistitem omnium huius seculi Hebraeorum Doctorum agnoscunt, qui pulchra methodo, brevitate, perspicuitate, eo quae ab aliis confuse, prolixe, obscure olim fuerunt, congesta, tradit...." Theological Faculty of Strasbourg to Johannes Buxtorf, Strasbourg, September 23, 1628, Basel UB Ms G I 61: 2, translated in Buxtorf-Falkeisen, *Johannes Buxtorf*, 12.

[13] Lebram noted, for example, that both Petrus Martinius and Antoine Chevallier, two of the most important Protestant grammarians of the late sixteenth century, attributed their content to Kimhi. "Hebräische Studien," 337-340. Sebastian Münster's mature grammatical works were, to a large extent, Latin translations of Levita's works with his own annotations. Karl Heinz Burmeister, *Sebastian Münster: Versuch eines biographischen Gesamtbildes*, Basler Beiträge zur Geschichtswissenschaft, no. 91 (Basel: Helbing & Lichtenhahn, 1963), 45.

[14] Arabists such as Guillaume Postel and Joseph Scaliger were important exceptions to the rule of Christian ignorance of Arabic during the sixteenth century.

the presentation and organization of Hebrew grammar resulted
more from authors' differing perspectives on grammatical and
pedagogical theory than from new breakthroughs in Hebrew
philology.[15]

Historical treatment of grammatical research demands that
grammars be studied not only as analyses of the language that they
describe, but also as documents reflecting the linguistic and pedagogical theories current when they were written.[16] For Christian
scholars of the Renaissance, Latin grammar served as the basis for
description for all other languages, including their own vernacular
languages and oriental languages. Reuchlin, for example, based his
De Rudimenta on the organizational pattern of Priscian's Latin
grammar.[17] During the sixteenth century Latin grammatical study
came to a methodological crossroads. Latin grammarians of late
antiquity such as Priscian and Donatus taught that grammar was
adduced through a combination of formal and semantic features. In
the Middle Ages a group of grammarians known as the *modistae*
developed a system of universal grammar based on the categories
of scholastic philosophy.[18] Roger Bacon thought that "in all languages, however much they may vary in surface details or
'accidents,' the underlying 'substance' is the same."[19] Some grammarians went on to make a distinction between the *verbum oris* or
discourse, and the *verbum mentis* or underlying mental syntax
common to all languages. Since the mental syntax was inaccessible
to the grammarian via formal linguistic markers it could only be

---

Buxtorf's correspondent Thomas Erpenius had to make a special effort in order to
learn the language. See J. Brugman, "Arabic Scholarship," in: *Leiden University
in the Seventeenth Century: An Exchange of Learning*, ed. Th. H. Lunsingh
Scheuleer and G. H. M. Postumus Meyjes (Leiden: E. J. Brill, 1975), 202-4.

[15] Lebram was the first scholar to mark the importance of grammatical theory
for Christian Hebraists in "Hebräische Studien," 337-351.

[16] G. A. Padley, *Grammatical Theory in Western Europe 1500-1700: Trends
in Vernacular Grammar*, (Cambridge: Cambridge University Press, 1985), xiii-
xiv.

[17] Hermann Greive, "Die hebräische Grammatik Johannes Reuchlins *De
rudimentis hebraicis*," *Zeitschrift für die alttestmentliche Wissenschaft* 90 (1978):
397-398.

[18] "The grammatical theory of the Modistae rests on the study of words and
the properties of these words as the "signs of things" which are, however, capable of signification." G. L. Bursill-Hall, "Mediaeval Grammatical Theories,"
Canadian Journal of Linguistics 9 (1963): 47.

[19] Padley, *Vernacular*, 234.

analyzed logically and philosophically.[20] This was particularly true for syntactical "anomalies" such as ellipsis where only a part of the "correct" construction was expressed.[21] Many Renaissance era grammarians rejected philosophical approaches to grammar, favoring instead more purely descriptive grammatical studies. A few scholars, notably Thomas Linacre and Julius Caesar Scaliger, disagreed and continued to analyze Latin grammar using a philosophical approach.[22] By the end of the sixteenth century, however, Renaissance descriptivism had run its course. The tasks that Latinists had set for themselves, the purification of Latin grammar according to classical usage and the establishment of reliable texts of the Latin classics, had largely been achieved. Scholars were faced with the choice either of returning to a more philosophic methodology or of adopting the more radical formalism of Petrus Ramus and his followers.[23]

Petrus Ramus was a professor at the University of Paris from 1545 until his tragic death on August 26, 1572, during the St. Bartholomew's Day Massacre.[24] He believed that each of the three basic liberal arts—logic, rhetoric and grammar—had its own role in education and that these roles should never be confused.[25] The only role that logic could play in grammatical analysis was to un-

---

[20] Ibid.

[21] Ibid., 235. See also W. Keith Percival, "Deep and Surface Structure Concepts in Renaissance and Medieval Syntactic Theory," in: *History of Linguistic Thought and Contemporary Linguistics*, ed. Herman Parret, Foundations of Communication (Berlin and New York: Walter de Gruyter, 1976), 239.

[22] Ibid., 232-244.

[23] Ibid., 220 and G. A. Padley, *Grammatical Theory in Western Europe 1500-1700: The Latin Tradition* (Cambridge: Cambridge Univ. Press, 1976), 57. On J. C. Scaliger specifically see Jean Stéfanini, "Jules César Scaliger et son De causis linguae Latinae," *History of Linguistic Thought*, 317-330.

[24] For information on Ramus' life and works see Walter J. Ong, *Ramus, Method and the Decay of Dialogue* (Cambridge, MA: Harvard Univ. Press, 1958) and Padley, *Vernacular*, 9-83.

[25] Grammatical instruction was traditionally divided between all three branches of the *trivium*. "Word order was treated in rhetoric, while basic intrasentential relations (subject and predicate, dependency relations between adjectives and nouns, and so forth) were referred to the logician. The result of this distribution was to break up the study amoung all three branches of the *trivium*." W. Keith Percival, "Grammar and Rhetoric in the Renaissance," in: *Renaissance Eloquence: Studies in the Theory and Practice of Renaissance Rhetoric*, ed. James J. Murphy (Berkeley: Univ. of California Press, 1983), 325.

cover the basic relationships between parts of speech through observing their use and to arrange them in an appropriate order.[26]
Ultimately, he thought, the structure of all knowledge, grammatical
or otherwise, could be expressed by pairs of dichotomous concepts
that were logically linked in a hierarchical chain connecting all
branches of knowledge. To take a grammatical example, he thought
that words could be divided into six different types. If a word
could either express number (singular or plural) then it was either
a noun or a verb; if it could not express number it was an adverb
or a conjunction. Nouns and verbs could be further distinguished
from one another by the fact that nouns express gender and case,
while verbs express tense and person. Adverbs (which included
prepositions and interjections) and conjunctions, had no morphological markers, and could be identified by their function in a sen-
tence.[27] He tried to restrict semantic analysis of words to lexicography, arguing that grammar concerned itself only with what was
consignified—number, gender, comparison, case, person, tense and
by the endings of words themselves.[28] This was an important
weakness in his system because syntax, an aspect of grammar that
Ramus thought particularly important, cannot be analyzed formally
without recourse to the logical relationships underlying surface
realizations.[29]

Ramus' theory of grammar was reflected in at least three pedagogical practices followed by Ramist grammarians. Ramus thought
that teachers should concentrate upon imparting the most general
grammatical precepts first, without cluttering their presentation
with exceptions, and that they should use plenty of examples and
exercises to help students learn them.[30] He insisted that those precepts which apply to several grammatical categories be discussed
only once, when they first appear in the book, and that were not to
be repeated later in the work. This approach had the effect of re-
ducing the traditional division of grammar from four parts, etymology (i. e. morphology), syntax, prosody, and orthography, to

---

26 Padley, *Vernacular*, 22-23 and Ong, *Ramus*, 245-6.
27 Padley, *Vernacular*, 33-34.
28 Ibid., 24.
29 Ibid., 45, and Ong, *Ramus*, 259-60.
30 Padley, *Vernacular*, 22-24.

two: etymology and syntax.[31] His binary pairings of elements lent themselves readily to graphic representation in the flow charts of concepts for which Ramist pedagogy is best known.[32]

Buxtorf was trained in Ramist philosophy as a student both in Dortmund and at Herborn. The entire teaching faculty of Herborn was adamantly Ramist during Buxtorf's time. Johannes Piscator was an especially well-known Ramist scholar and reprinted numerous editions of Ramus' books with his own commentary.[33] Whether because of their Ramist teaching philosophy or for other reasons a number of Herborn alumni went on to became important philologists. Georg Pasor and Matthias Martinius compiled significant Greek lexicons and Johannes Buxtorf himself acquired no small reputation as a grammarian and lexicographer.[34]

Buxtorf's *Thesaurus Grammaticus Linguae Sanctae Hebraeae*, first printed in 1609, was his principal grammatical work and provides the most complete account of his ideas on grammatical theory.[35] In addition to a lengthy treatment of Hebrew grammar Buxtorf also included treatises on Hebrew poetry, Yiddish literature, and on reading unvocalized Hebrew.[36] Buxtorf revised *Thesaurus Grammaticus* twice, first in 1615 and then again in 1620.[37] The 1620 edition was reprinted twice, in 1629 and 1651, and then Johannes Buxtorf II revised the book yet again in 1663.[38] Since the third edition reflects Buxtorf's mature thought on Hebrew grammar it will be the focus of this study.[39] But in order

---

[31] Ibid., 25 and Ong, *Ramus*, 250.

[32] See for example Ong, *Ramus*, 31, 202, 261, 300.

[33] Menk, *Herborn*, 210. For a bibliography of Piscator's works, see Steubing, "Lebensnachrichten," 137-138.

[34] Menk, *Herborn*, 268-270.

[35] *Thesaurus Grammaticus Linguae Sanctae Hebraeae* (Basel: Konrad Waldkirch, 1609). Prijs no. 199. The pattern of organization employed in this work was repeated almost without alteration in his subsequent grammars, notably *Epitome Grammaticae Hebraeae* (Basel: Konrad Waldkirch, 1613) and *Grammaticae Chaldaicae et Syriacae*, as even a casual inspection of their chapter titles reveals.

[36] These three treatises are discussed below and in chap. 5.

[37] Prijs nos. 216 and 224.

[38] Prijs nos. 229, 255 and 270.

[39] It is also the most readily available text for scholars since there is a modern reprint. *Thesaurus Grammaticus Linguae Sanctae Hebraeae* (Basel: Haered. Ludovici Regis, 1651; reprint ed., Hildesheim: Georg Olms Verlag, 1981). All subsequent references to *Thesaurus Grammaticus*, unless otherwise indicated, are to this edition.

to assess Buxtorf's contributions to Hebrew grammar properly, some discussion of his theory of grammar is in order.

The best indicators of Ramist influences upon Buxtorf's grammatical studies are his choice of pedagogical model for *Thesaurus Grammaticus* and his use of Ramist dichotomies as its organizing principle.[40] The Hebrew grammar that Buxtorf used as his model in composing *Thesaurus Grammaticus* was Petrus Martinius' *Grammatica Hebraea*. Martinius organized his grammar along fairly strict Ramist lines, dividing up all of grammar into two parts, morphology and syntax. Hebrew words were subdivided into those which could indicate number and those which could not (nouns and verbs, and adverbs and conjunctions).[41] Nouns and verbs were further distinguished because nouns could indicate number and gender, while verbs could indicate these things and also time and person.[42] There were two declensions of nouns, those whose plural endings were אִים and תֹ, and all verb constructions could be divided in "light" and "heavy" constructions (those with and without doubling of the second root letter).[43] However, Martinius' pervasive use of dichotomies sometimes produced bizarre results. He took the traditional division of Hebrew consonants into five categories, classified them as either *semivocales* or *mutae*, and then subdivided these further into binary pairs.[44] In his zeal to organize Hebrew particles according to binary pairs Martinius was forced to classify them as either adverbs or conjunctions. Following Ramus he classified prepositions as adverbs.[45]

Buxtorf followed Martinius' pattern of organization to a large extent in *Thesaurus Grammaticus*. He divided his work into two parts, treating morphology and syntax, and also retained the formal distinction between first and second declension nouns. Buxtorf did reorganize his subject matter in many places, introducing distinc-

---

40   Lebram noted Buxtorf's indebtedness to Martinius in "Hebräische Studien," 349 and n. 115.

41   Ibid., 337-8.

42   Martinius gave the following definitions for noun and verb: "Nomen, est vox numeri cum solo genere," and "Verbum est vox numeri & generis cum tempore & persona." Petrus Martinius, *Grammatica Hebrae Recens ab auctore emendata & aucta* (La Rochelle: Hieronymus Haultinus, 1590), 37, 56. Buxtorf's well-annotated copy is Basel UB FA VII 25.

43   Ibid., 38, 47, 59.

44   Ibid., 20-26.

45   Ibid., 151.

tions not found in Martinius. For example, he divided irregular verbs into those that lacked a root letter and those which had a quiescent root letter.[46] He also divided vowels into two categories, proper and improper. Proper vowels were either long or short and "improper" vowels was his designation for simple and composite shewa.[47]

Buxtorf was prepared, however, to adjust his manner of presentation to accord with the realities of Hebrew grammar and was less doctrinaire than Martinius about forcing everything into ramistic dichotomies. While he noted that he and Martinius were in essential agreement about the nature of Hebrew consonants, he did not further subdivide them the way Martinius had done.[48] In his discussion of irregular verbs Buxtorf noted four kinds of quiescent constructions, Pe Yod, Ayin Yod, Lamed Aleph and Lamed He, but did not attempt to divide them further into pairs. In sharp contrast to Martinius, Buxtorf divided particles into four different kinds, adverbs, prepositions, conjunctions and interjections, without creating a hierarchical structure to organize them.[49]

In common with many other German Ramists of this period, Buxtorf was not a convinced advocate of Ramist philosophy of language, and he was not averse to borrowing both concepts and terminology from Aristotelian grammarians.[50] His definition of the preposition, for example, was taken from Julius Caesar Scaliger's *De causis linguae Latinae*.[51] When explaining the syntax of conjunctions he explained some features according to the analogy of Latin grammar, quoting from the works of Lorenzo Valla and Donatus.[52] Buxtorf often discussed varieties of ellipsis, pleonasm, and enallage common in biblical Hebrew within his general treatment of syntax, phenomena explicable in logical rather than formal

---

[46] *Thesuarus Grammaticus*, 164, 188.
[47] Ibid, 8. Martinius discussed *shewa* in his chapter on syllables and not with vowels at all. *Grammatica*, 28-33.
[48] *Thesaurus Grammaticus*, 1-8.
[49] Ibid., 325-332.
[50] Ong, *Ramus*, 298-300.
[51] *Thesaurus Grammaticus*, 328, quoting *De causis linguae Latinae* (Lyons: Sebastian Gryphium, 1540), bk 8, chap. 152. In the first edition of *Thesaurus Grammaticus* (Basel: Konrad Waldkirch, 1609) Buxtorf quoted from *De causis* an additional 4 times on pp. 4, 7, 22-23 and 27 (see *De causis*, 84-85, 23-24, 94).
[52] *Thesaurus Grammaticus*, 593.

terms.[53] He was also willing, in common with modist grammarians, to posit linguistic phenomena on the basis of philosophical premise, rather than on the morphology of Hebrew itself. The best example of this is his elaborate derivation of a case system for Hebrew.

The idea that Hebrew had cases in the way Latin and Greek did not originate with Buxtorf. Johannes Reuchlin, for example, posited the existence of six cases—nominative, accusative, dative, genitive, ablative and vocative—in his *De Rudimenta*.[54] Petrus Martinius also thought that Hebrew had a case system, although he devoted little discussion to it.[55] Buxtorf's conception of a case system for Hebrew grew out of his understanding of syntax. He defined syntax as that part of grammar in which the structure of words that appeared together were described. These structures could be either conjunctive or disjunctive. A conjunctive grammatical structure could be expressed either through agreement between words or through structures where one word governs another.[56] The governance of one word over another was expressed, in Buxtorf's view, through cases. He thought that Hebrew had five cases: nominative, genitive, accusative, dative and ablative.[57] Instances of the nominative case required no special discussion and Buxtorf thought that the genitive case was expressed in Hebrew by "bound constructions" between two nouns, or between nouns and

---

[53] Ibid., 374-381, 407-417, 430-435, *passim*. Although Martinius was aware of these phenomena he devoted less discussion to them than Buxtorf did. *Grammatica*, 156-161, 196.

[54] Johannes Reuchlin, *De Rudimentis Hebraicis libri tres* (Pforzheim: Thomas Anshelm, 1506; reprint ed., Hildesheim: Georg Olms, 1974), 556. See also Louis Kukenheim, *Contributions à L'Histoire de la Grammaire Grecque, Latine et Hébraïque à L'Époque de la Renaissance* (Leiden: E. J. Brill, 1951), 104 and n. 3.

[55] Martinius, *Grammatica*, 184-7. *Pace* Lebram, "Hebräische Studien," 338.

[56] "Syntaxis est secunda pars Grammaticae, quae vocum structuram interpretatur. Structura est, qua voces diversae inter se vel conjunguntur, vel conjunctae distinguuntur, ut illinc sermonis puritas, hinc sententiae claritas evidentius elucescat.... Conjunctio vocum sit vel Convenientia vel Rectione. Convenientia est, quando vox voci in certis accidentibus citra rectionem convenit. Rectio, quando vox vocem certo sine flexionis aut certis accidentibus regit." Buxtorf, *Thesaurus Grammaticus*, 333-334.

[57] Buxtorf mentioned a sixth case, vocative, in his Aramaic grammar but not in any edition of his *Thesaurus Grammaticus*. See *Grammaticae Chaldaicae*, 251.

infinitives, participles or adjectival nouns.[58] Verbs could take accusative, dative or ablative objects, and prepositions could govern
either accusative or ablative constructions.[59]

The case structure of Hebrew could, however, only be derived
semantically, according to Buxtorf, as his eight rules for the use of
the ablative case illustrate. Five of the eight involved the use of the
preposition בְּ. A verb with בְּ could indicate a cause, an instrument
or a mode of action. It was also used with verbs of sale or appraisal
for value, and with verbs of quiet or movement in a "significant
place," such as one's house, field or the Lord's temple.[60] The
prepositions בְּ or מִן (or a simple object without preposition) could
be used with selected verbs of quantity or lack.[61] Either בְּ or עַל
were commonly used with verbs of praise and exultation.[62] The
other three rules involve the use of the preposition מִן. It could be
used in comparisons, with verbs of prohibition, removal, absti-
nence or other expressions of distance and separation, or with
verbs of motion from a significant location.[63] That prepositions
alone are insufficient as formal markers of case is apparent from
Buxtorf's previous discussion of the accusative and dative cases: בְּ
can be used in either accusative or dative constructions, and עַל can
be used in some circumstances to indicate the accusative case.[64]

The conceptual origin of Buxtorf's ablative case for Hebrew is
readily apparent from his descriptions. The Latin ablative of separation, comparison, and means were the direct or indirect inspiration for at least half of Buxtorf's rules for use of the Hebrew ablative. Buxtorf doubtless thought that these case identifications were
inherent in the nature of language, and that he merely identified in

---

[58] Although a number of verbs in Latin take genitive objects, Buxtorf felt that
the equivalent Hebrew expressions appeared either in the accusative or ablative
cases. Ibid., 355-74, 446.

[59] "Verbum finitum regit Nomen, Pronomen vel Participium (quatenus usum
Nominis habet) in aliquo casu nunc nude & simpliciter, nunc intercedente aliqua
praepositione, & id quidem frequentissime." Concerning prepositions Buxtorf
wrote, "Praepositiones separatae regunt vel Accusativum, vel Ablativum, quos,
tanquam motus aut quiotis causam vel terminum, Verbo adjiciunt." Ibid., 445,
553.

[60] Ibid., 480-2, 486-7
[61] Ibid., 483-4.
[62] Ibid., 484-5.
[63] Ibid., 483, 485-7.
[64] Ibid., 452, 471, 474, 478.

Hebrew what was even more obvious in Latin. For the Latin-speaking student of Buxtorf's day his discussion of cases was doubtless helpful in providing hints for how to translate certain Hebrew syntactical constructions into Latin. Whatever Buxtorf's justification for his case system would have been, and he offered none in *Thesaurus Grammaticus*, it is obviously deduced from Latin rather than a feature inherent within Hebrew itself.

Buxtorf himself, however, considered his greatest contribution to grammatical study to be practical rather than theoretical.[65] He strove to provide far more examples from the Bible for grammatical constructions, both common and unusual. Since Hebrew was not a living language (at least for Christians), examples of good style were especially important for illustration and imitation.[66] Buxtorf also tried to provide explanations for unusual morphological and syntactic structures drawn from the best authorities, medieval Jewish grammarians and biblical commentators.

While the use of grammatical works such as Kimhi's *Michlol* was not uncommon by Christian Hebraists in preparing textbooks, Buxtorf went to great lengths to demonstrate his debt to Kimhi, Levita and other Jewish authorities.[67] When explaining unusual biblical Hebrew constructions, whether morphological or syntactical, Buxtorf often referred to medieval Jewish commentaries, particularly to David Kimhi and to Abraham Ibn Ezra. For example, when he discussed the occurrence of a single Yod as the plural form of some masculine nouns he quoted the explanations of Rashi and Ibn Ezra as alternative explanations for two specific instances

---

65 "Conscripsi Thesaurum Grammaticum, in quo methodice linguae proprietatem et usus complexus sum." Johannes Buxtorf to Philippe du Plessis de Mornay, Basel, September 8, 1613, Basel UB Ms Autogr. Slg. Geigy Hgb 736.

66 "Modus omnino duplex est: vel enim usu addiscenda, vel ex praeceptis. Usu addiscuntur linguae peregrinae, Gallica, Italica, Hispanica, Anglica & aliae: non sic Hebraea, cujus usus inter Christianos non in vulgo, sed in Scholis tantum est.... Ad Praecepta ergo deveniendum. Hinc tanto facilius lingua addiscetur, quanto ea fuerint absolutiora: absolutiora, tam in legitima sui conformatione, quam declaratione per copiam exemplorum & usum loquendi." Johannes Buxtorf to the Estates General of Holland, Basel, March, 1609, *Thesaurus Grammaticus*, ff.):(4v-):(5r.

67 Buxtorf quoted Kimhi's מכלול forty four times, his שרשים seven times, Levita's טוב טעם six times and הרכבה four times in *Thesaurus Grammaticus*.

of the phenomenon.[68] In Buxtorf's treatment of ellipsis in nominal constructions he quoted Ibn Ezra's solution to one instance of it in Isa. 40: 10.[69]

Thesaurus Grammaticus was well received by Buxtorf' contemporaries and exercised a lasting influence upon the study of Hebrew grammar. Both Thomas Erpenius and Constantijn L'Empereur, professors of Hebrew at the University of Leiden, recommended it to their more advanced students.[70] Sixtinus Amama, one of Buxtorf's correspondents, was impressed with Buxtorf's discussion of Hebrew syntax in *Thesaurus Grammaticus*, but less so with his discussions of morphology, preferring Martinius' work. In order to have the best of both works he printed book 1 of Martinius with book 2 of Buxtorf under the title *Grammatica Martino-Buxtorfiana*.[71] *Thesaurus Grammaticus* was printed six times during the seventeenth century, indicating a fairly steady demand for the book.[72] Gesenius judged it to be a watershed work, clearly superior to any Hebrew grammar that had previously been written by either Jewish or Christian authors.[73] Emil Kautzsch still considered the *Thesaurus Grammaticus* a useful resource in his own studies in 1879.[74]

While *Thesaurus Grammaticus* was Buxtorf's most substantial grammatical work it was far from his only book on the subject. In addition to a primer written for beginning Hebrew students, he composed an important Aramaic grammar and also brief introduc-

---

[68] *Thesaurus Grammaticus*, 79. Cf. Wilhelm Gesenius, *Gesenius Hebrew Grammar*, ed. E. Kautzsch and A. E. Cowley, 2d English ed. (Oxford: Clarendon, 1910; reprint ed., Oxford: Clarendon, 1983), para. 87f, g.

[69] *Thesaurus Grammaticus*, 345.

[70] Van Rooden, *Theology*, 63, 186.

[71] See Lebram, "Hebräische Studien," 341 and Van Rooden, *Theology*, 65-66, 112.

[72] See below, Appendix 1, nos. 103-110.

[73] "Sein *Thesaurus grammaticus linguae sanctae* ... übertrifft an Ausführlichkeit, Genauigkeit und Methode alle frühern und die rabbinischen Grammatiken weit, wenn man gleich an Materie und Form die Bildung des Verfassers nach den letztern erkennt. Die Syntax ist schon ausführlich behandelt, aber vieles dahin gezögen, was der Formenlehre gehört." Wilhelm Gesenius, *Geschichte der hebräischen Sprache und Schrift. Ein philologisch-historische Einleitung in die Sprachlehren und Wörterbücher der hebräischen Sprache* (Leipzig: Friedrich Christian Wilhelm Vogel, 1815; reprint ed., Hildesheim: Georg Olms, 1973), 110.

[74] Kautzsch, *Buxtorf*, 9.

tions to both medieval Hebrew and to Yiddish. Buxtorf was best
known among Hebrew students throughout seventeenth- and eigh-
teenth-century Europe as the author of an extremely popular
Hebrew grammar. He published the first edition under the title
Praeceptiones Grammaticae de Lingua Hebraea, in 1605.[75] He revised it somewhat and reprinted it in 1613 under the title *Epitome
Grammaticae Hebraea*.[76] Between 1613 and 1790 the work was
reprinted 27 times and appeared twice in English translation, a
"best-seller" among Hebrew grammars.[77] Since Buxtorf wrote this
grammar for beginning students he kept his presentation as simple
as he could, giving few rules to memorize and leaving out many
exceptions to grammatical rules.[78] Eleven Psalms, together with a
number of important theological prooftexts, were included in the
Epitome as translation exercises.[79]

Apart from his *Thesaurus Grammaticus*, Buxtorf's
Grammaticae Chaldaicae et Syriacae may have been his most
significant grammatical contribution. The work followed the same
pattern laid out in *Thesaurus Grammaticus*: it was divided into two
parts describing morphology and syntax and included many examples to illustrate grammatical rules. Buxtorf ambitiously tried to
provide a grammatical description for biblical Aramaic, Syriac (in

---

[75] Buxtorf, *Praeceptiones Grammaticae*. Prijs no. 189. Less than three years
later Buxtorf reported that it was quite well received. "Edideram ante biennium
Epitomen brevissimam Grammaticae Hebraeae, maxime pro usu Gymnasii nostri
Basileensis. Ea praeter spem sic excepta est, ut et Herbornae, et aliquot Scholis in
Palatinatu nostraque Helvetia publice discenda proponatur." Johannes Buxtorf to
Konrad Vorstius, Basel June 8, 1608, Bibliotheca Rosenthaliana (Amsterdam
UB) Brieven-collectie, no. 110.
[76] *Epitome Grammaticae Hebraea* (Basel: Konrad Waldkirch, 1613). Prijs no.
210.
[77] See Appendix 1, nos. 14-43, 102.
[78] "Maxime vero ii, qui primum linguam vel artem discere incipiunt, nec in
prolixioribus, nec in gravioribus, quam captus ingenii ipsorum ferat, sunt
exercendi. Alioquin enim vires vel cito flaccescunt, vel oneri plane succumbunt.
Habitus itaque hic brevissima de lingua Hebraea Praecepta, in quibus
Grammaticae fundamentum solide sternitur." Buxtorf added that those readers
who wished more detailed discussion could always consult his *Thesaurus
Grammaticus. Epitome Grammaticae Hebraea* (Basel: Konrad Waldkirch, 1617),
ff. (:) 4r, (:) 5v-6r.
[79] These passages were Genesis 3:14-15 and 49: 8-10, Deut. 18:15-19, Isa.
7:10-14, 9:6-7 and 11:1-5, Jer. 23:5-6, Dan. 9: 24-25, Mic. 5:2, Hag. 2:7-10,
Zech. 6:11-13, and 9: 9-10, Mal. 3:1 and 4:5-6 together with Psalms 6, 9, 12,
15, 22, 23, 57, 110, 117, 121 and 130. Ibid., 98-119.

Hebrew characters), targumic Aramaic, and talmudic Aramaic. This had the effect of producing rather crowded paradigms and notes but must have been particularly useful for students interested in the Peshitta and Targum.[80]

Buxtorf's grammar represents a new departure for Christian study of Aramaic. Most other grammars of Aramaic written by Christians had concentrated upon biblical Aramaic since this was the dialect most necessary to theology students.[81] Buxtorf thought that other dialects of Aramaic were important for explaining anomalies in biblical Hebrew. Targumic Aramaic was especially important for Christians to learn because the Targum bore witness to the coming of Christ.[82] His concern that Christian students be exposed to a variety of Aramaic dialects is best expressed by his choice of exercises included in the third part of the book. He included 123 pages of texts with Latin translations and notes, including selections from biblical Aramaic, Targums Onkelos, Jonathan, Pseudo-Jonathan and Yerushalmi and the Writings, the Peshitta, the Talmud (Babylonian and Jerusalem), and the Zohar.[83] He also included a dowry agreement and formula of divorce, the latter from Maimonides' *Mishneh Torah*.[84] These readings show how broad Buxtorf thought a biblical philologist's understanding of Aramaic should be in order to understand the Hebrew Bible text.

Buxtorf's two other attempts at grammatical description, his discussions of unpointed (post-biblical) Hebrew and Yiddish were far more modest efforts than his other grammars. Buxtorf encouraged his students to consult rabbinical Bible commentaries in his classes at the University of Basel, but his only published grammati-

---

[80] See, for example, his discussion of declination of nouns and pronouns with suffixes in *Grammatica Chaldaica*, 24-27, 36-42.

[81] "Hoc tamen in illis desideratum, quod vel in solo Daniele & Esra explicando occupati fuerint, vel usum & differentiam dialectorum Chaldaicarum non satis per exempla declaraverint." Johannes Buxtorf to the Counsellors and Senators of Bremen, Basel, March 15, 1615, Ibid., f.):(4v.

[82] Ibid., ff.):(3v-):(4r.

[83] Buxtorf chose Daniel 5:1-30 as an example of Biblical Aramaic, Exod. 20: 1-17 for Targums Onkelos and Jonathan (together with Obadiah for Jonathan), Gen. 49: 8-10 for Targums Yerushalmi and Pseudo-Jonathan, and Psa. 23 and Prov. 9: 7-12 for the Writings. His sole specimen for the Peshitta was Matt. 6: 5-13. For the Babylonian Talmud he chose Sanhedrin, ff. 108-9, and for the Jerusalem Talmud a selection from *Berakot* chap. 4. The Zohar selections were for Genesis, para. לֶךְ לְךָ and for Leviticus para. אַחֲרֵי מוֹת.

[84] *Grammaticae Chaldaicae*, 389-403.

cal aid was *Instructio Brevis ad lectionem Rabbinicam absque punctis vocalibus*, a short appendix to the first edition of *Thesaurus Grammaticus*. He justified the importance of the essay by arguing that since the only Jewish books that used vowel points were Bibles, prayer books, and some school books, Christian Hebraists who seriously wished to utilize Jewish sources in their work had to learn how to read unpointed Hebrew.[85] His two principal suggestions were to learn biblical Hebrew very well, paying close heed to the rules of grammar given in *Thesaurus Grammaticus*, and to be alert for post-biblical linguistic developments, especially in vocabulary. Buxtorf was fairly sanguine about the continuity between biblical and medieval Hebrew. He provided a number of examples (all with Latin translation and some with notes) from *Hiskuni*, the biblical commentary of Hezekiah ben Manoah,[86] four sample letters, selections from *Berahot*, Bahya ben Asher's *Kad ha-Qemah*, and from an unidentified work entitled *Hakme ha-Musar*, to illustrate how far biblical Hebrew could bring a student in reading post-biblical Hebrew.[87]

Written Hebrew had not, however, remained static, and Buxtorf warned his readers to take note of the ways it had changed. A number of words from biblical Hebrew had acquired different meanings, and new words had been added to the language. The sources of these new words included Aramaic and also non-Semitic languages since the Jews usually adopted the language of their country of residence. Hence the Hebrew they spoke was of rather uneven quality.[88]

Beyond his two principles Buxtorf advised that students use such study aids as were then available. Both Sebastian Münster and Gilbert Génébrard had written introductions to reading rabbinic Hebrew, although they had by no means exhausted the subject.[89] The Aramaic grammars of Mercier, Bertramus, and Martinius

---

[85] Ibid., 613.
[86] This commentary was printed in חמשה חומשי תורה (Basel: Conrad Waldkirch, 1606-1607), Prijs no. 191A-B.
[87] Ibid., 622-642.
[88] Ibid., 643-644.
[89] Sebastian Münster, *Chaldaica Grammatica* (Basel: Johann Froben, 1526), and Gilbert Génébrard, *Eisagoge: Ad Legenda et intelligenda Hebraeae et Orientalium sine punctis scripta* (Paris: Aegidius Corbinus, 1587).

were also helpful.[90] For lexicons Buxtorf suggested those composed by Münster, David de Pomis, and Guido Fabricius, although these were all incomplete.[91] Another desideratum was a guide to Hebrew abbreviations, a gap in the literature that Buxtorf himself planned to fill.[92]

Buxtorf was unsatisfied with this rather general advice and planned to revise and expand his introduction to rabbinic Hebrew. Although he promised to publish this enlarged version in the next printing of *Thesaurus Grammaticus*, he decided against it, preferring to print it separately.[93] Buxtorf's plan to write and publish a more extensive introduction to post-biblical Hebrew, like so many of his projects, apparently fell victim to the length of his work list and was never written.

Buxtorf's introduction to Yiddish was intended primarily for German Christians who wished to read the language, although he suggested that others might find at least the alphabetic tables useful for deciphering Hebrew manuscripts written in Ashkenazic cursive script.[94] He included discussion of its consonants, vowels and syllables, stressing peculiarities in pronunciation but providing no further discussion of its grammar.[95] The most interesting aspects of this essay are, however, its Yiddish title list and the variety of reading exercises that Buxtorf selected. Nearly all of the titles that he lists can be readily identified with books from the Buxtorf family library. Buxtorf made extensive use of Yiddish books in his works, particularly in *Juden Schul*.[96]

---

[90] Jean Mercier, *Tabulae in Grammaticen linguae Chaldaeae, quae & Syrica dicitur* (Paris: Guillaume Morelium, 1560), Cornelius Bertramus, *Comparatio grammaticae hebraeae et Aramicae* (Geneva: E. Vignon, 1574) and Petrus Martinius, *Grammatica*.

[91] Sebastian Münster, עָרוּךְ *Dictionarium Chaldaicum* (Basel: Johann Froben, 1527), David de Pomis, צמח דוד (Venice: G. di Gara, 1587) and Guy Lefèvre de la Boderie, *Dictionarium syro-chaldaicum* in the Antwerp Polyglot, *Biblia Sacra, hebraice, chaldaice, graece et latine* (Antwerp: C. Plantin, 1569-72), vol. 7.

[92] Ibid., 646-647. Buxtorf mentioned the lists of Münster and Mercier, but felt that they were unsatisfactory. See below, chap. 5.

[93] *Lexicon Hebraicum et Chaldaicum* (Basel: Konrad Waldkirch, 1615), 959. See Prijs, *Drucke*, 326, 328.

[94] Buxtorf noted that several of these were preserved in the Palatine Library in Heidelberg. *Thesaurus Grammaticus*, 659.

[95] Ibid., 663-670.

[96] Ibid., 660-662. The Yiddish books that he cited in *Juden Schul* are Yiddish list nos. 12, 14, 18, 19, 20, 21, 24, 25. See Appendix 3.

The Yiddish reading exercises include Psalm 23, several letters, selections from the Solomon ibn Verga's *Shebet Yehudah*, and two excerpts from the Talmud translated into Yiddish.[97] Perhaps the most intriguing, and potentially defamatory, selection was Solomon ibn Verga's account of David "Eldavid" (Alroy), a Jew who claimed to be the Messiah.[98] In the second edition Buxtorf added one of Maimonides' letters in which he described a messianic pretender in Yemen.[99]

The diversity of his grammatical studies indicates the philologically diverse education that Buxtorf felt a Christian Hebraist needed in order to engage in biblical research. Biblical Hebrew was basic to his concerns but was only the first step in Hebrew education. In order to draw upon the resources of Jewish tradition for biblical philology and interpretation, scholars had to know both Aramaic and rabbinical Hebrew. Talmudic Aramaic and Yiddish, though less useful for biblical studies, were important for the study of Jews and Judaism. Grammatical studies alone, however, were not enough to provide access for Christians to the resources of Jewish tradition. Appropriate lexicons for the various Jewish languages and dialects were also a scholarly necessity.

If, as Dr. Johnson said, a lexicographer is a harmless drudge, then Johannes Buxtorf was one of the great drudges of his time. Between 1600 and his death in 1629 he was continuously at work compiling lexicons of various sizes for both students and scholars. While Buxtorf's dictionaries of biblical Hebrew and Aramaic were among his most often reprinted works, his *Lexicon Chaldaicum, Talmudicum et Rabbinicum* was perhaps his most enduring contribution to lexicography. Buxtorf composed three different biblical dictionaries over the course of his career. The first of these, *Epitome Radicum Hebraicarum*, he reluctantly wrote at the request of his colleague Amandus Polanus during the final four months of 1600.[100] Polanus wanted a dictionary inexpensive enough for all of

---

[97] Ibid., 671-690.

[98] See Solomon ibn Verga, שבט יהודה, ed. Azriel Shochet (Jerusalem: Mossad Bialik, 1946-1947), 74-77.

[99] Ibid., 683-690. This letter was first added in the 1615 revision of *Thesaurus Grammaticus*. Prijs, *Drucke*, 328.

[100] ספר השרשים קצור *Epitome Raducum Hebraicarum* (Basel: Konrad Waldkirch, 1600). Prijs no. 171. Buxtorf told Kaspar Waser, "Tuo exemplo D. D. Amandus me incitavit, ut et ego foris caniculares utiliter studiosis Theologiae

his theological students to own for themselves. Such a book would be useful for public theological disputations, where arguments over the meaning of Hebrew words were common, and also for the students' private study of the Hebrew Bible.[101] A book intended for student purchase, however, had to be relatively short in order to minimize its production costs. Buxtorf told Kaspar Waser that he planned to limit the dictionary's size to between ten and twelve gatherings of paper. Since the book was printed in 12° it was to be no more than 288 pages long.[102] The least expensive Hebrew dictionary that was then available for students to purchase was F. Raphalengius' abridgement of Santes Pagninus' *Thesaurus Linguae Sanctae*, and that cost at least one *Reichstaler*.[103] Size and cost are not, however, the only comparisons that may be drawn between Pagninus' work and Buxtorf's *Epitome*.

Prijs' comment that the Hebrew title of *Epitome radicum Hebraicarum* should have been entitled *"Abridgement of Sefer ha-Shorashim"* is not far from the truth.[104] Most Christian Hebraists beginning with Reuchlin used Kimhi's *Sefer ha-Shorashim* as the point of departure for their lexicographical works.[105] For the letters Gimel, Lamed, and Sade Pagninus' *Epitome Thesaurus Linguae Sanctae Hebraeae* listed 234 roots while Kimhi listed

---

et hebraeae linguae impenderem, et ad brevem Epitomen Lexici alicujus hebraici conficiendam hortatus est. Recusare nec potui nec debui." Johannes Buxtorf to Kaspar Waser, Basel, September 7, 1600, Zürich ZB Ms S-155: 40.

[101] "Adhaec in disputationibus Theologicis, in quibus frequentissimae controversiae de vocibus Hebraeis incidunt, in lectionibus item Hebraeis...." Amandus Polanus to the Reader, Basel, August 18, 1600, *Epitome Radicum*, 4.

[102] "Libellus erit decem aut ad summum 12 foliorum...." Buxtorf to Waser, Basel, September 7, 1600, Zürich ZB Ms S-155: 40. The final printed work was 504 pages long, foliated a-x in 12• and so required 23 folio pages. Prijs, *Drucke*, 278.

[103] "... Epitome seu compendium a Raphelengio editum Dalero et amplius venditur: neque etiam ubique prostat, nec omnibus emitur. Reliqua Lexica magna sunt." Buxtorf to Waser, Basel, September 7, 1600, Zürich ZB Ms S-155: 40. Although Sanctes Pagninus was almost as important as Sebastian Münster in advancing Hebrew studies among Christians during the sixteenth century, he has remained virtually unstudied. See Timoteo M. Centi, "L'Attivita Letteraria di Santi Pagnini (1470-1536) Nel Campo delle Scienze Bibliche," *Archivum Fratrem Praedicatorum* 15 (1945): 5-51 and G. Lloyd Jones, *Discovery*, 40-44.

[104] "קצור ספר השרשים" Cf. Prijs, *Drucke*, 279.

[105] Greive, "Reuchlin," 407 and Centi, "Pagnini," 28-36.

235.[106] Both Kimhi and Pagninus discussed many more words than this, but these other words were listed as sub-entries under their roots. Pagninus' lexicon made this clear by printing the roots in particularly large type and sub-entries in somewhat smaller type, both located flush with the left margin. Buxtorf owned a copy of Pagninus' *Epitome* and it probably served as his base text for *Epitome radicum Hebraicarum*.[107] Of the 240 entries Buxtorf gave under the letters Gimel, Lamed and Sade 164 of them correspond to a root listed by Pagninus. The remaining entries were generally drawn from sub-entries given by Pagninus (or Kimhi).[108] In 35 cases Buxtorf gave as his listing a word that Pagninus also thought would be a better entry rather than the root letter.[109] Buxtorf drew his Latin definitions primarily from the Latin Bible translations of Pagninus and of Franciscus Junius and Immanuel Tremellius.[110]

As he did in his later grammatical works Buxtorf made use of Jewish sources for clarifying obscure words in *Epitome radicum Hebraicarum*. The biblical commentaries of Rashi, Ibn Ezra, and David Kimhi were frequently the source of his explanations. These citations together with references to Saadia's Daniel commentary, to Levi b. Gerson's Job commentary and to the Masora suggest that Buxtorf's most important resource for lexicographical study was

---

[106] Kimhi gave three entries not found in Pagninus: ציר, מתלהלה and צפת, while Pagninus listed two not found in Kimhi: לא and לך.

[107] Buxtorf's copies of these works are Sanctes Pagninus, *Epitome Thesaurus Linguae Sanctae Hebraeae*, ed. F. Raphalengius (Antwerp: C. Plantin, 1588), Basel UB FA II 42 and David Kimhi, ספר השרשים (Venice: Marco Antonio Justiniani, 1552), Basel UB FA III 6/2. He also owned a revised version of the entire work: *Thesaurus Linguae Sanctae Hebraeae*, ed. Jean Mercier, Antoine Chevallier and Cornelius Bertramus (Leiden: Bartholemaeus Vincentius, 1575), Basel UB FA VI 11b. This book contains extensive marginalia in his hand.

[108] Buxtorf surprisingly cited Kimhi's ספר השרשים, only once in *Epitome Radicum*, in his discussion of the root נוא on p. 218.

[109] Pagninus noted in many places the root followed by the words "inde sit" and a derivative form of the word. Some examples where Buxtorf's entry follows Pagninus suggestions occur in his discussions of גבול, גבינה, גבורה, גביש and גדיש. See Buxtorf, *Epitome*, 41-42, 44, and Pagninus, *Epitome*, 41-43.

[110] "Deinde significata omnium vocum ad probatissimas Bibliorum versiones, maxime Santis Pagnini & Immanuelis Tremelii ac Francisci Junii, ita sunt accomodata; ut hoc etiam nomine utilitatem inde sitis copiosam habituri." Polanus to the Reader, Basel, August 18, 1600, *Epitome radicum*, 4. On these translations see Lloyd Jones, *Discovery*, 41-42, 50-52.

the second edition of the Bomberg rabbinical Bible.[111] He referred three times to Rabbi Anshel's Yiddish language biblical dictionary, and several other times to Yiddish Bible translations.[112] These references, however, were relatively uncommon. Only about half of the entries under the letters Gimel, Lamed, and Sade (107 out of 226 total entries) had biblical verse references, much less references to other Hebrew books.

Although it was only printed once, Buxtorf's *Epitome radicum Hebraicarum* was important since it was the ancestor, direct or indirect, of all his subsequent biblical dictionaries. His *Epitome Radicum Hebraicum et Chaldaicum* of 1607 hearkened back to *Epitome radicum Hebraicarum* both in the similarity of their titles and also in Buxtorf's comment that the latter was "nove aucta." Buxtorf considered his *Manuale Hebraicum et Chaldaicum* the lineal descendant of *Epitome Radicum*. The second printing of *Manuale* bears the notation "fourth revised edition;" the first edition being *Epitome radicum Hebraicarum* and the second a lost work with no known extant copies.[113]

If *Epitome radicum Hebraicarum* was an unplanned interruption in Buxtorf's schedule undertaken at another's behest, his second lexicon, *Epitome Radicum Hebraicum et Chaldaicum*, was a carefully crafted work, appearing only when its author was satisfied with it. Privately he again compared his work with Pagninus' *Thesaurus*, but this time he felt that his lexicon superseded the latter work. He provided not only more definitions of words, but more extensive commentary as well.[114] He revised the work some-

---

[111] For references to Rashi see *Epitome radicum*, 190, 256, to Ibn Ezra, 107-108, 241, 257, 266, 295, 298, 315 and to Kimhi, 155, 169, 171, 195, 199, 238, 287 passim. He also made reference to R. Saadia's Daniel commentary on 266, to Levi b. Gerson's Job commentary on 199, and to the Masora on 432.

[112] Anshel, אנשל 'ר ספר (Krakow: Isaac b. Aaron Prostitz, 1584). See *Epitome radicum*, 38, 113, 194. For his references to Yiddish Bible translations, see pp. 38, 195, 244, 257 and 265.

[113] Prijs satisfactorily explained the bibliographic confusion surrounding the sequence of Buxtorf's lexicons. The second edition of *Manuale* was mentioned by Daniel Tossanus, *Oratio*, 10 and such information as is available about it is related by Prijs, *Drucke*, 293, 343. The third edition of *Manuale*, however, is a drastic abridgement of the *Epitome Radicum* of 1607.

[114] "Doctis expositus est pretiosus Sanctes Pagnini Thesaurus. Raphelengius Epitome vide contracta, plurimum hactemus juventi profuit. Ipsius laboribus ego adjicere aliquid conatus sum, significatis aliisque pluribus copiosius propositis."

what and published it in 1615 under the title *Lexicon Hebraicum et Chaldaicum*.[115]

In its form Buxtorf's *Lexicon* is organized in much the same way as Pagninus' was. Roots are printed in the largest Hebrew type on the page, and other derivative forms appear under it in smaller type, as do cross-references from one root to another. The work differs from Pagninus, however, in that Buxtorf often devoted more space to certain words that were either philologically complex such as חוּל and יָדַע, or theologically significant such as the divine names. For the Tetragrammaton alone Buxtorf devoted ten pages of discussion.[116]

In his arrangement of roots Buxtorf followed the lead of Kimhi and Pagninus with relatively few differences. Kimhi listed a total of 235 entries under the letters Gimel, Lamed and Sade, while Buxtorf gave 223 main entries, 202 of which are identical with Kimhi's. In thirteen cases Buxtorf altered the root form given by Kimhi to a greater or lesser degree, usually following a suggestion made either by Kimhi himself or by Pagninus.[117] Buxtorf himself altered the form of entries only three times.[118] Another thirteen

---

Johannes Buxtorf to Konrad Vorstius, Basel, June 8, 1608, Bibliotheca Rosenthaliana (Amsterdam UB), Brieven-collectie, no. 110.

[115] Although the foliation for *Epitome Radicum Hebraicum et Chaldaicum* (Basel: Konrad Waldkirch, 1607) and *Lexicon Hebraicum et Chaldaicum* (Basel: Konrad Waldkirch, 1615) are the same, Buxtorf did revise their contents. Under the letter Gimel, for example, the former has 239 entries, the latter 231. The pagination differs as well, *Epitome* has 38 pages of discussion on Gimel and goes from pp. 107-147, while *Lexicon* has only 32 pages and goes from pp. 92-124. Another major difference between the two works, his appendix *Lexicon Breve Rabbinico Philosophicum* is discussed below. Since this printing of the *Lexicon* was the the last one that Buxtorf edited before his death it will serve as the basis of discussion.

[116] For Buxtorf's entries on אלה, שׁדי, and יהוה see *Lexicon*, 78, 137-138 and 154-164.

[117] Examples of roots where Buxtorf followed suggestions by Kimhi include גף גב, גרשׁ, לגם, לוה, לצר and צפת. I have used a reprint edition of Kimhi's lexicon for my analysis in this section: David Kimhi, ספר השׁרשׁים *Radicum Liber sive Hebraeum Bibliorum Lexicon*, ed. J. H. R. Biesenthal and F. Lebrecht (Berlin: G. Bethge, 1847; reprint ed., Jerusalem: n. p., 1967), 53, 63, 65, 177, 180, 182, 317. For roots where Buxtorf followed suggestions made by Pagninus, see his discussion of the roots גוד, למג, צוא and צוֹן. *Epitome*, 44, 166, 315-316. For Buxtorf's entries see *Lexicon*, 93, 101, 119, 181, 382, 388, 415, 627 and 651.

[118] In two cases he changed monosyllabic forms into geminate ones, צב and גת, in one instance, צְנֵצֶת, he changed the entry from masculine to feminine, following Kimhi's first example rather than his entry. *Lexicon*, 124, 627, 645.

entries from Kimhi's dictionary appear as secondary entries under other roots in Buxtorf's *Lexicon*. Nine of these are quadraliteral forms that Buxtorf variously analyzed either as geminate or final He verbs, or as derivative forms whose fourth root letter could be ignored for purposes of classification.[119] Buxtorf added fourteen new entries to his *Lexicon* beyond what he derived from Kimhi, six of them taken from biblical Aramaic.[120] Buxtorf's *Lexicon*, while much larger in scope than Kimhi's *Shorashim*, is still clearly a derivative of it from the perspective of the number of roots analyzed.

Although Buxtorf consulted Jewish sources in the preparation of his *Epitome Radicum* his use of them in the *Lexicon* is far more extensive. Among the 231 words, roots and sub-references given by Buxtorf under the letter Gimel only thirty seven are explained with the help of extra-biblical Jewish sources.[121] The bulk of these, again, are drawn from the biblical commentaries of Rashi, Ibn Ezra, Kimhi, and Levi b. Gerson.[122] Other commentaries cited were those of Bahya b. Asher and Simon Darshan.[123] Kimhi's dictionary was quoted three times.[124] Talmudic references appear five times.[125] Curiously Buxtorf made little or no use of secondary quotations from Kimhi's *Shorashim*; he did not cite either Jonah Ibn Janah or the Talmud, although Kimhi cited the latter twenty two times when discussing words beginning with Gimel.[126]

Buxtorf's frequent use of Jewish sources did not, however, often lead him to assign different definitions to words than his predecessors. Of the 92 roots beginning with Gimel that were listed in

---

[119] Buxtorf analysed גרר, מתלהלה, צלל and צפף as geminate forms, צעצע as final *He*. The other quadraliteral forms were גנוך, גלמד , גבעל and צרפת. *Lexicon*, 95, 114, 117, 122, 383, 641, 649, 647 and 651.

[120] The biblical Aramaic entries are גדבר, גזבר, גֶּשֶׁם, צְלָה, לְוָת and עֲבָא. The remaining entries are גוּף, לא, לוֹ, לחח, לחן, לחן, צַנְתְּרוֹת, and צפף. *Lexicon*, 97, 104, 105, 123, 377, 384, 388, 389, 627, 640, 646 and 650.

[121] In contrast to Buxtorf's practice in *Epitome Radicum*, however, practically all entries have biblical references included.

[122] Rashi was cited ten times, Kimhi eight times, Ibn Ezra ten times and Levi b. Gerson's Job commentary, five times. The Masora was quoted twice.

[123] *Lexicon*, 108-109.

[124] Ibid., 93, 121 and 123.

[125] See his discussion of גד, גֵּיא, גִּיל and גָּלְמוּד. Ibid., 97, 110, 114.

[126] Kimhi cited Ibn Janah in his discussions of גלש, גיא, גוי, גדל, גדד, גבש, גבן; גם and גרם; he quoted the Talmud in his discussions of גדה, גדל, גדש, גוב, גוש, גוע, גיל, גיף, גלד, גלל, גלם, גפר, גרד, גרס, גרף and גשם. סֵפֶר השרשים, 53-65.

Pagninus' *Epitome*, Buxtorf did not disagree with any of the definitions. In several cases such as גְּבִישׁ, גדד and גדף, he wished to assign a more technical definition than Pagninus did, defining them
as "pearl," "to muster troops," and "to blaspheme" respectively.[127]
Buxtorf made a grave error in his definition of *goy* (גּוֹי), suggesting that it referred only to Christians in post-biblical Hebrew,[128]
which was why, he added, the censors of the Basel Talmud often
replaced it with "Samaritans," (כּוּתִיים).[129] Buxtorf was incorrect on
this point, of course, since Kimhi made it clear that *goy* referred to
anyone who was not an Israelite.[130] Buxtorf also devoted an extensive discussion to the word גֵּיא, "valley." Although the phrase
"Valley of Hinnon" only occurs a few times in the Hebrew Bible
and once in the New Testament (Matt. 5:22), its associations with
ancient Israelite idolatry, and later with the Christian concept of
Hell, made it worthy of an extended explanation. Buxtorf primarily
drew upon Kimhi's comments on 2 Ki 23: 11 and Ps 27:13 and
Rashi's discussion of Jer 7: 31 in describing the valley's identification with idolatry. He also quoted from BT *Sanhedrin* 52 and BT
Nedarim 39.[131]

The continuity of both the form and definitional content with
the dictionaries of Kimhi and Pagninus in Buxtorf's *Lexicon* is
striking. His intention was clearly not to break new philological
ground but rather to refine existing works by providing far more
references to other Jewish sources, particularly to biblical commentaries. This preoccupation with biblical commentaries is a reflection of Buxtorf's pedagogical practice since he frequently encouraged his students to learn enough medieval Hebrew to use these

---

[127] For גְּבִישׁ Pagninus wrote "Genus lapidis preciosi: Iob 28, 18," for גדד,
"Cogere & ducere exercitum ... Supere exercitu: Genes. 49. 19 ... ," and for גדף,
"Exprobrare, conviciari." *Epitome*, 41-43. Buxtorf followed Levi b. Gerson's
comment in Job 28:18 in his definition of גְּבִישׁ, for גדד he suggested "Turmatim
convenire," and for גדף "Blasphemavit." *Lexicon*, 96, 97, 100.

[128] "Atque ita quod ante Christum fuit generale nomen, id post Christum
fecerunt speciale, & ad solos Christianos restrinxerunt. Turcas enim non Gojim,
sed יִשְׁמְעֵאלִים Ismaelitas: Aethiopes, כּוּשִׁיים appellant, & ita aliae quaeque gentes
Christo non addictae, speciali nomine ipsos vocantur." *Lexicon*, 102-103.

[129] "Ex quo autem libri ipsorum censurae Christianorum in quibusdam locis
fuere sujecti, pro גּוֹיִם, declinandae invidiae causa, substituerunt כּוּתִיים Cuthiim, ut
in Opere Talmudico Basileae edito, factum. Cuthaeos autem Samaritanos olim
vocarunt quod venerint ex Cutha, de qua 2 Reg. 17. v. 24." *Lexicon*, 103.

[130] ספר השרשים, 57. Kimhi, "גוי ... כלומר שהוא מגוי אחר שאינו מישראל."

[131] *Lexicon*, 108-110.

commentaries.[132] When he did provide comparative material from other Semitic languages it was all drawn from Jewish sources, primarily the Targums and the Talmud.

The other major source of material available for comparative Semitic philology during the early seventeenth century was Arabic. Buxtorf wished to learn the language but was unsuccessful in doing so. When he read in 1611 that a revision of Schindler's *Lexicon Pentaglotton* would soon be printed he told Kaspar Waser that he hoped to use it to help him read Arabic books.[133] In 1614 he attempted to teach himself from a grammar, but apparently without much success. He was forced to admit in 1617 that he did not know Arabic.[134] While he could not be faulted for not trying, Buxtorf's ignorance of Arabic placed limits on the kinds of philological observations that he could make, and hence on his contribution to Hebrew lexicography.

Manuale Hebraicum et Chaldaicum was a pedagogical adaptation of the much larger *Epitome Radicum Hebraicum et Chaldaicum* written in 1607. The need that Polanus identified in 1600 for an inexpensive Hebrew dictionary still existed and Buxtorf apparently decided that a ruthless abridgement of his larger dictionary would be a better solution than reprinting either his *Epitome radicum* or the first edition of *Manuale*.[135] A comparison of the entries for Gimel reveals just how thorough this paring was. Buxtorf listed 239 words in his *Epitome Radicum Hebraicum*

---

[132] See above, chap. 1.

[133] "...quod ex Catalogo librorum Francof. video, plane simile Lexicon à Schindlero confectum, nunc ibi sub prelo esse, excerpto quod Arabicum adjectum ipsi sit, cujus linguae ego peritiam nullam habeo, ut seq usum, ab librorum Arabicorum defectum." Johannes Buxtorf to Kaspar Waser, n. p., April 8, 1611, Zürich ZB Ms S-162: 32. The title page inscription on Buxtorf's copy reads, "D. M. Joanni Buxdorfio mittit Joan. Rulandius (the publisher)." Valentinus Schindler, *Lexicon Pentaglotton* (Hanau: Hans Jacob Henne, 1612), Basel UB FA II 9.

[134] "Ego Arabica degustare tentabo, quantum ex mutis praeceptoribus id licet." Johannes Buxtorf to Bartholomaeus Rülich, Basel, August 4, 1614, Magdeburg SA, Abt. Kothen C 18, 31: 155r. When responding to a question about his knowledge of Arabic Buxtorf told Wolfgang Ratich, "Arabica zu befordern hab ich kein mittel...." Johannes Buxtorf to Wolfgang Ratich, Basel, March 30, 1617, Magdeburg SA, Abt. Kothen C 18, 30: 185v.

[135] "Conscripsi Thesaurum Grammaticum .... Edidi et Epitomen Radicum, sub lexici brevis forma. Ex utroque excerpsi compendia pro tyronibus et scholis trivialibus." Johannes Buxtorf to Philippe du Plessis de Mornay, Basel, September 8, 1613, Basel UB Ms Autogr. Slg. Geigy Hgb. no. 736.

et Chaldaicum in 38 pages; in *Manuale* he gave 188 entries in only 13 pages.[136] He achieved this reduction by eliminating practically all verse references and notes on Jewish sources.

Both the *Lexicon* and *Manuale* were runaway best-sellers by the standards of the Hebrew book market. Throughout the seventeenth century the *Lexicon* was reprinted at least every ten years in Basel and several times elsewhere. It was printed fourteen times in Basel, twice in Amsterdam and three times in London before 1800. During the nineteenth century it was reprinted in 1824, 1833 and 1845, testifying to its continuing appeal. The *Manuale* was only printed six times during the seventeenth century, although two of these printings were pirate editions. It was reprinted again in 1807.[137]

The commercial success of these two dictionaries was to a large degree a reflection of their pedagogical usefulness to Buxtorf's contemporaries. The *Lexicon* particularly enjoyed an excellent reputation among scholars. Even Richard Simon felt that he could recommend it without reservation.[138] Buxtorf's fame as a lexicographer, however, was not a result of his work in biblical Hebrew, but in post-biblical Hebrew and talmudic Aramaic.

Buxtorf's work with post-biblical Hebrew began quite early in his career. He soon became dissatisfied with all of the available dictionaries, both those composed by Christians and by Jews. In a letter to Joseph Scaliger Buxtorf neatly summarized the dilemma shared by most Christian Hebraists. The most recently composed lexicon, David de Pomis' *Semah David*, was very incomplete; he filled the margins of his own copy with further notes.[139] Münster's lexicon was no longer available for purchase, and Guido Fabricius'

---

[136] Since the *Epitome* was printed in 8° and the *Manuale* in 12° the thirteen pages of the latter would only fill up about nine pages in the former.

[137] See below, Appendix 1, nos.78-94, and 95-100.

[138] "La plus part de ceux qui se vantent aujourdhui de sçavoir la Langue Hebraïque, n'ont presque point eu d'autre maitre que le Dictionnaire de Buxtorfe, qu'ils ont jugé etre le meilleur, parce qu'il est le plus abregé & le plus methodique." Richard Simon, *Histoire Critique du Vieux Testament* (Rotterdam: Renier Leers, 1685; reprint ed., Frankfurt/M: Minerva G. M. B. H., 1967), 359.

[139] "De Lexico Davidis de Pomis tuum cognovi judicium. Certe neque meum aliud est .... Multa, plurima, infinita desiderantur; probe novi. Testatur id meum exemplar, in quo omes margines aliis vocibus complevi." Johannes Buxtorf to Joseph Scaliger, Basel, March 17, 1607, London: British Library Ms Add. 5158: 25, printed in *Sylloges*, 2: 366.

lexicon, which that was printed with the Antwerp Polyglot, was equally hard to find.[140] Since the *Aruk* of Nathan b. Yehiel was far too difficult for most students to use Buxtorf himself was already thinking about writing a lexicon to satisfy the need.[141]

Buxtorf began to compile his rabbinical dictionary in 1608, according to his son.[142] In 1610 he had completed several letters and hoped to finish the entire work within two years.[143] He apparently planned to write a work of roughly the same size as his *Lexicon Hebraicum et Chaldaicum*, but the longer he wrote the more material became incorporated in his later entries.[144] His brief glossary of rabbinic Hebrew, published as an appendix to *Lexicon Hebraicum et Chaldaicum*, was composed during this period, although it was not intended in any way to replace the larger work.[145] Buxtorf's overly full work schedule also slowed his

---

[140] Buxtorf later felt that neither of these works were worth using. When Sixtius Amama asked him whether a revision of Münster's dictionary would be worth publishing he was emphatic that it would not be. "Respondi, meo consilio istud Lexicon nec cum bono publico, nec cum honore alicujus privato, excudi posse, tum propter immanem Radicum et vocum confusionem, tum propter innumeros errores, quorum Drusius ne centesimam partem cognovit, non dicam millesimam." Fabricius' lexicon was equally bad since "quaedam Munsteri correxit, sed plura retinuit et excripsit." Johannes Buxtorf to Wilhelm Schickhard, Basel, October 10, 1627, Stuttgart, WLB Cod. hist. 2° 563, transcribed in F. Seck, *Wilhelm Schickhard Briefwechsel*, 4 vols. (Tübingen: Typescript, 1975).

[141] "Si mihi ut animus, ita otium esset, cogitarem de hoc opere." Johannes Buxtorf to Joseph Scaliger, Basel, March 17, 1607, London: British Library Ms Add 5158: 25, printed in *Sylloges*, 2: 366.

[142] "Commendabit se ipse ... cum Lexico Thalmudico et Chaldaico ante viginti annos inchoato...." Johannes Buxtorf II to Petrus Cunaeus, Basel, September 3, 1628, Leiden UB Ms Cun 2:100, printed in *Epistolae*, 161-2.

[143] "Si vita ad biennium supersit, spero me absoluturum. Aliquot alphabeti literas jam expetivi." Johannes Buxtorf to Johannes Uytenbogaert, Basel, March 15, 1610, Leiden UB Ms Pap 2, and printed in *Praestantium ac Eruditorum*, 938-940.

[144] "Nam cum initio hos labores aggrederetur, nequaquam tam completum & diffusum opus, sed brevem tantum Epitomen ad forman Lexici sui Hebraici proponere cogitavit: undefactum, ut ultra dimidium literarum ordinem eam rationem tenuerit & observavit." Johannes Buxtorf II to the Rulers of the States of Groningen, Basel, February, 1639, printed in *Lexicon Chaldaicum, Talmudicum et Rabbinicum*, f. (*)4v.

[145] *Lexicon Breve Rabbinico-Philosophicum* (*Lexicon*, 865-960) was more of an accident than a publication. Buxtorf's printer prevailed upon him to compose a glossary of rabbbinic Hebrew as an appendix to the lexicon in order to keep his presses from being idle for the final two weeks before the Frankfurt book fair. Prijs, *Drucke*, 326, quoting *Lexicon Hebraicum et Chaldaicum*, 954.

progress on the lexicon, since he was often forced to lay it aside in favor of other projects. By 1617 he had reached the letter Ayin.[146] Between 1617 and 1619 he worked on the rabbinical Bible and probably had no time to devote to the lexicon. Finally in 1628 he completed the first draft.[147] His manuscript work was in no shape to be published, however. Buxtorf was forced to revise entries from the earlier letters of the alphabet so that they would be of comparable length with the later ones. He died before he finished revising the entries under Bet.[148]

The younger Buxtorf inherited essentially a skeleton of a lexicon, not a completed work, from his father.[149] His responsibilities as a new professor at the university, familial calamities, and oversight of the printing of his father's *Concordantiae* effectively forced him to lay aside the talmudic lexicon for a number of years. His only activity with regard to the *Lexicon* was to explore the possibilities of having it printed in Leiden.[150] Only in 1634 or 1635 was he finally able to begin the arduous task of editing his father's work.[151] By June of 1637 he had completed the entries for the letter Mem, and the work was finally printed in 1639-1640.[152] While he modestly attributed the work to his father there can be no doubt that he himself contributed a great deal to its content, and any ex-

---

146 "Mein vor etlich Jahren angefangenes Lexicon Chaldaicum Rabbinicum et Talmudicum hab ich verfertiget biß zu und Literae ע. Im ubrig hab ich materi genuch, muß nur Zeit und arbeit daran werden, alles in ordnung zu bringen und zusammen zu schreiben." Johannes Buxtorf to Wolfgang Ratich, Basel, March 30, 1617, Magdeburg SA, Abt. Kothen C 18, 30: 185v.

147 Johannes Buxtorf II to Petrus Cunaeus, Basel, September 3, 1628, Leiden UB Ms Cun 2:100, printed in Cunaeus, *Epistolae*, 161-2.

148 "Cum autem absolutis ultimis literis, cogitaret praecedentes quoque in eandem formam redigere, & caeteris aequales redere, inevitabili Fati lege, in secunda litera Beth calamum deponere, & cursum sistere jussus fuit Anno M DC XXIX." Buxtorf II to the Rulers of the States of Groningen, Basel, February, 1639, *Lexicon Chaldaicum, Talmudicum et Rabbinicum*, f. (*) 4r.

149 "Eousque quidem ab eo vivente fuit perductum, ut totam Alphabethi seriem perfecerit & absolverit, atque ita sceleton totius operis reliquerit, sed multis partibus mutilum & imperfectum. . . . Unde factum, ut & in inextricabili fere confusione & maxima inaequabilitate Opus post se reliquerit." Ibid.

150 Van Rooden, *Theology*, 204. See Daniel Heinsius to Johannes Buxtorf II, August 9, 1632, Basel UB Ms G I 59: 252, printed in *Catalecta*, 471-2.

151 "In tertiam jam annum protrahitur editio ...." Johannes Buxtorf II to Petrus Cunaeus, Basel, March 24, 1638, printed in Cunaeus, *Epistolae*, 171-2.

152 Johannes Buxtorf II to Petrus Cunaeus, Basel, June 18, 1637, printed in Cunaeus, *Epistolae*, 168-9. For a description of the work see Prijs, *Drucke*, 365-370.

amination of the work's substance rightly belongs to a study of the younger Buxtorf.[153]

The international community of scholars of the seventeenth century, particularly Protestants, recognized the importance of linguistic access to post-biblical Hebrew literature, whether directly through translations or indirectly through their use by Christian scholars. For non-theologians, access to Jewish literature meant the ability to read works written in Hebrew by Jewish authors in a variety of disciplines, including law, medicine and philosophy.[154] Theologians recognized the value of Jewish literature for biblical interpretation and, of course, for anti-Jewish polemics.[155] The enthusiasm with which scholars greeted the younger Buxtorf's publication of the *Lexicon Chaldaicum, Talmudicum et Rabbinicum* should be understood in this light. Constantijn L'Empereur thought that it was a milestone in the study of Hebraica. "A work which is truly worthy of eternity. If a large number of translated texts from the Talmud were further to be added to it as a manual, we should finally be able to penetrate everywhere into it without the aid of the Jews."[156] Twenty years later John Lightfoot acknowledged how important the talmudic lexicon was to his own work on New Testament backgrounds. He wrote,

---

[153] Several smaller studies of the sources of Buxtorf's *Lexicon Chaldaicum* have already appeared. David Kaufmann's identification of the ערוך הקצור manuscript with Bern Burgerbibliothek Cod. 200, 3 with the one used by Buxtorf in his talmudic lexicon is correct as his marginalia on ff. 101v, 111v and on the right inside cover attest. Buxtorf II borrowed it from Samuel Hortin of Bern (Hortin to Buxtorf II, Burgdorf, February 11, 1636, Basel UB Ms G I 63: 12, and February 10, 1637, Basel UB Ms G I 63: 14). See David Kaufmann, "Buxtorf's Aruchhandschrift, wiederaufgefunden." *Monatsschrift für Geschichte und Wissenschaft des Judentums* 34 (1885): 185-192, 225-233. Carlos Gilly discussed Buxtorf II's use of Postel's Latin translation of *Bereshit Rabba* in "Guillaume Postel et Bâle. Quelques additions à la Bibliographie des manuscrits de Guillaume Postel," in *Guillaume Postel 1581-1981*, Actes du Colloque International d'Avranches 5-9 septembre 1981 (Paris: Éditions de la Maisnie, 1985), 43-45.

[154] "Sunt in eo multa Juridica, Medica, Physica, Ethica, Politica, Astronomica, & aliarum scientiarum praeclara documenta, quae istius gentis & temporis historiam mirifice commendant." Buxtorf II to the Rulers of the States of Groningen, Basel, February, 1639, *Lexicon Chaldaicum*, f. (*)3r.

[155] Van Rooden, *Theology*, 148, 151, 153, 165-183. Katchen also discussed the value of Latin translations of Hebrew books in *Christian Hebraists and Dutch Rabbis*, 65-100, 161-259.

[156] Constantijn L'Empereur to James Ussher, n. p., March 1, 1641, Leiden UB Ms. Thysiana 164, 6, quoted in Van Rooden, *Theology*, 183.

It pleases you, most honored sir, to speak of my skill in the Talmudists, which if it be any (and how small it is I well know) is wholly due to you and to your incomparable father. Ploughing with your oxen [using your lexicons], I have sowed; and if any crop comes of it, it is yours. And what Christian is there, I ask, who reads over the Talmudic writings, that owes not the same tribute? So much is the whole Christian world indebted to the great name of Buxtorf.[157]

Since Lightfoot was the first scholar to apply talmudic material systematically to the study of the New Testament, the Buxtorfs made a substantial, though indirect, contribution to that field as well.[158] If, as Schoeps affirmed, the seventeenth century saw the greatest interest among Christians for talmudic studies of any era before or since, then the Buxtorfs and their talmudic lexicon played an important part in this development.[159]

Hebrew was taught among Christians as a classical language in the seventeenth century and could only be learned through the use of books, with or without the help of an instructor. Johannes Buxtorf's works in grammar and lexicography were important contributions to Hebrew pedagogy. His larger scholarly works such as *Thesaurus Grammaticus* and *Lexicon Hebraicum et Chaldaicum* were expansions and revisions of existing works, making extensive use of Hebrew language sources. Buxtorf's references to these sources gave his readers both insight into specific linguistic problems and also an example of how they could solve other problems. Discussions of Kimhi and Levita were not necessarily the last word on any subject in Buxtorf's opinion, and he favored the fullest possible use of other works, particularly biblical commentaries, in grammar and lexicography.

If Buxtorf's grammars and lexicons represented an advance in Hebrew learning in the abstract, they also reflected the pedagogical needs of seventeenth-century schools and students. Buxtorf composed his grammars according to a modified Ramist pattern at a

---

157 John Lightfoot to Johannes Buxtorf II, Hereford, February 1, 1663, Basel UB Ms G I 62: 11, printed in John Lightfoot, *The Whole Works of the Rev. John Lightfoot, D. D. Master of Catharine Hall, Cambridge*, 13 vols (London: J. F. Dove, 1825), 1: 100 (English translation) and 13: 426 (Latin original).
158 Stephen Neill, *The Interpretation of the New Testament 1861-1961* (London: Oxford Univ. Press, 1964), 292-4. For a recent study of John Lightfoot, see Schertz, "Christian Hebraism."
159 Schoeps, *Philosemitismus*, 134.

time when Ramism was the leading educational theory espoused by German Reformed educators.[160] His pocket-sized Hebrew grammars and lexicons were inexpensive enough to be purchased by students and were designed to provide enough information to bring students to the modest level of Hebrew learning which most seminarians then (as now) sought. By recasting linguistic information gleaned from a variety of Jewish sources into appropriate pedagogical forms, Buxtorf forged a key to unlock not only the Hebrew Bible, but also post-biblical Jewish literature on biblical studies.

In order to learn to use post-biblical Hebrew properly, however, students required better instruction, and more and better textbooks on the subject. Although Buxtorf's works on post-biblical Hebrew literature, apart from his *Lexicon Chaldaicum*, were rather limited in scope they were designed to provide more advanced instruction in the peculiarities of this literary corpus, and to aid those teachers who wished to provide a level of instruction comparable to their colleagues in Greek and Latin literature.

---

[160] Menk, *Herborn*, 205-206.

CHAPTER FIVE

POST-BIBLICAL HEBREW LITERATURE
IN THE CONFESSIONAL ACADEMY

Hebrew studies during the sixteenth and seventeenth centuries was a discipline informed and influenced by two rather different intellectual traditions: Renaissance humanism and academic theology. Those Christian Hebraists who were hired to teach Hebrew at schools or universities served as instructors in theology, Hebrew, or both. Although the professorships in Hebrew language at Cambridge, Oxford, Leiden, Louvain, and Paris had been established through the impetus of the humanist ideal of trilingual education, the Hebraists who taught in these institutions were forced to justify their existence through their usefulness to the university community. In practice this often meant that they were little more than adjunct members of the theology faculty. At Leiden University, for example, the professor of Hebrew taught theological common places (systematic theology) since the university's charter did not provide for a professorship in common places, and yet the theology faculty needed a lecturer in it.[1] If Hebrew instruction were to involve anything more than teaching grammar, lecturing on the philological aspects of individual biblical books, and on theology, then Hebraists had to make a case for the Christian study of extra-biblical Hebrew literature. They also had to be prepared to offer instruction in Hebrew composition, specifically in letter-writing and poetry.[2] Only when they could provide instruction on a level comparable with their other colleagues on the Arts faculty would Hebrew be recognized as a full-fledged humanist language by other scholars within the Academy.

Johannes Buxtorf felt that for Hebrew education to improve, more study aids were necessary. In a letter written three years before his death to Hieronymus Avianus, a younger Hebraist who was

---

[1] Van Rooden, *Theology*, 50-54.

[2] Lebram attributed the failure of Hebrew to establish itself in the early modern university to its unsuitability as a language of scholarship when compared with Latin or Greek. J. C. H. Lebram, "Hebräische Studien," 322-323.

writing a book on Hebrew poetics, Buxtorf was unusually forth-coming about his professional motives. Hebrew students did not suffer from a lack of talent but from a lack of linguistic helps. As an educator Buxtorf felt that he had to do something to remedy the situation and had composed two works dealing with Hebrew com-position and another with bibliography.[3] If the study of Latin and Greek letters required such specialized works, then Hebrew re-quired no less.[4]

Latin rhetoric enjoyed a privileged place in Renaissance educa-tion. The ability to write and speak well in Latin was a professional necessity for those who aspired to high office in both church and state. Erasmus and other educational theorists urged the importance of excellence in the composition of letters and neo-Latin verse upon generations of teachers and students.[5] Well-crafted learned correspondence in particular played an important role within the international community of scholars. Wallace K. Ferguson noted, "at a time when there were no learned journals in which scholars could have their articles published, letters, whether intended to be printed or merely to be circulated in manuscript, served much the same purpose."[6] Among the scholars of Renaissance Europe, letters were virtually the only way to maintain contacts with colleagues, and literary friendships were a particularly important aspect of academic life.[7] The model of Latin letters was unavoidable for

---

[3] "Quo majorem usum & fructum juventus harum literarum videbit, tanto ardentius ad eas discendas flagrabit. Non defectus elegantium ingeniorum, sed defectus subsidiorum, quibus ad solidiorem cognitionem hujus Linguae pervenirent, ab acriori studio hactenus multos vel absterruit, vel penitus avertit. Hîc succurere pro modulo meo mihi hactenus fuit propositum." Johannes Buxtorf to Hieronymus Avianus, Basel, July 3, 1626, printed in Avianus, *Clavis Poeseos Sacrae* (Leipzig: Gottfried Gros, 1627), ff. b6r-v. While Buxtorf only mentioned his works on poetry and letter-writing in this letter, it is clear that he wrote *De Abbreviaturis* with the same student audience in mind.

[4] "Cum enim ista in Lingua Latina & Graeca istum habeant usum, cur non & in Lingua sancta Hebraea eundem habere possint?" Ibid., f. b6r.

[5] See Judith Rice Henderson, "Erasmus on the Art of Letter-Writing," in: *Renaissance Eloquence: Studies in the Theory and Practice of Renaissance Rhetoric*, ed. James J. Murphy (Berkeley: Univ. of California Press, 1983), 331-355. Joseph S. Freedman gave an interesting reconstruction of pedagogical prac-tice during this period in "Cicero in Sixteenth- and Seventeenth-Century Rhetorical Instruction," *Rhetorica* 4 (1986): 243.

[6] Quoted by Henderson, "Erasmus," 339.

[7] Trunz, "Späthumanismus," 166-169.

those Christian Hebraists who wished to teach composition of Hebrew letters.

The interest of Christian Hebraists in Hebrew letter-writing during the sixteenth century was essentially practical: those who wished to correspond with Jews had to be able to read and write Hebrew. Elias Levita carried on at least some of his correspondence with Christians in Hebrew.[8] Together with Paul Fagius he composed *Nomenclator* as an aid to would-be authors of Hebrew letters and verse.[9] Sebastian Münster received a number of Hebrew letters written by Jewish correspondents and planned to publish an anthology of them, a work he never completed.[10] By the seventeenth century, Hebrew letter-writing became a somewhat more common expression of the learning of Christian Hebraists, due in part to the efforts of Johannes Buxtorf.

Buxtorf himself began to write Hebrew letters to other Christian Hebraists quite early in his career. He wrote at least four Hebrew letters to his friend Kaspar Waser before 1600.[11] Another of his Hebrew letters, written to Johannes Drusius, earned him a

---

[8] Levita's two extant Hebrew letters to Christians were written to Sebastian Münster and to Johann A. Widmanstadt. Levita to Münster, Venice, 16. Adar 291 (= March 5, 1531), originally printed in David Kimhi, *Commentarium Rabi David Kimhi in Amos Prophetam*, trans. Sebastian Münster (Basel: Henricus Petrus, 1531), f. Aleph 2r, and reprinted with a translation by Moritz Peritz, "Ein Brief Elijah Levita's an Sebastian Münster, nach der von letzterem 1531 besorgten Ausgabe desselben auf's Neue herausgegebenen und mit einer deutschen Uebersetzung und Anmerkungen versehen," *Monatsschrift für Geschichte und Wissenschaft des Judentums* 38 (1894): 258-260, and with Hebrew text only in Prijs, *Drucke*, 497. Levita's letter to Johann A. Widmanstadt, n. p., 8. Siwan 1543 (= May 11, 1543) is preserved in Munich, Bayerische SB Ms Oefeleana 249, and printed in Weil, *Élié Lévita*, 244-246.

[9] Elias Levita, שמות דברים *Nomenclator* (Isny: Paul Fagius, 1542; reprint ed., London: Moshe Rosenfeld, 1988). Rosenthal described it as "an alphabetic listing of Hebrew words and terms which would enable a writer to compose Hebrew letters, prefaces, poems epigrams and the like from either a Latin or a German draft." Frank Rosenthal, "The Study of the Hebrew Bible in Sixteenth Century Italy," *Studies in the Renaissance* 1 (1954): 87.

[10] "Alios...epistolas, quas idem Elias et alii multi Judaei ad me scripserunt, alio tempore evulgabimus, quo multiplex tibi sit formula Hebraice scribendi." Kimhi, *Commentarium*, f. 3v, printed in Prijs, *Drucke*, 524, n. 1.

[11] Six Hebrew letters from Buxtorf to Waser are extant. Buxtorf to Waser, Basel, n. d. (c. 1598-1600), Zürich ZB Ms S-149: 125, 1; idem to idem, n. p., July 28, no year, Zürich ZB Ms S-149: 125, 2; idem to idem, n. p., n. d., Zürich ZB Ms S-149: 125, 3; idem to idem, Basel, April 29, 1594, Zürich ZB Ms S-149: 125, 4; idem to idem, Basel, 1596, Zürich ZB Ms S-149: 125, 5; and idem to idem, December 28, 1593, Zürich ZB Ms S-149: 125, 6.

pretty compliment. In a letter that Drusius later published, he told Buxtorf that he could have written "nothing more learned or elegant."[12] Buxtorf continued to exchange Hebrew letters with Drusius, and later did so with the Drusius' son as well.[13] He also carried on a considerable correspondence with Jews, mainly with regard to the printing business.[14]

Buxtorf thought about publishing a collection of exemplar letters as early as 1599. He told Kaspar Waser that he had heard from the Jews who worked for Waldkirch that printed collections of letters existed, and that he had actually seen one himself.[15] Unfortunately, its Jewish owner refused to part with it.[16] Over the following four years Buxtorf had considerably better luck in collecting source materials on composing letters. He obtained copies of *Iggerot Shelomim* and *Megillat Sefer*, two important collections of letters, and he discovered some of Israel Siforno's correspondence with German and Italian rabbis written while he edited the Basel Talmud.[17] When Drusius heard, presumably from students

---

[12] "Legi epistolam tuam, quam Ebraice scriptam ad me Basilea misisti. Quaeris quid sentiam? nihil ea doctius, nihil elegantius." Johannes Drusius to Johannes Buxtorf, n. p., n. d. (before 1595); the original letter has not been preserved, but it is printed in Drusius, *De Quaesitis*, 153.

[13] Only one of Buxtorf's letters to the elder Drusius is extant: Johannes Buxtorf to Johannes Drusius, September 13, 1597. A copy is preserved in Leeuwarden: Friesland Provincial Library Ms. 731 and it is printed in Fuks, "Brievenboek," 13-14. Several other Hebrew letters in the collection written by Buxtorf to Drusius' son, together with the latter's responses were also published by Fuks.

[14] See above, chap. 2.

[15] A number of Jewish authors had already written works on how to compose Hebrew letters before Buxtorf's day. David B. Ruderman provided a good bibliography on the pedagogical use of letter-writing in *The World of a Renaissance Jew. The Life and Thought of Abraham ben Mordecai Farissol*, Monographs of Hebrew Union College, no. 6 (Cincinnati: Hebrew Union College Press, 1981), 178 n. 42.

[16] "Inter caetere...Libellos quosdam de conscribendis epistolis hebraicis intelligo enim a Judaeis nostris, aliquot ejusmodi esse Venetiis editos in quibus variae habentur formae scribendi epistolas hebraicas, salutandi amicos, inscriptionum et omnia quae ad hunc usu requiruntur. Unum hujusmodi vidi, sed nec prece nec pretio impetrare a pessimo Judaeo possum." Johannes Buxtorf to Kaspar Waser, Basel, May 1, 1599, Zürich ZB Ms S-150: 32.

[17] אגרות שלומים (Augsburg: Hayim Schwarz, 1534), and מגלת ספר (Cremona: n. p., 1566). The British Library of London kindly provided me with microfilms of both works for use in this study (call nos. 1978.b.38 and 1978.b.12). Buxtorf mentioned Siforno's letters in *Sylvula Epistolarum Hebraicarum Familiarium* (Basel: Konrad Waldkirch, 1603), 1, and Johannes Buxtorf to Johannes Drusius,

who had first studied in Basel, that Buxtorf had a book of Hebrew letters he urged Buxtorf to publish it.[18]

Buxtorf's first work on Hebrew letters, *Sylvula Epistolarum Hebraicarum,* was little more than an anthology of models for composition.[19] He translated twelve of the sixty-two letters into Latin and appended a list of the abbreviations that were used in the book.[20] Buxtorf expressed the hope that his book would make it as simple for students to compose letters in Hebrew as it was for them in Latin or Greek. In order to make full use of the book, however, one had to have a good grasp of the grammar and vocabulary of biblical Hebrew, a dictionary for post-biblical Hebrew (he recommended David de Pomi's *Semah David*), and some knowledge of Aramaic grammar.[21] To Drusius' delight Buxtorf dedicated the work to him.[22]

Johannes Uytenbogard and Daniel Heinsius, 1610, *Institutio*, f. *3v. See Prijs, *Drucke*, 524-527. The Basel Talmud (Prijs no. 124) was printed between May, 1578 and autumn of 1580. While the orignial letters have not survived, Buxtorf's stylistic notes on them are preserved in Basel UB Ms A XII 20, pp. 50-120. A. M. Habermann printed some of Buxtorf's notes on these letters in "Fragments of Letters from the Archive of Israel Sifroni in Basel," in his *Studies in the History of Hebrew Printers and Books* (Jerusalem: Rubin Mass, 1978), 272-289 (Hebrew).

[18] "Iam ante per literas enixe flagitasti, praestantissime Drusi, ut quem aliquot ex Schola tua Hebraica discipuli doctissimi, apud me viderant, Epistolarum Hebraicarum libellum, tecum filii tui causa huius linguae studiosissimi ... amice communicarem." Johannes Buxtorf to Johannes Drusius, Basel, August 1, 1603, printed in *Sylvula Epistolarum*, f. 1v.

[19] The Hebrew portion of the book was a virtually unaltered reprint of אגרות שלומים (Augsburg: Hayim Schwarz, 1534). It was printed and distributed as two different works: one with a Hebrew title page for the Jewish market, and one with Latin title page, Buxtorf's Latin introduction and translations for Christians. See Prijs nos. 185A-B. The latter book was *Sylvula Epistolarum*. The Buxtorf family library copy, Basel UB FA VIII 4, contains Buxtorf's marginalia and some editorial markings relating to Buxtorf's other work on letter-writing, *Institutio Epistolaris Hebraica* (Basel: Konrad Waldkirch, 1610).

[20] Although the translations are numbered 1-10, Buxtorf actually translated twelve letters since translation no. 1 is for Hebrew letters 43-45. These letters were also printed together (with Latin translation) in *Institutio* as Hebrew letter no. 19.

[21] Buxtorf, *Sylvula Epistolarum*, 2-4.

[22] "Superioribus nundinis, si recte mea curata sunt, binas a me literas accepisti, una cum libellis, Elohim & Tetragrammaton. Ex iisdem potuisti cognoscere, quam grata mihi fuerit dedicatio Epistolarum Hebraicarum vel potius judaicarum, quanquam in stilo nonnihil desidero." Johannes Drusius to Johannes Buxtorf, Franker, February 21, 1605, Basel UB Ms G I 59: 257, partially reprinted in *Institutio*, f. *6r.

Sylvula Epistolarum Hebraicarum won Buxtorf the respect of one of the most brilliant and irascible scholars of the seventeenth century, Joseph Scaliger. Scaliger wrote to Buxtorf, congratulating him on what he had published. He was certain that the work would awaken a love for Hebrew in many a student.[23] At the same time, he urged Buxtorf not to be satisfied with what he had written. What students really needed was a manual for composing Hebrew letters that thoroughly explained its rules and provided illustrations. No Hebraist was better qualified than Buxtorf to undertake such a task, and he, Scaliger, would be among Buxtorf's first pupils to profit from its publication.[24] By this time Buxtorf badly needed Scaliger's encouragement, since his *Sylvula Epistolarum Hebraicarum* apparently had not been well received by students in Basel itself. Buxtorf commented in his response to Scaliger that very few of his own students had made any progress in Hebrew, but if Scaliger thought that a manual of Hebrew letters would stimulate the study of Hebrew, then he would undertake the task.[25]

Buxtorf's second publication on Hebrew letters, *Institutio Epistolaris Hebraica*, was a far more ambitious work than the first.[26] Buxtorf had shortly before overseen production of a reprint edition of *Megillat Sefer*, a collection of 113 letters that was in-

---

[23] "Hoc sine dubio accendet juventutem nostram amore Hebraismi, quae non odio literarum Hebraicarum a lectione librorum Judaicorum aliena est, sed inopia magistrorum." Joseph Scaliger to Johannes Buxtorf, June 1, 1606, Basel UB Ms G I 59: 363, printed in Scaliger, *Epistolae*, 522.

[24] Quemadmodum igitur, quia non habent, qui eos manu ad fontem deducat, aut saltem ad illud studium accendat, non dubium est, si novum aliquod opus nacti sint, ex quo doctrinae illius institutiones, exempla, & praecepta haurire possint, quin ex illa copia tanto propensiores sint ad Hebraismum amplectendum, quantum ex inopia ab eo deterrebantur. Nullus hodie vivit, qui eam provinciam melius administrare possit, quam tu. Quod si hoc a te impetramus, ego primus in discipulis tuis nomen profiteor meum." Ibid., 522-523.

[25] "In nostris Academiis paucissimi sunt, qui eousque in studio Hebraeo progrediuntur, ut vel scriptitare vel balbutire aliquid Hebraeum audeant, unde non magnopere mihi iste labor cordi fuit. Si tamen hoc qualicunque labore industria Studiosorum incitari & promoveri posset, libenter hoc praestarem." Johannes Buxtorf to Joseph Scaliger, Basel, April 3, 1606, Utrecht UB Ms 987: 237-238; printed in *Sylloges*, 2: 364.

[26] All references to *Institutio* are to the 1629 edition. Prijs noted that Buxtorf II made only small changes to this edition apart from adding a long appendix. *Drucke*, 351-352.

---

tended for the Jewish market.[27] Taking 80 letters from *Megillat Sefer* and adding a further 20 from *Iggerot Shelomim*, Buxtorf assembled a new collection for the use of Christian students.[28] The organizational pattern that he imposed upon the *Institutio Epistolaris* bore no resemblance to either of his sources. He divided the work into two books consisting of 50 letters each, providing vocalized texts, Latin translations, and critical notes for each letter in book one. None of the letters in book two were pointed and translations were provided only for the first ten letters.[29] By grading the level of difficulty and the amount of helps given, Buxtorf hoped both to help beginners and to challenge more advanced students. What distinguished *Institutio Epistolaris* from other earlier collections of Hebrew letters, however, was not the number or difficulty of its model letters or the critical notes given for the sake of beginners, but rather Buxtorf's introduction to the book.

The first eighty pages of *Institutio Epistolaris* comprised a textbook for the composition of Hebrew letters. Since Buxtorf consciously limited his discussion to the composition of private letters rather than to philosophical, theological, or philological treatises, he had little trouble reconciling Ciceronian rules of composition with Hebrew practice.[30] Cicero thought that letters were essentially written conversations between friends and hence should be written briefly and clearly, using simple diction.[31] Accordingly, Buxtorf's definition of a letter was a simple restatement of Cicero's, and the latter's admonitions on style he copied in his chapter on expression

---

[27] מגלת ספר (Basel: Konrad Waldkirch, 1610). Prijs no. 203. The British Library of London kindly suppled me with a microfilm of the book (call no. 1978.b.46).

[28] Buxtorf reprinted eight letters that he had translated into Latin from his earlier edition of אגרות. These were (in order of their appearance in *Institutio*): book 1, letters 9 (#10), 19 (#1), 20 (#2), 26 (#5), 27 (#6), 30 (#7), 49 (#3) and 50 (#4). Prijs, *Drucke*, 316.

[29] Ibid.

[30] This limitation was also forced upon Buxtorf to some degree, since מגלת ספר is essentially an anthology of letters in the private style. *Institutio*, 68. On the Hebrew epistolary styles current in Buxtorf's day, see Ludwig Blau, introduction to Leon Modena, *Leo Modenas Briefe und Schriftstücke: Ein Beitrag zur Geschichte des hebräischen Privatstils*, ed. Ludwig Blau (Strasbourg: Karl J. Trübner, 1907), 3-4.

[31] Henderson, "Erasmus," 332 n. 2, 352.

(*sermo*).[32] Since the form of Hebrew prose used in letters was modeled upon biblical Hebrew, Buxtorf emphasized the pedagogical importance of these letters for helping students attain a better grasp of Hebrew.[33] Concentrating upon the private style also had the added benefit of teaching the only kind of composition that Christian students were likely to need when composing letters to Jews.[34] The appended Hebrew letter from a Nuremberg area Jew served to remind Buxtorf's readers that instruction in Hebrew letter-writing had practical benefits as well as heuristic ones.[35]

Buxtorf divided his discussion of the elements of Hebrew letters into three parts dealing with the essence of a letter (*res*), including both the constant formal elements that defined it (*stata*) and the different categories of letters as defined by Latin rhetoricians, the manner of expression (*sermo*), and a chapter on the importance of imitation and exercise for developing a good epistolary style.[36] Buxtorf devoted the bulk of his work to the formal parts of a Hebrew letter. He discussed the salutation (*exordio*), opening paragraph (*narratio*), conclusion (*clausula*) and superscript (*superscriptio*), explaining each element and giving numerous examples. These examples were important not only for the sake of eloquence, but also to ensure that an appropriate tone was employed in composition. In his discussion of forms of address, for example, he gave salutation formulae for wealthy men, learned rabbis, great men, honorable old men, heads of households, and

---

[32] Buxtorf, *Institutio*, 7-8, 69-74.

[33] "In hoc numero cupio esse omnes, qui per sanctae linguae Hebraeae accuratiorem, cognitionem, firmius & solidius de vera Verbi Dei, quod Hebraice conscriptum est, interpretatione judicare solicite cupiunt, quorum conatus omni studio juvare, ut animus est, ita vitam & vires inter tot nunc circumvallantes nos calamitates, Deus elementer suppeditet." Ibid., 80.

[34] Curiously some scholars criticized Buxtorf's work on letter-writing for this reason. "Memini, quosdam viros doctos improbasse meum studium in edendis Epistolis Hebraicis, & de earum conscribendarum ratione, quod vile judicarent, locutiones lacras ad vulgarem & profanum usum accommodare." Buxtorf to Avianus, Basel, July 3, 1626, printed in *Clavis*, f. b8r.

[35] Buxtorf wrote, "Hebraea lingua pudorem etiam rebus inanimatis tribuit. Unde ne sequentes paginas pudeat vacuas exire, ornabo eas epistola honoraria, quam a docto Rabbino ad me perscriptam, Lectori benevolo in auctarium deferant (read: deferam)." Ibid., 357-359, printed in Prijs, *Drucke*, 317, 528.

[36] Ibid., 8, 69, 75.

friends. He also gave suggestions on seasonal references to festivals such as Passover and Yom Kippur.[37]

Buxtorf mentioned several times that he drew many of the example formulae from actual Hebrew letters written to the editor of the Basel Talmud, but these were not the only manuscript letters to which he had access.[38] He himself had had at least a decade of experience reading and writing business letters in Hebrew and drew upon his own correspondence for some examples.[39] Buxtorf kept extensive notes on Jewish letters usage in his study notebook, following a practice that Latin teachers routinely admonished their students to adopt.[40]

Buxtorf divided all letters into three general categories: serious (*serium*), learned (*doctum*), and private (*familiare*). Under "serious" letters he gave a host of categories common in Latin manuals including letters of persuasion, dissuasion, exhortatory, vituperation, consolation etc., without mentioning any specifically Hebrew examples.[41] "Learned" letters he divided into philological, philosophical, and theological works. Under the first and third of these categories Buxtorf mentioned *responsa*, and under the second "letters" composed by Nahmanides and Maimonides, the latter

---

[37] Ibid., 20-27. Nearly all of the temporal and seasonal formulae (11 of 14), and three of the honorific ones, the formula of address for an honorable old man and two for leaders (pp. 20-21), were taken from a list printed in ספר מגלת (Basel: Konrad Waldkirch, 1610), ff. A2r-4r.

[38] Ibid., *3v, 30, 61.

[39] He explicitly mentioned one letter that he received from Elijah Loanz, the Rabbi of Hanau, whose salutation he reproduced as an example on pp. 27-28.

[40] For example, in his discussion of one kind of concluding phrase Buxtorf gave twelve examples, nine of which he drew from his notes on the subject. See Basel UB Ms A XII 20, f. 102, examples 2, 4, 6, 7, 8, 9, 10, 14, 15 and cf. *Institutio*, 51. The examples on p. 102 were assigned other numbers that correspond to the order in which they appear on the page in *Institutio*, suggesting that notebook was written before the book. On the use of notebooks, see E. Catherine Dunn, "Lipsius and the Art of Letter-Writing," *Studies in the Renaissance* 3 (1956): 140.

[41] Erasmus gave a list of the three major classes of letters, persuasive, encomiastic and judicial, together with their subdivisions, in *On the Art of Writing Letters*, ed. J. K. Sowards, in *The Collected Works of Erasmus*, vol. 25 (Toronto: Univ. of Toronto Press, 1985), 71.

available in Latin translation.[42] Buxtorf indicated that his discussion would focus upon writing Hebrew letters in the private style.[43]

Writers could only achieve a pure Hebrew epistolary style through careful use of expression and the imitation of worthy models. Letters were to be simple, brief and clear in their formulation.[44] Following Cicero's dictates raised some problems for would-be Hebrew writers, however. Since Hebrew was not a spoken language among Christians, how could "simplicity" of diction be determined? Buxtorf proposed following the Jews' example and regarding biblical words as being the equivalent of popular speech.[45] The Jews associated a good Hebrew style with the language of the Bible.[46] He urged his readers to use the language respectfully, avoiding unnatural, overly clever constructions, and twisting the language. Written illustrations should guide the writer. When no biblical word or phrase was appropriate, then one commonly used by learned rabbinical writers could be employed.[47]

Aside from following Hebrew usage present within the Bible itself, the best way to learn elegant and pure Hebrew diction, according to Buxtorf, was to imitate good examples of composition. Accordingly, he discussed the suitability of three different letter collections as stylistic models: *Megillat Sefer, Iggerot Shelomim,* and Samuel Archevolti's *Mayan Gannim.* The latter two books did not contain, he thought, particularly good examples of style,

---

[42] Ibid., 67-68. The two works are Moses Nahmanides, אגרת הקדש (Basel: A. Froben, 1581), and Moses Maimonides, אגרת...על גזרת משעטי הכוכבים, trans. Johannes Isaac Levita, (Cologne: Maternum Colinum, 1555).

[43] Ibid., 68.

[44] Ibid., 69.

[45] "Atqui Hebraeus sermo nobis Christianis non est naturalis, multo minus quotidianus: quomodo ergo ejus simplicitatem scripto assequemur? Imitemur Judaeos. ... Simplicem & quotidiano sermoni similem stilum, acquiremus ex libris Veteris Testamenti Hebraicis, in quibus solis hodie linguae simplicitas, puritas, gravitas, venustas & decentia omnis comprehenditur." Ibid., 70.

[46] Buxtorf quoted the Yiddish saying of approval, "Unde quem Judaei Germani ab usu & peritia linguae Hebraeae summe commendare volunt, de eo dicunt, "Er schreibet eitel *pasuk laschon,* id est, puro puto stilo biblico in scribendo utitur." Ibid., 74. See Arthur M. Lesley, "Jewish Adaptations of Humanist Concepts in Fifteenth- and Sixteenth Century Italy," in: *Renaissance Rereadings: Intertext and Context,* eds. Maryanne Cline Horowitz, Anne J. Cruz and Wenday A. Furman (Urbana: Univ. of Illinois Press, 1988), 56-58, 63-64.

[47] "Ad hanc virtutem primo adhibeas verba propria: fugias aliena atque audacius translata, aut prave flexa & detorta: lectis atque illustribus utaris, in quibus plenum quiddam & sonas inesse videatur." Ibid., 73.

Iggerot because its diction was not purely biblical and *Mayan* because of its rather florid prose. Archevolti made extensive use of metaphor, allegory, hyperbole and rather grandiose diction, "not adorning but deforming" his compositions.[48] Students were to look to their models for appropriate formulae, words and especially figures of speech, such as parables, allegories, and proverbs. For the figures of speech, Buxtorf strongly recommended that students consult *Pirke Abot* and several of Johannes Drusius' works.[49]

Buxtorf's *Institutio Epistolaris* was intended to serve as a textbook for instruction in composing Hebrew prose. While the application of Ciceronian standards of composition to Hebrew composition might seem inappropriate to readers of a later century, it was unavoidable to Hebraists of Buxtorf's day. Curiously Cicero's ideas on private epistolary style and the standards of Hebrew style expressed by the sample letters in Buxtorf's anthology complement each another. While Buxtorf may have treated some prose styles unfairly, notably that of Samuel Archevolti, his purpose was not to teach every style of Hebrew composition, but only what he, and some Jewish authorities, considered to be the "best" style. Prijs thought that parts of Buxtorf's treatment have yet to be superseded, a rather unusual distinction for a literary manual written 370 years ago.[50]

Institutio Epistolaris Hebraica was not a commercial success as so many of Buxtorf's other textbooks were. It was only reprinted once, in 1629. Buxtorf's son supervised its reprinting, and he added an appendix containing a number of letters written by Maimonides, Nahmanides, David Kimhi, Samuel Ibn Tibbon, and other scholars on philosophical and theological topics to the book. While no pedagogical reason was given for their inclusion, these letters may have been added to offset some of the work's bias in

---

[48] "Nam stilus in eo sublimior, metaphoris, allegoriis, hyperbolis, plenus, gravis & grandiliquus saepe usque ad vitium, quo ipso faciem epistolarem non ornat sed deformat ...." Ibid., 76.

[49] Ibid., 76-77. The two Drusius books mentioned are *Proverbiorum classes duae* (Franeker: Aegidius Radaeus, 1590), and *Proverbia Bensirae ... Accesserunt Adagiorum Ebraïeorum ...* . (Franeker: Aegidius Radaeus, 1597).

[50] See Prijs, *Drucke*, 316. More recently Roberto Bonfil echoed Prijs' judgement in "Una 'Enciclopedia' di Sapere Sociale. L'epistolario ebraico quattrocentesco di Josef Sark," *Revista Critica di Storia della Filosofia* (Firenze) 40 (1985): 116, n. 7.

favor of personal correspondence; they may also reflect the younger Buxtorf's philosophical interests.[51] If students were to learn to read more technical post-biblical Hebrew they needed examples of the treatment of theological and philosophical topics.[52]

Composition of Hebrew letters never became a standard element of Hebrew instruction in European universities as Buxtorf hoped, but his manual may have aided the private study of later Christian Hebraists. Buxtorf II used it in teaching, as can be seen from Johann Jacob Buxtorf's notebook of 1658, which contains translations from *Institutio Epistolaris*. Johann Heinrich Hottinger purchased seven copies of the book from Ludwig König during 1645, probably for classroom use.[53] A number of Christian scholars active during the seventeenth century were known to have corresponded with Jews in Hebrew for various reasons, among them Johannes Buxtorf II and his friend Johann Heinrich Hottinger.[54] Since Buxtorf's *Institutio Epistolaris* was the only work of its kind, the existence of these letters suggests that the book did not go completely unread.

The other aspect of Hebrew composition that Buxtorf addressed in his works was poetry. His essay *Tractatus Brevis de Prosodia Metrica* was written for the first edition of *Thesaurus Grammaticus* and reprinted in every subsequent edition.[55] While he provided some analysis of biblical poetry, the bulk of Buxtorf's discussion concerned post-biblical metrics. He hoped that his introduction to Hebrew poetics would incite students to a greater love for the

---

[51] Carlos Gilly, *Spanien und der Basler Buchdruck*, 70-72.

[52] Ibid., 351-3. Johannes Buxtorf II mentioned his work reprinting the *Institutio* in a letter to Petrus Cunaeus, Basel, March 20, 1629, Leiden UB Ms Cun 2: 102, printed in Cunaeus, *Epistolae*, 164-165.

[53] On Johann Jacob Buxtorf's notebook, Basel UB Ms A XII 3, no. 12, see my description in "Buxtorf Family Papers," in: Prijs, *Handschriften*, 77, ms 60/12. See also Ludwig König to Johann Heinrich Hottinger, n. p., January 5, 1645; idem to idem, Basel, August 27, 1645; and idem to idem, Basel, July 2, 1645, Zürich ZB Ms F 55: 7, 9, 11.

[54] J. W. Wesselius mentioned a number of instances where Jews and Christians corresponded in Hebrew during the seventeenth century in "Johannes Drusius the Younger's Last Journey to England and his Hebrew Letter-Book," *Lias* 16 (1989): 172-173, nn. 5-11. Buxtorf II's correspondence is preserved in Basel UB Ms G I 62: 321-358; parts of it have been published. See Burnett, "Buxtorf Family Papers," 87-88. Braunschweig's correspondence with Hottinger is preserved in the Zürich ZB, Ms F 85, ff. 526-575.

[55] Buxtorf, *Thesaurus Grammaticus*, 625-658.

Hebrew language and would encourage them to try their hand at composing their own Hebrew verse.[56]

The use of meter and rhyme in Hebrew poetry was the first question addressed in the *Tractatus*. The idea that biblical Hebrew poetry could be scanned according to the rules of Greek and Latin poetry originated with Philo and Josephus. The latter suggested that Moses composed the Song of the Sea (Exod. 15: 1-8) in hexameter verse.[57] Buxtorf thought that Hebrew poetry in general could be defined either metrically or by the use of rhyme.[58] He argued that scansion of biblical Hebrew verse involved counting the total number of syllables rather than applying the Greco-Latin quantitative system.

> Meter (in the Bible) consists of a certain number of syllables, according to R. Mosche Schem Tobh (ibn Habib) and other Hebrews... [A] metric line is completed with a single half-verse (*versus*), or by two hemistichs, or even three or four strung together so that one פָּסוּק or verse will include a tristichon or tetrastichon.... Each hemistich has either an equal number of syllables, or else one or the other will go beyond the number.... Of the exceeding meter, that is when one hemistich or the other has a greater number of syllables, there are infinite examples, and almost all of the sacred songs are so defined, in which either the extra number is absorbed by a speeding up of the time-measuring, or the deficiency is filled out and made complete by a smooth varying and drawing-out of the voice.[59]

Buxtorf thought that the biblical poets were much less concerned about exact syllabic equivalence of hemistichs than the Greek and

---

[56] "Quantitatis & pedum rationem, quam exquisite & perspicue ex usu ipso exposuimus, ita ut juventus studuii hujus amore inflammata, imitationis viam hîc planam & expeditam habeat." Ibid., 658.

[57] James Kugel, "The Influence of Moses ibn Habib's *Darkhei Noam*," in: *Jewish Thought in the Sixteenth Century*, ed. Bernard Dov Cooperman, Harvard University Center for Jewish Studies: Texts and Studies, no. 2 (Cambridge, MA: Harvard Univ. Press, 1983), 324, n. 39, quoting Josephus, *Jewish Antiquities*, II, 16: 14. For Philo's views of Hebrew poetics see Israel Baroway, "The Hebrew Hexameter: A Study in Renaissance Sources and Interpretation," *English Literary History* 2 (1935): 66-67. My discussion of of Buxtorf's ideas of Jewish poetics owes much to Kugel's fine essay.

[58] "Numerus poëticus est vel Metrum vel Rhythmum." Buxtorf, *Thesaurus Grammaticus*, 627.

[59] Ibid., 628-629, translated by Kugel, "Influence," 315. Adele Berlin translated a larger portion of Ibn Habib's discussion of poetic meter in *Biblical Poetry through Medieval Jewish Eyes*, Indiana Studies in Biblical Literature (Bloomington: Indiana Univ. Press, 1991), 115-118.

Latin poets were about the exact conformity of their verses to recognized meters.

In his discussion of the nature of metric feet, Buxtorf used a curious mixture of terms drawn both from medieval Jewish poetics and from traditional analysis of Greek and Latin poetry. He described biblical verse in terms coined by medieval Jewish scholars, referring to each biblical Hebrew poetic line as a *Bayit* that consisted of two Hemistichs, the former called the *Delet*, and the latter, the *Soger*.[60] Buxtorf fully identified the kinds of metric feet used in post-biblical Hebrew poetry with classical units of scansion. He did so by taking the two basic metric "feet" of medieval Hebrew poetry, the *tenua* and the *yated*, and correlating various combinations of them with classical feet.[61] The *tenua*, for example, he called a semi-spondee; two of them together formed a spondee, and three of them consecutively were defined as a *molossus*.[62] The *yated* Buxtorf incorrectly identified with the classical iamb, following the description by Solomon Almoli.[63] If a semi-spondee was added to the iamb then a *bachius* was formed, and if a semi-spondee preceded the iamb then it would be scanned as a cretic foot.[64]

Armed with these familiar scansion units Buxtorf set about the task of analyzing Hebrew versification. He identified 23 types of meter in all, most of them involving combinations of different kinds of metric feet.[65] Five metric schemes he identified as

---

[60] Ibid., 627-628. See Dan Pagis, "Hebrew Metrics in Italy and the Invention of Hebrew Accentual Iambs," (Hebrew) *ha-Sifrut* 4 (1973), English summary, xxxiii. What later grammarians considered short and long vowels within Hebrew, e. g. *segol* and *sere*, have no relevance for this kind of scansion.

[61] "Hebrew-Spanish prosody distinguished between short and long syllables, the short corresponding to a consonant vocalized by a semi vowel (*sheva* or *hataf*), the long by a full vowel (*tenua*). The *sheva* was considered dependent upon the *tenua* which followed it." Ibid., xxxiii.

[62] As examples of semi-spondee, a spondee, and a *molossus* Buxtorf suggested אָב, סָפַר, and כַּפִּים. Buxtorf, *Thesaurus Grammaticus*, 631.

[63] "Iathed autem dicitur quodlibet scheva mobile, ubi praeterea aliqua motionum accedit, qualis est dictio שְׁמוֹר shemor." *Libellus de Metris Hebraicis e Grammatica R. Davidis Iehaiae, cuius inscriptio*, למודים, in Génébrard, *Eisagoge*, 150.

[64] Buxtorf, *Thesaurus Grammaticus*, 631-632. For a brief explanation of Latin meters see B. L. Gildersleeve and Gonzalez Lodge, *Gildersleeve's Latin Grammar*, 3d ed. (New York: University Publishing Co., 1898), 456-457.

[65] Buxtorf's meters bear little resemblance to those mentioned by Almoli, whose meters were derived from Abraham Ibn Ezra's classic discussion in *Sefer*

"simple" because they involved the use of only spondees or semi-spondees.[66] The composite schemes he classified according to the number of feet per line, whether two, three, four, five or six.[67] For example, he identified three different kinds of Tetrameter verse schemes in Hebrew. These patterns were:

> spondee, iamb, spondee, spondee
> iamb, spondee, iamb, spondee
> and spondee, iamb, spondee, iamb.[68]

To illustrate the first pattern Buxtorf gave an example drawn from Ibn Ezra's poetry.[69]

קוּמָה אֱלֹהִים עֶזְרָתָה
לִי וַעֲנֵה בַּצָּרָתָה

Buxtorf drew his other Tetrameter examples from Elias Levita's *Capitula Cantici*, from the liturgical poem *Adon Olam*,[70] and from Ibn Gabirol's poetry, leaving the reader with the false impression that he had analyzed a good deal of poetry before coming to his conclusions.

The Jewish sources that Buxtorf used to illustrate his metric analysis of Hebrew were, in fact, fairly limited. Gilbert Génébrard's translation of Solomon Almoli's *Shekel ha-Qodesh* provided ten example verses, including all of his quotations from Ibn Gabirol, Ibn Ezra, Maimonides, and Judah ha-Levi.[71] He also drew examples from Elias Levita's *Capitula Cantici*, a series of di-

---

Sahot. See Abraham Ibn Ezra, *Sefer Sahot de Abraham Ibn Ezra: edición crítica y versión castellana*, ed. and trans. Carlos del Valle Rodriguez, Bibliotheca Salmanticensis Dissertationes, no. 1 (Salamanca: University of Salamanca, 1977), 146-159 and Pagis, "Hebrew Metrics," xxxiii, xxxviii.

[66] "Simplex, quod ex meris syllabis longis, spondeis vel semispondeis constat." Buxtorf, *Thesaurus Grammaticus*, 637.

[67] The only exception to this was Buxtorf's discussion of pure cretic verse, a poetic form he thought barbaric. Ibid., 656-657.

[68] Ibid., 641-643. Please note that Hebrew scansion patterns, like Hebrew itself, must be read from right to left.

[69] Ibid., 641. Buxtorf drew the Ibn Ezra example from Almoli, *Libellus de Metris*, 158.

[70] Kugel, "Influence," 314.

[71] Buxtorf, *Thesaurus Grammaticus*, 641-644, 646-647, 650-652.

dactic poems on Hebrew grammar, and Hai Gaon b. Sherira's *Shire Musar Haskel*.[72] Nearly all of the other examples analyzed by Buxtorf were drawn from dedicatory or introductory poems printed in books, including Levita's poems for the second Bomberg rabbinical Bible, and his own *Masoret ha-Masoret* and *Tishbi*, and introductory poems from the *Zohar*, David Gans's *Semah David* and Kimhi's *Miklol*.[73]

Although Buxtorf devoted some of his discussion to medieval Hebrew metrics, he was clearly at least as interested in relatively recent Hebrew verse, particularly in the kinds used to compose honorific verses given in the beginnings of books. The latter concern tallied neatly with the pedagogical purpose of the *Tractatus*. If Hebrew were to come into more common use as a humanistic language, then would-be users needed both instruction and models for its more common poetic uses. Buxtorf himself had composed Hebrew verses for specific occasions and expected his students to learn the skill.[74] It was not his remarks on Hebrew meter that had the most lasting impact upon subsequent scholarship, however, but his discussion of the role of rhyme in Hebrew poetry.

Rhyme was not an essential quality of Hebrew poetry, either from the biblical period or later, according to Buxtorf. "Rhyming verse was not cultivated in a manner other than what might be produced spontaneously and happen quite by chance, not that it seem to be summoned up by some belabored attention."[75] Buxtorf did, however, allow for the possibility of rhyming verse. Jerome wrote in his introduction to the book of Job, "Sometimes as well a sweet jingling rhythmical effect is achieved by the poetic arrangement being set free from the laws of meter." Buxtorf understood Jerome's use of the word "rhythmus" to mean "rhyme" as it did in

---

[72] Ibid., 633-634, 638, 641-644, 647-648. Buxtorf consulted Elias Levita, *Capitula Cantici* (Basel: Johann Froben, 1527), Prijs no. 27, and Hai Gaon, שירי מוסר השכל, trans. Jacob Ebert (Frankfurt/O: n. p., 1597), ff. A4v-6r. Buxtorf's copy of the latter book is Basel UB FA VIII 13.

[73] Buxtorf, *Thesaurus Grammaticus*, 639, 644, 648, 652, 653, 655.

[74] For example, he wrote a laudatory Hebrew poem for Kaspar Waser's *Archetypus Grammaticae Hebraeae* (Basel: Konrad Waldkirch, 1600), appearing on f. a8v (Prijs, *Drucke*, 274) and another honoring Balthasar Crosniewicius when the latter received his doctorate in theology. *Carmina Gratulatoria*, f. A2v.

[75] Buxtorf, *Theasurus Grammaticus*, 629, translated by Kugel, "Influence," 315-316.

Latin of the early modern period.[76] To this slight misunderstanding of Jerome Buxtorf added a wrongly understood illustration, taken from Moses Ibn Habib's *Marpe Lashon*.

> R. Mosche Shem Tov...wrote in the pamphlet מרפא לשון that he had seen during his long wanderings, on a certain high mountain the tombstone of Amaziah the king of the Jews, on which he was able to read these words incised, the rest having been obliterated by age:
>
> שאו קינה בקול מרה לשר גדול לקחו י-ה לאמציה
>
> He understood from the similar endings of these words, that rhyming verse was then in use at the time when the Israelites still dwelt in their own land.[77]

Habib's point was to prove that Spanish style verse, using *tenuot* and *yetedot*, existed in biblical times. Buxtorf apparently thought that the inscription was a poem in which the every second word was the end of a stich, and rhymed with the word at the end of the next stich (e. g. קינה and מרה).

Hebrew rhyme, according to Buxtorf, was essentially a matching of endings. Following Solomon Almoli he distinguished between three kinds of rhyme. The *Shir ober* (שׁיר עֹבֵר) required that the final letters of corresponding words match. The final two letters of corresponding words had to be alike in the second variety, *Shir raui* (שׁיר רָאוּי). For final type of rhyme, the *Shir mishibbah* (שׁיר מְשֻׁבָּח) the final three consonants had to match.[78] With respect to the practice of Hebrew rhyme Buxtorf added nothing beyond what Almoli had already written.

Poetry was rather marginal to Buxtorf's scholarly concerns and the *Tractatus* was a mere appendix to a larger, more important work. It does illustrate, again, the importance of Jewish authorities in Buxtorf's philological discussions of any aspect of Hebrew literature. While he demonstrated some ingenuity (perhaps too much) in identifying so many different Latin meters with the quantitative forms of Hebrew verse, his theoretical discussion of Hebrew poetry was derived almost entirely from Moses Ibn

---

76 Ibid., 626. Kugel, "Influence," 324, nn. 39 and 43. Kugel translated the quotation from Jerome, *Praefatio in Libro Job, MPL* 28: 1081-2.

77 Ibid., 635-636, trans. by Kugel, "Influence," 316.

78 As examples of rhymed pairs Buxtorf suggested as examples for type (1) אָבַד and בָּדָד, (2) לֵאמֹר and לִשְׁמֹר and (3) דְּבָרִים and גְּבָרִים. *Thesaurus Grammaticus*, 636. Cf. Almoli, *Libellus de Metris*, 152-153.

Habib's *Marpe Lashon* and Solomon Almoli's *Sheqel ha-Qodesh*. His purpose in writing *Tractatus* was also similar to theirs: to explain the principles of Hebrew meter and to compile examples of different metrical patterns for would-be poets to emulate.[79] While it is difficult to assess its pedagogical usefulness for teaching the composition of Hebrew verse, Buxtorf's explanations of meter would have been easily understood by his Latin-educated readers. Further research on Hebrew verse composed by Christians is necessary before an assessment of the importance of Buxtorf's contribution to this rather unusual field can be made.[80] After the elder Buxtorf's death, five scholars sent Hebrew verses as expressions of homage to Buxtorf II, which he had printed with Daniel Tossanus' funeral oration.[81]

The nature of Hebrew verse continued to be a hotly debated topic among Christian Hebraists throughout the seventeenth century, and Buxtorf's *Tractatus* played a part in the discussion. Buxtorf's correspondent Franciscus Gomarus, perhaps with the *Tractatus* in mind, composed a systematic description of biblical verse, analyzed according to classical meter.[82] Jean Le Clerc disagreed strongly with Buxtorf's views on rhyme and tried to prove that rhyme was the sole structural constant of biblical poetry.[83] Buxtorf's contributions to this debate and to Hebrew composition in general were, however, insignificant when compared with his immensely important work in the field of Hebrew bibliography.

De Abbreviaturis Hebraicis was one of Buxtorf's most significant works on post-biblical Hebrew literature. It provided a key to Hebrew abbreviations, catchword titles for parts of the Talmud and the Pentateuch, and a bibliography of books written in Hebrew and Yiddish. By his own account Buxtorf had planned only to write a treatise on abbreviations, but when he discovered that so many of

---

[79] Ibid., 309.

[80] George A Kohut, "The Hebrew Letters of Jacob Alting," in: *Festschrift für Aron Freimann zum 60. Geburtstage*, Soncino-Blätter, Bd. 4., ed. Alexander Marx and Herrmann Meyer (Berlin: Soncino-Gesellschaft, 1935), 70.

[81] Tossanus, *Oratio*, 23-24, 31-32, 35, 37, 48. See Prijs, *Drucke*, 354-355.

[82] Israel Baroway, ""The Lyre of David:" A Further Study of Renaissance Interpretation of Biblical Form," *English Literary History* 8 (1941): 119-142.

[83] Kugel, "Influence," 318-319.

them represented either parts of the Talmud, the Bible or other books he decided to compile a bibliography as well.[84]

The extensive use of abbreviations in Hebrew books and manuscripts was a major obstacle for Christian readers to overcome as they studied post-biblical Jewish literature. Other Christian Hebraists before Buxtorf's time, notably Sebastian Münster, Jean Mercier, and Johannes Quinquarboreus, had published lists of them. Quinquarboreus' own work was quite extensive, discussing 571 different abbreviations in 91 pages.[85] Buxtorf, however, found them to be unsatisfactory and produced a much longer work of his own to replace them.

Buxtorf began his discussion with an introduction explaining the kinds of abbreviations in use among the Jews. He divided them into two classes, proper and improper. Proper abbreviations were those in which each letter was the first letter of another word. To illustrate a proper abbreviation Buxtorf used the example ז"ל, meaning "of blessed memory." He further divided proper abbreviations into those in use generally among Hebrew authors and those unique to specific authors or kinds of literature. The authors of the Talmud, the Masora and prayer books, together with grammarians and kabbalistic authors had their own abbreviations.[86] By "improper" abbreviations Buxtorf meant truncated words, which were often used

---

[84] "Animus erat, Abbreviaturas Hebraicas dumtaxat, post alios omnes lucidius explicatas, & dilatatas, hoc tempore proponere. His per accidens in media via accessere, Operis Talmudici recensio, & Bibliotheca Rabbinica. Animadvertebam enim, plura ex his abbreviate proponi apud Scriptores, quam a me inter Abbreviaturas relata. Ut ergo quam minimum in talibus desideraretur, libros & capita Talmudica perfecte; Rabbinicos libros, quot cursim potui, in aciem disposui." Johannes Buxtorf's dedicatory letter to Philippe du Plessis de Mornay, Basel, August 7, 1613, *De Abbreviaturis*, f.):(3r.

[85] Quinquarboreus wrote that he used the works of five Christian authors in compiling his work: Johannes Cellarius, Sanctes Pagninus, Matthaeus Aurogallus, Sebastian Münster and Jean Mercier. *De Notis Hebraeorum Liber, Hoc est De Literis Multarum Literarum vim habentibus, quae hactenus à viris doctissimis ex variis Hebraeorum authoribus sunt excerptae* (Paris: Martinum Juvenem, 1582), 2-3.

[86] "Speciales sive privatae, quae in auctore aliquo certo, certo libro, certa ac speciali aliqua materia magis usurpantur, quarum ussu alibi incommodus esset. Sic Grammatici, Masorethae, Talmudici suas habent privatas abbreviaturas; sic in libris precum, in libris ritualibus, in libris Cabalisticis aliisque similibus, certae ac speciales abbreviaturae sunt." *De Abbreviaturis*, 4.

in the masoretic apparatus of Hebrew Bibles, but sometimes in other kinds of books as well.[87]

Buxtorf's treatment of abbreviations was not, however, simply a list of cryptic symbols and their meanings. In common with his predecessors Buxtorf took the opportunity to discuss the concepts inherent in the terms represented by the abbreviations. Among the abbreviations beginning with the letter Resh, for example, thirty six rabbis are listed and Buxtorf provided brief capsule biographies for many of them.[88] Under the abbreviations אט"בח and את"בש Buxtorf gave an explanations of the kabbalistic concepts.[89]

Buxtorf also took full advantage of the work of other Christian Hebraists on Hebrew abbreviations in his own treatise. He consulted Galatinus' *Opus de Arcanis Catholicae Veritatis*, and Reuchlin's *De Arte Cabalistica* for kabbalistic abbreviations.[90] He owned copies of both Mercier's and Quinquarboreus' books and used them in his discussion.[91] The latter work probably served as the basis of *De Abbreviaturis*, and a comparison between the two books is revealing. Buxtorf's book had 639 entries while Quinquarboreus' had 571, a difference of only 68, which suggests that the difference in coverage was only about ten percent. A closer examination of Buxtorf's work belies this first impression. Under the letter Aleph, for example, Buxtorf discussed 86 abbreviations while Quinquarboreus listed only 60. Of these, 38 are unique to Buxtorf's work, but only 10 are unique to the latter. Moreover, Buxtorf's treatment of those entries that are common to both books is generally more detailed. For twelve entries in which both Buxtorf and Quinquarboreus gave more than one definition, the former listed more possibilities.[92]

---

[87] For example, the use of אונק׳ for אונקלוס, and וגו׳ for וגומר. Ibid., 4-6.

[88] Ibid., 154-170.

[89] Ibid., 25-28, 37-38. See Cecil Roth and Geoffrey Wigoder, eds., *Encyclopaedia Judaica* (Jerusalem: Macmillan, 1971-1972), s. v. "Acrostics," by Nahum M. Sarna and Yehuda A. Klausner.

[90] Buxtorf, *De Abbreviaturis*, 20, 38 and 84. Quinquarboreus also used Reuchlin's *Cabalistica*. See *De Notis*, 17, 27, 41 *passim*.

[91] Jean Mercier, *Tabulae in Grammaticen linguae Chaldaeae, quae & Syrica dicitur* (Paris: Guillaume Morelium, 1560), Basel UB FB III 5/4, and Quinquarboreus, *De Notis*, Basel UB FB I 10. Cf. Buxtorf, *De Abbreviaturis*, 30, 64, 135, 168.

[92] See the entries for "א"ת, א"א, א"ה, א"ח, א"יה, א"ם, א"נ, א"ע, א"ק, א"ש, and א"תל in *De Abbreviaturis*, 12-14, 22-23, 26, 28-32, 34, 36-38, and in *De*

In addition to his printed sources Buxtorf also consulted some manuscript notes on abbreviations composed by Pierre Chevallier, one of the censors for the Basel Talmud.[93] Chevallier apparently used either Mercier or Quinquarboreus as his base text and added a number of his own corrections. Isaac Casaubon, a friend and colleague of Chevallier's at Geneva before the latter's death, apparently gave Buxtorf his copies of Chevallier's personal notes.[94] These notes Buxtorf put to good use in expanding upon some of Quinquarboreus' entries.[95]

In common with Mercier and Quinquarboreus, Buxtorf also made extensive use of Jewish sources to explain Hebrew abbreviations.[96] The most obvious places to look were lexicons and Buxtorf used David Kimhi's *Sefer ha-Shorashim*, Nathan b. Yehiel's *Aruk*, and Elias Levita's *Tishbi* and *Meturgemann*.[97] Buxtorf also gathered further examples of abbreviations from other books, and in-

---

Notis, 7-11, 13-17. Only in one instance, א"אכ, did Quinquarboreus propose more definitions than Buxtorf did, two instead of one. *De Abbreviaturis*, 15 and *De Notis*, 8.

[93] *Abbreviaturae quibus Rabbini in suis commentarijs utuntur, transcriptae ex Cevallerii autographo, emendante Isaaco Casaubono. Genevae Anno 1596 Mense Majo*, Basel UB Ms Ki Ar 190a, ff. 2r-7r. The notes treat only abbreviations beginning with the letter Aleph. Whether these pages are only a fragment of a larger collection that has not been preserved is unclear. On Pierre Chevallier see Wackernagel, *Matrikel*, 2: 259, and Prijs, *Drucke*, 176, 180.

[94] Isaac Casaubon was one of the premier scholars of classical and patristic Greek of the seventeenth century. See Pattison, *Isaac Casaubon*. In the only extant letter from Casaubon to Buxtorf the former told Buxtorf of his friendship with Chevallier and offered to lend Buxtorf a copy of Münster's *Dictionarium chaldaicum* (Prijs no. 26) that had once belonged to Jean Mercier and then to Chevallier and was full of their marginalia. Isaac Casaubon to Johannes Buxtorf, Paris, February 12, 1610, Basel UB G I 62: 99-100, printed in Buxtorf, *Catalecta*, 461-463.

[95] For example in the entry for "א Buxtorf added the word אֲוִיר, and in א"א he added the phrase אֲנִי אָמַר, both of which are noted by Chevallier. Compare Chevallier's discussion of "א, א"א, א"אא, א"בד, א"בי, א"ה, א"בח, אט"בח, and ח"א in *Abbreviaturae*, Basel UB Ms Ki Ar 190a, ff. 2r-4v, with the corresponding entries in Buxtorf, *De Abbreviaturis*, 12-14, 17, 19, 23-26 and *De Notis*, 7-10.

[96] Quinquarboreus used Elias Levita's תשבי, and the third part of מסורת המסורת which dealt with masoretic abbreviations a number of times in his discussion. *De Notis*, 12-13, 22-23, 26, 28-29, *passim*.

[97] See Buxtorf, *De Abbreviaturis*, 149, 186, 202 and 226 for the ערוך, p. 90 for מתורגמן, p. 147 for ספר השרשים and pp. 87, 109-110, 147 and p. 187 for תשבי.

cluded references to Judah b. Samuel, *Hasidim, Abqat Rokel, Kaphtor* and Abraham ibn Daud, *Sefer ha-Qabalah*.[98]

In addition to his treatment of abbreviations, Buxtorf also included two short sections with the catchword titles for various parts of the Talmud and Pentateuch. The use of *incipits* to identify books or parts of books was hardly a foreign concept to Christian Hebraists of the seventeenth century, but they were unfamiliar with the specific standardized catchword titles used by Jewish authors. By providing alphabetically arranged tables of these catchwords Buxtorf sought to help students overcome this difficulty. He thought that the use of catchword titles was only one part, however, of a much broader problem for Christians who wished to study post-biblical Hebrew literature: the bibliographic problem.

If Christian scholars were to have access to the world of post-biblical Hebrew literature, they first had to know the names of Jewish authors and the titles of their books as well as the subjects which they addressed. Without this information most Jewish scholarship was, practically speaking, unknown and unknowable. Buxtorf's *Bibliotheca rabbinica* was one of his most important contributions to scholarship, because in it he set a standard for describing Hebrew and Yiddish books and provided substantial information on the availability of Jewish books in his own day. His bibliographic work was the first step on the long road that led to Steinschneider's Bodleian library catalog and beyond.

Buxtorf's Christian predecessors had by and large contented themselves with rather sketchy listings.[99] Sebastian Münster's *Catalogus quorundam librorum sacrae linguae, qui hodie extant* gave little more than authors' names. His entry for Moses and David Kimhi, for example, stated that they wrote "various works."[100] Konrad Gessner's bibliography made reference to some

---

[98] Ibid., 91, 110, 177-9.

[99] Hebrew bibliography, in the modern sense of the phrase, was an invention of Christian scholars of the Renaissance. See Moritz Steinschneider, *Bibliographisches Handbuch über die theoretische und praktische Literatur für hebräischen Sprachkunde* (Hildesheim: Georg Olms, 1976), XIV-XVII, and Shimeon Brisman, *A History and Guide to Judaic Bibliography*, vol. 1: *Jewish Research Literature*, Bibliographica Judaica, no. 7 (Cincinnati and New York: Hebrew Union College Press and KTAV, 1977), 2-5

[100] "Rabbi David Kimhi Hispanus: & Rab. Moses Kimhi, varia scripserunt." Sebastian Münster, *Grammatica Hebraea Eliae Levitae Germani, per Seb.*

Jewish authors and their books, particularly those that were translated by Christian Hebraists.[101] In Gessner's entry under Elias
Levita, for example, all of the works (with one exception—a book
printed in Rome) that he cited were editions or translations by Paul
Fagius or Sebastian Münster. None of the Bomberg press Venice
imprints are mentioned.[102] Gessner organized his bibliography by
author, an arrangement that would not have helped Christian
Hebraists in their study of medieval Hebrew literature, since Jewish
authors from the Middle Ages through the eighteenth century very
often cited books by title, rather than by author.[103] He also gave
only Latin translations of the titles, not their actual Hebrew names
in the Hebrew alphabet. Michael Neander's *Catalogus librorum
quorundam praecipuorum in variis linguis* was based on Gessner's
bibliography but was arranged by subject rather than by author.
The list of Hebrew books he provided for the Liberal Arts illustrates how limited Neander's knowledge of Hebrew bibliography
was: only four books were named, each of them a diglot printing
containing a Latin translation.[104] His discussion of Hebrew Bibles
did contain one feature that Buxtorf may have copied: a description
of the contents of the Bomberg 1517 and 1525 rabbinical Bibles.[105]

The work which Buxtorf probably found most useful in
preparing his bibliography was Gilbert Génébrard's *Index
Librorum Rabbinicorum Editorum.*[106] Génébrard compiled a list

---

Munsterum versa & scholijs illustrata (Basel: Froben, 1552), unfoliated
appendix.
    [101]   Gessner's first edition was 1545; I consulted Konrad Gessner,
Bibliotheca Instituta et Collecta, ed. Josias Simler (Zürich: Christoph Froschover,
1583).
    [102] Ibid., 179.
    [103] On the manner of citation, see Brisman, *Guide,* vol. 1, 5.
    [104]   Michael Neander, *Sanctae linguae Hebraeae Erotemata* (Basel:
Bartholomäeus Franco, 1567), 556-557. Buxtorf's copy was Basel UB FA VII
5b. The imprints mentioned by Neander are listed in Appendix 4, the Buxtorf
Hebrew Library, nos. 53, 121, 134, 136.
    [105] Ibid., 401-405. Cf. Buxtorf, *De Abbreviaturis,* 264-268. Buxtorf thought
highly of Neander's grammar. He wrote in the margin of one of his books,
"Haec eadem vide apud Neandrum in sua Gram. heb. copiosius et elegantius."
See Elia Schadaeus, *Oratio de Linguae Sanctae Origine Progressu, & Varia
Fortuna, ad Nostrum usque Saeculum* (Strasbourg: Jodocus Martinus, 1591), f.
C5v, Basel UB FA VIII 1.
    [106] Gilbert Génébrard, *Eisagoge,* 145-148. Cf. Steinschneider, *Handbuch,*
XVI.

of 107 "entries," most of which were titles of Hebrew books.[107] More important than the actual number of titles listed, however, was the way in which he described them. He gave the title in Hebrew, sometimes adding a transliteration in Latin characters to supply the vocalization, and then a Latin translation of the title. Occasionally Génébrard gave the name of the author and the subject of the work as well. He never supplied information on whether or not an item had appeared in print. He also did not arrange the titles in any particular order. With the exception of the latter two deficiencies this manner of bibliographic description is remarkably similar to Buxtorf's approach. Since Buxtorf made such extensive use of Génébrard's translation of *Sheqel ha-Qodesh* (which appears in the same book on the page following the *Index*) his use of Génébrard's bibliographical format as a model is reasonably certain.

What set Buxtorf's *Bibliotheca rabbinica* apart from its predecessors was the structure of individual "bibliographic entries," the information they contained, and the plethora of sources he used to compile them. In the past scholars have been misled by the literary structure of the *Bibliotheca* and have assumed that the number of entries in it corresponded to the number of books that Buxtorf described.[108] A careful analysis of the entries themselves, however, reveals that he used at least three different types. The most common form included a book title (in Hebrew characters), a transliteration,[109] and translation of the title into Latin, a short description of its contents, the author (if it was not an anonymous or classical ancient Hebrew text) and the place and date of publication (for

---

[107] "Deficeret tempus & charta enumerandis variis libris Eliae, R. Iehuda Ben bilham, R. Ioseph Kimhi, filiorum eius, R. Mose & R. David, R. Saadiae, R. Abraham b. Paritsol, R. Mose Gerundensis & aliorum." Genebrard, *Eisagoge*, 148. Some of the words or phrases on the list are names of authors (such as Moses b. Nahman and Levi b. Gerson) and others are explanations of terms such as "דקדוקים‎," as "Grammaticae variorum," ibid., 146.

[108] Brisman, *Guide*, 4 gives the number as 324; the actual number of entries within the bibliography proper is 325 and a further 31 Bible imprints are listed separately on pp. 264-270.

[109] Buxtorf explained that transliteration was necessary in order to make oneself understood when speaking with Jews about books. "Noveris primo nomina librorum Latine scripta esse ad forma pronunciationis judaicae, quibus Thau lene sive raphtum semper ut S effertur. Id eo fine, ut si quis eos à judaeis petat, sciat eos ipsorum more nominare." *De Abbreviaturis*, 335.

printed works).[110] There are also "see-references," directing the
reader from a colloquial or abbreviated form of the title to the
main entry.[111] Finally, Buxtorf also had four entries containing no
titles at all, in which he described particular genres of Hebrew literature, such as Midrash.[112] Moreover, Buxtorf often mentioned
several books with the same title, or even different ones, under the
same entry.[113] Clearly an approach other than simple enumeration
of titles is necessary to calculate accurately the number of works
Buxtorf discussed.

Buxtorf's *Bibliotheca rabbinica* contains bibliographic notations
for manuscripts, printed books, and titles that cannot be positively
identified as either. Buxtorf mentioned only five manuscripts: three
which had once belonged to Joseph Scaliger, one which he himself
owned, and another manuscript work by R. Elijah Loanz, which he
presumably learned of while the latter lived near Basel during
1599-1600.[114] Imprints are those items for which a specific printing location or year of production is indicated, for which a print
format (folio, octavo etc.) is given or, in the case of some Yiddish
books, whether the book was written in Yiddish or Hebrew.[115]
Using these criteria 198 printed books can be adduced from
Buxtorf's listings. A further 210 titles are listed that cannot be

---

[110] Ibid., 5. Occasionally, however, titles are listed twice. See, for example,
כסף משנה and מגיד משנה, commentaries on Maimonides' *Mishneh Torah*, are listed
under the latter and separately. *De Abbreviaturis*, 291, 298, 300-301.

[111] See the entries for ילמדנו, סמק and תורת כהנים in *De Abbreviaturis*, 293,
313, and 332.

[112] For the entries on חדושים, מדרש, פירוש, תוספתא and see ibid., 289, 301,
320 and 331.

[113] The entry for ספרא, for example, mentions to two books by that title. The
entry for אמרי בינה refers to two separate imprints of the *Zohar* that are not mentioned under that entry. See *De Abbreviaturis*, 313-314, 275.

[114] Ibid., 271, 313, 324, 332. On the Scaliger manuscripts, see below.
Buxtorf owned a copy of אבקת רוכל, Basel UB Ms R III 3. On Elijah Loanz' stay
in Basel, see above, chap. 2.

[115] Although no publication data was given in Buxtorf's list of Yiddish titles
(first published in his *Theasurus Grammaticus* of 1609), Buxtorf probably
owned 24 of the 25 titles listed when he composed it (he probably did not own
Yiddish Booklist no. 16), although he probably disposed of several before he
composed his *Bibliotheca rabbinica* (notably nos. 9, 22. Cf. *De Abbreviaturis*,
283, 299). This information has been helpful for resolving the identity of several
Yiddish books mentioned but not sufficiently described in *Bibliotheca rabbinica*.
De Abbreviaturis, 302, 313, 297, 311, 304, and Appendix 3, Yiddish Booklist,
nos. 9, 10, 11, 17, 23, 24.

more narrowly identified.[116] These entries usually contain only author and title (127), less commonly only a title (37), and sometimes a citation from another book where Buxtorf found the work being described (46).[117] Some of these "undescribed" titles were, in fact, printed books, thirteen of them probably owned by Buxtorf himself, yet he did not include publication information for them. By this reckoning Buxtorf actually listed 413 bibliographic "items."[118]

Buxtorf used a variety of sources to compile his *Bibliotheca rabbinica* including books he owned, those he helped to print, books he saw for sale at the Frankfurt book fair or the wares of travelling Jewish book sellers, reports from his correspondents and titles mentioned by Jewish authors. Scholars have long recognized that the *Bibliotheca rabbinica* reflects Buxtorf's personal library to some degree.[119] The Buxtorf family sold its library to the city of Basel in 1705, and Johann Ludwig Frey composed an inventory of the books and assigned them library call numbers. These call numbers are essentially the same as the present day ones for *Bestände* FA and FB, which contain the vast majority of Buxtorf family books.[120] For the purposes of this study it is assumed that if a book in the 1705 inventory corresponds to one described in the

---

[116] Buxtorf was aware of the shortcomings of some of the title entries. He wrote in his introduction, "Ergo, Lector benevole & docte, quae hîc nec annotata, nec explicata, (quae scio plurima esse) tu adde & explica: libros quos habes aut videris, nominato, argumentum dicito, locum impressionis, sujicito, eaque vel mecum, si placet communicato, vel hisce meis initijs apposita, sub tuo nomine publicato." Buxtorf, *De Abbreviaturis*, 259.

[117] Of these records with citation, 25 of them contain author, title and citation, and 20 have only the title and reference. Menahem M. Slatkine drew attention to the importance of citations as a source for titles for Buxtorf's *Biblitheca* in his *Origins of the Earliest Hebrew Bibliography* (Tel Aviv: n. p., 1958), 25 (Hebrew).

[118] These bibliographic "items" include include marginal commentaries to the Bible, to *Midrash rabba*, to Maimonides' *Mishneh Torah* and to Aristotles' *Ethics*. Buxtorf, *De Abbreviaturis*, 290-291, 298, 300-301, 310.

[119] Slatkine, *Origins*, 25, and Brisman, *Guide*, 4.

[120] For example Buxtorf's copy of *Abodah Zara* (no. 29) has the call no. A. 1. 6. in Frey's catalog. See Johann Ludwig Frey, *Index Librorum Buxtorfianorum Bibliothecae Publiae*, Basel UB Ms AR I 31. A printed version of the Buxtorf library catalog also exists: [*Kleiner Katalog der Buxtorfschen Bibliothek*] (Basel: Johann Brandmüller, 1705), Basel UB Fr Gr D VII 109.

Bibliotheca rabbinica, or if Buxtorf cited it in his works before 1613, then he owned it.[121]

Following these assumptions Buxtorf probably owned no more than 138 of the titles, including fourteen from the "undescribed" category.[122] He cited five of them, Abraham ibn Daud, *Sefer ha-Qabalah*, Isaac Abravanel, *Nahlat Abot*, Gedaliah Ibn Yahya, *Shelshelet ha-Qabalah*, Judah ha-Levi, *Kuzari*, and Moses Cordovero, *Pardes Rimonim* within the bibliography itself when discussing other titles.[123] Buxtorf curiously did not list at least nineteen books that he probably owned. He may have excluded ten of them because they were Yiddish language works.[124] Although Buxtorf does mention Yiddish books in *Bibliotheca rabbinica*, they are usually translations of Hebrew originals.[125] Seven of them could also have been excluded because they were translations of parts of the Bible into Yiddish, and Buxtorf devoted comparatively little space to Bible imprints in *Bibliotheca rabbinica*, preferring to concentrate his attention on post-biblical Jewish works. Four other omissions are not so easily explained. Buxtorf neglected to mention two of Elias Levita's works, *Tub ha-Taam* and *Tishbi*, as well as Hai Gaon, *Shire Musar* and David de Pomi's, *Semah David*, all of which he used extensively in his grammatical and lexicographical works before 1613.[126] The omission of such important Hebrew works, together with Buxtorf's lack of description for the seven books he did own, suggest that he may not have been as careful in composing the *Bibliotheca* as hitherto assumed.

Buxtorf's involvement in the book trade gave him many opportunities to learn of far more books than he actually owned. He

---

[121] Although both of these assumptions are open to question in individual cases, a reconstruction of the Buxtorf's library for 1613 is useful both in providing an upper limit on the proportion of books mentioned in the *Bibliotheca* that he could have owned, and also as an analytical tool for the completeness and accuracy of his citations. He demonstrably owned many of the books listed and also a few that are not mentioned in *Bibliotheca* at all.

[122] Appendix 4, nos. 45, 48, 52, 54, 82, 85, 87, 102-3, 107, 119-120, 128, 139, 4*, and 5*.

[123] Buxtorf, *De Abbreviaturis*, 324 (Abraham b. David), 314 (Abravanel), 315 (Judah Halevi) and 278-280, 307, 315, 318, 324, 327 and 329 (Gedaliah) and 322 (Cordovero).

[124] Appendix 4, nos. 13-15, 19-21, 60, 109, 141, 143.

[125] Buxtorf, *De Abbreviaturis*, 270, 297, 299, 302, 304, 311, 313 and 325-6.

[126] Appendix 4, nos. 68, 76, 80-81 and 83.

worked for both Waldkirch and König as a corrector and for the city of Basel as a censor for their products. Walter Keuchen, a former student who likewise worked as a Hebrew censor in Hanau, served informally as a representative for Buxtorf until at least 1619 in Hanau and in nearby Frankfurt, locating a number of valuable items, including a manuscript copy of Ibn Ezra's astronomical works sometime after 1613.[127] Buxtorf also visited the Frankfurt book fair on several occasions and took other opportunities to view the wares of Jewish booksellers.[128] Presumably some of the more sketchily described printed books that he listed are works that he had seen and then later described from memory.[129]

Other Christian Hebraists provided Buxtorf both with information about their holdings and, occasionally, with books. Buxtorf's descriptions of three manuscripts that had belonged to Joseph Scaliger, as well as an early printing of Moses Kimhi's grammar *Mahalak Shebile ha-Daat*, came either from Scaliger himself or from another of Buxtorf's Leiden correspondents, since Scaliger had donated his library to the University of Leiden in his will.[130]

---

[127] Keuchen was a student in Basel during 1605 and served as rector of the *Hohen Landeschule* in Hanau from 1612-1622. Wackernagel, *Matrikel*, 3: 52. On Keuchen's activities on Buxtorf's behalf see Kayserling, "Richelieu," 79. For a description of the Ibn Ezra manuscript see Moïse Schwab, "Manuscrits Hébreux de Bâle," *Revue des études juives* 5 (1882): 253. The last known item that Keuchen provided for Buxtorf was Moses Isserles' מחיר יין (Cremona: Vincent Conti, 1559), Basel UB FA V 39/1, which bears the inscription "Ex dono Walter Keuchen 13. September 1619."

[128] Buxtorf mentioned seeing two imprints and a third one that was present "among the Jews of Frankfurt" ("apud judaeos Francofurti." *De Abbreviaturis*, 279, 283 and 298. Buxtorf once complained to Kaspar Waser, "Judaei non libenter mecum amplius libros communicant, nec aliunde quam Francofurto comparandi occasionem habeo." Buxtorf to Kaspar Waser, Basel, July 14, 1609, Zürich SA Ms E II 383: 853-4.

[129] For example, when describing the book כלי יקר Buxtorf wrote, "...habens (nisi fallor) adjunctum textum cum punctis." Buxtorf, *De Abbreviaturis*, 298.

[130] Ibid., 302, 313, 332. Two of the three manuscripts mentioned are Leiden UB Mss. Scal. 3 and 4. The third, Scaliger's excerpts from the Jerusalem Talmud, are not a part of the Leiden UB collection. Scaliger's copy of מהלך שבלי הדעת, 3d ed. (Ortona: Gerson Soncino, [1519]) is bound with Ms Scal. 13. See Moritz Steinschneider, *Catalogus Codicum Hebraeorum Bibliothecae Academiae Lugduno-Batavae* (Leiden: E. J. Brill, 1858), 541-4, and Albert van der Heide, *Hebrew Manuscripts of Leiden University Library*, Bibliotheca Universitatis Leidensis Codices Manuscripti, no. 18 (Leiden: Universitaire Pers, 1977), 3-4, 63.

Buxtorf asked Drusius for a list of all Hebrew books that he owned, presumably to be included in the *Bibliotheca*.[131] Occasionally his friends passed on more than information. Thomas Erpenius, professor of Hebrew at Leiden University, gave Buxtorf one of the books mentioned in *Bibliotheca rabbinica*.[132] He later provided Buxtorf with a number of Arabic books.[133] Buxtorf himself was rather generous to his friends in this regard and mentions two books that he gave to Scaliger, one to Drusius and one to an unidentified friend.[134]

Citations of titles in books was the other source of information that Buxtorf used in composing *Bibliotheca rabbinica*. He gave citations as the sole source of his information for forty-five titles. Buxtorf consulted both Christian and Jewish sources. He acknowledged using Galatinus' *Opus de Arcanis Catholicae Veritatis*, Reuchlin's *De Arte Cabalistica*, and Münster's printing of the Gospel of Matthew in Hebrew and introduction to *Sphaera Mundi*, together providing nine titles.[135] Génébrard's *Index* may have provided as many as fourteen titles.[136]

Jewish authors were far more important sources of citations both in terms of number and the quality of information provided. Buxtorf's four principal sources are the histories of Abraham Saba,

---

131 Drusius responded, apologetically, that he could not give a quick answer to Buxtorf's question. "Catalogum librorum Ebraicarum quos habeo qui plurimi sunt difficulter colligere possum quia dispersi per meam bibliothecam nec certo positi ordine. Tamen videbo quid possim." Johannes Drusius to Johannes Buxtorf, n. p., February 8, 1613, Basel UB Ms G I 59: 260; Basel UB Ms G 2 II 24 is a transcription of the letter. No list of Drusius' library has been preserved among the Buxtorf family papers in Basel UB.

132 Buxtorf, *De Abbreviaturis*, 310.

133 Among the Arabic books given to Buxtorf were *Proverbia Arabica* (Leiden: Erpenius, 1614), and *Passio Domini nostri Jesu Christi secundum Matthaeum* (Leiden: Erpenius, 1613), Basel UB FA VI 1/1-2, and an Arabic Pentateuch (Leiden: Erpenius, 1622), Basel UB Fr Gr A IV 28.

134 Ibid., 304, 305, 310, 311. See Johannes Buxtorf to Joseph Scaliger, Basel, April 3, 1606, Utrecht UB Ms 987: 237-238, printed in *Sylloges*, 2: 363, and Johannes Drusius to Johannes Buxtorf, n. p., August 10, 1607, Basel UB Ms G I 59: 259.

135 Ibid., 271, 283, 302, 311, 313, 315, 324 and 329. The two Münster works quoted are Appendix 4, nos. 24, 53.

136 See Buxtorf, *De Abbreviaturis*: 272-3, 280, 284, 295, 297, 302-3, 309, 314, 329, 331: אור עמים, בית יעקב, אותיות לר עקיבה, אור עיניים, דרשות על תורה, עבודת הלו, משלי שועלים, מלחמות יי, מחנרת עמנואל, כבוד אלהים, ישר, ייחוס הצדקים, תולדות יצחק, שערי הגמול.

David Gans, and Gedaliah Ibn Yahya, and Jacob Luzzatto's kabbalistic work *Kaphtor*, providing among them twenty-five additional titles.[137] He identified titles with the help of ten other books in the course of *Bibliotheca rabbinica*, including one, *Shebile emunah*, that is not even listed within it.[138] Four of these books were quoted by page number but no imprint information about them is provided in the book. Presumably Buxtorf found many other titles in other Hebrew books that he did not acknowledge using, since a further 208 titles are essentially undescribed in the bibliography.

Buxtorf thought that the Christian academic public, Christian missionaries to the Jews, and would-be Jewish converts would all benefit from his bibliography. He wanted schools to be able to make the fullest possible use of what he termed "profitable" Hebrew literature. With the help of his *Bibliotheca rabbinica* scholars would be able to "separate gold from dung" and make use of "such wisdom as the Jewish synagogue once professed."[139] Similarly, Buxtorf hoped to provide a listing of those books that Jews actually used so that Christians would be able to learn more about them, presumably in order to persuade them to convert. He also hoped that at least a remnant of Jews would recognize their "errors and blindness" through the Scripture and the "best of their own books."[140]

Buxtorf's bibliography of Hebrew books was by any standard an important contribution to the study of Hebrew literature. The type of bibliographic description he used remained the standard format until well into the twentieth century, and successive editions of his

---

[137] Ibid. Books referred to by David Gans appear on pp. 270, 276, 300 and 321; those by Gedaliah on pp. 278-280, 307, 315, 318, 324, 327 and 329; those by Luzzatto on pp. 273, 284, 300, 307-8, 321 and 326, and one by Abraham Saba on p. 321. The four books are Appendix 4, nos. 57, 69, 82 and 101.

[138] Ibid., 314. See Appendix 4, nos. 54, 77, 87, 119-120, 125, 139, 153 and 159. Buxtorf also quoted from Ibn Ezra's biblical commentaries and once from Maimonides' introduction to the Talmud. Ibid., 298, 306 and 313-14.

[139] "Sic tandem tela haec caepta pertexetur, & scient nostrae quoque scholae, quam Synagoga judaica sapientiam olim professant, & quam hodie doctrinam profiteatur. Licebit & hîc aurum ex stercore colligere, & margaritas pretiosas simo reconditas reperire." Buxtorf, *De Abbreviaturis*, 259.

[140] "Sic tandem quoque fiet, ut judaei ex verbo Dei & propriis ipsorum libris, erroris & caecitatis tanto melius convinci, de veritate eruditi, & ad salutem adduci & converti possint. Quod fieri ut nobis Christianis optandum , ita quoque opera danda, ut fieri commode per nos possit, ad quod subsidium admirabile praebebit librorum, quibus ipsimet Judaei utuntur, familiaris cognito." Ibid., 260.

book were carefully consulted by other bibliographers, both Jewish and Christian.[141] The work was not, however, without flaws both in its content and organization. While Buxtorf clearly intended to provide as much information as possible about printed Hebrew books, he failed in a number of instances. Several Hebrew books that he edited for publication in Basel, notably Levita's *Tub ha-Taam* and *Tishbi* were not even mentioned in the bibliography.[142] The omission of many Yiddish titles was also a weakness. Among the books Buxtorf left out was Moses b. Enoch Altschuler's *Brantspiegel*, one of the most important sources for his *Juden Schul*. Even when describing books that he both owned and listed, Buxtorf often did not indicate whether they were published or not. Although Buxtorf gave the impression of providing detailed extensive bibliographic descriptions of the books he discussed, he left out many details he could easily have provided.

Buxtorf also systematically withheld information on Basel Hebrew imprints that were produced while he lived in the city. Of the twenty Basel Hebrew imprints mentioned in *Bibliotheca rabbinica* only four were printed between 1598 and 1613.[143] Although he provided entries for ten other Basel titles, Buxtorf did not indicate that they were printed there.[144] Of the eighteen different prayer books printed in Basel during these years not one was noted in *Bibliotheca rabbinica*.[145] Buxtorf served as the municipal censor for Basel during most, if not all, of these years and would probably have been obliged to read each of these books. Moreover, he was entitled to one copy of each work as a part of his payment, and

---

[141] Slatkine, *Origins*, 25, and Brisman, *Guide*, vol. 1, 6-15.

[142] Prijs nos. 172 and 188. Buxtorf's personal copy of טוב טעם (Basel UB FA VIII 34, Appendix 4, no. 76) contains extensive corrections, presumably added to prepare it for publication.

[143] These were Isaac Alfasi, ספר רב אלפס, Nathan b. Yehiel, ערוך, and a Hebrew Bible printing and a Yiddish חומש (Prijs nos. 158, 182, 186 and 207). *De Abbreviaturis*, 269-270, 273-4, 317.

[144] These titles included the Isaac Tyrnau, מנהגים, and the Yiddish מנהגים, Isaac Düren, שערי דורא, Solomon Loria, עמודי שלמה, Elia Louans, רנת דודים, Jacob Weil, שחיטות ובדיקות, Solomon b. Mordecai, מזבח הזהב, Jacob Pogetto, ראשית חכמה הקצר, Moses de Leon, החכמה הנפש, and ספר מגלת. Cf. *De Abbreviaturis*, 275-6, 301, 302, 304, 311, 316, 323-4, and 326, and Prijs nos. 152, 164-6, 173, 179, 187, 194, 196, 202, 203 and 206.

[145] Cf. תפלה מכל השנה, סליחות, מעמדות, מחזור, זמירות, ברכות המזון in *De Abbreviaturis*, 283, 288, 302, 305-6, 313 and 333. Cf. Prijs nos. 153b, 169, 170b, 200b, 163a, 157, 150, 167 and 148, 153a, and 170a.

seventeen Hebrew Basel imprints from this time are part of the Buxtorf family library.

The reasons Buxtorf left Basel Hebrew imprints out of *Bibliotheca rabbinica* are unclear. Until 1612 the authorities had allowed a number of Jewish books to be printed in Basel, but by 1613 they may have had a change of heart. Except for the rabbinical Bible of 1618-1619, which was authorized because it would benefit Christians, no other Jewish books were printed in Basel during Buxtorf's lifetime. The last time that city council discussed Jewish printing was on May 22, 1616, when they flatly refused permission to allow Talmud tractate *Berachot* to be printed in Basel.[146] The apparent change of policy in Basel may have occurred because its leaders now believed that to allow Jewish printing was to support Judaism. Seven years earlier the princely council of Hanau felt obliged to consider whether a Christian state should allow Jewish printing and to assess whether permitting it would expose Hanau to attacks from confessional opponents.[147] Alternatively, Buxtorf may not have specified Basel imprints since they were only manufactured there, and no longer for sale in the city.[148]

Buxtorf's reluctance to associate Basel with Jewish printing was consistent in that he tended to avoid associating Protestant cities with Jewish printing. He mentioned only three specifically Jewish books that had been printed in Protestant cities during his lifetime;

---

[146] Achilles Nordmann, "Geschichte der Juden in Basel seit dem Ende der zweiten Gemeinde bis zur Einführung der Glaubens- und Gewissensfreiheit. 1387-1875," *Basler Zeitschrift für Geschichte und Altertumskunde* 13 (1914): 27, n. 1. See also Mordecai Gumplin to Johannes Buxtorf, n. p., n. d., Moscow: Russian State Library, Günzburg Collection, Ms. 1213, ff. 11b-12b (Copy held by the Jewish National and University Library, Institute of Microfilmed Hebrew Manuscripts, Jerusalem).

[147] Stephen G. Burnett, "The Regulation of Hebrew Printing in Germany, 1555-1630: Confessional Politics and the Limits of Jewish Toleration," in: *Infinite Boundaries: Order, Re-Order and Dis-Order in Early Modern German Culture*, ed. Max Reinhart and Thomas Robisheaux, Sixteenth Century Essays and Studies (Kirksville: Sixteenth Century Journal Publishers, forthcoming).

[148] Only seven years after its printing in Basel, Buxtorf hinted that *Iggeret Shelomim* (1603) was no longer available in Basel. "Alter *Iggeret Shelomim*, qui hic Basileae ante paucos annos recusus, apud Judaeos Francofurti venditur." *Institutio*, 76. See above, chap. 2 concerning the marketing of Basel Judaica books.

all of the other books he listed were printed in Catholic cities.[149]
Apparently even the production of licit Jewish books, those which
contained no "anti-Christian blasphemy," was considered a support
to the Jewish religion and hence a questionable economic activity.

Organizationally the bibliography suffers from an insufficient
system of cross-references. Imprints were sometimes divided
among two or more entries. For example, Buxtorf mentioned only
the Venice 1606 printing of the Mishnah under the heading
Mishnah, but the careful reader could also find another printing
(Venice: G. de Gara, 1609) by consulting the entry for the Mishnah
commentary *Kaph Nahat*.[150] Abravanel's *Nahlat Abot* is itself a
commentary on *Pirke Abot*, a relationship which was not explained
in either entry.[151] Although no specific imprints of the *Zohar* were
mentioned under the entry *Zohar*, two of them, Cremona and
Venice, are listed under the entry for *Imre Binah*.[152] Buxtorf
clearly had a concept of main entries and used cross references on
occasion to refer readers to them, but he did not apply his system
consistently, and the result is less than satisfactory.

Buxtorf's contemporaries immediately appreciated the importance of *De Abbreviaturis* for their studies. One of the most striking testimonies to Buxtorf's efforts came for R. Jacob Roman, a
scholar living in Constantinople who read the book and sent the
younger Buxtorf a list of other Hebrew books that were not listed
in *Bibliotheca rabbinica*. According to Buxtorf II, Roman planned
to translate the entire work from Latin into Hebrew for the benefit
of Jewish readers.[153] The best indication for the work's lasting
significance, however, is that it stimulated others to take up where
Buxtorf left off. While some such as Cardinal Jean de la Pause
Plantavit and Johann Heinrich Hottinger were largely dependent

---

[149] These are Isaac Alfasi, ספר אלפס (Basel: Konrad Waldkirch, 1602),
Nathan ben Yehiel, ערוך (Basel: Konrad Waldkirch, 1599), and Shabbethai
Sheftel Horowitz, שפע טל (Hanau: [Hans Jacob Henne], 1612). Buxtorf, *De
Abbreviaturis*, 273, 317, 330. Buxtorf listed the following locations for seven-
teenth century Judaica printers (not including Bible printers): Hanau and Prague
in the Holy Roman Empire, Venice, Franeker in the Netherlands (translations by
Johannes Drusius), Cracow and Lublin in Poland, and Basel itself.

[150] Ibid., 298, 310.

[151] Ibid., 310, 318-9.

[152] Ibid., 275, 286-7.

[153] Buxtorf, *De Abbreviaturis*, ed. Johannes Buxtorf II (Basel: Ludwig
König, 1640), 435-472. See also Prijs, *Drucke*, 371.

upon Buxtorf for the listings in their bibliographies, others, including Giulio Bartolocci, Shabbethai Bass, and Johann C. Wolf, expanded the number of titles many times beyond what Buxtorf listed, to the lasting benefit of later scholars.[154]

Buxtorf considered it his educational mission in life to provide better textbooks in order to encourage Hebrew learning; he achieved a measure of success in achieving this goal. Advanced students of Hebrew were able to derive much benefit from Buxtorf's works on composing letters, poetics, and bibliography. His bibliography opened the world of Jewish learning to Christian pedagogues in the most practical way possible, by providing a list of books which most scholars had no idea existed. His composition textbooks played a less substantive but no less important role in promoting Hebrew learning. Public demonstrations of learning presented on specific occasions, usually in the form of orations or poetry, were a characteristic of early modern university life.[155] By providing guides to composing Hebrew prose and poetry, Buxtorf opened the way for other Hebraists to participate in these literary events which, although they often pained both the speakers and auditors, were nonetheless part and parcel of seventeenth-century academic culture.[156]

Buxtorf's books had an impact not only within schools and universities, but also outside of them. Advanced study in Hebrew during the seventeenth century remained to a great extent either a matter for independent study or study with a tutor.[157] Buxtorf's three works were designed for self-study, and only further research can establish the extent to which his works encouraged greater Christian use of post-biblical Hebrew literature. His *De*

---

[154] Brisman, *Guide*, vol. 1, 6-17.

[155] Wilfried Barner tellingly illustrated this point by discussing the immense literary productivity of Christoph Kaldenbach, professor of Poetry at the University of Tübingen from 1656-1698 in *Barockrhetorik: Untersuchungen zu ihren geschichtlichen Grundlagen* (Tübingen: Max Niemeyer, 1970), 432-433.

[156] Grafton and Jardine noted that MA candidates at Tübingen during the 1580's were required to present short essays in Greek on philosophical topics at their graduation ceremony, "no doubt to the utter boredom of their audiences." Anthony Grafton and Lisa Jardine, *From Humanism to the Humanities. Education and the Liberal Arts in Fifteenth- and Sixteenth-Century Europe* (Cambridge: Harvard Univ. Press, 1986), 119.

[157] For example, John Lightfoot was basically self-taught in Rabbinics. Schertz, "Christian Hebraism," 19-20.

Abbreviaturis, however, was unquestionably one of the most important books in Hebrew studies written during the seventeenth century since it made Christian intellectuals aware of the range and breadth of Jewish scholarship in a way that no work had done before. When Buxtorf had studied at Herborn, the faculty had recognized the potential importance of Jewish books relating the the liberal arts, but they had no practical way of identifying those which might be of use to professors and students. Subsequent generations of Christian scholars did not suffer under this handicap. Appropriately enough, the final revision of Buxtorf's *De Abbreviaturis* was made in 1708 by a professor at Herborn to encourage the use of Jewish literature almost a century after the book first appeared.

Buxtorf did not encourage his students to become proficient in Hebrew for the love of learning alone, but rather he hoped that his students would put their linguistic knowledge to work, particularly in the service of the church. His editions of the Bomberg rabbinical Bible, a Hebrew Bible concordance, and *Tiberias*, his introduction to masoretic studies, were all works written to make the fruit of Jewish biblical scholarship more accessible to theologians. Buxtorf's chief preoccupation was not so much with the biblical text itself as with the masoretic apparatus which had been assembled to preserve the text from corruption. Since Buxtorf considered the Bible to be the "effective cause" of the Christian faith, preoccupation with the individual words of the Hebrew Bible was an significant philological task with important theological ramifications.

CHAPTER SIX

A HEBREW TEXTUS RECEPTUS:
BUXTORF AND THE TEXT OF THE HEBREW BIBLE

Theology, the queen of sciences, demanded a rigorous course of professional training from her seventeenth-century subjects, both Protestant and Catholic. Theology students were obliged to study the Liberal Arts and theology proper; they were also required to learn Hebrew and Aramaic so that they could read the Old Testament in its original languages.[1] For Protestants the need to know Hebrew was an outgrowth not only of the humanist trilingual ideal but was also a logical extension of their insistence upon the theological principle of sola scriptura. A theologian had to understand the word of God accurately so as to edify the faithful, settle controversies, and parry the attacks of opponents, including both theologians of other Christian confessions and adherents of other religions.[2] Professors of Hebrew were responsible for providing their students with this philological grounding; their courses were considered in some ways to be a part of the theological studies curriculum. Johannes Buxtorf took his theological responsibilities very seriously. By producing a new version of the Bomberg *Biblia rabbinica* he sought to provide theologians with what he considered the most important tools for interpreting the Old Testament. He also edited and published a concordance to the Hebrew Bible as an aid to textual study and biblical interpretation. While both Protestant and Catholic interpreters had previously used these Jewish philological tools, Buxtorf advocated a far greater role for them in theological studies, reflecting not only a concern that theology be based upon the Bible in its original languages, but also perhaps the emerging Reformed orthodox emphasis upon Scripture as the foundation and "cause" of all true religion.[3]

The Venice *Biblia rabbinica* of 1525 was one of the most important philological and theological works produced during the

---

[1] Muller, *Post-Reformation Reformed Dogmatics*, vol. 1, 270-271.
[2] Ibid., 273-274.
[3] Ibid., 304.

sixteenth century. It had a substantial impact upon Protestant theology and Bible translations even though its editors intended it primarily for a Jewish reading public.[4] Jacob ben Hayyim's intensive study of not only biblical but also Masora manuscripts resulted in a form of the biblical text that became accepted (at least among Christians) as the "received text."[5] It was also a triumph of the printer's art, requiring a massive capital investment by Daniel Bomberg for the purchase of the manuscripts necessary for its preparation and for the printing process itself.[6] All "rabbinical Bibles" produced after 1525 followed its format and, for the most part, its content. Very few Jewish scholars active during the sixteenth and seventeenth centuries had the technical knowledge of the Masora necessary to improve upon Ben Hayyim's work.[7]

While masoretic studies were almost unknown among Christian Hebraists of the sixteenth and seventeenth centuries, many of them could use the Targums and rabbinical Bible commentaries. A large number of translations and diglot editions of individual books of the Targum had been published for the use of Christians after 1500, and the entire Targum had been translated into Latin and printed in the Antwerp Polyglot.[8] Philological study of the

---

[4] Moshe Goshen-Gottstein, Introduction to *Biblia Rabbinica: A Reprint of the 1525 Venice Edition Edited by Jacob ben Hayim ibn Adoniya*, 4 vols. and separate introduction fascicle (Jerusalem: Makor, 1972), 7, 19.

[5] Idem, "Foundations of Biblical Philology in the Seventeenth Century: Christian and Jewish Dimensions," in: *Jewish Thought in the Seventeenth Century*, ed. Isadore Twersky and Bernard Septimus (Cambridge, MA: Harvard Univ. Press, 1987), 83-84.

[6] Jacob ben Hayyim ibn Adoniyah, *Introduction to the Rabbinic Bible, Hebrew and English*, ed. and trans. Christian D. Ginsburg, 2d ed. (London: Longmans, Green, Reader & Dyer, 1867), 41, 77-78.

[7] Perhaps the best-known critic of Ben Hayyim's masoretic work was Elias Levita, who nonetheless had a good deal of praise for it. "But although his edition is exceedingly beautiful, he committed many mistakes, and bore false testimony in many places. This, however is not to be wondered at, for the work was new, and every beginning is difficult." *The Massoreth Ha-Massoreth of Elias Levita, Being an Explanation of the Massoretic Notes of the Hebrew Bible*, trans. Christian D. Ginsburg (London: Longmans, Green, Reader & Dyer, 1867; reprint ed., New York: KTAV, 1968), 94-95. Goshen-Gottstein in his introduction to *Biblia Rabbinica*, 12 mentions Solomon ben Judah Norzi author of שׁ מנחת (first published in 1742-44) and Menahem di Lonzano ben Judah, author of אור תורה (1618) as two prominent seventeenth century Jewish critics of Ben Hayyim's work.

[8] For example, Imanuel Tremellius translated the minor prophets into Latin in *Jonathanae, filii Uzielis, antiquissimi et summae apud Hebraeos antoritatis,*

Aramaic language, however, remained where Elias Levita left it in the mid-sixteenth century. The Christian Aramaic and Syriac grammars printed during these years were rudimentary works written for beginning students. Better educated Christian Hebraists could read medieval Hebrew and often consulted Jewish biblical commentaries.[9] These commentaries became standard sources for Protestant commentators on the Old Testament and for Bible translators.[10] Until Buxtorf edited the Basel rabbinical Bible edition of 1618-19, however, no single Christian scholar, Protestant or Catholic, took upon himself the task of editing the entire Hebrew Bible text with masoretic notes, Targums, and biblical commentaries. Buxtorf's project was a truly audacious undertaking for his time.

If any Christian Hebraist of that generation was amply prepared for such a task, it was Buxtorf. As a grammarian and lexicographer, he had become sensitive to small variations in Hebrew and Aramaic vocalization. He had also worked as a corrector for a Hebrew Bible edition in 1610-11.[11] As an instructor he used Jewish Bible commentaries frequently and also encouraged his students to do so. The most recent Venice edition of the rabbinical Bible was printed in 1568, and both it and other older editions were too ex-

---

Chaldaea paraphrasis in duodecim minores Prophetas (Heidelberg: Martinus Agricola, 1567), and Paul Fagius translated Genesis 1-4 in his *Exegesis sive expositio dictinum hebraicis literalis in quatuor Geneseos* (Isny: P. Fagius, 1542).

[9] Both Sebastian Münster and Konrad Pellikan translated several of Levita's works and Pellikan even translated several of the biblical commentaries into Latin and German, although he never published these translations. See Burmeister, *Münster*, 77-81, and Christoph Zürcher, *Konrad Pellikans Wirken in Zürich 1526-1556*, Zürcher Beiträge zur Reformationsgeschichte, vol. 4 (Zürich: Theologischer Verlag, 1975), 7.

[10] For example, Martin Bucer made extensive use of these commentaries in his Psalms commentary of 1529. Both Sebastian Münster and Imanuel Tremellius made extensive use of Jewish commentaries in their Latin translations of the Old Testament. Lloyd Jones, *Discovery*, 44-48, 51-52, 73-74 and Burmeister, *Münster*, 89-97.

[11] "Editionem Bibliorum hebraicorum molimur, et habet hic examplar ex quo de forma utcuique judicare poteris. Correctura mecum praeerit aliquis doctus judaeus, ut et inter ipsos tanto melius distrahi possint." Buxtorf to Waser, Basel, February 7, 1608, Zürich ZB S-160: 45. Presumably this Bible edition is Prijs no. 207, which was only printed between 1611 and January 26, 1612, and edited by Mordecai b. Joseph Judah Wahl of Frankfurt. Steinschneider noted "cura Jo. Buxtorf. pat." in StCB p. 64, n. 395, to which Prijs added "jedoch ohne Quellenangabe" *Drucke*, 320.

pensive for most students to buy. Buxtorf expressed his concern that students should be able to purchase their own copies of the rabbinical Bible in his appeal to the Basel city council for permission to print the Bible edition.[12]

The Basel edition of the Bomberg *Biblia rabbinica* was the most technically demanding of all Buxtorf's printed works.[13] Buxtorf and his co-workers labored for three years to prepare the *Vorlage* and to print the new edition. Ludwig König had to seek permission first to print the rabbinical Bible and then hire the Jewish correctors necessary for such a complex project.[14] The actual printing began between the mid-August and mid-September of 1618.[15] According to the colophon, production ended on the 24 of *Ab*, 379 (= August 4, 1619), but since this date also appeared on the colophon of the Bomberg *Biblia rabbinica* edition of 1524-25 (reprinted unchanged in the 1546-48 and 1568 editions) it is suspect. Prijs suggested that the probable completion date was sometime during *Ab* of 379, between July 12 and August 10 of 1619.[16]

Abraham Braunschweig, the chief printer, gave an unusual glimpse into the workings of König's print shop in his introduction to a list of corrections supplied at the end of the work.[17] While he praised the acumen of Buxtorf the chief editor, he also begged the

[12] Beck and Buxtorf reported that rabbinical Bibles cost between 30 and 50 *Reichsthaler*, a sum far beyond the reach of most scholars. They argued that the Bible should be published, "das auch solche Bibel in ihren ursprunglichen Sprachen, zu mehrere fortpflanzung, erkundigung und erhalltung Göttliches worts, zu erbawung der in Gottswort studierenden und diser Sprachen liebhabenden Jugend, auch zu mehrer underrichtung aller deren gelehrten so Gottes wort in seinen Original und ursprunglichen Sprachen...lehren und erklehren...." Sebastian Beck and Johannes Buxtorf, *Bericht uber das Biblisch Truck, so man jetzt und zu trucken begehret*, September 5, 1617, Basel SA, Handel und Gewerbe, JJJ 1.

[13] Prijs no. 219. Prijs gave an elaborate description of the technical qualities of the work from a printing point of view in *Drucke*, 331-343.

[14] Sebastian Beck and Johannes Buxtorf, *Bericht*, September 5, 1617, Basel SA, Handel und Gewerbe, JJJ 1 and Basel SA, Basel Stadt, Protokolle, Kleiner Rat, Bd. 15, f. 198r, September 6, 1617.

[15] Prijs noted that Buxtorf's Latin introduction is dated August 22, 1618, that the title page of the Pentateuch has the year 378, and the title page for the Prophets gave 379 as the year of printing. In 379 the Jewish New Year fell on September 20, 1618. Prijs, *Drucke*, 334.

[16] Ibid.

[17] Braunschweig's introduction was reprinted with an accompanying French translation by J. Derenbourg in "L'Édition de la Bible Rabbinique de Jean Buxtorf," *Revue des études juives* 30 (1895): 70-78.

indulgence of his readers for a product which was less than perfect. Each working day he and his fellow employees were required to set and print three folio pages of text. Since most of the typesetters could not read Hebrew the Jewish correctors worked under severe time pressure and had numerous errors to correct. Even the process of correction provided the chance for new errors to creep in at the hands of the typesetters. Furthermore, Christian typesetters worked on Saturdays without any supervision or help from the Jewish correctors, with predictable results.[18]

As editor-in-chief of the project Buxtorf worked on a somewhat different schedule than the printers, but he probably felt the time pressure almost as acutely. He wrote to Benedict Turrettini on June 22, 1618, that he had finished his preparatory work on the Hebrew text of the Pentateuch and was working on Judges. He had completed his Targum corrections up to Isaiah.[19] By June 26, 1619, he had completed work on both the Targums and the Masoras.[20]

Buxtorf did not plan simply to reprint one of the existing Venice editions, but rather to assemble the best features of them all into one work. Buxtorf used the *Biblia rabbinica* of 1546-48 as his *Vorlage* and added materials from the other two editions.[21] He took the commentaries of Abraham Ibn Ezra to Isaiah and the minor prophets from the 1524-25 edition, and portions of the *Masora magna* from the 1568 printing and had them included in his edi-

---

[18] Ibid., 75-76.

[19] "Pentateuchum jam absolvimus, et pergimus nunc in libro Judicium... In Targum corrigendo jam perveni usque ad Iesaiam." Johannes Buxtorf to Benedict Turrettini, Basel, June 22, 1618, Geneva: Archives Turrettini, Fonds 1, Dd 4.1.

[20] "Ego plus laboris habui in corrige(ndo) Targu(m) et Masora, quam in Novo exemplari. Targum absolvi; in Masora adhuc...res restant." Johannes Buxtorf to Benedict Turrettini, Basel, June 26, 1619, Geneva: Archives Turrettini, Fonds 1, Dd 4.3.

[21] "Tertius labitur annus, quando typographus noster Ludovicus König...de Bibliis magnis Hebraicis, Venetiis tertio quartoque editis, suis quoque typis edendis (novo certe Germaniae exemplo) consilia secum mecumque iniret." Buxtorf to the Estates General of the Netherlands, Basel, April 1, 1620, *Tiberias*, fol., f. ***3r. Prijs noted that despite differences in pagination of their appendices, the pagination of the Basel *Biblia rabbinica* accords most closely with that of the Venice 1546-48 edition. He provided a detailed table of comparisons in *Drucke*, 334, 529-531. The three Venice editions Buxtorf used are StCB p. 11, no. 52 (1524-25), p. 24, no. 125 (1546-48), and pp. 36-37, no. 206 (1568).

tion.[22] Targum Yerushalmi was also reprinted from the 1568 edition.[23]

Buxtorf planned to improve his edition of the rabbinical Bible in several editorial respects as well. In his introduction to the *Biblia rabbinica* Buxtorf discussed in turn each of the four constituent part of the rabbinical Bible: Hebrew Bible text, Targum, biblical commentaries, and the Masora. He also planned to compose introductions to the Hebrew text, rabbinical Bible commentaries, and Masora which would be published separately from the rabbinical Bible itself.[24] *Tiberias*, his introduction to the Masora, was the only work that was actually published.[25]

Buxtorf planned to reprint the biblical text without alteration, reproducing it down to the last vowel point and accent, since only an impious man would alter the text of the Bible.[26] To a great extent he was able to realize this goal. A survey of one hundred verses reveals no variation between the consonantal Hebrew text of the Basel rabbinical Bible and its ultimate hypearchetype, the second edition of the Bomberg rabbinical Bible of 1524-25.[27] A com-

---

[22] In both cases Buxtorf used his personal copies as the originals. His copy of the Venice 1524-25 edition is Basel UB Fr Gr A I 17, and of the Venice 1568 is Basel UB FA I 2a-c. Both of these works contain printers' markings indicating which portions were to be copied. Ibid., 334.

[23] Targum Yerushalmi appears neither in the Bomberg 1525 nor 1546-48 rabbinical Bibles. Prijs, *Drucke*, 529.

[24] "Sed de quatuor harum partium, quae in hoc Opere biblico continentur (Text, Targum, Masorah and commentaries) ampliori usu...specialem & sufficientem Instructionem una cum completo hoc Opere, Deo annuente, proponemus, ad quem Christianum & benevolum quemque Lectorem hoc tempore remittimus...." Buxtorf, Latin introduction to *Biblia rabbinica* , f. (1)v, dated August 22, 1618. See also Johannes Buxtorf II's introduction to, *Lexicon Chaldaicum et Syriacum* (Basel: L. König, 1622), f. **2v. Both are quoted in Prijs, *Drucke*, 335.

[25] Buxtorf was also able to complete the Targum commentary *Babylonia* before his death. According to Buxtorf II he also began his textual commentary on the Hebrew Bible but was unable to complete it: "Commentarium Hebraicum, in quo de lingua Hebraica, et Hebraeorum codicum puritate agere volebat, inchoavit, et jam aliquo usque perduxit, sed non absolvit." Johannes Buxtorf II to James Ussher, Basel, August 26, 1633, printed in Ussher, *Works*, 15: 567.

[26] "Textum Hebraeum in antiquissima & verissima sua puritate & substantia, in minimo etiam apice, reliquimus. Impius enim, quisquis ei aliquid vel addiderit vel detraxerit, aut quovis modo in eo quid mutaverit." Johannes Buxtorf, introduction to the *Biblia rabbinica*, f. (1)v.

[27] The verses surveyed were Deut 1:1-46, Hosea 1:1-2:25, and Esther 1:1-22. I compared Buxtorf's text with that of the *Biblia rabbinica*, 4 vols (Venice: Daniel Bomberg, 1524-25; reprint ed., Jerusalem: Makor, 1972) since the latter repre-

parison of the occurrence of *Methegs* in each edition of the biblical text also reveals their close similarity.[28] In the same hundred verses the Bomberg second edition has 177 methegs and the Buxtorf Bible 174, 170 of which are common to both, a variation of about six percent. Only 11 occurrences are unique to either Bible.[29] Since the Christian print shop workers who set the type for the Bible were illiterate in Hebrew and had no understanding of the appropriate placement of accents, perhaps even this variation is not as significant as it might otherwise seem.

Buxtorf considered the Targum to be an important aid for Christians in biblical studies and theology. It helped the reader to understand obscure passages in the Hebrew Bible and it plainly testified to the promised Messiah.[30] He understood that the Targum was a paraphrase and not a word-for-word translation and sometimes contained midrashic elements.[31] He was not, therefore, tempted to purge "additions" from the Targum in order to bring it into closer accord with the Hebrew in the way that the editors of the Antwerp Polyglot had done.[32]

Buxtorf followed the consonantal Targum text of his *Vorlage* fairly closely. Bacher noted that the Basel edition, with very few exceptions, contained the printing errors of the Second Venice

---

sents the hypearchetype of the textual family to which the Buxtorf edition belongs.

[28] Menachem Cohen has demonstrated that "light" *metheg* use is a particularly helpful clue for separating medieval biblical manuscripts into their respective families. For a summary of his findings see Menachem Cohen, "Systems of Light *Gayot* in Medieval Biblical Manuscripts and their Importance for the History of the Tiberian System of Notation," *Textus* 10 (1982): 44-83. Jordan S. Penkower applied Cohen's method (using both "light" and "firm" *methegs*) in his analysis of the first and second editions of the Bomberg rabbinical Bible in his work "Jacob ben Hayyim and the Rise of the Biblia rabbinica," 2 vols. (Ph.D. Diss., Hebrew University of Jerusalem, 1982), English summary, xxv-xxvi.

[29] *Methegs* unique to the Venice Second edition in these passages are Deut. 1:1 בְּעֶרְבָה, 1:4 אַחֲרֵי, 1:30 הַהֹלֵךְ, 1: 32 תֵּלְכוּ, Hosea 2:4 כִּי-הִיא, 2:9 וְלֹא and Esther 1:6 בְּחַט-וְשֵׁשׁ. Methegs unique to the Buxtorf Bible in the same verses are Deut. 1:31 נְשָׂאֲךָ, 1:32 בַּיהוָה, Hosea 1:4 כִּי, and Esther 1:12 הַסָּרִיסִים.

[30] Buxtorf to the Estates General of the Netherlands, Basel, April 1, 1620, in *Tiberias*, fol., f. ***3r.

[31] "Targum quinque libellorum, nempe, Ecclesiastis, Canticorum, Thren., Ruth, Esther similem dialectum continent, nisi quod prolixitate alias quasque paraphrases superant, & quandoque in fabulosas opiniones Rabbinicas egrediuntur." Johannes Buxtorf, *Grammaticae Chaldaicae*, 365.

[32] Moshe H. Goshen-Gottstein, "The "Third Targum" on Esther and Ms. Neofiti I," *Biblica* 56 (1975): 308-312.

rabbinical Bible. He provided a list of 25 "errors" common both to the Venice 1516-17 and 1524-25 rabbinical Bibles and to the Basel edition, and 26 errors unique to the Basel Targum text.[33] Of the 47 errors he identified in the Venice 1524-25 Bible, 37 appear in the Basel edition.[34] Significantly almost half of Abraham Braunschweig's errata list is made up of misprints from the Targum.[35] The presence in the Basel Bible of so many "errors" that originated in the Venice rabbinical Bibles suggests that most of the "corrections" Buxtorf made affected the consonantal text minimally.

While he followed the consonantal Targum text of the Bomberg rabbinical Bible closely, Buxtorf considered its vocalization to be in a shameful state of disrepair.[36] He decried the haphazard use of vowel letters and the inconsistent vocalization he found in the Venice Bible editions.[37] His goal in editing the Targum of the Basel rabbinical Bible was to purge the text of grammatical impurities. As the editors of the Complutensian and Antwerp Polyglots had begun, so he would continue.[38]

Even Buxtorf, however, recognized that the Targums were composed in at least two distinct dialects, and he tried to make al-

---

[33] Wilhelm Bacher, "Kritische Untersuchungen zum Prophetentargum," *Zeitschrift der Deutschen Morgenländsichen Gesellschaft* 28 (1874): 41-42. The nature of Bacher's "errors" is less important for this study than for their importance as textual peculiarities suggesting a common origin.

[34] Ibid., 40-41.

[35] *Biblia rabbinica*, ff. K 1v-2r.

[36] "Textum Chaldaeum...ad antiquam, veram & perpetuam linguae priscae Chaldaicae analogiam, libris Esrae & Danielis pulcherrime praemonstratam, redegimus, & ab inepta & insigniter deformi punctatione, quam editiones Venetae continent, vindicavimus." Johannes Buxtorf, introduction to the *Biblia rabbinica*, f. (1)v.

[37] "Praeterea sunt etiam adhuc vestigia in textu Hebraeo, ante usum apicum vocalium, fuisse vocalibus insertas literas vocales, lectionis in linguis Orientalibus matres אי, quae in editionibus Venetis in Targum relictae fecerunt ibi miras anomilias et formas ineptis, si mas propter imperitos Grammaticos istarum literarum non pauca in textu Hebraeo adhuc relicta quando puncta fuerunt adscripta, unde & varietas lectionis quaedam nata." Johannes Buxtorf to Louis Cappel, Basel, January 1, 1623, Zürich ZB Ms. F 45: 247r.

[38] "Haec ipsa, admirabili diligentiae exemplo, in laudatissimo Complutensi Opere primum tentata fuere, & plenius etiam in Opere Regio Hispanico, per Christophorum Plantinum Anno Christi M. D. LXXII. impresso, exculta. Infinita tamen in his meliori curae posterorum, fuerunt relicta. Nihil enim unquam simul fuit coeptum & perfectum." Johannes Buxtorf, introduction to the *Biblia rabbinica*, f. (1)v.

lowance for this diversity in his editorial practice. Targum Onkelos and Jonathan he felt were written in a dialect directly descended from biblical Aramaic. Divergences from biblical Aramaic grammar in them were better understood as grammatical errors rather than as linguistic developments.[39] In using biblical Aramaic as his standard Buxtorf followed the practice of Franciscus Raphalengius, who edited the Targum for the Antwerp Polyglot. Buxtorf felt that he had no recourse but to impose uniformity on conflicting sources using grammatical analogy.[40]

Buxtorf treated the Targums of the Hagiographa rather differently. They were translated much later than Onkelos and Jonathan in a distinctive dialect which, Buxtorf felt, had its own integrity and purity. He attempted to respect this by relying more on comparison with other parts of the Targum and with ancient authorities to restore obviously corrupt words and passages. Buxtorf's attempt to give these Targums special treatment ultimately created a multitude of new textual variants unique to his edition.

The editorial decisions which resulted in the published Targum text are recorded and augmented with additional examples in *Babylonia,* Buxtorf's exhaustive textual commentary on the Targum. He planned to publish it as the second of his four proposed appendices to the Basel rabbinical Bible.[41] *Babylonia* was to be Buxtorf's improvement upon Raphalengius' *Variae lectiones et*

---

[39] "Fundamentum in Daniele & Esra pono. In his enim purissimus, & elegantissimus linguae nitor, ut tunc in florentissimo Babyloniae regno excolebatur, vivide perspicitur. Post quadringentos, & amplius, annos, linguae nitor iste primaevus defloruit...Posteaquam enim Judaei ex Babylonia reduces, diu Hierosolymam occupassent, magis magisque Babylonicam linguam corrumpebant, sic ut ipsorum sermo Hierosolymitanae dialecti nomen tunc acciperet. Inde Talmud Babylonicum, & Hierosolymitanum: inde Targum speciale, in V. Mosis, & alios aliquot libros biblicos Hierosolymitanum appellatum." Johannes Buxtorf to the Counsellors and Senate of Bremen, Basel, March 15, 1615, in *Grammaticae Chaldaicae,* ff.):(4v-5r.

[40] Merx argued that Buxtorf's procedure was not entirely unreasonable. "Buxtorfs Verfahren war also nicht neu, sondern Weiterbildung einer schon vorhandenen Methode, und sagen wir einer nothwendigen Methode, denn wonach soll sich ein Herausgeber richten, wenn die Handschriften verschieden sind, ausser nach der grammatischen Analogie?" Adalbert Merx, "Bemerkungen über die Vocalisation der Targume," *Verhandlungen des fünften internationalen Orientalisten-Congresses* 2, 1 (*Abhandlung und Vorträge der semitischen und afrikanischen Section,* 1) (1882): 159.

[41] *Babylonia, sive Commentarius Criticus in Universum Targum, sive Paraphrasin Bibliorum Chaldaicum,* Basel UB Ms. F IX 41.

annotatiunculae, quibus Thargum, a textual commentary for the Targum of the Antwerp Polyglot, although his own effort was far more comprehensive.[42] He began work on it in conjunction with his editorial work on the Bible project, and continued with it even after the Bible was published. His dissatisfaction with his own work on the Targum text is evident from the numerous marginal notes in his personal copy of the Basel rabbinical Bible. He also wished to provide, as it were, a complete witness to the entire Targum text.[43] He was still working on it in 1625, to the puzzlement of one correspondent who felt Buxtorf could use his time better by responding to Louis Cappel's critique of his book *Tiberias*.[44] Buxtorf completed work on the manuscript before he died but never published it.

Feeling a responsibility for his father's unpublished works Buxtorf II added some further notes to *Babylonia*, particularly in the Pentateuch. He owned a manuscript copy of Targum Onkelos from which he drew a number of variant readings.[45] In 1656

---

42 Franciscus Raphalengius, *Variae lectiones et annotatiunculae, quibus Thargum, id est Chaldaica Paraphrasis infinitis in locis illustratur et emendatur*, in the *Biblia sacra, hebraice, chaldaice, graece et latine*, 8 vols. (Antwerp: C. Plantin, 1569-72), 8: 1-32. (Each tractate in volume 8 has its own pagination). *Babylonia* comprises 836 quarto pages of commentary.

43 Buxtorf II claimed in the subtitle of *Babylonia* that the work would address "Non solum innumerae mendae et corruptelae quae in targumim editionum Venetarum occurrunt, sub censuram revocantur…." Adalbert Merx, "Johannes Buxtorf's des Vaters Targumcommentar Babylonia [Part 1]," *Zeitschrift für wissenschaftliche Theologie* 30 (1887): 285. He wrote to James Ussher, "Haec (i. e. censored portions) & alia loca in commentario Chaldaico parentis diligenter sunt annotata, & ex antiquis exemplaribus restituta." Johannes Buxtorf II to James Ussher, Basel, August 26, 1633, printed in Ussher, *Works*, 15: 568.

44 "Rogo igitur Te vehementer, ut de Apologia tua cogites. Si enim ille Crypticus (i. e. Cappel) invalesceret, qua ratione tyro ad lectionem Hebraeam adduceretur, & vocata in dubium punctatione biblica, quae tandem certitudo in Textibus aequivocis manebat? Variae sunt artes Diaboli, ut Scripturam divinam è medio tollat, vel ejus sensum ita attenuet, ne animus fidus habeat, ubi immotè consistat…Miror etiam ea apud Te latere diutius, quae collegisti in restituendis Commentariis Hebraeorum Targumicis, quae Tibi videbantur peculiare volumen suffectura." Laurentius Fabricius to Johannes Buxtorf, Wittenberg, August 24, 1625, Basel UB Ms G I 61: 210, printed in Buxtorf, *Catalecta*, 434-436. On Cappel and *Tiberias*, see below.

45 *Targum Onkeli in V Lib. Moses*, Basel UB Ms AN IX 1. See *Babylonia*, f. 44v on Deut. 2:25 אֵימְתָךְ = Onkelos ms. f. 188d; f. 51v on Deut. 28: 29 בְּטִיהֲרָא = ibid., f. 216b, and f. 55v on Deut. 33: 29 פְּרִיקַת = ibid., f. 225a. For a description of the manuscript itself see Prijs, *Handschriften*, 21-22. The three examples given above and all other comments on the Onkelos manuscript in *Babylonia* are

Buxtorf II received a letter from Samuel Clark, one of the scholars involved in the London Polyglot project, urging him to send *Babylonia* to England in order to have it published, and in January of 1657 Buxtorf II did so.[46] Unfortunately the manuscript arrived too late to be included in any of the principal volumes of the Polyglot, although Clark did use it as a source for his own textual commentary on the Targum.[47] Bishop Walton and his team were still interested in publishing the manuscript, reassuring Buxtorf II several times on this point, although they never actually did so.[48] Finally, upon the death of Walton, Buxtorf II decided that he had waited long enough and asked for the manuscript back so that he could publish it himself.[49] Buxtorf II himself died without publishing *Babylonia*, and since his death only portions of it have appeared in print.[50]

The elder Buxtorf used an impressive array of sources when writing *Babylonia*, most of them books from his own library. He consulted, naturally, the Venice rabbinical Bibles that he had used previously for his rabbinical Bible edition, but he also referred extensively to Targum texts printed in the Antwerp Polyglot and in

---

written in the hand of Buxtorf II in a lighter shade of brown ink than the rest of the work. The younger Buxtorf's script from later in his life can be distinguished relatively easily from his father's handwriting.

[46] Samuel Clark to Johannes Buxtorf II, London, October 2, 1656, Basel UB Ms G I 62: 21, printed in *Catalecta*, 450-451, and Buxtorf II to Clark, Basel, March 8, 1657, London: British Library Ms. Add 22 905, f. 4r-v.

[47] Clark in the introduction to *Variae Lectiones et Observationes in Chaldaicam Paraphrasin, Biblia sacra, complectentia textus originales...versionesque antiquarum...*, 6 vols. (London: Thomas Roycroft, 1657), 6: 17.

[48] See the three letters from Brian Walton to Johannes Buxtorf II, London, October 15, 1658, Basel UB Ms G I 62: 6, London, December 22, 1659, Basel UB Ms G I 62: 7-8, and London, February 28, 1661, Basel UB Ms. G I 62:9-10, all published in *Catalecta*, 446-449. See also Merx, "Bemerkungen," 160-161.

[49] Johannes Buxtorf II to Samuel Clark, Basel, March 1, 1661, London: British Library Ms Add 22 905, f. 47r.

[50] Genesis 1:1-23 was published in *Catalecta*, 348-351, and Adalbert Merx himself published the entire commentary on Ecclesiastes and Esther, and for I Samuel 2, Psalm 68 and Isa. 11 in "Johannes Buxtorf's des Vaters Targumcommentar Babylonia," *Zeitschrift für wissenschaftliche Theologie* 30 (1887): 280-300 [Part 1], 462-471 [Part 2], and ibid. 31 (1888): 41-48 [Part 3].

the Complutensian Polyglot.[51] References to two appendices of the
Antwerp Polyglot, Raphalengius's textual commentary and Guido
Fabricius's Aramaic lexicon, also appear from time to time.[52]
Buxtorf consulted several Targum editions for specific parts of the
Bible, including a Venice Pentateuch edition with three Targum
texts (including the Jerusalem Targum) and the "Psaltero
Nebiense," a polyglot Psalter edited by Augustinus Justinianus.[53]
Since *Babylonia* was to be a commentary on vocalization as well,
Buxtorf made extensive use of lexicons such as Nathan ben Yehiel's
Aruch, Elias Levita's *Meturgeman*, and Kimhi's *Sefer ha-
Shorashim*. He did not, however, have access to manuscripts of any
portion of the Targum. His commentary was designed to refine and
improve upon the Targum text as it appeared in the Venice rab-
binical Bibles.

Buxtorf's discussion of the book of Esther in *Babylonia* illustrates his understanding of textual corruption and the critical
methods he employed to "cleanse" the Targums of such corruption.[54] He commented on 186 words and phrases in his discussion
of Esther and proposed 135 changes to the Targum text.[55] Only 61

[51] Basel UB held the copy of the Antwerp Polyglot that Buxtorf used (FG I 2-
8), and Buxtorf's personal copy of the latter work was Basel UB FA II 9a, 10,
10a, 10b, 10c, 10d.
[52] Raphelengius, *Variae*, and Guido Fabricius, *Dictionarium syro-
chaldaicum*, the former in vol. 8 and the latter in vol. 7 of the Antwerp Polyglot.
For a summary of the contents of the entire Polyglot see B. Rekers, *Benito Arias
Montano (1527-1598)* (London and Leiden: The Warburg Institute and E. J.
Brill, 1972), 53, n. 1.
[53] חמשה חומשי תורה, 3 parts (Venice: Aaron Pesaro, 1590/1) [Basel UB FA
VII 2a-b, Nr. 1], and *Psalterium, Hebraeum, Graecum, Arabicum et Chaldaeum,
cum tribus Latinis interpretationibus*, ed. Augustinus Justianius (Genoa: Nicolai
Justiani Pauli, 1516).
[54] See *Babylonia*, Basel UB Ms F IX 41, ff. 403v-411r, printed in Adalbert
Merx,"Johannes Buxtorf's des Vaters Targumcommentar Babylonia," *Zeitschrift
für wissenschaftliche Theologie* 30 (1887): 297-299, 462-471 and idem,
"Johannes Buxtorf's des Vater's Targumcommentar Babylonia (Schluss),"
Zeitschrift für die wissenschaftliche Theologie 31 (1888): 41. Although Merx's
transcription is useful, he did not for the most part distinguish between the work
of the elder and later additions by the younger Buxtorf. In the Esther commentary
alone Buxtorf II made additions to verses 1:22, 2:7, 9, 12, 22 and 7:4, although
Merx notes only 1:22 on 465 and n. 1. In this study only the elder Buxtorf's
comments have been noted unless specifically stated.
[55] In 17 instances Buxtorf gave several alternatives rather than definitive solu-
tions. See 1:3, 9, 11, 2:1, 5, 10, 14, 3:2, 4 (two words), 9, 4:5, 5:3, 6:1, 13,
and 8:7, 8.

of these changes appear in the Basel rabbinical Bible, and Buxtorf wrote 31 more in the margin of his personal copy of the Basel rabbinical Bible.[56] His reasons for proposing changes must be deduced from the changes themselves, since his comments are often vague. In 51 instances he claimed that the text was corrupt (*prave, mendose*), the sense was obscure or incongruous (*sensus obscurus, incongrue*) or that there were grammatical errors (*inepte pro*). In 47 cases he wrote simply that his changes "should be read" (*legendum*), were "better" (*melius*), "possible" (*forte, potius, possit*), or "more correct" (*rectius*)." More tentatively he suggested other changes (*puto, videtur, proponendum*).

Buxtorf left the Targum consonantal text of Esther substantially unchanged, even where it departed from the Hebrew text. He noted two substantial "additions," in 1:1 and 9:14, but he felt no need to delete them.[57] He criticized the editors of the Antwerp Polyglot in numerous places for their widespread excision of material.[58] Although he was aware of the second Targum to Esther Buxtorf made virtually no use of it, since he wished to "cleanse" the Esther text he had at hand. He credited the second Targum as his inspiration for suggested changes in only two cases.[59]

Buxtorf made few substantive changes to the consonantal text of Targum Esther. He deleted seven words, added four and substituted five words or phrases. In three instances the change brought the Targum reading into closer accord with the Hebrew text.[60] The addition of יָת in 5:14 may reflect Buxtorf's tendency to bring the Targum text into closer accord with biblical Aramaic. The other fourteen changes do not correspond in any way to the Hebrew text

---

[56] Basel UB FG II 19-20.

[57] In 1:1 Buxtorf gave a Latin translation of the addition and suggested that it was a quote from BT *Megilla* 10b, and noted the addition of a description of the execution of Haman's sons following the word צליבו. Merx, "Babylonia [Part 1]," 297, and "Babylonia [Part 2]," 471.

[58] Buxtorf commented in Esther 1:1, "Hijus libri Targum in Regiis (i. e. the Antwerp Polyglot) majori ex parte castratum est." Merx, "Babylonia [Part 1]," 297. He criticised omissions and deletions made in the polyglot text in 1:13, 3:13, 4:2, and 5:2.

[59] Buxtorf suggested adding a phrase from the second Targum in Esther 4:5: "Hic post vocem מַלְכוּתָא inseri possit ex secundo Targum מַ...מַלְכָּא דִי הֲוָה קָאִים...juxta Hebraeum מִסְרִיסֵי הַמֶּלֶךְ." In 9:12 he used a phrase from it to replace the expression in his *Vorlage*. Merx, "Babylonia [Part 2]," 466-67, 471.

[60] See 2:19 where וְיתוב was repointed to וְיְתֵב, 3:14 where בְּכָל is deleted and 7:6 where אֶסְתֵּר, is added.

and were made to "improve" the verses' readability.[61] Most of the changes proposed by Buxtorf were at the level of morphology and syntax.

The majority of emendations which Buxtorf proposed for Targum Esther may be broadly divided into three categories: correction of transmission errors, changes in morphology, and changes in syntax. The two principal kinds of transmission errors that he found in Targum Esther were metathesis and confusion of look-alike consonants.[62] Buxtorf corrected five words in Esther on the basis of metathesis.[63] He made fifteen changes in single letters, many of which are well-recognized examples of look-alike consonants. These include ד and ר, כ and פ, ה and ח, ב and כ, and ס and ם.[64] That Buxtorf realized that this sort of error did occur is clear from his comment on תוּגְדָן in 8:6.[65]

Most of the changes to the text of Targum Esther which Buxtorf proposed were changes in vocalization. He based a few of these, as he promised in his introduction, on the analogy of forms in other parts of the Targum, and on "other ancient authorities," particularly from talmudic Aramaic and Syriac. Buxtorf used words found in other parts of the Targum as models to emend words in five verses of Esther, and explained obscure words with Targum references in three others.[66] He followed talmudic Aramaic forms in four verses and quoted the Talmud in four other places to illus-

---

[61] Buxtorf deleted עַל in 1:16, וּמְסַח וְיוֹמָא in 2: 20, כְּתִיב in 3:12 and בְּעִזְקַת in 8:8 because he felt that they were "superfluous" in some way (usually because they followed a close synonym). He added וּבְכָל in 4:4 and לָא in 6:1, and the deletion of כבר in 5:14. For the five other substituted forms see דְּתִלַּת in 1:3, וְיִמְחָרָא in 3:4, לְמִמְנֵי in 3:9, יָאֵי in 5:14 and רְחִמוֹי in 6:13.

[62] There is also one instance of dittography, לְלְבְרַת 2:15.

[63] See דְּמַחֲתָן in 1:6, וְגָזֵי in 2:1, חַוֵּיתָא in 2:10, אִתְגְּרִישׁ in 6:1 and בָּאוּזְנִיקָא in 7:4.

[64] ר/ד: תִּגְדָא in 4:11, 5:2 and 8:4, and שְׁהִיד in 6:1; כ/פ: וְהָרְכֵי in 10: 1, ה/ח: חֲתַךְ in 4:5, ב/כ: כְּנַסוּ in 2:21 and ס/ם: וּבְסִיס in 1:7. Other pairs where only one letter changed include ת/ח: וּמַעֲהָא in 9:23, צ/ד: וְאִתְקַדְּרוּ in 8: 10, כ/א: אַרְאוּנִין in 8:9, ק/כ: דְּעַקְרוֹי in 5:14, פ/ת: וּמְסַח in 2:20, ה/מ: כַּד פַּח in 2:1 and ז/ג: גְּנֵי in 1:3.

[65] "תוּגְדָן Mendose pro תִּתְדָן judicabitur , condemnabitur. Facilis transitus literae ת in ג." Merx, "Babylonia [Part 2]," 470.

[66] See פַּג in 2:1, בְּחַזוּ in 2:2, דְּמְנַתַּר in 2:12, תִּגְדָא and in 4:11. For Buxtorf's illustrative use of Targum verses see his comments on 1:6, 2:21 and 10:3. He re-pointed קְרָא in 6:1 on the analogy of קַנָּא, a form more common in targumic than in biblical Aramaic. See Marcus Jastrow, *A Dictionary of the Targumim, the Talmud Babli and Yerushalmi, and the Midrashic Literature*, 2 vols, (London: Trübner, 1886-1913; reprint ed., Brooklyn, NY: P. Shalom, 1967), 1388.

trate the meaning of words.[67] In 6:1 Buxtorf proposed replacing an obscure word with an appropriate one found in Syriac, and in 2:2 noted use of הֲוָה as a modal verb in a manner similar to Syriac usage.[68] Buxtorf also made occasional use of both Nathan ben Yehiel's *Aruch* and Elias Levita's *Meturgeman* to record their unusual textual readings and explanations and to correct their errors or omissions.[69]

Since the "Jerusalem" dialect of Aramaic contained a higher proportion of Greek and Latin loan words than the Aramaic of Onkelos and Jonathan, Buxtorf pointed them out in his commentary.[70] On seven occasions he "corrected" Aramaic words so that they more closely reflected the Greek words from which they were derived.[71] He also noted the Greek or Latin etymologies of a further eight words in Esther.[72]

In spite of his good intentions Buxtorf also made a number of changes which brought words into closer grammatical conformity with biblical Aramaic. He did so in part because he felt that the editors of the Venice rabbinical Bibles used vowel letters unnecessarily often and believed that it was his responsibility to correct these editorial "mistakes."[73] For example, he deleted the first Yod in אִיטָמוֹסִי (2:5) and אִיזְדַבְנָא (7:4) as unnecessary. In 1:3 Buxtorf

---

[67] See Buxtorf's comment on דְּנְבּוֹן in 4:7 and his use of רְחַטָנִין in 3:13, 15 and 8:1. Jastrow, *Dictionary*, 1473. For talmudic illustrations see 1:6, 2:12, 14 and 7:4.

[68] See his comments on שָׁהִיד in 6:1 and on הֲוַת עָבְדַת in 2:20.

[69] Buxtorf mentioned unusual readings given by Levita in his remarks on וְדַשְׁרִין in 1:6, בְּנַסוּ (accepted by Buxtorf) in 2:21, בַּחֲרֵיה in 3:2. Elias Levita, מתורגמן (Cologne: Birckmannum, 1560), ff. 29b, 14b, 6b, 112a (s. v. עצץ), 111a. Buxtorf mentioned Nathan b. Yehiel's *Aruch* in his comments on מִילְתָא in 3:7 and on בָּאוֹנִיקָא in 7:4. Nathan ben Yehiel, ערך השלם *Aruch Completum*, ed. Alexander Kohut 8 vols. in 4 (Vienna: Georg Bróg, 1878-92), 8: 242 (referring to the second definition of תמא in his discussion of 3:7) and 5: 326 for 7:4 [נוז]). He corrected mistakes and omissions in Levita's work in his remarks on עֲצוּצָא in 5:1 and on שָׁהִיד 6:1, and in the *Aruch* for תְּגְרָא in 4:11, ibid., 8: 202 (תִּיגְרָא).

[70] "(Hierosolymitana dialectus) habet et plura vocabula Graeca et Romana, quam priores paraphrastae." Buxtorf, *Dialectorum*, Basel UB A XII 3, f. 4v.

[71] See דְּאִיטָמוֹסִי in 2:5, אִיקְנִין in 2:17, דִּיטַגְמָאָה in 4:8 and 8:13, טִימִין in 7:4, אַרְאוּנִין in 8:9, and וְהַכְרְכִי in 10:1.

[72] See Buxtorf's comments on 1:14, 2:12, 21, 3:8, 7:6 and 8:2.

[73] For example, he wrote, "Orthographiae anomalia creba in literis ו & י geminatis, non quidem in Daniele & Esra, sed in Targum, id est, paraphrasi Bibliorum Chaldaica, maxime editionis Venetae, rarius in Regiis Plantinianis." *Grammaticae Chaldaicae*, 2.

changed a Peal participle with a double Yod, וַאֲיָיתִין, to the biblical Aramaic form וְאָתִין (with the Peal Perfect form וְאָתוֹ as an alternative). He also changed four forms which contained "unnecessary" internal Alephs.[74] His repointing of מִשְׁתָּא to מִשְׁתֵּא in 1:9 reflects the biblical Aramaic usage.

Nearly half (69) of the changes Buxtorf proposed involved changes in morphology. The most apparent reason for most of them is to even out rough places within the Targum text itself. In 5:14, for example, Buxtorf changed four verb forms to imperfect third person masculine singular in order to maintain continuity of subject.[75] He altered the gender reference of three verbs and four nouns or prepositions in order to achieve concord. On several occasions he commented that this was a common problem in Targum Esther.[76]

Other changes reflect grammatical considerations. Buxtorf emended four verbs in Esther that he considered defectively written, three Ithpeel or Ithpael forms, and one defectively written Aphel infinitive. He changed the conjugation in three cases so that the verb fit better into its context.[77] On eight occasions he took noun forms with either an אָא or a אָה ending and deleted the ending, making them into construct forms.[78] In similar fashion he deleted the objective suffixes of לְמִסְבָּה in 5:1 and of רַגְמֵיה in 5:14. Other morphological changes are less explicable. Buxtorf substituted one form of third person feminine singular suffix for nouns and prepositions (הָא) for another (אָה), although he recognized

---

[74] See וַהֲווֹיאָן in 1:3, וּבְנָאָן in 2:3, מְסָאֲנִין in 5:14, and דַּיָּרָאֵי in 9:27.

[75] See changes to חַב, זְרוֹק, סָמוּן and יְגַלֵּי. For other examples of ememdations to ensure subject agreement see וְכַבְּשִׁין in 1:3, דְּשַׁמְשִׁין in 1:10, דְּאִתְעֲבִידָא in 2:7, דְּאִסְתַּמְמוּ in 5:14, and אִתְעֲבִידַת in 7:6.

[76] See גְּזֵרַת and דְּחַיְּיבַת in 2:1 and הַשְׁרִית in 6:13 and for the changes in nouns and prepositions see לְכוּלְהוֹן in 1:3, בְּמַלְלוּתְהוֹן in 1:17, לֵהּ in 2:18 and לָךְ in 5:3. See Buxtorf's comments ad loc in Merx, "Babylonia," 298-99, 464 and 468.

[77] See אַגְלִיאַת in 2:6, לְשָׁחֲצָאָה in 4:1 and תֶּהֱפוֹךְ in 5:14. Buxtorf commented on this kind of change in 4:1. See Merx, "Babylonia," 466. For the Aphel form see לְאַשְׁקָא in 1:7 and for the remaining three changes see מְפַלְחָה in 1:11, יַשֵּׁר in 5:8 and יְאַבֵּד in 6:1.

[78] See כּוּרְסֵיה in 1:2, מַדְבְּחָא and דְּבְכוּרְסֵיה in 1:14, וּמַלְכוּתָא in 1:19, חַוֵּיתָא in 2:10, כּוּרְסֵיה in 5:1, כּוּלֵיה in 6:1 and בְּעִזְקְתָא in 8:8. In one case Buxtorf simply substituted the final ה for a final א (See מַלְכוּתָה in 2:4).

both forms as valid in his *Grammaticae Chaldaicae*.[79] Beyond these patterns of change Buxtorf revocalized many other words.[80]

Buxtorf made relatively few changes in syntax to Esther. He proposed that word order be changed on two occasions[81] and suggested twenty-one changes involving waw conjunctive, the relative pronoun Dalet and prepositions. The most common change Buxtorf made was to add a Dalet in order to make genitive constructions plainer.[82] The other changes that he proposed involving Waw and Dalet do not fit any particular pattern.[83]

The editorial patterns evident in Buxtorf's textual commentary on Esther suggest that four considerations played an important role in his textual decisions. He wanted the Targum to reflect the Hebrew original, although he made few actual emendations to fulfill this wish, reflecting his concern to respect its textual integrity. Grammatical correctness played an important role in Buxtorf's editing, not only in Targums Onkelos and Jonathan, but also for the Targums of the Hagiographa. His preoccupation with grammatical order impelled Buxtorf to make numerous textual changes so that incongruities in the text, whether of person, gender, or verb construction, were smoothed out. Finally, he showed some awareness of transmission errors and a willingness to make textual changes in the Targum, using them as the basis for his decision. The latter point is especially striking when compared with the deferential attitude Buxtorf took toward the received Hebrew text. While only an impious man would change the Hebrew Bible text, the Targum could be corrected as necessary.

---

[79] See עֲלָה and רֵישָׁהָא in 1:11, עֲלָהָא in 1:15 and רְבוּתָהָא in 2:9, and *Grammaticae Chaldaicae*, 38.

[80] For example, he changed קַדְמְיָתָא to קַדְמִיתָא in 1:1 and אֶתְפְּרַע to אִתְפְּרַע, in 3:1.

[81] See יְדוֹי in 3:9 and בְּמוֹקְדוֹנִין דְּדַהֲבָא in 8:15.

[82] Buxtorf seemed to favor the genitive construction in which the first word was in the determined state and the second had a relative pronoun. See מַלְכוּתֵיהּ in 1:2, דְּכַרְנְיָא in 2:23, דְּעַמָּא מָרְדְּכַי in 3:6, עֵצוּצָא in 5:1, סְטוּמְתָּא in 8:2 and יוֹמָא נִיסָא in 9:12. Buxtorf added Dalet only to genitive forms in 1:19 (פַּרְסָאֵי), 8:15 (בִּדְהַב) and 9:30 (מַלְכוּת).

[83] Buxtorf proposed adding Dalet in his comments on 2:21 (דְּמִטּוֹל), 2:2 (דַּהֲווֹ) and 5:14 (דְּאִסְתַּחֲמִמוּ). He wished to add a waw conjunctive in 1:3 (מִטּוֹל), 6:1([סְכַן]) and 9:23 (מַתְּנָן), and to delete them in 2:12 (אַנְפְּקִינוֹן), 6:1 (וּמַטְרַד) and 10:1 (וְהַכְּרְכֵי).

If Buxtorf's goal for his Targum edition was to impose a kind of grammatical uniformity on the disorderly texts printed in the Venice rabbinical Bibles, then he succeeded. But what did his "cleansing" of the text accomplish for Targum studies in general? Richard Simon thought that Buxtorf had rushed in where even Elias Levita had feared to tread when he applied a grammatical standard to the Targum and made textual corrections accordingly. Levita stated in the introduction to *Meturgeman* that he did not think himself capable of composing an Aramaic grammar for the Targums because of the dramatic variations in both consonantal text and in vocalization present in the manuscripts.[84] Buxtorf's failure to consult Targum manuscripts of any kind in the preparation of the Basel rabbinical Bible was his greatest mistake. In limiting himself to printed editions, eschewing the use of manuscripts to prepare the Targum text, and in choosing to "correct" the Targum text assembled by Bomberg's editors for the Venice rabbinical Bibles, Buxtorf ensured the idiosyncratic quality of his own work. Simon argued that Buxtorf's critical method, particularly his use of a grammatical standard, was based on an illusion.[85]

Even in his attempts to safeguard the linguistic purity of the Targums written in the "Jerusalem" dialect Buxtorf actually compromised its integrity. Since he used forms drawn from other Targums, the Talmud, Syriac and even Greek and Latin as models to emend words in Targum Esther, what he created was a "mixed text" which reflected the grammatical patterns of at least three Aramaic dialects. Buxtorf's readiness to seek grammatical clues in

---

[84] Levita wrote (in the Latin translation quoted by Simon), "Plurimi rogarunt me, an condi posset Grammatica in haec Targumim, respondi uti sentiebam, nimirum, me non posse, eo quod exemplaria inter se variarent, tam in dictionibus quam in literis, & omnino in punctis, quae admodum variant." Richard Simon, *Disquisitiones criticae de variis per diversa loca & Tempora Bibliorum Editionibus* (London: Richard Chiswel, 1684), 102.

[85] "On ne s'arrêtera donc pas toûjours aux ponctuations qui sont dans les Paraphrases Caldaïque imprimées, ni aux Traductions Latines, ou il y a assez souvent de l'erreur: & de-plus, tout ce que nous avons qui appartient à la Grammaire Caldaïque, est defectueux, & ne peut pas servir de regle infaillible; parce que les Juifs, qui ont negligé pendant un tres-long tems cette étude, n'ont pû rétablir parfaitement la Langue Caldaïque; outre que la methode dont Buxtorfe & les autres Reformateurs se sont servis pour corriger la vielle ponctuation du Caldéen, est sujette à illusion." Richard Simon, *Histoire critique du Vieux Testament*, 2d ed. (Rotterdam: Reinier Leers, 1685; reprint ed., Frankfurt a. M.: Minerva, 1967), 300.

other dialects of Aramaic together with his willingness to emend the Targum in order to create a more logical, readable text unfortunately motivated him to create a linguistic curiosity. Buxtorf's edition of the Targum is of more interest to modern scholars as an example of seventeenth-century editorial practice than as a witness to the Targum text. Any value that it has in this respect is derived entirely from its parent text, the Venice rabbinical Bible of 1546-48.

Buxtorf considered the Jewish Bible commentaries that were to be printed in the margins of the *Biblia rabbinica* to be works both useful and dangerous for Christian readers. They were indispensable for any interpreter who wished to find the literal sense of many biblical passages, because the commentators were such excellent grammarians. The commentaries also contained "perverse and false" interpretations, particularly in those passages which discussed the Messiah. Surprisingly Buxtorf let these passages stand without censoring them because, he claimed, they stood as a testimony to the unbelief of the Jews, and hence were a fulfillment of what Moses and the prophets had predicted.[86]

Buxtorf's claim to have left "Jewish blasphemies" in the rabbinical Bible commentaries was somewhat disingenuous. The most objectionable passages in the commentaries, those which would invite a prohibition on sale of the Bible edition in the Holy Roman Empire, Italy and elsewhere, had already been excised from his *Vorlage*.[87] In David Kimhi's commentary on Isaiah chaps. 1-35, for example, the words "Christians," "heretics," and "Jesus" occur eleven times, while in the Venice 1546 printing ten of the eleven

---

[86] "Est in iis mel, est in iis fel. Melleum, quod ad linguae Hebraicae proprietatem melius explicandam, quodque ad literalem Grammaticumque Scripturae sensum genuine illustrandum facit commodumque est, suscipimus, quod & omnes alii viri docti, quotquot accuratiorem & perfectiorem linguae Hebraicae cognitionem inter Christianos assecuti sunt, hactenus fecerunt. Felleum, quod in rerum tractatione perversa aut falsa occurit, & maxime in iis locis qui de promisso Messia, ejusque persona & officio agunt, id totum ipsis relinquimus, ut sit contra eos loco testis perpetui, ut Moses loquitur Deut. 31: 26, quod caecitate percussi sint, ut idem praedixerat Deut 28: 28." Johannes Buxtorf, introduction to the *Biblia rabbinica*, f. (1)v.

[87] I discussed the measures used by German imperial and territorial authorities during the seventeenth century to control the Jewish book trade in "Hebrew Censorship in Hanau," 203-205.

were removed.[88] The censors also made some attempt to remove all references to Rome; the critical edition of Kimhi's commentary contains twelve references to Rome and Romans, but there are only five occurrences in the Venice printing.[89] In some cases, such as Kimhi's discussion of the young woman (*almah*) in Isa 7: 14, they removed whole sentences at a time.[90] It is also possible that Buxtorf's copy of the Venice 1546 Bible was expurgated, a process which would have removed still more potentially offensive material.[91]

In fact, Buxtorf did censor his *Vorlage* rather carefully and removed many words and phrases which had escaped the attention of earlier censors. Where the editors of the Venice 1546 Bible had left five occurrences of "Rome," Buxtorf reduced them to one, in Isa. 30:6. The other places where the word occurred he either deleted it or changed it to "Edom," "Samaria," or "Babylon."[92] Buxtorf also deleted or changed Kimhi's comments which contained "Edom" or the "Kingdom of Edom" as well, since he knew that these names were often used to signify Christianity or

---

[88] נצרים occurs six times (2:19, 2:21 (2x), 2:23, 11:14 and 34:1), מינים occurs twice, both times in 7:15, and ישו occurs three times in 2:19, 2:21 and 7:15. נצרים was retained in Isa. 11: 1 because it was not used pejoratively. In addition to Buxtorf's *Biblia rabbinica*, I have used *The Commentary of David Kimhi on Isaiah*, ed. Louis Finkelstein, Columbia University Oriental Studies, vol. 19 (New York: Columbia Univ. Press, 1926), and *Miqraot Gedolot*, 4 vols (Venice: Daniel Bomberg, 1546-1548) [Oxford: Bodleian Library, Opp. fol. 7].

[89] In the critical edition רומי occurs twelve times in 21:12, 24:16, 25:2, 26:5, 30:6, 34:1 (4x), 9 (2x), and verse 16, while the Venice 1546 printing has it only in 21: 2, 24: 16, 25: 2, 30: 6 and 34:9. In 34: 1 and 34: 9 the word אדום was substituted for רומי. Replacing offensive words with more inocuous ones was a fairly common censorial practice in Italy and one which Buxtorf himself used quite frequently. See Popper, *The Censorship of Hebrew Books*, 57-59, 79-80.

[90] For the sake of convenience I will identify the excised material in 7:14 by page and line number in Kimhi, *Commentary*, 49. The censors removed about three lines beginning with the words following העלמה הרה at the end of line 15 and picking up Kimhi's discussion with the phrase והעלמה הזאת about half way through line 19. Other places where Kimhi's commentary was "abridged" include Isa. 7:15 and 34:1.

[91] On the pervasiveness of expurgation, see Isaiah Sonne, *Expurgation of Hebrew Books—the Work of Jewish Scholars. A Contribution to the History of Censorship of Hebrew Books in Italy During the Sixteenth Century* (New York: New York Public Library, 1943).

[92] Buxtorf used אדום in Isa. 21:2, כותא in 24:16, בבל in 25:2, and deleted it entirely in 39:4.

Christendom.[93] He made other less obvious, but no less tendentious, textual changes as well. Where Kimhi stated in his comment on Isa. 35: 8 that the nations (*goyim*) would not walk on the highway of holiness, Buxtorf substituted the word "wicked," (*reshaim*), forcing Kimhi to follow Isaiah's wording.[94] While editing and censoring the biblical commentaries he took careful notes on places containing offensive or blasphemous remarks because he hoped ultimately to compile a textual commentary on the biblical commentaries.[95] Buxtorf clearly made an effort to edit out what he considered to be obvious instances of blasphemy or derogatory remarks about the Christian faith.

Buxtorf's work on the rabbinical Bible commentaries was sharply criticized by later scholars. Richard Simon said that the Jews considered it a poor edition since it not only left uncorrected the numerous errors of the Bomberg rabbinical Bible editions, but multiplied them still further. Furthermore Buxtorf did not use any manuscripts of the commentaries to revise his printed text.[96] Others, such as James Ussher, deplored the absence of some of the censored material.[97] Buxtorf's later critics, however, did not take

---

[93] Buxtorf, *Juden Schul*, 458-459. אדום and מלכות אדום occur twenty seven times in the critical edition; Buxtorf censored them in 24:17, 27:1, 34:1 (5x), 5, 7, 16 (2x), 17 and 35:1 (3x), 4; the word/phrase occurs eleven times in the Buxtorf Bible: 1:18 (4x), 11:11, 14, 12:8, 24:5, 25:10 (2x) and 27:2. Buxtorf replaced Edom with יון in 24:17 and 34:5, and with כותא in 34:1, 34:16 and 35:1.

[94] The Venice 1546 text of Kimhi's commentary contained גוים.

[95] "Ad haec, collegerat illa loca omnia pater meus, et in praefatione, quam illis praefigere volebat proponere voluit. Quia autem post absolutam editionem aliud consilium ceperat, de triplici commentario addendo, Masorethico scilicet Chaldaico, et Hebraeo, in commentarium Hebraicum ista reservabat, vel in peculiarem tractatum quam parabat de blasphemiis Judaeorum contra Christianos." Johannes Buxtorf II to James Ussher, Basel, August 26, 1633, printed in Ussher, *Works*, 17: 566-567.

[96] "Mais bien qu'il prétende que son Edition est plus exacte que les autres, les Juifs cependant ne l'estiment pas beaucoup, à cause des fautes qui s'y rencontrent, sur tout dans les Commentaires des Rabbins, ou il a laissé les erreurs des Copistes qui étoient dans les Editions précedentes, & il y en ajoûté de nouvelles. Il seroit necessaire d'avoir de bons Exemplaires manuscrits de ces Commentaires de Rabbins, pour les corriger en une infinité d'endroits...." Simon, *Histoire critique du Vieux Testament*, 513. Jacob b. Hayim devoted relatively little effort to editing the biblical commentaries in the 1525 Rabbinical Bible. See Jacob b. Hayim, *Introduction*, 84, and Goshen-Gottstein, "Introduction," 11 and n. 25.

[97] "Where by the way you may note, that in the last edition of the Masoritical and Rabbinical Bible, printed by Bombergius, both this (referring to Ibn Ezra's

into account the very strict constraints under which he edited and
printed the Jewish biblical commentaries. Buxtorf II recalled later
that the city council of Basel had insisted that the rabbinical Bible
be strictly censored so that it contained no instances of blasphemy
against Christ or slurs against Christians or the Christian religion.
He noted significantly that anyone who knew how much trouble his
father had experienced on account of the Bible edition would understand why he had been careful about such passages in the commentaries.[98]

Buxtorf felt that the Masora played an extremely important role
both in indicating true readings and preventing textual corruption.
Therefore he was appalled at the number of discrepancies he found
in the course of his revisions. He would spare no effort in correcting these errors as well.[99] Buxtorf's corrections in the *Masora
magna* and *parva* serve to underscore his belief that he was printing
an inviolable Hebrew biblical text. Jacob ben Hayyim, who compiled the Masoras (*parva*, *magna* and *finalis*) that were printed in
the 1524-25 Venice rabbinical Bible reported that his own work
reflected the collation of many manuscripts and that it did not al-

---

comment on Gen. 37: 35) and divers other passages elsewhere have been cut out
by the Romish correctors, which I wish our Buxtorfius had understood when he
followed that mangled and corrupted copy in his late renewed edition of that great
work." James Ussher, *An Answer to a Challenge Made By a Jesuit in Ireland*
(1625), printed in *Works*, 3: 320.

[98] "Deinde quod illa quae contra Christianos faciunt non fuerint restituta,
factum esse, partim mandato et voluntate magistratus nostri qui ea lege permisit
editionem illam, ut ne quid vel in Christum blasphemi, vel in Christianos et
Christianam religionem maledici et contumeliosi in iis relinqueretur. Et qui novit
persecutiones et odia gravissima, quae occasione Bibliorum istorum in hac ipsa
urbe contra se excitavit pater meus, non mirabitur, ipsum sibi ab istius modi
Judaeorum cavillis exprimendis cavisse." Johannes Buxtorf II to James Ussher,
Basel, August 26, 1633, printed in Ussher, *Works*, 17: 566.

[99] "Tertia horum Bibliorum pars Massora vocatur, estque Critica sacra super
textum Hebraeum, ejus genuinam lectionem indicans & adversus omnem
corruptionem & depravationem eum firmissime muniens, unde Sepes Legis ab
Hebraeis appellatur...Massoram majorem & minorem non raro inter se
discrepare, aliaque typographica menda non pauca incidisse observavimus. Haec
talia in prima editione, in qua ex manuscriptis omnia excudebantur, fuisse
commissa, non est mirum: at in sequentibus editionibus à Correctoribus Hebraeis
ista non fuisse deprehensa vel correcta inexcusabilis est socordia. Nos vero his
singulis, opera Hebraei cujusdam adjuti, quotiescunque nostram
animadversionem & censuram incurrerent, curatricem manum adhibuimus,
labesque & maculas, quascunque deprehendimus, diligenter eluimus." Johannes
Buxtorf, introduction to the *Biblia rabbinica*, f. (1)v.

ways agree with the Hebrew Bible text printed with it.[100] In cases
where biblical manuscripts and Masora manuscripts disagreed and
Ben Hayyim was unable to resolve the conflict satisfactorily, he assumed that either there was an error in the Masora or that the
Masora was correct, reflecting a manuscript that he had not
seen.[101] Judging by Buxtorf's printed justification of the changes he
made in the Masora of the Basel rabbinical Bible, he thought that
only the Masora could err.

In the folio version of *Tiberias* Buxtorf published a critical
commentary on the Masora in which he justified changes that he
had made in the Basel rabbinical Bible. He also proposed some
additional corrections in it.[102] The changes he wished to make in
the *Masora magna* and *parva* for the book of Isaiah illustrate
Buxtorf's rather conservative approach in matters masoretic.
Buxtorf made 28 of the 41 proposed changes on the basis of masoretic notes in other parts of the Bible.[103] In five instances he corrected the *Masora parva* of given passages with information drawn
from *Masora magna* on the same word or phrase.[104] In both cases
Buxtorf corrected the Masora on the basis of the biblical text that
he had before him. In three instances Buxtorf detected instances of
textual corruption within the masoretic notes themselves.[105] The

---

[100] Jacob ben Hayyim, *Introduction*, 79-80. For a discussion of the
terminology and function of these parts of the Masora see Israel Yeivin,
Introduction to the Tiberian Masorah, trans. and ed. E. J. Revell, The Society of
Biblical Literature Masoretic Studies, no. 5 (n. p.: Scholars Press, 1980), 64-80.

[101] Penkower, "Jacob ben Hayyim," English summary, 1: xvi. Goshen-
Gottstein argued convincingly, that Jewish scholars resisted the idea that any
printed Bible edition faithfully reflected the whole Hebrew text without error or
question in his "Foundations," 83-86. Elsewhere he wrote that scholars such as
Norzi and Lonsano felt that parts of the biblical text did indeed require revision,
but that 99% of it was beyond dispute. They thought in terms of "one traditional
text which had suffered scribal corruptions in some minor details." Goshen-
Gottstein, introduction to the *Biblia Rabbinica*, 12

[102] Buxtorf, *Tiberias*, fol. (Basel: Ludwig König, 1620), 80-114.

[103] Isaiah 1:16, 23; 2:3; 3;1, 18; 7:14; 8:2; 10:33; 11:12; 14:10; 23:6; 28:23
(2x); 28:29; 30:25; 31:1; 33:16; 34:11; 40:12, 16; 47:11; 48:8; 49:21; 50:3; 58:1,
4; 61:4 and 65:23. Buxtorf's notes on Isaiah are on ibid., 94-96.

[104] Isaiah 7:3; 16:9; 25:3; 40:16 and 48:18.

[105] In Isaiah 19:5 Buxtorf argued that a scribe had copied part of Jonah 2:6
into the Masora magna quotation of Jonah 2:4, in 37:33 he deleted one וְלֹא from
וְלֹא וְלֹא לֹא וְלֹא וְלֹא on the basis of dittography and in 38:16 he noted that נדיא
should be ודיא, a נ/ו interchange.

remaining five changes are less easily characterized.[106] In none of
these instances did Buxtorf defer to a masoretic reading; to him the
Masora was of use only to the extent that it reflected the phenomena of the Hebrew Bible text of Jacob ben Hayyim.

Buxtorf claimed to have made extensive use of a Masora
manuscript which he borrowed from the Heidelberg University
Palatina collection through the courtesy of its librarian, Janus
Gruter, and several unnamed governmental officials.[107] Prijs noted
that since Buxtorf received the manuscript no earlier than
December of 1619 he probably had little time to consult it as
Tiberias was printed shortly afterward.[108] If Buxtorf did consult
the manuscript, he followed very few of its readings. Only four of
the 41 comments Buxtorf made on the *Masora magna* and *parva* of
Isaiah also appear in the manuscript and Buxtorf followed only one
of them, כְּמוֹ in 14:10.[109]

The "errors" in the Masora that Buxtorf wished to correct were
inconsistencies with the biblical text and inconsistencies within the
masoretic notes themselves. That the differing Masora readings
could reflect biblical manuscripts which differed from Ben
Hayyim's text was not one of Buxtorf's working assumptions, although he had read Ben Hayyim's Bible introduction and so must

---

[106] Isaiah 5:27 refers the reader to the *Masora finalis* which indicates 5:27
without there being a master list of occurances in either location. In 3:11, 42:7
and 43:8 Buxtorf made smaller changes within the Masora magna of each verse
and in 45:12 he deleted a critical note printed in parentheses which came at the
end of the Masora magna reference.

[107] "Hinc natus primo Commentarius Criticus, qui Castigationes in universam
masoram continet ad quarum verificationem magnopere in plerisque profuit &
consensit Masora manuscripta in pergameno, quam ex Bibliotheca Illustrissimi
Principis Palatini, opera viri clarissimi D. Jani Gruteri eram consecutus, cujus
tamen usum optassem citius mihi contigisse." Buxtorf to the Estates General of
the Netherlands, Basel, April 1, 1620, *Tiberias*, fol., f. ***3v. See also Janus
Gruter to Johannes Buxtorf, Heidelberg, December 8, 1619, Basel UB Ms G I
60:7; a German translation is printed in Buxtorf-Falkeisen, *Buxtorf*, 28-29; the
manuscript is Basel UB A III 1. See also Umberto Cassuto, *I Manoscritti Palatini
Ebraici Della Biblioteca Apostolica Vaticana e la Loro Storia*, Studi e Testi, no. 66
(Vatican City: Biblioteca Apostolica Vaticana, 1935), 58-59.

[108] Prijs, *Drucke*, 533, n. 2. The manuscript contains the *Masora magna* and
Masora parva to the former and latter prophets, to Psalms, and to the Megillot.
The bulk of it dates from the twelfth or thirteenth centuries. See Prijs,
Handschriften, 24-25.

[109] Basel UB A III 1, f. 45b. The other references to Isaiah passages in the
manuscript which Buxtorf did not follow are לְרָשָׁע in 3:11 (f. 44b), וְנֶהֱרַ in 19:5
(f. 46a) and תַּרְשִׁישָׁה in 23:6 (f. 46a).

have been aware of the problem.[110] His work as an editor was to "improve" the existing Venice rabbinical Bible by eliminating inconsistencies and errors in the Masora, just as he had "cleansed" the Targum text of errors. In striving for consistency between the text and the Masora he differed little from the accepted scribal standards of Jewish copyists.[111] Although he did not use the term, Buxtorf believed that the Ben Hayyim biblical text was a *Textus receptus* and that its Masora should reflect its phenomena.[112] What other Masora manuscripts might attest was not as important for him as for Ben Hayyim.[113]

Buxtorf's hope to create a corrected version of Ben Hayyim's Masora were doomed to failure in any case both because of his choice of *Vorlage* and the ineptitude of the printers. Prijs noted that the *Masora finalis* of Buxtorf's *Vorlage* was the most error-ridden of the three Venice editions, and its short-comings were compounded by printing mistakes made by the Basel printers.[114] For example, the concluding formula from a list of Babylonian and Palestinian variants, which was misplaced in the third Venice edition, was actually printed seven pages before the list began in the Basel Bible.[115] The catch word phrase "the letter Waw" was printed on the third to last page of the *Masora finalis*, long after all listings for that letter.[116] Buxtorf attempted, however, to remedy some of the worst deficiencies of his *Vorlage*. He reprinted the entries for lists 13 and 14 from the Venice 1568 Bible since they

---

[110] Ben Hayyim's introduction was printed on ff. a2r-3v, of the Basel rabbinical Bible and Buxtorf quotes it in *Tiberias* (quarto edition), 46-47. See idem, *Introduction*, 42.

[111] "The question of absolute precision and relative correlation between text and massoretic notation thus became a major touchstone for judging the quality of a codex." Moshe Goshen-Gottstein, "The Aleppo Codex and the Rise of the Massoretic Bible Text," *Biblical Archaeologist* 42 (1979): 149.

[112] Ibid., 158-162, and idem, "Foundations," 82-83.

[113] Richard Simon's (inevitable) criticism of the Masora of the Buxtorf Bible was that he had not consulted Masora manuscripts. *Lettres Choisies de M. Simon, ou L'on Trouve un Grand nombre de faits anecdotes de Literature*, 2d ed., 4 vols. (Rotterdam: R. Leers, 1702-1705; reprint ed., Frankfurt a. M.: Minerva, 1967), 1: 22, 25.

[114] "Das ist nun allerdings die fehlerhafteste, von der II., die Editio princeps der Masora enthaltenden, und von der mit dieser fast identisch IV. am meisten abweichende." Prijs, *Drucke*, 334.

[115] The list began on *Biblia rabbinica,* f. 65b and its concluding formula appears on f. 62a. Ibid., 335.

[116] See *Biblia rabbinica*, f. 28b, and Prijs, *Drucke*, 335.

were missing from his *Vorlage*.[117] He also added new entries in several places where previous editions had merely given "see" references to entries in the *Masora magna*.[118] Perhaps, again, Buxtorf's illiterate Christian printers are to blame for some of the evident errors in the *Masora finalis*, since the *Masora magna* and *parva* show evidence of a good deal of careful correction.

The Basel rabbinical Bible became a standard tool for research among Christian scholars and would remain so, in spite of its well-known weaknesses, until the end of the nineteenth century.[119] It served as one of the sources used in compiling the Paris Polyglot of 1628-45 but exercised greatest influence upon the London Polyglot.[120] Brian Walton, who edited the latter work, acknowledged that he and his fellow workers had made extensive use of Buxtorf's Hebrew and Targum texts in the critical work which went into their Bible edition.[121] Samuel Clark, as has been noted, was also able to put *Babylonia* to use in his critical commentary on the Targum in volume six of the Polyglot.

The Buxtorf Bible was, however, in the end merely a further revision of the 1546-1548 printing of Jacob ben Hayyim's rabbinical Bible. Any differences between it and Ben Hayyim that were not the result of inept printing reflect Buxtorf's understanding of editorial practice and, to a lesser degree, his theological predisposition. He used no manuscript sources in his revision, only the rules of grammar and his own seemingly limitless patience to compile exhaustive notes in order to eliminate inconsistencies. This appar-

---

117 Prijs, *Drucke*, 334 and 530-531.
118 For example, Prijs noted that Buxtorf gave complete listings for חמש on f. 32, col. a and לעיניהם on f. 49, cols. d-e. *Drucke*, 530.
119 Kautzsch used it when he consulted the Targum text or medieval Jewish Bible commentaries. *Buxtorf*, 7-8. Merx noted that since Targum editions published before the Buxtorf Bible were difficult to obtain and more recent editions did not contain texts for the entire Targum, the Buxtorf Bible was still often used for Targum studies in his day. "Babylonia," 280. J. Derenbourg published Abraham Braunschweig's introduction to the errata list in part to warn exegetes that many "authentic variants" in the Buxtorf Bible were probably printing errors. "L'Édition de la Bible Rabbinique," 70.
120 Ernst Friedrich Karl Rosenmüller, *Handbuch für die Literatur der biblischen Kritik und Exegese*, 4 vols. (Göttingen: Vandenhoeck & Ruprecht, 1798-1800), 3: 319.
121 Brian Walton, *Biblicus Apparatus Chronologico-Typographico-Philologus* (Zurich: Bodmerianus, 1673), 265. See also Brian Walton to John Lightfoot, n. p., April 14, 1656, printed in Lightfoot, *Works*, 13: 358-59.

ently endless capacity for work would serve Buxtorf well when he edited another of his massive projects, a new edition of the Hebrew Bible concordance of Isaac Nathan b. Kalonymus.

Jacob ben Hayyim praised Isaac Nathan ben Kalonymus' Bible concordance because he found it a useful tool for his work on the Masora.[122] By contrast, Buxtorf found it to be poorly organized and incomplete when he revised the Masora for the Basel rabbinical Bible. He also disagreed with many of Isaac Nathan's parsings of Hebrew words and consequently with their incorrect placement within the concordance. He felt that a thorough revision of the entire concordance was necessary.[123]

Buxtorf envisioned three principal uses for his edition of the *Concordantiae*.[124] It was to be a useful tool for helping scholars find quickly the Bible passages they sought. The *Concordantiae* would also be an important lexical aid since all forms of a given verb, noun or other word as it appeared in the Bible were listed

---

[122] Jacob ben Hayyim, *Introduction*, 80-81.

[123] "Disponuntur in formam Lexici, ut quaelibit vox, qua forma, et quiotes in tota Scriptura extet, primo intuitu vel levi momento inveniatur. Sic erit quoque Masora perfecta et illustris, eius Masorae, quae hodie extat, innumerabiles defectus et errores detegens. Multos locos, qui hactenus in Concordantiis defuerunt, addo. Confusionem corrigo in radicibus veluti הגה ponitur in יגה: Quiescentia et Defectiva secunda radicali plerumque sunt confusa, veluti ידי et דוד, item נדד et דוד. Sic סלה et סלל confusa, נמל et מול, ירק et רוק, et aliae radices pluriame, quae in Concordantiis sunt confusae." Johannes Buxtorf to Peter Cunaeus, Basel, June 24, 1625, Leiden UB Ms. Cun 2:91, printed in Cunaeus, *Epistolae*, 145-47. Buxtorf used as his *Vorlage* the third edition of *Concordantiae Bibliorum Hebraeorum* (Basel: Ambrosius Froben, 1581).

[124] While Buxtorf II's preface to the *Concordantiae* is the source for most of this discussion, his father clearly had these goals in mind when he selected the complete title for the work that he had composed by 1625. See the manuscript copy of the title page enclosed in Buxtorf's letter to Peter Cunaeus, Basel, September 15, 1625, Leiden UB Cun 2:93. Buxtorf's proposed title reads, "Concordantiae Bibliorum Hebraicae, nova et artificiosa methodo dispositae, quam plurimis locis deficientibus expletae, Radicibus antea confusis, distinctae, et mendis sublatus castigatae: Quibus Primum Locus quaesitus, exerto quasi digito, in momento ostenditur, aut facillimo saltem jucundissimoque labore invenitur: Secundo Lexici Hebraici omnibus vocibus flexilibus completi, forma absoluta proponitur. Denique Masora perfecta , quoties scilicet, quâ formâ, quo loco, libro, capite et versu ununiquodque vocabulum in textu Hebraeo invenitur, numerato traditur, Cum praefatione multiplicem harum Concordantiarum usum declarante. Pars secunda, voces indeclinabiles et chaldaicas aliusque in prioribus Concordantiis desideratas, complectens." The proposed title differs little from the one assigned by Buxtorf II.

together in one place.[125] Finally, he hoped to create a useful tool for masoretic studies. Indeed, Buxtorf felt that his concordance would be an improvement upon the Masora since the latter did not contain notes on every word in the Bible and did not give book, chapter and verse references in its lists as his concordance did.[126]

Although there was a felt need among Protestant theologians and philologists for a new Hebrew Bible concordance, Buxtorf had more difficulty getting this work published than any of his other books. He began work on the concordance revision after *Tiberias* was printed in 1620. By June of 1625 he had completed all entries for the letter Pe and in September he began work on the letter Shin.[127] The draft was completed by May of 1626, but seven more years would pass before the book finally appeared in print.[128]

The Hebrew Bible concordance, like the rabbinical Bible edition, was an extremely expensive work to print and it would be purchased only by a relatively small group of customers. It also required the services of a printer with an ample supply of Hebrew type and assistants who had experience with Hebrew language printing.[129] Buxtorf did not have enough money to finance its publication and he had reservations about Ludwig König's ability to print it.[130] André Rivet offered to arrange for its printing in

---

[125] "Omnes Radices cum suis derivatis omnibus, sed et singularum vocum formae universae, appositis statim singulorum vocabulorum locis, in quibuscunque per universam Scripturam occurrunt, quod in nullo hactenus Lexico factum." Johannes Buxtorf II, preface to *Concordantiae Bibliorum Hebraicae et Chaldaicae*, ed. Bernhard Baer (Stettin: E. Schrentzelius, 1861), (unpaginated).

[126] "Plurimae adhuc sunt, quarum Masora nulla extat. Hic numeratur omnes et singulae, exceptis nimirum nominibus propriis, et paucis quibusdam particulis, quarum fere nullus numerus. Masora libros et capita non solet indicare. Hic sunt in promptu." Ibid.

[127] Johannes Buxtorf to Peter Cunaeus, June 24, 1625, and idem to idem, Basel, September 15, 1625, Leiden UB Ms Cun 2:93, printed in Cunaeus, *Epistolae*, 151-52.

[128] Johannes Buxtorf II to Wilhelm Schickard, May 7, 1626, WLB Cod. hist. 2° 563 and Dr. F. Seck's unpublished edition of Schickard's correspondence, *Wilhelm Schickard Briefwechsel*, 4 vols. (Tübingen: Typewritten, 1975).

[129] Buxtorf gave an elaborate description of the Hebrew font varieties he felt were necessary to print the *Concordantiae* in his letter to André Rivet, Basel, April 24, 1628, Leiden UB Ms BPL 285 I, f. 99.

[130] Buxtorf told Cunaeus, "Quando et ubi imprimi aliquando possint, nondum scio, sed reliqua omnia subsidia desunt. Industriam edito requiret non levem." Buxtorf to Cunaeus, September 15, 1625, Leiden UB Cun 2:93, printed in

Leiden by the Elzevier press, which served the University of Leiden, but Buxtorf decided against it.[131] In the end he decided to have König print the work after all.

Presumably Buxtorf still had to raise money for the project, or at least to discover whether there was sufficient interest to warrant publication of the concordance. He arranged to have a single folio page of the concordance printed as a sample late in 1628, and then, for the Spring book fair at Frankfurt, he had a second sample of two folio pages printed.[132] These samples elicited a warm response from scholars in many parts of Protestant Europe. He received an official letter of encouragement from the theological faculty of Strasbourg University and another from André Rivet, who wrote on behalf of other interested Leiden University faculty.[133] Johann-Georg Dorsch, a theologian at Strasbourg, and Sixtius Amama and Matthias Pasor, both philologists, urged Buxtorf to print it.[134] Two scholars, Wilhelm Schickhard and Louis Cappel, sent suggestions

---

Cunaeus, *Epistolae*, 151-52. "Concordantiae ante annum absolutae sunt. In Lexico dimidia litera ש restat. Revisione et emundatione reliqua opus habent. Noster typographus König, consocer meus obtulit se ad impressionem, sed vix inter nos conveniet. Plura de his ad nundinas Francofurtenses." Johannes Buxtorf to Wilhelm Schickhard, Basel, August 12, 1627, WLB Cod. hist. 2° 563 and Seck, *Schickhard*.

[131] André Rivet to Johannes Buxtorf, Leiden, March 27, 1628, Basel UB Ms G I 59: 38.

[132] "Scripserat vero chartu filius meus ad D. D. Altingium, et ad D. D. Petrum Cunaeum ac simul folium unum Speciminis Concordantiarum mearum Hebraicarum nova methodo dispositarum, quod praecedentibus meis literis promiseram." Johannes Buxtorf to André Rivet, Basel, November 7, 1628, Leiden UB Ms BPL 285 I, f. 100. Buxtorf II described the second sample in a letter to Peter Cunaeus. "Otium ad literas scribendas subripuit mihi adjunctum specimen Concordantiarum, quod absolvendum erat, ut Typographus Francofurtum secum sumere possit. Nam ut tanto melius ratio totius operis constet, duo intergra folia imprimi curavimus, quo plenior habeatur materia. Hîc imprimentur, et propediem continuatis operis procedent. Quaedam enim praeparatoria adhuc ad Apparatum operis requiruntur." Johannes Buxtorf II to Peter Cunaeus, Basel, March 20, 1629, Leiden UB Ms Cun 2:102, printed in Cunaeus, *Epistolae*, 164-65.

[133] Theological Faculty of Strasbourg to Johannes Buxtorf, Strasbourg, September 23, 1628, Basel UB Ms G I 61: 2-3, partially translated in Buxtorf-Falkeisen, *Buxtorf*, 12, and André Rivet to Johannes Buxtorf, Leiden, March 15, 1629, Basel UB Ms G I 59: 40.

[134] Johann-Georg Dorsch to Johannes Buxtorf, Strasbourg, June 12, 1629, Basel UB Ms G I 61: 48, Sixtius Amama to Johannes Buxtorf, n. p., June 16, 1629, Basel UB Ms G I 59: 262, and Matthias Pasor to Johannes Buxtorf II, Oxford, January 12, 1629, Basel UB Ms G I 59: 237-238.

on how the organization of the concordance could be improved.[135] Perhaps the most welcome response, however, came from Hieronymus Avianus, who represented Gottfried Grosse, a bookseller in Leipzig. He wished to arrange for rights to sell the concordance at the Leipzig book fair once it was printed.[136] The printed samples of the concordance had served their purpose.

Two final problems threatened the printing of Buxtorf's Bible concordance. For reasons unknown to the Buxtorfs, König did not buy enough paper of the proper grade and so was unable to begin printing the concordance in July of 1629, as he had planned.[137] About this time the plague epidemic which would claim Johannes Buxtorf's life also broke out in the city.[138] On September 7 he showed the first signs of infection and on the 9th he put in his last day of work on the concordance, correcting the rubric for *Adonai*. On September 13, 1629, he died.[139] The elder Buxtorf had only lived long enough to see the first six leaves printed.[140]

Fortunately for subsequent Hebrew scholars, Buxtorf's Bible concordance was also the first work that he composed together with his son. Buxtorf II had worked with his father for at least four years on the concordance before the latter's death.[141] He had been responsible for some of the less agreeable tasks, such as

---

[135] Wilhelm Schickhard to Johannes Buxtorf, Tübingen, November 10, 1628, Basel UB Ms Ki Ar 26b: 4, and in Seck, *Schickhard*. Cappel's suggestions are undated (Basel UB Ms G I 62: 109).

[136] "Hinc si futurus nundinis in lucem prodirem, ex Francfurti a Dn König illud mihi assignatum ministro Godfridi Grosii, bibliopolae Lipsiensis, traderetur, hinc ab hoc continuo eidem meo nomine pecunia gratissimo animo Vr Excell. reddenda exolvenetur. Modo interea de quantitate debeti pretii certior fierem per literas, quae Argentoratum missis facili negotio postmodum huc promorebuntur." Hieronymus Avianus to Johannes Buxtorf, Leipzig, May 6, 1629, Basel UB Ms G I 61: 237.

[137] "Sed nescio quo fato tunc novum impedimentum supervenit. Nihil desiderabatur nisi Charta. Ita cum adfertur, deprehenditur nec quantitatem nec qualitatem convenientem habere, uti pactum erat, et a Parente desideratum. Cujus chartari ire an typographi culpa id acciderit nescio." Johannes Buxtorf II to Benedict Turrettini, Basel, July 12, 1629, Geneva: Archives Turrettini, Fonds 1, Dd. 5.6.

[138] Ibid.

[139] Kautzsch, *Buxtorf*, 44-45.

[140] "Concordantias lugeo, in quarum natalibus ipse obiit; Non enim nisi sex prima folia impressa vidit." Johannes Buxtorf II to Peter Cunaeus, n. p., January 1, 1630, printed in Cunaeus, *Epistolae*, 166.

[141] Johannes Buxtorf II to Benedict Turrettini, Basel, February 21, 1625, Geneva: Archives Turrettini, Fonds 1, Dd. 5.1.

preparing the second printed sample on extremely short notice, but he also composed the entire concordance to the Aramaic portions of the Bible. Buxtorf II immediately took over as editor of the concordance upon his father's death, and its printing continued at a slow but deliberate pace.[142] He devoted much of the two intervening years to a final thorough revision of the manuscript.[143] In the summer of 1630 Buxtorf II's wife died, and the stress brought on by that traumatic event together with his exhaustion from overwork forced him temporarily to give up work on the concordance. König then decided to reprint two of Buxtorf I's works, *Lexicon Hebraicum et Chaldaicum*, and *Manuale Hebraicum et Chaldaicum*, so that the presses would not remain idle. As a consequence, work on the concordance was delayed still further.[144] By the spring of 1631, however, printing began again. Buxtorf's dedicatory foreword is dated August 20, 1631, and the date on the title page is 1632.[145] While the organizational scheme of the work was worked out by the father, both father and son were responsible for the work as it appeared in print.

Isaac Nathan b. Kalonymus organized his concordance by placing all words derived from the same root in a single list, each word

---

[142] "Concordantiarum opus continue procedit, gradu tamen testudineo, et quandoque interrupto, ut Iustuo eis istius modi temporibus fieri solet." Johannes Buxtorf II to Benedict Turrettini, Basel, October 14, 1629, Geneva: Archives Turrettini, Fonds 1, Dd. 5.7. By January 1, 1630 entries for the letter Gimel were already in press. Buxtorf II to Peter Cunaeus, n. p., January 1, 1630, printed in Cunaeus, *Epistolae*, 166.

[143] "Autographum Patris diligenter recognovi, Concordantias Chaldaicas de novo concinnavi, quaecunque operi illustrando inservire mihi videbantur, adjeci, omnia quam eleganter...edi curavi & nunc post integri biennii labores continuos, ad umbilicum, Dei gratia, perduxi." Buxtorf II in the preface to the *Concordantiae* (unpaginated), quoted by Prijs, *Drucke*, 357. See also Johannes Buxtorf II to Peter Cunaeus, Basel, March 20, 1629, Leiden UB Ms Cun 2:102, printed in Cunaeus, *Epistolae*, 164-65.

[144] Johannes Buxtorf II to Wilhelm Schickhard, n. p., November 11, 1630, WLB Cod. hist. 2° 563, and Seck, *Schickhard*. The two works are Prijs nos. 233 and 234.

[145] "Concordantias Hebraeas intra trium mensium spatium absolutas iri." Johannes Buxtorf II to Wilhelm Schickhard, Basel, April 21, 1631, WLB Cod. hist. 2° 563 and Seck, *Schickhard*. A few exemplars of the *Concordantiae* (such as Darmstadt LB call no. V 1145), have a title page bearing the date 1629. The Darmstadt copy does, however, have the foreword of August 20, 1631, suggesting that either a printer's error was responsible for the date, or that some title pages were printed in 1629 in the hope that the work would be released in that year.

appearing according to its occurrence in the Bible, without regard
to its grammatical form.[146] Buxtorf found this arrangement clumsy
and organized his concordance analytically, listing each word derived from a given root according to its grammatical form, and
only within these narrower categories according to the order it occurred in the Bible. For verbs he listed forms by conjugations, and
beneath this rubric in each of its forms (Perfect, Participle,
Imperfect, Infinitive, Infinitive with suffix, etc.) by person, number and gender.[147] Nouns he listed by their absolute form, then
those which had an affix (conjunction and preposition) and finally
those which had suffixes.[148] This arrangement made it far easier to
look for specific grammatical forms, a feature that was particularly
important for masoretic studies.

Besides reorganizing the order of occurrence for words within
categories, Buxtorf also made other changes to Isaac Nathan's concordance. He gave definitions of the roots in Latin as well as
Hebrew to aid Christian users. Buxtorf II reported that the definitions were assigned largely by his father.[149] The elder Buxtorf also

---

[146] Heinrich Ernst Bindseil, *Concordantiarum Homericarum Specimen cum
Prolegomenis in quibus Praesertim Concordantiae Biblicae Recensentur
earumque Origo et Progressus Declarantur* (Halle: Hendeliis, 1867), XVI-XXI.

[147] For example, he listed occurances of the verb אָבָה according to the follow-
ing order: תֹּאבוּ, תֹּאבֶה, יֹאבֶה, תֹּאבֶה, תֹּאבָא, אֹבִים, אָבִיתֶם, אָבוֹא, אָבוּ, אֲבִיתִי, אָבָה, and
יֹאבוּ.

[148] Under the word אָב Buxtorf listed the forms כְּאָב, לְאָב, וְאָב, הָאָב and וּכְאָב
as well as the absolute form. Then he went on to do the same for אַב, אָבִי, אָבִינוּ,
etc. For a discussion of Buxtorf's pattern of organization see Bindseil,
Concordantiarum, XXIX-XXXIII.

[149] "Dictum est de vocum Hebraicarum dispositione: sequitur *Interpretatio
illarum Latina*. Haec singulari studio, et summo judicio adhibitis et collatis variis
interpretationibus a Patre conscripta est, paucisque ante ejus obitum septimanis
absoluta, qua multis obscuris locis mirabili brevitate, et unico saepe verbo,
maxima lux infertur." Johannes Buxtorf II claimed that the definitions were taken
from his father's lexicographical works in his introduction to the *Concordantiae*,
(unpaginated). Prijs suggested that the definitions were copied from Mario de
Calasio's *Concordantiae Sacrorum Bibliorum Hebraicorum*, 2 vols. (Rome:
Stephanum Paulum, 1621) in *Drucke*, 358. Apart from Buxtorf II's explanation,
Prij's suggestion is unlikely because Buxtorf I felt that the work was riddled with
errors, particularly in its Latin definitions. "Exemplar Concordantiarum
Romanarum cum versione Latina a typographo habeo commodato. Sed non est ad
gustum meum. Errores priorum repetiit. Difficultatem quaerendi eandem
objiciunt, quam priores. Haec per versionem Latinam non sublata sed aucta. In
longis enim Radicibus tanto plura folia sunt perlustranda." Johannes Buxtorf to
Wilhelm Schickhard, Basel, September 7, 1626, WLB Cod. hist. 2° 563, and in
Seck, *Schickhard*.

claimed to have added many entries for words to his edition which did not appear in his *Vorlage*. The only categories of words that he excluded were certain undeclinable particles and proper nouns. He also corrected numerous typographical errors present in his *Vorlage*.[150]

If Buxtorf's *Concordantiae* was eagerly anticipated by his contemporaries who were Hebraists, it was just as gratefully received when it appeared. Johannes Baldovius, a professor at the Lutheran university of Helmstedt, devoted his inaugural lecture at that institution to the proper use of this work.[151] Its enduring worth is best illustrated by the fact that it was reprinted by Bernhard Baer in the nineteenth century. Unlike so many of Buxtorf's works which were antiquated by subsequent scholarship, scholars continued to benefit from the *Concordantiae*.

Buxtorf's critical work on his rabbinical Bible edition and Hebrew Bible concordance reflects traditional Jewish masoretic scholarship, the methods of late Renaissance humanism, and the theological needs and ideals of emerging seventeenth-century Reformed orthodoxy. His acceptance of Jacob ben Hayyim's recension of the Hebrew Bible text as the received text, preserved by the Masora, is entirely consistent with his views of the historical provenance and preservation of the Hebrew Bible text which he would later offer in his book *Tiberias*. Historical tradition and the masoretic apparatus together testified to its near miraculous preservation and to its absolute integrity. The Jewish Bible commentaries were a rich source for philological and sometimes theological insights to aid the interpreter in his work. The Bible concordance Buxtorf considered an improvement on the Masora, providing a more complete listing of textual minutiae for the continued preservation of the Hebrew Bible text. Buxtorf's *Biblia rabbinica* and Bible concordance together contained nearly every tool

---

[150] Bindseil, *Concordantiarum*, XXXII. "Multos locos, ubi hactenus in Concordantiis defuerunt, addo...Plurimos etiam errores typographicos invenio, & leves & graves, censura dignos." Johannes Buxtorf to Peter Cunaeus, Basel, June 24, 1625, Leiden UB Ms. Cun 2:91, printed in Cunaeus, *Epistolae*, 145-47.

[151] Johannes Baldovius, *De Johannis Buxtorfii laboribus, quos potissimum in Concordantiis Hebraicis exantlavit atque de earundem usu et perfectione* (Helmstedt: Jacob Lucius, 1639). (HAB Sig. 202.70 Qu (17)).

that a theologian might need for serious study of the Old
Testament.

In his editing of the Targum text, by contrast, Buxtorf worked
with an entirely different set of critical assumptions which were
closer to the normal canons of editing and textual criticism.[152] That
the Targum text had suffered at the hands of its copyists was only
too clear to him. He recognized transmission errors in the form of
metathesized letters, dittography, and confusion of one letter for
another. He was willing to impose grammatical concord on
Targums Onkelos and Jonathan using biblical Aramaic as his standard. He tried to respect the linguistic integrity of the Targums to
the Hagiographia by using analogous forms from later Aramaic
dialects to explain obscure words and expressions. Buxtorf's editing procedures for the Targum were designed to correct mistakes
caused by copyists' errors, none of which apparently marred the
Hebrew Bible text.

Dogmatic considerations played an important role in how
Buxtorf approached the biblical text. What he considered appropriate procedures for editing the Targum were inappropriate for
work on the Hebrew biblical text. Buxtorf's intensive work on the
Masora to the *Biblia rabbinica* and his revision of Isaac Nathan's
Hebrew Bible concordance were motivated in part by apologetic
concerns. He sought to defend the integrity and authenticity of the
received Hebrew Bible text, both consonants and vowels, by using
Jewish scholarship. What Buxtorf implicitly assumed in his detailed
work on the Hebrew Bible text he openly explained and defended
in his book *Tiberias*.

---

[152] Cf. Cappel's comments on Stephanus' *Castigationes in Marci Tulli
Ciceronis*, quoted by Peter T. Van Rooden, *Theology*, 224 and n. 186.

CHAPTER SEVEN

TIBERIAS AND THE VOWEL POINT CONTROVERSY

The post-Reformation arguments over the origin and antiquity of the Hebrew vowel points reveal the first indications of a shift in academic biblical studies from exegesis which treated the Bible as an internally self-consistent book of doctrine to the more strictly textual exegesis associated with modern biblical interpretation.[1] Johannes Buxtorf played a crucial role in these debates by furnishing an historical model explaining the fixation of the entire Hebrew Bible text as he knew it—consonants, vowel points and accents— which accorded closely with Jewish tradition and with the emerging Reformed orthodox doctrine of Scripture. He felt that the theological stakes were too high to treat this rather technical issue as a question over which people of good will might differ. His opponents, particularly Louis Cappel, argued that the theological aspects of this philological question were not decisively important and that the question should be debated only on philological grounds. While the Buxtorfs, both father and son, always had supporters in the scholarly world, many others were convinced by Cappel and accepted his critical approach to textual study, laying the methodological groundwork for nascent biblical criticism later in the seventeenth century.[2]

The integrity of the received Hebrew Bible text was already a problem for Christian scholars during the Middle Ages.[3] Raymond Martini thought that the vowel points were of late origin, inventions of Ben Naphtali and Ben Asher, and that the emendations of the scribes (*Tikkune ha-Soferim*) were "simply a few of the many willful corruptions and perversions introduced by the Jews into the sacred text, to obliterate the prophecies about the incarnation of the

---

[1] Muller, "Vowel Points," 53.
[2] Georg Schnederman, *Die Controverse des Ludovicus Cappellus mit den Buxtorfen über das Alter der hebräischen Punctation* (Leipzig: Hundertstund & Preis, 1878), 1-2 and J. C. H. Lebram, "Ein Streit um die hebräischen Bibel und die Septuaginta," in: *Leiden University*, 30, 33-34.
[3] Eugene F. Rice, Jr., *Saint Jerome in the Renaissance* (Baltimore: Johns Hopkins Univ. Press, 1985), 173-175.

Deity."[4] Martini's accusations was repeated by Christians long after his death and may even have elicited a Jewish response from R. Solomon ibn Aderet.[5] Nicolas de Lyra popularized Martini's views through his *Postilla,* as did Petrus Galatinus in his *De Arcanis Catholicae Veritatis.*[6] Jaime Pérez of Valencia also thought that the vowel points were invented after the time of Christ. He argued that variations among the Greek versions of the Old Testament were best explained by the translators' use of unpointed originals. Jerome too had used an unvocalized *Vorlage* in his opinion.[7]

By the eve of the Reformation many scholars had come to realize that the accepted Latin Bible had itself suffered from textual corruption and needed to be restored. Catholic humanists such as Johannes Reuchlin and Santes Pagninus sought to correct errors in the Latin Old Testament by comparing it with the Hebrew Bible.[8] The vowel points were not at issue, however, in humanist polemical exchanges with more conservative Catholic theologians, or indeed during the first decades of the Reformation. Many of the leading Protestant reformers thought that the vowel points were a human addition to the Hebrew Bible text. Luther considered them an imperfect aid to the reader, noting that since they were un-

---

[4] Christian D. Ginsburg, introduction to *The Massoreth Ha-Massoreth of Elias Levita, Being an Explanation of the Massoretic Notes of the Hebrew Bible,* trans. Christian D. Ginsburg (London: Longmans, Green, Reader & Dyer, 1867; reprint ed., New York: KTAV, 1968), 45-46. See Raymond Martini, *Pugio fidei Adversus Mauros et Judaeos, cum Observationibus Josephi de Voisin, et Introductione Jo. Benedicti Carpzovii* (Leipzig: Haeredum Friedrich Lanckisius,1687; reprint ed., Farnborough Hants: Gregg International, 1969), pars iii, dist. iii, cap xxi, 895.

[5] Martini is probably the scholar refered to in R. Solomon b. Abraham ibn Adret's apologetic treatise. See *R. Salomo b. Abraham b. Adereth: Sein Leben und seine Schriften nebst handschriftlichen Beilage,* ed. J. Perles (Breslau: Schletter'schen Buchhandlung, 1863), 32-34 (Hebrew section), and Norman Roth, "Forgery and Abrogation of the Torah: A Theme in Muslim and Christian Polemic in Spain," *Proceedings of the American Academy for Jewish Research* 54 (1987): 226-228.

[6] See Nicolaus de Lyra's comment on Hosea 9:12 in *Postilla super totam Bibliam,* 4 vols. (Strasbourg: J. Preuss, 1492; reprint ed., Frankfurt/Main: Minerva GmbH, 1971), 2: ff. GGG7r-v and Petrus Galatinus, *De Arcanis Catholicae Veritatis* (Basel: Johann Heruagius, 1561), book 1, chap. 8, 19-26.

[7] Wilfrid Werbeck, *Jacobus Perez von Valencia: Untersuchungen zu seinem Psalmenkommentar,* Beiträge zur historischen Theologie no. 28 (Tübingen: J. C. B. Mohr, 1959), 99-101.

[8] See Rice, *Jerome,* 176 and Lloyd Jones, *Discovery,* 40-43.

known to Jerome they must have been invented later.[9] Zwingli also pointed out that the vowel points were never mentioned by Jerome. The variety of ways that names were transliterated in the Septuagint and Latin translations and numerous other translation errors suggested to him that the translators were forced to vocalize the Hebrew text for themselves as they worked.[10] Calvin held the vowel points in higher regard, and while believing that the vowel points were an invention of the rabbis, "approved of alterations in pointing only after critical examination of the meaning of the text."[11]

The appearance of Elias Levita's *Masoret ha-Masoret* (1538) caused both Protestant and Catholic theologians to reconsider the canonical status and interpretive importance of Hebrew vowel points. Levita challenged the traditional Jewish view that the consonantal text and its vocalization were given by God to Moses when he received the Law on Mount Sinai.[12] In his third preface to *Masoret* he argued that the vowel points were invented by Jewish scholars after the composition of the Talmud. The vocalization of the biblical text thus occurred after both the closure of the biblical canon and the fixation of the consonantal text. Levita came to this realization while working on *Sefer ha-Zikronot*, an enormous masoretic commentary which he completed in 1536.[13] In 1539 Sebastian Münster printed *Masoret ha-Masoret* and translated its three prefaces into Latin, allowing for a much wider Christian readership.[14] Unfortunately for most Christian scholars he did not

---

[9] Muller, "Vowel Points," 53-54, citing Martin Luther, *Enarratio in Genesin (1535-1545)*, WA 46, 683.

[10] Ulrich Zwingli, *Complanationis Isaiae Prophetae, Foetura Prima, Cum Apologia que quidque sic versum sit*, in *Huldreich Zwinglis Sämtliche Werke*, CR, vol. 101 (Zürich: Berichthaus, 1956), 98-101.

[11] Muller, "Vowel Points," 54, quoting Jean Calvin, *Praelectionum in duodecim prophetas minores*, part 1, in: *Opera quae supersunt omnia*, CR, vol. 72 (Braunschweig: C. A. Schwetschke et Filium, 1890; reprint: New York: Johnson Reprint Corporation, 1964), col. 306.

[12] Levita, *Massoreth*, 103-104.

[13] See Ginsburg, introduction to Levita, *Massorah*, 34 and Weil, *Élie Lévita*, 94-95, 299-300. Levita had already been thinking along these lines, however, as his letter of 1531 to Sebastian Münster attests. See Peritz, "Ein Brief Elijah Levita's," 258-260.

[14] Buxtorf attributed the popularity of Levita's position directly to Münster's Latin translation."Inter Christianos etiam eo rariores, quòd nunquam Latinè iste Liber conversus sit, ut & alibi dixi. At quòd paucula inde Sebatianus Munsterus

translate the rest of the book and it remained accessible only to those few capable of reading it in Hebrew.[15]

Levita's arguments for a post-talmudic dating of the vowel points were advanced as a small part of a larger philological treatise, without any reference to the interconfessional battles among Christians over the use of the Bible in theological formulation. Protestant theologians, for the most part, ignored Levita's work.[16] Catholic polemicists, however, quickly recognized that Levita's work could be a powerful new weapon for their debates with Protestants. Robert Bellarmine codified four major lines of argument in his *Controversies* which countless later theologians recycled in their debates with Protestants: that Church Tradition existed prior to the canonical Bible; that the biblical text was imperfect and insufficient; that the biblical text was obscure; and that Church Tradition was of divine origin.[17] By arguing for the post-canonical origin of the vowel points Catholic polemicists could contend that the Hebrew Old Testament was not perspicuous and interpreters were almost entirely dependent upon human tradition in the form of the vowel points to understand it at all. Catholic polemicists also argued that the Jews had corrupted the Hebrew Bible text by changing the consonantal text and adding the vowel points to obscure prophecies about Christ. The Latin Vulgate did not suffer such indignities and was a more certain source of doctrine.[18]

Wilhelmus Lindanus was one of the first polemicists to make extensive use of Levita's arguments.[19] Johannes Isaac Levita, a

---

aliquando, transtulit, id causam praebuit, quare plurimi doctrinâ praecellentes viri Theologi & Philologi, de Masora & Masorethis, sinistra nimiùm conceperunt prejudicia." *Tiberias Sive Commentarius Masorethicus* (Basel: Ludwig König, 1620), f.):(2v. See Prijs no. 188.

[15] Konrad Pellican translated the rest of *Massoreth*, but it remained unpublished (Zürich ZB Ms. Car I 96). See Ginsburg's introduction to *Massoreth*, 42 and n. 36.

[16] Muller, "Vowel Points," 54-55. One important exception was Matthias Flacius Illyricus in his *Clavis Scripturae Sacrae. De Sermone Sacrarum Literarum, in duas partes divisae*, ed. Theodor Suicerius (Frankfurt and Leipzig: Hieronymus Christian Paulus, 1719), part 2, tract. 6, cols. 649-651.

[17] Heiner Faulenbach, *Die Struktur der Theologie des Amandus Polanus von Polansdorf*, Basler Studien zur historischen und systematischen Theologie, Bd. 9 (Zürich: EVZ-Verlag, 1967), 73.

[18] Rice, *Jerome*, 185-187.

[19] Wilhelmus Lindanus, *De optimo Scripturas genere* (Cologne: Maternum Cholinum, 1558). Other Catholic controversialists who used this sort of argu-

Jewish convert who was professor of Hebrew at the Catholic academy in Cologne, wrote a blistering response to Lindanus which later Protestant apologists found quite useful.[20] He stressed that the vowel points were essential to understanding the meaning of the Hebrew Bible text, noting that, "He that reads the Scriptures without the points is like a man that rides a horse *achalinos*, without a bridle."[21] A number of later Catholic polemicists used Elias Levita's arguments concerning the age of the vowel points in their works, notably James Gordon and Pierre Coton who were both contemporaries of Buxtorf.[22]

After the initial work of Elias Levita, Jewish scholars played a relatively small part in the ensuing debate.[23] Azariah de Rossi was

---

mentation included Gilbert Génébrard and Melchior Cano. See Muller, "Vowel Points," 55-56.

[20] Johannes Isaac Levita, *Defensio Veritatis Hebraicae Sacrarum Scripturarum, adversus Libros tres Reveren. D. Wilhelmi Lindani S. T. Doctoris, quos de optimo Scripturas interpretandi genere inscripsit* (Cologne: Jacob Soterem, 1559). Buxtorf's copy of the latter book is Basel UB FA VIII 47. Both William Whitaker, *A Disputation on Holy Scripture Against the Papists*, ed. and trans. William Fitzgerald (Cambridge: Cambridge Univ. Press, 1849), 159 and Franciscus Junius in his *Animadversiones ad controversiam secundam Christianae fidei* (Leiden: C. Plantin, 1600), 93-94 made use of Levita's *Defensio*.

[21] "Eum, qui sine punctis et accentibus Scripturam legit, similem esse homini equitanti equum *achalinoton* effrenem," quoted by Johann Gerhard, *Loci Theologici*, 10 vols. (Leipzig: J. C. Hinrichs, 1885), 1: 146 (book 1, chap. 15) and John Owen, *Of the Divine Original, Authority, Self-Evidencing Light, and Power of the Scriptures*, in *The Works of John Owen, D. D.*, ed. William H. Goold, (London: Johnstone and Hunter, 1853), vol. 16, 371. Isaac hinted, however, that he thought the vowel points to be a later addition to the consonantal text. See Faulenbach, *Die Struktur der Theologie*, 109 and n. 246.

[22] James Gordon, *Controversarum Epitomen* (Cologne: Johannes Kinchium, 1620), 23-24 (St. Paul MN: Lutheran Brotherhood Foundation Reformation Library, text-fiche); and Pierre Coton, *Genève Plagiaire* (Paris: Sebastien Chappelet, 1618), col. 20 (St. Paul MN: Lutheran Brotherhood Foundation Reformation Library, text-fiche).

[23] For accounts of several scholars of Buxtorf's generation or later who did participate see David Kaufmann, "Lazarus de Viterbo's Epistle to Cardinal Sirleto Concerning the Integrity of the Text of the Hebrew Bible," *Jewish Quarterly Review* o. s. 7 (1894-95): 278-296, Cecil Roth, "Immanuel Aboab's Proselytization of the Marranos," *Jewish Quarterly Review* 23 (1932-33): 126 and Yosef Hayim Yerushalmi, *From Spanish Court to Italian Ghetto. Isaac Cardoso: A Study in Seventeen-Century Marranism and Jewish Apologetics* (New York: Columbia University Press, 1971), 422-432. Interestingly enough Cardoso actually cited Johannes Isaac Levita's book in his discussion (p. 427 and n. 37).

the only Jew to publish a direct response to Levita's *Masoret*.[24] De Rossi first summarized Levita's position and then gave several counter arguments. He disputed Levita's interpretation of BT *Nedarim* 37a-b where Nehemiah 8:8-9 is discussed, and pointed out that other eastern languages such as Syriac, Aramaic, Persian, and Arabic also had vowel points. Taking a point from Levita's *Masoret*, he argued that the uncertainty of an unpointed text ran counter to God's command in Deut. 27: 8 that the law be written very plainly.[25] He even quoted a letter from the Church father Jerome to Evagrius which suggested that Jerome knew of the vowel points.[26] The most important point, however, which Azariah made was his rebuttal of Levita's contention that there was absolutely no mention of the vowel points in the Talmud or other ancient works. Levita wrote,

> I shall do battle against those who say that they were given on Sinai, and then state who invented them, and when they were originated and affixed to the letters. But if anyone should prove to me, by clear evidence, that my opinion is opposed to that of our Rabbins of blessed memory, or is contrary to the genuine Kabbalah of the *Sohar*, I will readily give in to him, and declare my opinion as void.[27]

De Rossi noted that passages in both the *Zohar* and *Sefer ha-Bahir* refer to the vowel points by name. Since, he argued, their authors lived before the composition of the Mishnah, Levita's position was not defensible. The argument and the quotations which supported it would reappear repeatedly in subsequent works which argued for the antiquity of the vowel points.[28]

Amandus Polanus von Polansdorf, professor of Old Testament at the University of Basel from 1596-1610 was, apart from Buxtorf himself, the scholar most responsible for making the age

---

[24] Azariah de Rossi, מאור עינים, 2 vols in 1 (Vilna: R. Romm, 1864-1866), 472.

[25] Ibid., 470-474. Azariah's arguments are summarized in Ginburg's introduction to *Massoreth*, 52-53.

[26] Ibid., 476-477. See Jerome to Evagrius the Presbyter, *MPL* 22: 680-681, and Ginsburg's introduction to *Massoreth*, 53 and n. 4.

[27] Levita, *Massoreth*, 121 and n. 75.

[28] De Rossi מאור עינים, 472-3. Perhaps the first Christian to employ De Rossi's quotations was Pierre Chevallier in his annotations to Antoine Cevallier's *Rudimenta Hebraicae Linguae, Accurata methodo & brevitate conscripta*, ed. Pierre Chevallier (Geneva: Fransiscus Le Preux, 1590), 27.

of the vowel points an issue of theological principle.[29] In his magnum opus, the *Syntagma Theologiae Christianae*, Polanus composed a locus which responded to Catholic polemics specifically. At the heart of Polanus' position is the notion that "adequate written representation of words required some sort of vowel symbol."[30] He made heavy use of Johannes Isaac Levita's *Defensio*, reproducing in outline form many of his arguments.[31] He also used Pierre Chevallier's notes in Antoine Chevallier's *Rudimenta*.[32] He (and Buxtorf) may also have been influenced by Hugh Broughton who held a similar position. He visited Basel in 1598 and published a Latin translation of his Daniel commentary there the following year.[33] Most intriguingly, Polanus argued that Hebrew text was reliable and pure because it had been edited by the Men of the Great Synagogue, a suggestion he found in Bellarmine's *Controversies*.[34] While no direct evidence exists that Polanus and Buxtorf worked together to arrive at their respective positions, the two men knew

---

[29] Muller, "Vowel Points," 57-58, and Faulenbach, *Polanus*, 106-110. Muller discussed the significance of Polanus' contribution to the emerging Reformed orthodox doctrine of Scripture in his *Post-Reformation Reformed Dogmatics*, vol. 2: *Holy Scripture: The Cognitive Foundation of Theology* (Grand Rapids: Baker Books, 1993), 111, 169-174, passim.

[30] Robert D. Preus, *The Theology of the Lutheran Reformers: A Study of Theological Prolegomena* (St. Louis: Concordia Publishing House, 1970), 308. Although Preus did not mention Polanus in this passage he discussed the general acceptance of this principle both among Protestants and Catholics. Cf. Amandus Polanus von Polansdorf, *Syntagma Theologiae Christianae* (Geneva: Jacob Stoër, 1617), I.xxvii.

[31] Ibid.

[32] Ibid., where reference was made to ספר הבהיר and Zohar passages which de Rossi quoted. See Chevallier, *Rudimenta*, 27. Buxtorf may have met Chevallier when he travelled to Geneva as a student since the latter served as professor of Hebrew at the Academy from 1587-1594.

[33] Ernst Staehelin, *Amandus Polanus von Polansdorf*, Studien zur Geschichte der Wissenschaften in Basel, vol. 1 (Basel: Helbing & Lichtenhahn, 1955), 39 and n. 105, and Prijs no. 160 for the Latin edition of Broughton's commentary. See Hugh Broughton, *Daniel his Chaldie visions and his Ebrew* (London: Gabriel Simson, 1596), ff. K2r-4v.

[34] "Omnes autem libros pertinentes ad religionis autoritatem esse in Canone Hebraeo manifestum est. Promo quia Esdras Propheta & Sacerdos, qui post captivitatem Babylonicam omnes libros Veteris Testementi recensuit & instauravit; ipsemet Bellarminus docet & fatetur … ." Polanus, *Syntagma*, I. xxxiv, quintum. Cf. Bellarmine, *De verbo Dei*, II i, in: *Opera omnia*, 12 vols. (Paris: Louis Vives, 1870-1874; reprint: Frankfurt a. M.: Minerva GMBH, 1965) vol. 1, 119-120. Bellarmine's position on the integrity and perpiscuity of the biblical text was not entirely consistant. See Lebram, "Streit," 35.

each other well, had worked together, and had even vacationed together.[35] Moreover, Buxtorf was well-grounded in theology and
was even offered Polanus' position as Professor of Old Testament
after his untimely death in 1610.[36] He was also well aware of the
theological implications of some of his philological research. The
appearance of both Polanus' *Syntagma* and Buxtorf's *Thesaurus
Grammaticus* in 1609, both of them containing a defense of the age
and integrity of the vowel points, was probably not accidental.

   Buxtorf was concerned with the integrity of the consonantal text
and to the origin and integrity of the vowel points and accents of
the Hebrew Bible from the very beginning of his scholarly career.
In 1593 he translated Elias Levita's *Masoret ha-Masoret* into Latin
for his own private use, as an exercise to improve his Hebrew.[37] He
told Kaspar Waser that he was preparing to publish a new edition
of Levita's *Masoret* and *De Accentibus*.[38] In 1606 he informed
Joseph Scaliger that he planned to study the age of the Hebrew
vowel points, presumably as preparation for his discussion on
Hebrew accents and vowel points in his *Thesaurus Grammaticus*
(1609). He noted that while Elias claimed that no mention of the
vowel points was made in early rabbinical literature, this was contradicted by the frequent references to them in the *Zohar* and *Sefer*

---

[35] Polanus and Buxtorf vacationed together in 1601 and 1603. Staehelin,
Polanus, 46, 48. Polanus may also have been involved in Hebrew printing, since
two letters written by Jews to Buxtorf include greetings to him as well. See Rabbi
NN to Johannes Buxtorf. Nuremberg, November 18/19, 1599, printed in
Buxtorf, *Institutio,* 358-359, and Prijs, *Drücke*, 528, and Isaac Eckendorf to
Johannes Buxtorf, n. p., n. d., Günzburg collection of the Russian State Library,
Moscow, Ms 1213, f. 8b (copy held by the Institute of Microfilmed Hebrew
Manuscripts, Jewish National and University Library, Jerusalem).

[36] Grynaeus' offer of a chair in theology to Buxtorf was a reflection of his
competence as a Hebraist, but also indicated his theological loyalty to Reformed
orthodoxy and his theological awareness and sensitivity. As head of the Basel
church, Grynaeus had sought since 1586 to mold both the Basel church and
theology faculty of the university into bastions of the Reformed confession and
he would not have offered anyone such an important position unless he trusted
the candidate without reservation. Cf. Geiger, *Die Basler Kirche*, 40-49.

[37] The only surviving copy of Buxtorf's translation is preserved in the Danish
Royal Library of Copenhagen Ms E dan. var. 13, 8°.

[38] Johannes Buxtorf to Kaspar Waser, Basel, December 23, 1593, Zürich ZB
Ms S-149:124, 1, and idem to idem, Basel , January 28, 1595, Zürich ZB Ms S-
150: 96. Basel UB FA VIII 34, nos. 1-2 was Buxtorf's working copy for the
proposed edition and contains many marginal corrections in his hand. Cf. Prijs
no. 189.

ha-Bahir. He still planned, however, "to consider other aspects of the matter more fully."[39] Buxtorf could not have known that Scaliger had already seen this argument in Chevallier's *Rudimenta Hebraicae Linguae,* and found it utterly unconvincing.[40]

Scaliger's response to Buxtorf was a foretaste of the response that his theory would receive after *Tiberias* was published. Scaliger wrote that the *Zohar* was written after the Talmud and so its attestation of an early date for the vowel points was not trustworthy. He argued on the analogy of Arabic that the Hebrew vowel points were a later grammatical development. In fact, both the Jews and Samaritans read only unpointed scrolls in the Synagogue, and so were quite capable of reading unpointed Hebrew. A number of passages in the Septuagint, he added, also suggested that the Hebrew *Vorlage* that the translators used was unvocalized.[41] In response to Scaliger's arguments Buxtorf argued that Jewish tradition reported an earlier dating than the Talmud for both the *Zohar* and *Sefer ha-Bahir.* According to David Gans' *Semah David* the author of *Sefer ha-Bahir* was Rabbi Jonathan ben Uziel, a contemporary of Hillel and Shammai.[42] The principal author of the *Zohar* was Rabbi

---

[39] "Incidi his diebus in librum Eliae Levitae, cui nomen, *Masoreth Hammasoreth,* (quem ante annos decem privati exercitii causa Latinum feci) ac disceptationem de origine & autoribus punctorum & accentuum Hebraicorum perlegi. Elias per מתקני הנקוד primos authores, ut puto, intelligit, ac si in monte Sinai data essent, scribit, futurum fuisse, ut id in priscorum scriptis alicubi reperiretur annotatum ... . At in priscorum libris nullam punctorum mentionem reperiri (Elias) ait. Huic Sententiae adversantur, qui ex libro Zohar, (quo vix alius antiquor) haec citant, quae in Cantico Canticorum leguntur ... לית לכל אתוון. Et in libro הבהיר, qui itidem satis antiquus: דאניש בגופא. Sed de hac materia alias amplius mihi cogitandum." Buxtorf to Scaliger, Basel, April 3, 1606, Utrecht UB Ms 987: 237-238; printed in *Sylloges,* 2: 362-364. For the *Zohar* quotation see ספר הזוהר, 21 vols. (Jerusalem: Yeshiva Bet Ulpana Rabatha, 1945-55), 21: 180-1 (Song of Songs section 602).

[40] Scaliger wrote in the margin of his copy next to Pierre Chevallier's discussion on the age of the vowel points, "Haec diatriba asiniana, falsa et idiotae hominis. Caveant studiosi." Quoted by Lebram, "Streit," 29, and 58, n. 130. Cf. Chevallier, *Rudimenta,* 21-27. Buxtorf himself took at least the *Zohar* quotation directly from de Rossi as it is several words longer than Chevallier's quotation, although he did attribute it to the latter in his *Thesaurus Grammaticus.*

[41] Joseph Scaliger to Johannes Buxtorf, Leiden, June 1, 1606, Basel UB Ms G I 59: 363; printed in Scaliger, *Epistolae,* 521-524.

[42] David Gans, צמח דוד (Prague: n. p., 1592), f. 35r.

Simeon ben Yohai who lived shortly before Rabbi Judah ha-Nasi although parts of it were written much later.[43]

Buxtorf's first published discussion of the age of the vowel points took the form of a long excursus in his *Thesaurus Grammaticus* of 1609.[44] He provided a summary of Levita's arguments for a post-talmudic dating of the vowel points, offered arguments for the antiquity of the vowel points drawn from Jewish tradition and Amandus Polanus' *Syntagma Theologiae Christianae* together with his own reflections on the necessity for inspired vowel points, and then gave a point by point rebuttal of Levita's arguments. Since many of these arguments reappear in *Tiberias* and in the works of Buxtorf's critics they are worth exploring in some detail. Levita thought that the vowel points and accents were invented after the composition of the Talmud for four reasons.[45] He noted that the vowel points are never mentioned in the Talmud, aggadot, midrashim and other ancient Hebrew books. In order to understand two talmudic passages, the story of Joab and his rabbi discussing the meaning of Deut. 25:19 and Mar Sutra's comments on Exod. 24:5, an unpointed, unaccented text must be assumed for them to make sense. In the former passage R. Dime of Nehardea argued that a teacher had to have good pronunciation and told the story of Joab and his rabbi to underline his point. Joab had ordered that the entire male population of Edom be slain in I Ki. 11:15-16 because his rabbi told him that Deut. 25:19 had commanded that the males, *zakar* (זָכָר), of Edom be obliterated. Then King David informed him that the Deut. text actually commanded that the memory, *zeker* (זֵכֶר), of Edom be obliterated, a rather important difference in vocalization. Joab drew his sword to kill the rabbi for

---

[43] Abraham b. Samuel Zacuto, ספר יוחסין (Krakow: n. p., 1580-81), f. 42. Buxtorf wrote, "In Jochasin pag. 42. notatur ab hoc Schimeone Zohar non esse absolutum, sed a discipulis ejus, neque evulgatum nisi post tempora רמבן, imo ipsum varh ne vidisse quidem." Johannes Buxtorf to Joseph Scaliger, Basel, March 17, 1607, London: British Library, Ms Add. 5158, f. 25; it is printed in *Sylloges*, 2: 366-367. Buxtorf's point on the authorship of the *Zohar* and ספר הבהיר are drawn directly from Azariah de Rossi, מאור עינים, 472. Buxtorf could have read de Rossi's book as early as 1603 since he quoted it in *Aus was Ursachen*, Basel UB Ms A IX 78, f. 43r.

[44] Buxtorf, *Thesaurus Grammaticus Linguae Sanctae Hebraeae* (Basel: Konrad Waldkirch, 1609), 55-64. Prijs no. 199.

[45] Levita, *Massoreth*, 127-131 and Buxtorf, *Thesuarus Grammaticus*, 56-59.

misleading him.[46] In the other passage Mar Sutra commented that a discussion of Exod. 24:5 had been necessary in order to know where to place a dividing accent, the implication being that it was not marked in the text.[47] Levita also pointed out that the names of every accent and vowel point were Aramaic, rather than Hebrew, the language in which Moses received the law on Mount Sinai. While Hebrew was a living language vowel points were not necessary. He related a discussion he once had with some middle eastern Christian scholars in Rome who read Syriac without any pointing and felt no need for any because they had known the language since childhood. Levita concluded his discussion by quoting passages from the works of Jonah ibn Janah and Abraham ibn Ezra which attributed the vowel points and accents to the scholars of Tiberias. Buxtorf added that Petrus Martinius and other Christian scholars argued that the Hebrew Bible did not have either accents or vowel points when the Septuagint was translated or during Jerome's lifetime.[48]

The four quotations from Jewish sources in the second part of Buxtorf's excursus are all drawn form Levita's *Masoret*.[49] David Kimhi stated flatly in his *Miklol* that the vowel points had been given on Mount Sinai.[50] R. Levi b. Joseph in his book *Semadar* suggested that the existence of the accents and vowel points in Moses' day were implied in Deut. 28: 8, since it commanded that the words of the law should be written *very plainly*. Since, for example, the root letters שלמה could mean "wherefore, retribution, Solomon, garment or perfect," when unpointed, pointing was necessary to make the meaning plain. The author of *Instruction for the Reader* too insisted that the accents were revealed to Moses on Mount Sinai.[51] Finally, Moses the Punctuator suggested in his *Treatise on the Vowel Points and Accents* that the vowel points

---

[46] BT *Baba Batra* 21b. See Levita, *Massoreth*, 128, n. 92.

[47] BT *Hagigah* 6b. See Levita, *Massoreth*, 128-129.

[48] Buxtorf, *Thesaurus Grammaticus*, 59. See Martinius, *Grammaticae*, 31-44.

[49] Buxtorf, *Thesaurus Grammaticus*, 59-61 and Levita, *Massoreth*, 121-129.

[50] David Kimhi, מכלול (Venice: n. p., 1550), f. 25b.

[51] The book ספר הסמדר is known only from quotations in Levita, Azariah de Rossi in מאור עינים and Samuel Archevolti in his grammar ערוגת הבושם (Venice: G. de Gara, 1602). The book הריית הקורא was composed by Judah Ibn Balaam on the Hebrew accents. Levita, *Massoreth*, 123.

were given on Mount Sinai, but were forgotten until Ezra revealed
them again. While Levita had not given these statements much credence and had disputed each one in turn, Buxtorf quoted them
without further comment as examples of the traditional Jewish
position.[52]

Buxtorf also quoted several more narrowly theological arguments for the antiquity of the vowel points which his colleague
Polanus had advanced.[53] The essence of these points is that because
Scripture was revealed by God through the prophets, "not only the
sense but also the words, the vowels and accents must have been
given by him, for without vowels the words cannot be recognized,
and without accents the meaning is disturbed."[54] If the vowel points
were essential to the meaning and were an invention of the masoretes then the Christian faith is built on a foundation of the masoretes, rather than on the prophets. The words of Christ in Matt.
5:18 concerning the importance of the jot and tittle show that the
pointing was no fifth century addition of the Tiberian Jews, but
that it was known and deemed an intrinsic part of the biblical text
during his lifetime.[55] Polanus' approach to the age and origin of
the vowel points is primarily theological. Buxtorf and his critics
would argue the issue on philological and historical grounds, although all were aware that their views had theological implications.
While Buxtorf did not cite Polanus explicitly in his later work
Tiberias he agreed with Polanus' position and made no secret of his
theological leanings.[56]

The final positive argument for the antiquity of the vowel points
addressed another aspect of the problem of textual validity; how
the proper pronunciation of the biblical text was preserved.
Buxtorf questioned Levita's contention that preserving authentic
readings for the unpointed Hebrew text was a relatively simple

---

[52] Moses the Punctuator's כללי הנקוד was published in the *Masora magna* of
the second edition of the Bomberg *Biblia rabbinica*. Buxtorf was not the first
Protestant apologist to use these quotations; both Polanus and Pierre Chevallier in
his annotations to Antoine Chevallier's *Rudimenta*, 21-27 had done so
previously.
[53] Buxtorf, *Thesaurus Grammaticus*, 61-64.
[54] John F. Robinson, "The Doctrine of Holy Scripture in Seventeenth
Century Reformed Theology," (Thèse de Doctorat ès Sciences Religièses,
Université de Strasbourg, 1971), 107.
[55] Ibid.
[56] Buxtorf, *Tiberias*, 130-131 and Robinson, "Scripture," 109.

matter while Hebrew was a living language. It took more than human ingenuity to differentiate sounds, words and verses accurately
against failures of memory. The vowel points were necessary to
preserve the meaning of the text and were of divine and prophetic
rather than merely human origin.[57]

Human agency in the form of institutions and scholars was,
however, required to preserve accurate copies of the Bible to settle
disputes and to serve as master copies for subsequent ones. Buxtorf
noted that Moses commanded that a written copy of the Law be
placed in the Ark as a testimony and that Hilkiah the Priest found a
scroll preserved in the Temple during the reign of Josiah.[58]
Maimonides mentioned a master scroll from a much later period in
his *Mishneh Torah*.

> The copy which we have followed in these matters is the famous Codex of
> Egypt which contains the twenty-four books, and which had been in
> Jerusalem for many years, in order that other codices might be corrected;
> and all followed it, & etc.[59]

Buxtorf was unable to answer the question of institutional responsibility of preservation of the Hebrew Bible satisfactorily for lack
of evidence and did not address the question in his later works.

Buxtorf concluded his excursus on the vowel points with a rebuttal of Levita's principal arguments.[60] To refute Levita's claim
that the most ancient Jewish literature never mentions accents or
vowel points Buxtorf quoted the two passages from the *Zohar* on
the Song of Solomon and *Sefer ha-Bahir* which he mentioned in his
letter to Scaliger, together with the references in Jewish histories

---

[57] "Ecquod enim acumen ingenii humani tantum quod ex solo auditu aut
praelectione nuda, tantum, sonorum differentiam, tot vocum diversitatem, tam
accuratam tot versuum & sententiarum per singula membra distinctionem,
distinctè complecti; ecquae memoria tam tenacissima fuit, quae ista omnia per tot
secula probè retinere, constanter ac nusquam impingente vel voce vel memoria,
alios docere, & posteritati secuturae adeò fidè tradere potuerit, ut indubitata
omnium veritas fidesque inter tam adversas & crebras ecclesiae Judaicae
tempestates, ad Masoretharum usque tempora pervenerit? Novo autem &
nunquam viso tali punctorum invento, Sacram Scripturam illustrare, ac genuinum
ejus sensum patefacere, divini potius & Prophetici, quàm humani fuit ingenii."
Thesaurus Grammaticus, 64-65.
[58] See Deut. 31: 26 and 2 Ki. 22: 8.
[59] Moses ben Maimon, *Mishneh Torah, Laws of Torah Scrolls*, VIII, 4,
quoted by Levita, *Massoreth*, 114 and n. 60.
[60] Buxtorf, *Thesaurus Grammaticus*, 66-69.

on the dates of these works' supposed authors. In Buxtorf's explanation of the talmudic explanation of Neh. 8: 8 he cited the commentaries of Isaac Alfasi, Rashi and Rabbi Nissim which favored
his position, a tactic he would use repeatedly in *Tiberias*. He quoted
Rabbi Nissim's interpretation of the passage in BT *Haggiga* to refute Levita's third point as well. Levita's argument using the story
of Joab and his Rabbi received a shorter shrift. Buxtorf dismissed
the episode as a fable unworthy of belief.[61] The final argument,
that the Aramaic names of the accents and vowels proved that
Moses and the prophets could not have known of them, Buxtorf
found uncompelling. They could have existed under other names
and only later been given Aramaic ones.[62]

The 1609 printing of *Thesaurus Grammaticus* was the only one
to contain this excursus on the age of the vowel points and accents.
Buxtorf explained its absence in the second edition of 1615 because
it was simply too large and important a topic to be explored in such
a limited space; it demanded a separate treatment.[63] Johannes
Buxtorf II confirmed that his father did not reprint this excursus
because he wished to treat the matter exhaustively in another work,
not because he had changed his mind.[64] Actually the elder Buxtorf
did change his position on some points and certainly presented his
arguments differently in *Tiberias* than he had in *Thesaurus
Grammaticus*.

Tiberias is Buxtorf's fullest and most impressive work on the
history of the biblical text. He conceived it as the first of four pro-

---

[61] "Secunda ratio tantum habet virium ad probandum, quantum meretur fidei
ad credendum. Ea autem fides ipsi debetur, quae millenis aliis fabulis
Talmudicis." Ibid., 68.

[62] "Figuris itaque antiquis nomina imposuerunt nova, pro ratione linguae tunc
temporis usitatae." Ibid., 69.

[63] "... de utraque materia (i. e. the excursus on the vowel points and the short
introduction to "rabbinical" Hebrew) prolixiora et luculentiora quaedam proximo
tempore proponere." preface to the reader, dated August 24, 1615 in *Thesaurus
Grammaticus*, (Basel: L. König, 1615), quoted by Prijs, *Drucke*, 328.

[64] "Hoc animo proposita fuêre ab ipso, quae primae Editioni Thesauri
Grammatici de hac quaestione inseruerat. Unde in posterioribus editionibus illa
iterùm expunxit; non quòd sententiam suam mutaverit, sed quia necessarium &
utile judicabat, atque etiam in animo habebat, pleniùs & absolutiùs totam illam
rem pertractare." Johannes Buxtorf II, *Tractatus de Punctorum Vocalium, et
Accentuum, in Libris Veteris Testamenti Hebraicis, Origine, Antiquitate, &
Authoritate: Oppositus Arcano Punctationis Revelato Ludovici Cappelli* (Basel:
Haeredum Ludovici König, 1648), f.)(3v.

posed guides to the four parts of the Basel rabbinical Bible edition: Hebrew text, Targums, rabbinical Bible commentaries and Masora.[65] It was published in 1620 in both quarto and folio formats, the latter meant to be bound with the Bible edition itself.[66] Both editions contain the historical first section and the practical second section, but only the folio edition contains the third section of corrections to the *Masora parva, magna* and *finalis*. Certain copies of the folio edition also contain the letter of dedication to the Estates General of the Netherlands.[67] The Estates General of Holland awarded him 200 Guilders for *Tiberias* as a token of thanks for dedicating it to them.[68]

Tiberias was composed to be a reference work for Christian students and scholars interested in studying the Masora. The first part is conceptual, offering a presentation of the history of the Masora (chaps. 1-11) and an explanation of its form (chaps. 12-20). The latter section included explanations of how individual verses, words and letters were preserved accurately and an introduction to the forms the Masora took and the types of critical marks used by the masoretes. The second part was more practical and included two separate lists of abbreviations (chaps. 2-3) and detailed explanations of technical terminology employed by the masoretes (chaps. 5-12).[69] Genesis chap. 1 was used as a practice text

---

[65] "Sed de quatuor harum partium, quae in hoc Opere biblico continentur (Text, Targum, Masorah and commentaries) ampliori usu ... specialem & sufficientem Instructionem una cum completo hoc Opere, Deo annuente, proponemus, ad quem Christianum & benevolum quemque Lectorem hoc tempore remittimus..." Johannes Buxtorf I's Latin introduction to his *Biblia rabbinica*, f. (1)v, dated August 22, 1618. See also Buxtorf II's introduction to *Lexicon Chaldaicum et Syriacum*, f. **2v, both quoted in Prijs, *Drucke*, 335.

[66] Prijs nos. 222A and 222B.

[67] Buxtorf, *Tiberias*, fol., 80-114. The letter of dedication is partially reprinted in Prijs, *Drucke*, 532-534. The Staats- und Universitätsbibliothek Bern kindly supplied me with a copy of the full letter (*Tiberias*, fol., ff. ***2v-4r). All references to *Tiberias*, unless otherwise indicated, are to the quarto edition.

[68] *Tiberias* was recognized by the Estates General on June 6, 1620. See J. G. Smit and J. Roelovink, eds. *Resolutiën der Staten-Generaal, 1610-1670*, vol. 4: *1619-1620*, Rijks Geschiedkundige Publicatiën, vol. 176 ('s-Gravenhage: Martinus Nijhoff, 1981), 490 and n. 3388b.

[69] This portion of *Tiberias* was an outgrowth of Buxtorf's preparatory work on the Basel *Biblia rabbinica*. "Haec dum inter laborandum notarem, simul peculiares masorae voces & locutiones observavi, quarum usus non adeo communis & tritus erat. Hinc natus primo Commentarius Criticus, qui Castigationes in universam masoram continet ... Deinde Clavis Masorae, quae

to illustrate the functions of the *Masora parva* and *Masora magna* (chaps. 13-14). In the final two chapters Buxtorf tied up loose ends in his discussion (chaps. 15-16).

A structural comparison between Levita's *Masoret ha-Masoret* and *Tiberias* reveals striking differences in emphasis. Levita's book contains three prefaces, the third discussing the age of the accents and vowel points.[70] The body of the work contains three sections, poetically called the two tablets of the law (each containing ten chapters which Levita called his "Ten Commandments") and the "broken tablet." In the first section Levita discussed vowel letters, and in the second he analyzed variant readings (*qere* and *kethib*), *qames* and *patah,* various accents, and a variety of technical terms used by the masoretes.[71] The final section, the "broken tablet," deals with masoretic abbreviations and contains a poem ascribed to Saadia Gaon which gives a summary of the statistics compiled by the masoretes for the entire Hebrew Bible.[72] Buxtorf, by contrast, used nearly half of his historical section to refute Levita's third preface and devoted the rest of part 1 and most of part 2 to material covered by Levita in his second and third parts. While Levita discussed how vowel letters were used in the entire first section of his book, Buxtorf practically ignored the topic.[73] The second section of *Tiberias* drew heavily upon the second and third parts of Levita's book but was intended to be both a primer for beginning students and a reference tool for more advanced scholars. Buxtorf's discussion of masoretic abbreviations, for example, contains explanations of fifty abbreviations compared to Levita's fifteen.[74] The two chapters illustrating the Masora for Genesis 1 have

---

voces & phrases masorae peculiares explicat, & ceu clavis, aditum in universam masorae cognitionem aperit." Buxtorf to the Estates General of the Netherlands, Basel, April 1, 1620, *Tiberias*, fol., f. ***3v.

[70] The first preface is a rhymed introduction and the second was written by Levita as an autobiography and defense of his dealings with Christians and of his willingness to instruct them in Hebrew. Levita, *Massoreth,* 86-101.

[71] Christian D. Ginsburg in his introduction to *Massoreth,* 41.

[72] Ibid., 271-278.

[73] Ibid., 145-179 and Buxtorf, *Tiberias,* 138-140.

[74] This difference did not go unnoticed among Buxtorf's contemporaries. "Novissimè Dn Buxtorfius occasione Bibliorum Basileensium, hanc materiam tripartito volumine, à Tyberitis denominato, ... altera Clavem fabricatur, quâ penetralia Masorae reseranter. Ubi Abbreviationes longe plures quàm Elias explicat ...." Wilhelm Schickhard, *Bechinath Happeruschim Hoc est Examinis*

no counterpart in *Masoret* but would have been quite useful for beginners. In Buxtorf's time Levita's book was also extremely rare, and he felt that there was a definite need for a textbook on the subject.[75]

Tiberias was written not only to serve as a textbook on the Masora, but also to refute Levita's position on the age of the vowel points. Buxtorf devoted six chapters (3-9) in the first part to describing Levita's arguments, supplying relevant historical description and offering elaborate rebuttals. Then in the next two chapters (10-11) he explained his own position, that the men of the Great Synagogue were responsible for adding the accents and vowel points.[76] Buxtorf's rebuttal of Levita can be divided into three parts: his sketch of Levita's views, an historical excursus on the schools of Tiberias, and his refutation of Levita's position in chaps. 8-9. According to Buxtorf two positions on the origins of the Masora were espoused in his day: that the sages of Tiberias were its author, or that it was written by the men of the Great Synagogue.[77] Since Levita's argument rested partially on an historical assumption that there were flourishing schools of masoretes in Tiberias after the composition of the Babylonian Talmud, Buxtorf began his rebuttal with a review of the history of the Tiberian schools as related by Jewish historians.[78] He gave a brief description of Tiberias, Yavneh, Sepphoris and Caesarea and their schools which is drawn mainly from the Talmud and from R. Benjamin of

---

Commentationum Rabbinicarum in Mosen Prodromus (Tübingen: Johann-Alexander Cellius, 1624), 59.

[75] Buxtorf, *Tiberias*, f.):(2v and Buxtorf to the Estates General of the Netherlands, Basel, April 1, 1620, *Tiberias*, fol., ff. ***3v.

[76] Ibid., 8-93 (chaps. 3-9) and 93-131 (chaps. 10-11).

[77] Levita's views were not unprecidented among Jewish scholars. Abraham ibn Ezra too believed that the vowel points were a later addition to the biblical text. See idem, *Sefer Sahot de Abraham Ibn Ezra: edición crítica y versión castellana*, ed. and trans. Carlos del Valle Rodriguez, Bibliotheca Salmanticensis Dissertationes, no. 1 (Salamanca: University of Salamanca, 1977), 131, ll. 8-10. Buxtorf also mentioned R. Jonah ibn Janah and R. Judah Hayyug of Fez as early proponants of this view. *Tiberias*, 13

[78] While there is no doubt today among scholars that there were flourishing schools of Massoretes in Tiberias and elsewhere after the composition of the Talmud the evidence for these schools remains fragmentary. See Israel Yeivin, *Introduction to the Tiberian Masorah*, trans. and ed. E. J. Revell, Society of Biblical Literature Masoretic Studies Series, no. 5 (n. p.: Scholars Press, 1980), 137-139.

Tudela's *Itinerum*.[79] Then he described their gradual demise between 230, when the Palestinian Talmud was said to have been
completed, and about 340 A. D. when Rabbi Hillel, the final principal of the Tiberias schools mentioned by Hebrew language histories, died.[80] Although these histories are silent about any further
activity in Tiberias they relate much about the Babylonian schools
which would remain important long afterward.[81] While Jerome
mentioned a Tiberian Jewish scholar in his Preface to the Book of
Chronicles (ca. 420 A. D.) this hardly proved the existence of a
school there.[82] Given the importance and prominence of the
Babylonian Jewish schools for a thousand years after their decline
in Palestine, Buxtorf asked, was it reasonable to assume that they
would yield all claim to the preservation and pointing of the Bible
to unknown scholars in provincial Palestine? Babylonian scholars
were able to promote the use of the Babylonian Talmud and to rel-
egate the Palestinian Talmud to obscurity; why were they unable to
impose their authority in matters masoretic? Determining the
pointing of the biblical text was, after all, not only a matter of
scholarly prowess, but also an assertion of religious authority over
the entire Jewish "church."[83] Finally, Buxtorf asked, if Elias is
correct and there are many masoretes, why are only those from
Tiberias mentioned?[84] Although masoretic schools such as Levita
posited would have been important enough institutions both to
command the respect of those in Babylon and to catch the attention
of later Jewish historians they did neither, calling their very existence into question.

---

[79] Buxtorf, *Tiberias*, 15-23.

[80] Ibid., 23-31.

[81] "Cui robur accedit inde, quod Chronica Hebraeorum post hunc Hillelem,
nihil quicquam amplius de Scholis aut Sapientibus Palaestinae referunt, sed
Babylonicas Scholas presse ad extremum terminum prosequuntur." Ibid., 30.

[82] Ibid.

[83] Ibid., 32-33.

[84] "[S]i ipsomet Eliâ fatente, Masorae authores per diversas generationes,
milleni fuerint & myriades, id est, plures & quasi innumeri, principium quoque
ipsorum & finis incertus, quomodo soli Tiberienses ejus authores dici possunt?"
Tiberias, 33. Buxtorf knew about about the "eastern" and "western" textual
readings from the standardized list of differences printed in the Bomberg Bible
editions. See Johannes Buxtorf I to Benedict Turrettini, Basel, June 22, 1618,
Geneva: Archives Turrettini, Fonds 1, Dd. 4.1. See also Yeivin, *Introduction*,
137-141.

After proving to his own satisfaction that Levita's masoretic
schools could not have existed after the completion of the
Babylonian Talmud, Buxtorf then turned to Levita's assumption
that the Masora had to have been composed after the Talmud's
completion. He noted that the Masora is mentioned by name in at
least one passage,[85] and that another passage testifies to the existence of *majusculum* and *minisculum* letters.[86] Still another passage
credited Moses himself with the division of verses in the law,
rather than to the Tiberian masoretes as Levita claimed.[87] Although
Levita attributed the elaborate gathering of statistics to the Tiberian
masoretes, BT *Kiddushim* 30 mentioned the existence of scholars
who tabulated such statistics.[88] Buxtorf also mentioned Jacob b.
Hayyim's judgement that the Masora carried higher authority than
the rabbis in the Talmud where the form of the biblical text is concerned.[89] Since the rabbis of the Talmud mentioned the Masora by
name and referred to the activities of the masoretes then, Buxtorf
concluded, it was reasonable to assume that the Masora was composed before the Babylonian Talmud was completed in the sixth
century.

In the ninth chapter of *Tiberias* Buxtorf concluded his rebuttal
of Levita by addressing the implications of Levita's central contention: that the Hebrew accents and vowel points were human inventions. His position was based upon a curious mixture of philological, historical, and barely disguised theological argumentation.
He began by contending that the very diversity of vocalization, use
of Dagesh and Mappik and of accents did not suggest the unified
results of one school of masoretes but a variety of conventions, reflecting the usages of individual biblical authors who naturally
followed the vocalization practices current in their own days.[90] In

---

[85] Ibid., 34-38 quoting BT *Megilla* 3a on Neh. 8: 8. Buxtorf also quoted a
talmudic proverb, "יש אם למקרא יש אם למסורת," which appears in BT *Kiddushin*
18b and BT *Sanhedrin* 4a.

[86] Buxtorf, *Tiberias*, 46-47, 153. For the significance of using larger and
smaller letters in the Hebrew text see F. E. Deist, *Towards the Text of the Old
Testament,* trans. W. K. Winckler (Pretoria: N. G. Kerkboekhandel Transvaal,
1978), 56-57.

[87] Buxtorf, *Tiberias*, 38-40, quoting BT *Megilla* 23b-24a and 22a.

[88] Ibid., 44-46.

[89] Ibid., 46-47, quoting Jacob b. Hayyim ibn Adoniyah's introduction to the
second Bomberg *Biblia rabbinica*. See idem, *Introduction*, 42.

[90] Ibid., 73.

support of his contention Buxtorf listed page after page of variants
punctuated by comments such as, "If the same people are the authors both of the pointing and of the Masora, then why are there
six exceptions to the common pointing?"[91] Buxtorf followed this
philological argument by rehearsing Levita's reasons for dating the
vowel points after the completion of the Talmud. His response was
in essence the same as he used in *Thesaurus Grammaticus*, but
contained far more quotations from both the Talmud and from its
principal commentators such as R. Nissim, R. Isaac Alfassi and
Rashi.[92] He concluded by arguing for the religious necessity of divinely inspired vowel points. Countering Levita's position that the
vowel points were not necessary while Hebrew remained a living
language, Buxtorf argued that without points there was no way to
ensure the transmission of correct readings and vocalization.[93]
Buxtorf maintained that the vowels are the soul (*anima*) of textual
readings, and that divinely inspired consonants alone were not
enough to enable interpreters to understand the Hebrew Bible.[94] If
the vowel points were not a part of the inspired biblical text then
some sort of interpretive standard, an "independent judge," was
needed by interpreters to settle these problems. The Septuagint was
unable to fulfill this role because it differed from the Hebrew not
only in the vocalization of individual words, but also in the consonantal text which lay behind it.[95] If the vocalization of the Hebrew
text were solely a work of human intellect rather than an intrinsic
part of the inspired biblical text then the result would be a plethora
of questions about individual verses which together could undermine the authority of the Word of God.[96] As a Protestant, Buxtorf

---

[91] "Si iidem sunt Punctationis & Masorae authores, quae causa fuit, ut ex tot
centenis tantum sex contra communem formam punctarint?" Ibid., 49. See also
pp. 50, 51, passim. Buxtorf gave 40 examples of vowel point and 12 of
accentual anomalies. See Laplanche, *L'Écriture*, 867, n. 18.

[92] Buxtorf, *Tiberias*, 81-89.

[93] Ibid., 91.

[94] Although Buxtorf and Polanus both ascribed their use of the body/soul
image to the quotation from ספר הבהיר, it is a notion which was also had firm
roots in Aristotelian grammatical theory. See Gershom Scholem's discussion in
Das Buch Bahir (Leipzig: W. Drugulin, 1923; reprint ed., Darmstadt:
Wissenschaftliche Buchgesellschaft, 1980), 85-90, 168.

[95] Buxtorf, *Tiberias*, 91-92 and *Thesaurus Grammaticus*, 61-62.

[96] Robert Preus wisely noted that Buxtorf and his successors never debated
the "inspiration of the vowel points" *per se*, as some have misrepresented it, but
rather argued over "whether the vowel points were part of the original auto-

felt the consequences of such a position were theologically danger-ous.[97]

Elias Levita's theory about the age of the Masora, the accents and the vowel points was unacceptable to Buxtorf for a variety of reasons. Historically there was no evidence that schools of ma-soretes existed in Tiberias during the period after the completion of the Talmud, and if they had they would have been ignored by the ascendant Babylonian scholarly community. Buxtorf argued that the rabbis of the Talmud were familiar with the Masora, men-tioning it by name and speaking of its various elements. The great diversity of conventions for vocalization and for accentuation sug-gested to Buxtorf not one school of masoretes in one location, but the many biblical authors living in different centuries. Levita's the-ory also raised questions about the religious authority of the Hebrew Bible, since it suggested a greater role for the subjective human reader than Buxtorf felt appropriate. Fortunately both Jewish and Christian tradition suggested a historically more plausible and religiously more acceptable alternative for the origin of the vocalized Hebrew text.

The Men of the Great Synagogue were, according to Jewish tradition, a group of scholars and prophets led by Ezra the Scribe in the early years after the Jews' return from the Babylonian Captivity.[98] Isaac Abravanel maintained that these men included, among others, the prophets Haggai, Zechariah and Malachi, Zerubbabel, Mordecai, Yeshua son of Yehoshedek the Priest, Nehemiah and Ezra himself.[99] Buxtorf drew upon not only the Talmud and later Jewish writings but also a number of Christian sources especially the Church Fathers when he described the Great

---

graphs, and thus whether they were inspired and are authentic." Robert Preus, *The Inspiration of Scripture: A Study of the Theology of the Seventeenth Century Lutheran Dogmaticians*, 2d. ed. (Edinburgh: Oliver and Boyd, 1957), 144-145.

[97] "Opus ipsorum (i. e. men who were not prophets) vocalium ascriptio, fuit *poal enuschi*, opus humanum, ac proinde authoritas istius lectionis, humana est, quae per se & ex se neminem hîc obligat. Si inventum humanum sunt, & authoritas ipsorum humana, removeri possunt, & sic lectio pro cujusque erit arbitrio. Quae tunc textus Hebraei firmitas, quae certitudo?" *Tiberias*, ff.):(3r-v.

[98] See Charles Taylor, *Sayings of the Jewish Fathers* (Cambridge: Cambridge Univ. Press, 1897-1900; reprint ed., Amsterdam: Philo, 1970), 110-111.

[99] Isaac Abravanel, נחלת אבות (Venice: Marcus Antonius Justinius, 1545), preface, quoted in Buxtorf, *Tiberias*, 95-96. This book was actually a new printing of *Pirke Abot* with Abravanel's commentary.

Synagogue and its work. He cited Tertullian, John Chrysostom, Irenaeus, Eusebius and Augustine on the work of Ezra in restoring the Scripture.[100] Then, in a clever rhetorical move, he quoted explanations of the importance of the Great Synagogue written by Robert Bellarmine and Gilbert Génébrard, two prominent Catholic polemicists. By so doing he demonstrated that Catholic theologians too attached great importance to the work of the Great Synagogue.[101] Génébrard, for example, thought that the Men of the Great Synagogue determined the canon and corrected the text of canonical books where necessary. He attributed the *Tikkune ha-Soferim* to Ezra himself.[102] Having established the historical and theological credentials of the Great Synagogue, Buxtorf then discussed their actual work.

The Men of the Great Synagogue were the first masoretes according to Buxtorf. They were responsible for closing the biblical canon and dividing it into the traditional three parts: Torah, Prophets and Writings.[103] They, and not the Tiberian masoretes, were responsible for the introduction of verse divisions throughout the Bible. Although verse divisions in the Septuagint sometimes differed from the Hebrew text this was to be explained as the result of poor copying.[104] Ezra and his colleagues also worked to guarantee the accuracy of individual words in the biblical text by correct copying, letter by letter, of the consonantal text and by correct vocalization of each word. Since they had access to the original auto-

---

[100] Buxtorf, *Tiberias*, 94-102.

[101] By quoting Bellarmine, Buxtorf also followed Polanus's theological reposte.

[102] "Hi praefuerunt concilio, quod centum viginti homines, quorum alii nobiles, alii plebei erant, de emendandis libris sacris, eorumque constituendo canone, juxta praescriptum Cabbalae inierunt ... Ejus (Esrae) consilio & opera praesertim libri sacri collati sunt & emendati: unde Tikkun sopherim, id est Correctio scribarum, appellatur Tikkun Esrae, ut in Masora Num. 12. quasi Esra Scribarum fuerit princeps." *Tiberias*, 105. The first part of the quotation came from Genebrardus, *Chronographia in Duos Libros Distincta* (Louvain: Johann Foulerum, 1572), f. 27v; I have been unable to find the second part (beginning with "Ejus").

[103] Buxtorf, *Tiberias*, 106-112.

[104] "Respondetur, Versuum illam differentiam, ut & innumerorum aliorum locorum discrepantiam in versione ista, non esse à primis illis interpretibus, sed à librariis & Scriptoribus, quorum quisque; nunc plures sententias conjunxit, nunc distraxit, prout in calamum fluerent, & animus scriptionis operi esset intentus, aut vagus, ut in magnis & longis operibus fieri solet." Ibid., 114-115.

graphs of each book (and some of them were themselves prophets) their work was entirely trustworthy.[105] This is not to say that Buxtorf could answer every possible question about the Great Synagogue's work from extant historical sources. Tradition was unclear as to whether the Ezra and his co-workers had invented the present-day vowel points and accents themselves or whether they were invented by others and fell into disuse and were only restored by the Men of the Great Synagogue.[106] It was also unclear whether they were also responsible for numbering each letter, word and verse in each book to find in each case which one was in the middle, keeping a record of unique occurrences of words, and other such work. This statistical work began before the Talmud was written, according to BT *Kiddushim*.[107] Buxtorf concluded his argument by quoting Azariah de Rossi's *Meor Enayim*, Gedaliah ibn Yahya's *Shelshelet ha-Qabalah*, Isaac Abravanel's introduction to *Pirke Abot*, and the grammarian Profet Duran to the effect that the Men of the Great Synagogue had composed the Masora.[108] Levita had admitted that most Jewish scholars believed that the Men of the Great Synagogue had composed the Masora and were responsible for the vowel points and accents. Buxtorf was convinced that they were correct and Levita was wrong.

---

[105] "Post Versuum distinctionem, à Viris Synagogae magnae voces singulae considerate fuerunt, in quibus duplex cura: una, quae scriptionem ipsarum juxta nudas consonas spectabat, altera quae lectionem & pronunciationem ipsarum juxta literas & vocales conjunctim. In scriptione vocum juxta literas, consulebant authentica primorum authorum exemplaria, quotquot tunc extabant in manibus ipsorum, aut sequebantur probatissimorum & plurium exemplarium fidem, an voces juxta nativam originis suae proprietatem, essent scriptae, quae voces cum quibus literis quiescentibus, plene essent scriptae, aut quae defective: quae literae & voces essent scriptae abundanter, & non lectae: aut contra, quae lectae fuerunt, cum tamen non essent in textu scriptae...." Ibid., 115.
[106] "An autem ipsimet viri synagogae magnae, Vocalium & Accentuum notas primo hîc invenerint, aut ab aliis inventas, sed in usu neglectas, restauraverint & perfecerint, ac Masoram de iis quoque conscribi curârint, facile nec dici, nec probari facile potest." Ibid., 117-118.
[107] "Ad extremum Viri synagogae magnae his omnibus non contenti, literas, voces & versus in singulis libris numerarunt, ut sciretur, quae litera, quae vox, qui versus in singulis libris medium occuparet . . . quae vox nonisi semel occurreret, & idcirco errorem aut corruptionem aliquam facile admitteret." Ibid. See BT *Kiddushin* 30a.
[108] Ibid., 120, 129-130. NB. The pagination of the quarto *Tiberias* goes from 120 to 129 due to a printer's error; the pagination continues consecutively after 129.

The proposed audience for Buxtorf's diatribe on the vowel points is not explicitly stated in *Tiberias*. While he focused his arguments against Levita his polemic was not directed against that long dead writer personally or against any other Jewish scholar. His most important aim was to counter Catholic polemical arguments. He argued that the fixation of the Hebrew Bible text, consonants, vowels and accents alike, was the work of Ezra and the other Men of the Great Synagogue, a position held, at least in principle, by many of the Church Fathers and more recently by Cardinal Bellarmine himself. To acknowledge Ezra's role in fixing the final form of the biblical text (including its vocalization in Buxtorf's opinion), as Bellarmine had, was also to reject Levita's position on the age of the vowel points. Buxtorf's identification of the Men of the Great Synagogue as the first masoretes was the result of a search for the most plausible institutional and historical setting for the fixation of the Hebrew Bible text. He argued that the phenomena of the text, both its regular and irregular features, were best explained by his position. His historical arguments could also have been directed against those Protestants who, like Scaliger, thought that the vowel points were a human invention. Buxtorf placed philology at the service of theology and wrote what appeared to be a conclusive statement on the origins of the Masora and vowel points.

Buxtorf's argumentation and impressive familiarity with Jewish tradition mask important flaws both in his methodology and canons of admissible evidence. His use of Jewish sources was in the final analysis dogmatic rather than critical. He assumed the purity of the Hebrew Bible text as he had it, giving no credence to the Targum, Greek and Latin versions as witnesses to its textual history. Buxtorf considered the Septuagint's evidential value as a witness to the Hebrew text to be questionable since it sometimes varied not only in vocalization but also in wording and verse division from the Hebrew. To judge the Hebrew text by its Greek translation would be like allowing a servant to judge his master.[109] He refused to acknowledge the possibility that early Hebrew may have been unvocalized, as books in contemporary Arabic were. The vowel points

---

[109] Buxtorf, *Tiberias*, 92. See also Buxtorf to the Estates General of the Netherlands, Basel, April 1, 1620, *Tiberias*, fol., f. ***3r.

of Arabic might have been a scholarly invention that was adopted for the convenience of readers, but Jewish tradition attested to the use of Hebrew vowel points by the Men of the Great Synagogue. Even Buxtorf's minute examination of the Hebrew text for variants in consonants, vocalization and accentuation took place within the confines of the Masora. He acknowledged that the Targum text had suffered from a wide variety of transmission errors, including metathesis of letters, mistakes in copying such easily confused letters as Dalet and Resh, but made no effort to apply these canons to evaluate the received Hebrew text as Cappel later would do.[110] Such a methodology was unthinkable to Buxtorf. Only an impious man would change the received Hebrew text.[111]

Buxtorf's argument for the antiquity of the vowel points was substantially the same in both the 1609 edition of *Thesaurus Grammaticus* and over ten years later in *Tiberias*. In both works he refuted Levita's four arguments and argued that oral tradition was insufficient to safeguard the proper vocalization of the text. His theological point of view was identical in both works. *Tiberias* differed from its predecessor in its elaborate historical analysis of the history of the Tiberian schools and of the contention that the talmudic writers were familiar with the Masora and its component parts. Buxtorf's lengthy treatment of the Great Synagogue was also a feature unique to *Tiberias*. While Buxtorf again used the two quotations from the *Zohar* to Song of Solomon and to *Sefer ha-Bahir* as historical testimonies to the antiquity of the vowel points he was less sure of when the *Zohar* was composed, and he stressed this particular argument less than he did in *Thesaurus Grammaticus*.[112] One element in the 1609 essay which did not

---

[110] On Cappel's later works see Van Rooden, *Theology*, 222-223.

[111] "Textum Hebraeum in antiquissima & verissima sua puritate & substantia, in minimo etiam apice, reliquimus. Impius enim, quisquis ei aliquid vel addiderit vel detraxerit, aut quovis modo in eo quid mutaverit." Johannes Buxtorf in the Latin introduction to his *Biblia rabbinica*, f. (1)v.

[112] "Plura alia in Zohar inveniuntur, quae antiquam punctorum memoriam alunt. Cabalisticam in istis testimoniis Theologiam Judaeis relinquimus: pro memoria duntaxat punctorum asserenda, nos ista adduximus, non fine alio. Sive etiam antiquitatem, sive novitatem sapiant, excutiant alii. Saltem incognita hactenus in nostris Scholis Hebraicis fuerunt, quo fine ad publicam notitiam ea produximus, & judicium aliis relinquimus." *Tiberias,* 80. See also p. 75. Buxtorf's doubts about the age of the *Zohar* first appear in his *De Abbreviaturis*, 167-168.

reappear in *Tiberias* was Buxtorf's discussion of the preservation
of the biblical text before and after the work of the Great
Synagogue.

Tiberias has received a mixed reception both from Buxtorf's
contemporaries and from subsequent scholarship. As a textbook on
the Masora it had no rival among Christians. Wilhelm Schickhard
recommended it to his students in 1621, a year after it was published.[113] André Rivet, who initially disagreed with Buxtorf's position on the vowel points, called it a "learned treatise."[114] It remained the principal source for Christian study of the Masora until
well into the nineteenth century when Emil Kautzsch encouraged
its use, and Julius Wellhausen praised it extravagantly.[115] Buxtorf's
discussions on the age of the Masora and the vowel points were also
initially welcomed and quickly found their way into anti-Catholic
polemics.[116] His position on the vowel points also became part of
the Lutheran dogmatic tradition through Johann Gerhard's *Loci
Theologici*.[117] Over a hundred years later Johann David Michaelis,
who became one of the fathers of German biblical criticism, wrote
his doctoral dissertation on the antiquity of the Hebrew vowel
points.[118] Not all Protestants, however, welcomed the appearance
of *Tiberias*.

---

[113] Schickhard, *Bechinath*, 59. This book comprises a series of disputations
conducted in 1621 (pp. 1, 39, *passim*).

[114] André Rivet, *Isagoge, Seu Introductio generalis, ad Scripturam Sacram
Veteris & Novi Testamenti* (Leiden: Isaac Commelinius, 1627), 102.

[115] Wellhausen wrote that *Tiberias* was "... das Product einer von keinem
Christen und wenigen Juden erreichten Gelehrsamkeit und dabei
bewundernswerth einfach." Quoted by Kautzsch, *Buxtorf*, 8.

[116] Preus, *Inspiration*, 140-141. Salomo Glassius, a professor of Old
Testament at the University of Jena wrote within his *Philologia Sacra* (Jena: T.
Steinmann, 1623) a response to a polemical work by Jesuit James Huntley
Gordon (1541-1620) using *Tiberias* as a major source for his arguments. "In iis,
quae contra Gordonum Jesuitam p. 15 et seqq. dissero, tuam de Tiberiensibus
secutus fui sententiam, quae in Commentario Masoretico solidissimè exposita
...." Salomo Glassius to Johannes Buxtorf, Jena, December 23, 1623, Basel UB
G I 61: 271v. See Laplanche, *L'Écriture*, 894, n. 71.

[117] Gerhard, *Loci Theologici*, 1: 141-151 (I, xiv-xv), *passim*. See also Preus,
Inspiration, 141-144 and Laplanche, *L'Écriture*, 306-307.

[118] Anna-Ruth Löwenbrück, "Johann David Michaelis's Verdienst um die
philologisch-historische Bibelkritik," in: *Historische Kritik und biblischer Kanon
in der deutschen Aufklärung*, eds. Henning Graf Reventlow, Walter Sparn and
John Woodbridge, Wolfenbütteler Forschungen, vol. 41 (Wiesbaden: Otto
Harrassowitz, 1988), 158.

Only two years after its publication *Tiberias* received its first refutation at the hands of one of Buxtorf's own correspondents, Louis Cappel.[119] Cappel was professor of Hebrew and Old Testament at the French reformed academy of Saumur. In the course of his education he had spent nearly two years at Oxford where he had studied Arabic and began to compose an Arabic lexicon.[120] Shortly after his appointment to Saumur in 1613 he began his studies in biblical philology and textual criticism. His lecture on the Tetragrammaton, delivered on June 22, 1614, attests to a preoccupation with methodology which would distinguish his later work.[121] He sent a copy of another lecture in which he argued that the vowel points were invented after the time of Christ to Buxtorf by way of his elder brother Jacques.[122] At the latter's request Buxtorf wrote back to him his reasons for disagreement with Louis Cappel's views.[123] Cappel was forced to leave Saumur because of war in 1621 and took refuge in Sedan where his brother taught theology. He completed his book *Arcanum Punctationis* in of 1622

---

[119] Although he is a pivotal figure in the history of biblical studies Louis Cappel has never been the subject of a scholarly biography. Laplanche's *L'Écriture* offers a broad discussion of his scholarly achievements and Schnederman's *Controverse*, 2-9 gives a short sketch of his life. See also J. H. M. Salmon, "Protestant jurists and theologians in early modern France: the family of Cappel," in *Renaissance and Revolt: Essays in the Intellectual and Social Hstory of Early Modern France*, Cambridge Studies in Early Modern History, (Cambridge: Cambridge Univ. Press, 1987), 54-72.

[120] Schnederman, *Controverse*, 6.

[121] "Oratio de SS. Dei nomine Tetragrammato hwhy ac genuina ejus pronunctiatione," printed in: *Arcanum Punctationis Revelatum. Sive De Punctorum Vocalium & Accentuum apud Hebraeos vera & germana Antiquitate, Diatriba* (Leiden: Johannes Maire, 1624), 313-332. See also Laplanche, *L'Écriture*, 214.

[122] L. Cappel later claimed that Jacques had passed the manuscript on to Buxtorf without his consent. Louis Cappel to Johannes Buxtorf, Sedan, July 10, 1622, Basel UB Ms G I 62: 107-109, printed in Buxtorf, *Catalecta*, 477.

[123] "Quaero, si per otium licet, lege oratiunculam hanc ex ea dare quid tibi videatur, scribe." Jacques Cappel to Johannes Buxtorf, n. p., September 9, 1619, Basel UB Ms G I 62:124. See also Johannes Buxtorf to Jacques Cappel, n. p. and n. d., Basel UB Ms Ki Ar 189:8. Since Jacques Cappel agreed with Buxtorf's position on the vowel points both before and after the publication of the *Arcanum* Buxtorf's response to Jacques probably gives his reaction to Louis' earlier lecture rather than to the *Arcanum*. Jacques Cappel told Buxtorf,"Quod de punctis Hebraeorum aliud sentit (i. e. Louis) quam ego ...." Jacques Cappel to Johannes Buxtorf, Sedan, June 23, 1623, Basel UB Ms G I 62: 122. Laplanche, *L'Écriture*, 214 and 867, notes 23 and 25.

and sent it in manuscript to Buxtorf, requesting that he critique the work and send both his response and the manuscript back.[124]

Cappel's thesis in the *Arcanum* is that the age of the Hebrew vowel points, accents, and Masora is primarily a philological question and should be treated as such.[125] He had, however, a theological motivation to pursue this line of argumentation. Cappel wished to deprive Catholic polemicists of Elias Levita's arguments and to use them as a part of his own theory of biblical interpretation. He argued that the consonantal Hebrew Bible text could be interpreted reliably without the aid of vowel points.[126] He was convinced that Buxtorf and others who opposed Levita's position were not only mistaken on philological grounds, but that they played into the hands of the Catholics by giving Levita's arguments to them.[127]

Several curious features of the *Arcanum* and the circumstances of its composition are more comprehensible when considered within the theological context of the early seventeenth century. Cappel did all that he could to avoid embarrassing Buxtorf publicly.[128] He sent his manuscript to him before publishing it and within the book itself rarely attributed Buxtorf's views to him directly, preferring to attack the *patroni punctorum*.[129] As a result he

---

[124] Louis Cappel to Johannes Buxtorf, Sedan, July 10, 1622, Basel UB Ms G I 62: 107-109, and *Catalecta*, pp. 477-478. See Schnederman, *Controverse*, 7-8.

[125] "Quaestio videntur ista Philologica, & ad Criticam magis quam ad Theologiam pertinens, proindeque magna esse debet in ejus definitione diversa sententium libertas." *Arcanum*, f. (b3)r.

[126] Laplanche, *L'Écriture*, 218-219.

[127] "Cumque in solvendis & refutandis illis argumentis laborare debuissent adversus Pontificios qui illis in nos utuntur, ut totam Scripturae authoritatem ab Ecclesiae testimonio pendere demonstrent, ipsi contra, ultro illis ea concedunt & largiuntur, adeoque fortius astringere conantur, conquisitis ad id undique omnis generis argumentis, quibus id efficere studebant, quod nobis propositum est hac Diatriba oppugnare." *Arcanum*, 283. See also Cappel's remarks on pp. 3-5.

[128] The reception of Scaliger's *Thesaurus temporum* by Protestants is another example of this kind of "confessional courtesy." Anthony T. Grafton, "Joseph Scaliger and Historical Chronology: The Rise and Fall of a Discipline," *History and Theory* 14 (1975): 173-174.

[129] Cappel told Buxtorf privately that the arguments which he criticised in the second part of *Arcanum* came from his brother Jacques, Chevallier's *Rudimenta*, and both Buxtorf's *Thesaurus Grammaticus* (Basel: Konrad Waldkirch, 1609) and *Tiberias*. Louis Cappel to Johannes Buxtorf, Sedan, July 10, 1622, Basel UB Ms G I 62: 107-109, printed in Buxtorf, *Catalecta*, 477-478.

and Buxtorf were able to maintain respectful relations even after the publication of the *Arcanum*.[130]

Cappel's reluctance to claim authorship of *Arcanum* should also be considered in light of a polemical battle that French Protestants were then waging over the the nature of Scripture with their Catholic foes. In 1618 Pierre Coton wrote *Genève plagiaire*, a scathing polemical book on the Geneva French Bible translation.[131] In it he claimed that the Hebrew Bible text in its present form was neither "pure, complete or certain."[132] The book elicited a flurry of responses from French Protestants including one by Jacques Cappel in 1620.[133] Before he published his own response to Coton, Benedict Turrettini wrote to Buxtorf asking for information on the history of the Hebrew Bible text.[134] In this poisonous atmosphere, when Cappel espoused several positions which were in agreement with Catholic ones, his reluctance to acknowledge the *Arcanum* is understandable.[135] While he expected his arguments to disarm Catholic polemicists in the long run the book had to be accepted by Protestants first to have an effect.[136]

While Cappel spared no effort to maintain the appearance of Protestant solidarity both with Buxtorf and with his fellow Huguenots, his *Arcanum* can only be described as a devastating re-

---

[130] See, e. g. Louis Cappel to Johannes Buxtorf II, Saumur, December 3, 1628, Basel UB Ms G I 62: 117, printed in *Catalecta*, 486-488. See Schnederman, *Controverse*, 12.

[131] William A. McComish, *The Epigones: A Study of the Theology of the Genevan Academy at the Time of the Synod of Dort, with special reference to Giovanni Diodati* (Allison Park, PA: Pickwick, 1989), 127-145.

[132] Pierre Coton, *Genève plagiaire*, col. 9, quoted by Laplanche, *L'Écriture*, 314.

[133] Laplanche, *L'Écriture*, 314-315. The (as yet unpublished) minutes of the Geneva Company of Pastors meetings between January 1618 and December 1619 reveal the concern with which the leaders of the Genevan church viewed Coton's book. See the extracts published by McComish, *Epigones*, 141-142, notes 27-38.

[134] Johannes Buxtorf to Benedict Turrettini, Basel, June 22, 1618, Geneva: Archives Turrettini Dd. 4.1. Cf. Benedict Turrettini *Défense de la fidélité des traductions de la S. Bible faties à Genève opposée au livre de Pierre Coton jésuite intitulé Genève plagiare* (Geneva: P. et J. Chouet, 1618), 53, 57 (St. Paul MN: Lutheran Brotherhood Foundation Reformation Library, text-fiche).

[135] Laplanche, *L'Écriture*, 315.

[136] Cappel's identity as the author of the *Arcanum* was never a well-kept secret among Protestants. Wilhelm Schickard identified him in print as its writer in 1624, the same year that the *Arcanum* was published. Van Rooden, *Theology*, 63 and n. 48.

buttal of Buxtorf's *Tiberias* and the theological position that it supported. Cappel refused to accept Buxtorf's historical and philological paradigm for discussing the age and significance of the vowel points. Instead he reexamined the evidence of Jewish history, the early Greek and Latin translations and the Church fathers, and the philological evidence, arguing that all of these supported Levita's position on the age of the vowel points. Cappel devoted the second part of his book to a point by point rebuttal of the objections which Buxtorf and others had raised against Levita's *Masoret*.[137] Many of the arguments which Cappel made were unoriginal; he was anticipated by Jacob Perez of Valencia, Zwingli, Petrus Martinius and Scaliger among others.[138] However, the way he formulated these arguments and answered Buxtorf were uniquely his own.

Cappel used both inferences from silence and from evidence in his response to Buxtorf's historical argument. He argued in chaps. 2-7 of the first part that Jewish tradition offers a "silent testimony" (*Testimonium tacitum*) to a later dating of the vowel points.[139] He stressed the convention of reading only unpointed scrolls in the synagogue, and the lack of any mention of the vowel points or accents in the Talmud.[140] To complete his rebuttal Cappel discussed each of the talmudic passages quoted by Buxtorf in detail.[141] Cappel felt that the silence of Jewish histories about the Tiberian masoretic schools reflected a lack of evidence for their existence, but that it was not proof that they never existed.[142]

---

[137] Ibid., 215-220. Schnederman's discussion of the *Arcanum* should be used with caution since the focus of his discussion is Cappel's polemics with Buxtorf II and he quoted much material from Cappel's later works.

[138] Cappel in fact emphasized that his position was nothing new for a Protestant; many of the sixteenth-century reformers agreed with him; *Arcanum*, 4. The list of Cappel's authorities that Schnederman quoted is drawn from the former's preface to *Vindicatiae Arcani punctationis*, a work that remained unpublished until after both Buxtorf II and Cappel had died. See prefatio to *Vindicatiae*, 13-23, printed in *Commentarii et notae criticae in Vetus Testamentum...Vindiciae hactenus ineditae*, ed. Jacques Cappel (Amsterdam: P. & J. Blaeu, 1689), quoted by Schnedermann, *Controverse*, 28-30.

[139] Schnederman, *Controverse*, 36-37.

[140] Ibid., 37-40

[141] Cappel, *Arcanum*, 245-261. Cappel devoted chaps. 15-17 of the second part to respond to Buxtorf's historical arguments against the Tiberian masoretic schools.

[142] Ibid., 248-249.

Cappel's historical argument was successful not because he was willing to use historical evidence to make inferences and Buxtorf was not, but because the inferences he made were better ones. Buxtorf's argument for the existence of the vowel points before the composition of the Talmud, for example, was a chain of inferences. Since the Talmud attested to the Masora by name, and described masoretic activities such as counting letters and using critical markings Buxtorf assumed that, by implication, the talmudic sages knew of the other parts of the Masora and used biblical texts which had accents and vowel points much like the Bomberg *Biblia rabbinica* Hebrew text.[143] If one accepted the testimony of some Jewish historians as to the dating of the *Zohar* and *Sefer ha-Bahir* then the vowel points were also attested before the composition of the Talmud.[144] The amazing success of the masoretes in fixing the form of the biblical text together with the apparently off-handed remarks in the Talmud about masoretic activities and elsewhere misled Buxtorf to believe that the Masora as he knew it was quite ancient. He was willing to infer from the silence of Jewish historians that the Tiberian masoretic schools could not have existed after the composition of the Talmud.[145] Buxtorf's willingness to use detailed philological argumentation belies Laplanche's claim that he was wedded to the use of authorities while Cappel used evidence.[146] Buxtorf's argument is unconvincing, however, because it did not analyze important evidence from outside of rabbinical Jewish tradition.

Cappel's weightiest objections to Buxtorf's *Tiberias* were philological rather than historical. He refused to rule out the evidence of the Septuagint and other Greek versions, the Targum and

---

[143] Buxtorf, *Tiberias*, 34-40, 46-47.

[144] Ibid., 75, 79-80. Since the Jewish historian Abraham Zacuto doubted that R. Simeon b. Yohai had written the entire *Zohar* Buxtorf was willing to leave the question of its dating open as early as 1607. Buxtorf to Scaliger, Basel, March 17, 1607, London: British Library Ms Add 5158: 25, printed in *Sylloges*, 2: 366-367. See also Buxtorf, *Abbreviaturis*, 167-168. Cappel noted the latter passage and used it to buttress his own arguments discounting the evidential value of the *Zohar* in *Arcanum*, 196.

[145] Buxtorf, *Tiberias*, 31-33.

[146] "Nous saisissons là le passage d'une conception de l'histoire à une autre: selon Buxtorf, le fait historique doit être transmis par une chaîne de témoins: selon Cappel, il suffit d'en déduire l'existence à partir de traces ou d'absence des traces." Laplanche, *L'Écriture*, 218.

the Church fathers as inadmissible or irrelevant.[147] That the early translations such as the Septuagint were made from unpointed Hebrew originals was undeniably true.[148] Cappel also discussed anomalies in vocalization and accent use, arguing that these were better explained by his theory.[149] By using the versions as witnesses to the original form of the Hebrew text together with the received Hebrew textual tradition Cappel was in effect depreciating the evidential value of the received Hebrew text in favor of the versions.[150]

Cappel thought that the age of the vowel points was a purely philological question, but he understood and addressed the theological questions which Polanus and Buxtorf raised.[151] Cappel asserted that the consonantal text of the Hebrew Bible was sufficient in itself to ensure accurate interpretation. The objections that Polanus and Buxtorf raised against this position focused on the potential uncertainty of individual words which, out of context, could mean a number of different things. Cappel believed that the individual words of Scripture should be interpreted within their immediate context and within the wider context of the Bible itself. The "principal of totality," as Laplanche called it, would solve nearly all interpretive problems, leaving only a few which the individual interpreter was free to solve as best he could.[152] Since Cappel was

---

[147] Ibid., 92. Buxtorf wrote to Cappel, after reading the *Arcanum*, concerning the Targum text, "Praeterea sunt etiam adhuc vestigia in textu Hebraeo, ante usum apicum vocalium, fuisse vocalibus insertas literas vocales, lectionis in linguis Orientalibus matres אוי, quae in editionibus Venetis in Targum relictae fecerunt ibi miras anomilias et formas ineptis, si mas propter imperito Grammaticos istarum literarum non pauca in textu Hebraeo adhuc relicta quando puncta fuerunt adscripta, unde & varietas lectionis quaedam nata." Johannes Buxtorf to Louis Cappel, Basel, January 1, 1623, Zürich ZB Ms. F 45: 247r.

[148] Cappel, *Arcanum*, 46-52. See Schnederman, *Controverse*, 42-45.

[149] Ibid., 73-91, 114-157.

[150] Goshen-Gottstein pointed out that the Polyglot Bible editions of this period were "an expression not only of Catholic philological-theological curiosity, but also a leveling down of the originals." "Foundations," 87.

[151] Cappel, *Arcanum*, 284-285 of the second part, where he introduced his theological discussion, Cappel quoted four of the eight theses from Polanus given by Buxtorf in *Thesaurus Grammaticus*, 61-64, and addressed two more in part 2, chaps. 14 (pp. 243-245) and 18 (pp. 262-266). He also quoted Buxtorf's principal argument from *Tiberias* regarding the need for an "independent judge" to ensure the meaning of the text is clearly understood. *Tiberias*, 92 and *Arcanum*, 285.

[152] Laplanche, *L'Écriture*, 218-219.

familiar with Arabic, another Semitic language which could be read without vowel points, he was predisposed to accept Levita's argument that the vowel points were not necessary to understand the Hebrew Bible.[153]

Cappel sent the *Arcanum* to Buxtorf in manuscript form with a letter on July 10, 1622.[154] He waited impatiently for its return, sending Buxtorf two letters admonishing him to send it back as quickly as he could.[155] Buxtorf's response was not to Cappel's liking. He restated his objections to using the early translations as evidence since they often differed from the Hebrew text not only with regard to vocalization but also lacked words which appeared in the "veritatem Hebraicam."[156] The Targum was hopelessly obscure as a guide to vocalizing the Hebrew text since the so-called "vowel letters," consonants which could be used to indicate vowels, were used in a completely haphazard way.[157] He asked Cappel not to publish the *Arcanum* for fear of its theological consequences to Protestantism.

> I honestly recognize that it is difficult to argue for the antiquity of the vowel points, yet you do not dispel my worries about the pernicious and dangerous consequences of affirming their recent origin. They compel me to believe that it is not judicious to discuss this problem with greater precision and depth in the schools, whether orally or in published works.[158]

---

[153] Ironically some of Cappel's points on reading Hebrew without vowels were drawn from Buxtorf's introduction to reading post-biblical Hebrew (unvocalized!) in his *Thesaurus Grammaticus* (Basel: Konrad Waldkirch, 1609), 612-647. See Laplanche, *L'Écriture*, 868, n. 31.

[154] Louis Cappel to Johannes Buxtorf, Sedan, July 10, 1622, Basel UB Ms G I 62: 107-109

[155] Louis Cappel to Johannes Buxtorf, Sedan, October 27, 1622, Basel UB Ms G I 62: 110, and idem to idem, Sedan, December 9, 1622, Basel UB Ms G I 62: 111. Cf also Johannes Buxtorf to Louis Cappel, Basel, January 1, 1623, Zürich ZB Ms F 45: 246r.

[156] "Patres Christiani textum Hebraeum vocarunt veritatem Hebraicam. At que sunt, erit meritas si lectio juxta vocales non sit vera, solida, authentica? Detractis vocalibus, an Graecos aut Latinos in Varietate Versionam imitabimur, ubi literas q(uae) p(ro)ponas exprimunt. Quid, ubi nec consonant, nec vocales referunt? Infinite occurrent lites, in quibus unus Judex nullus erit, si non sit una, solida et authentica textus Hebraeci lectio." Ibid., f. 246v.

[157] Ibid., f. 247r.

[158] "Hinc probe agnosco difficile esse argumentum de Antiquitate punctorum, interea etiam pessimas et periculosissimas consequentias ex novitate punctorum non satis ex animo meo revellis, quae etiam eò me pertrahunt ut putem non expedire publice hanc questionem subtilis et profundis in Scholis, vel voce vel

He promised to study the question further himself. Cappel wrote back to Buxtorf that he had discussed the theological questions with his brother Jacques (who disagreed with his position) and the latter did not consider them decisive.[159] Cappel sent the manuscript to Thomas Erpenius in Leiden to have it published and heard no more of it until he received a printed copy of it in the mail.[160]

The *Arcanum* received a mixed response from Protestants. French and Dutch Calvinists by and large accepted it both for scholarly and apologetic reasons.[161] Erpenius, in his introduction to the book, recommended it warmly. He himself had abandoned writing a book on the age of the vowel points because the *Arcanum* made it unnecessary.[162] Both André Rivet and Daniel Chamier, two important Huguenot theological thinkers, welcomed its appearance.[163] Within a year of its publication Chamier put the *Arcanum* to its intended use, as a weapon against the Catholics.[164] The bitter

---

etitis libris, tractare." Ibid., f. 247r, quoted by Laplanche, *L'Écriture*, 215, 867-868, n. 31.

[159] "Rationibus theologicis quibus scribis non plene a me tibi esse satisfactum, etsi primo frater vehementer movebat, tamen jam re diligentius excussa, non censet illud in iis inesse pondus atque robur, quod alii putant, existimatque illis in hac causa abstinendum potius esse, quam utendum aliisque esse pugnandum argumentis." Louis Cappel to Johannes Buxtorf, Sedan, March 1, 1623, Basel UB Ms G I 62:113, quoted by Laplanche, *L'Écriture*, 215 and 868 n. 32.

[160] Schnederman, *Controverse*, 8. Cappel may have become personally acquainted with Erpenius either in England or during his year in Leiden (1612-1613). J. W. Wesselius, Review of *Theology, Biblical Scholarship and Rabbinical Studies in the Seventeenth Century* by Peter T. Van Rooden, *Studia Rosenthaliana* 23 (1989): 215.

[161] Acceptance was not unanimous, however, among Reformed thinkers. Claude Sarrau said in a letter to Rivet written in 1642 that he was amazed to hear that there were still some at Leiden who defended the antiquity of the vowel points. Claude Sarrau to André Rivet, July 22, 1642, printed in *Correspondence intégrale d'André Rivet et de Claude Sarrau*, ed. Hans Bot and Pierre Leroy, 3 vols. (Amsterdam: APA-Holland University Press, 1978-1983), 2: 332-333, quoted by Van Rooden, *Theology*, 226 and n. 196.

[162] Thomas Erpenius to the Reader, Leiden, January 1, 1624 in *Arcanum*, ff. (a2)v- (a3)v. On Erpenius see J. Brugman, "Arabic Scholarship," in *Leiden University*, 202-215.

[163] Laplanche, *L'Écriture*, 220.

[164] Ibid. Jean Mestrezat, also used Cappel's arguments in his *Traicté de l'Escripture Sainte* (Geneva: J. Chouet, 1633). See Robinson, "Doctrine," 111-112, 235, n. 30.

controversy within Calvinist circles over the book would come only years after the death of the elder Buxtorf.[165]

Not all Protestants, however, thought that the *Arcanum* was a philological and theological breakthrough. Paul Tarnow of the Lutheran University of Rostock considered it theologically danger-ous and tried to convince fellow Lutheran Wilhelm Schickhard of the University of Tübingen, himself an eminent orientalist, to write a refutation as quickly as possible.[166] A number of scholars wrote to Buxtorf, demanding that he refute the book. Laurentius Fabricius, a professor of theology at the University of Wittenberg, said that the author of the *Arcanum* did the devil's work since his arguments cast doubt on the clarity of the Bible, and he insisted that Buxtorf respond to it.[167] Buxtorf did indeed gather materials to compose a response to Cappel, but, hampered by his numerous other writing and printing projects, he was never able to complete it.[168]

---

[165] Muller, "Vowel Points," 64-72, and Schnederman, *Controverse*, 14-21.

[166] "Rev. Dn. D. Tarnovius suis in literis ad Vos perferendis mentionem faciet Diatribes Punctationis Capelli, quam ut R[everendae] T[uae] V[enerabilitatis] examinet et refutet, instabit fortè. Aliquoties enim collocuti fuimus, unde percepi, se illam extirpatam potius quam repressam videre, detrimentum siquidem summum Reipubl. Christianae Eccl. allaturum esse censet ...." Daniel Lipstrop to Wilhelm Schickhard, Rostock, May 24, 1626, Stuttgart, WLB Ms Cod. histr. 2° 563. See also Paul Tarnow to Wilhelm Schickhard, Rostock, December 22, 1625, Stuttgart, WLB Ms Cod. histr. 2° 563. I consulted both of these letters in Dr. F. Seck's unpublished collection of Schickhard's correspondence, *Wilhelm Schickhard Briefwechsel*, 4 vols. (Tübingen: Typescript, 1975).

[167] "Rogo igitur Te vehementer, ut de Apologia tua cogites. Si enim ille Crypticus (i. e. Cappel) invalesceret, qua ratione tyro ad lectionem Hebraeam adduceretur, & vocata in dubium punctatione biblica, quae tandem certitudo in Textibus aequivocis manebat? Variae sunt artes Diaboli, ut Scripturam divinam è medio tollat, vel ejus sensum ita attenuet, ne animus fidus habeat, ubi immotè consistat." Laurentius Fabricius to Johannes Buxtorf, Wittenberg, August 24, 1625, Basel UB Ms G I 61: 210, printed in Buxtorf, *Catalecta*, 434-435.

[168] "Unde factum, ut multorum judicia denuo suspenderentur, & quid de hoc Arcano Revelato sentiendum sit, à Patre meo frequentissimis literis efflagitarent, avidissimeque expectarent. Cum vero tum temporis majoribus operibus occupatus esset, quorum absolvendorum magno desiderio tenebatur, ne tot praecedentium annorum exacti labores cum ipso fortassis intermorerentur, difficulter admodum se ab iis avelli passus est; hujusque materiae tractationem subinde de die in diem distulit. Et sic factum, ut antequam id aggrederetur, ex Dei Opt. Max. voluntate, his & aliis laboribus, praematura morte subductus fuerit Anno 1629." Buxtorf, *Tractatus*, f.)( )(r.

After Buxtorf died in 1629 his son became the target of these importunate correspondents.[169] At first he resisted the idea since he was committed to finishing his father's *Lexicon Chaldaicum, Talmudicum et Rabbinicum*. Buxtorf II was finally convinced of the need to refute Cappel's book in 1645 by the urgings of Andre Rivet and other Leiden theologians who had read Cappel's magnum opus *Critica Sacra* in manuscript and feared its theological impact if left unanswered.[170] Buxtorf's *Tractatus* was, in fact, only one of ten books written by Reformed theologians in the Netherlands, France and Switzerland against the theology of Saumur in a theological campaign orchestrated from Leiden by Andre Rivet.[171]

The differing approaches taken by Buxtorf and Cappel to resolving the age of the vowel points are indicative of changes occurring within the international community of biblical scholars during the early seventeenth century. Buxtorf represented an older tradition which combined biblical studies with the study of post-biblical Jewish works on the Bible, especially the medieval Bible commentaries. Cappel focused his attention more narrowly on the particulars of the biblical text itself, employing comparative philology and the versions to elucidate the Hebrew Bible verse by verse. The publication of two massive polyglot Bible editions between 1630 and 1660, the Paris Polyglot and the London Polyglot, attest to the popularity and influence of the new textual study of the Bible. Textual criticism became the chief concern of Old Testament scholars through the end of the eighteenth century.[172] Buxtorf's scholarly study of the Hebrew text, by contrast, could be supported easily by his edition of the *Biblia rabbinica*. He had no use for the

---

[169] "Post ipsius mortem crebrae ad me doctorum Virorum literae advolabant, quibus à me subinde, quaenam Parentis mei b. m. super isto Arcano fuerit sententia, quaeque silentii ejus causae, anxiè admodum sciscitabantur ... Mox, cum & ejus rei causas, & quod ego quoque in Parentis mei sententia persisterem, intelligerent, à me flagitabant, ut ego desertam hanc provinciam occuparem, atque tum ipsius Causae, in qua plurimum situm esse omnes judicabant: tum Patris mei, Vindicem agerem." Ibid., f.)( )(v.

[170] Frans Pieter van Stam, *The Controversy over the Theology of Saumur, 1635-1650. Disrupting Debates among the Huguenots in Complicated Circumstances*, Studies of the Institute Pierre Bayle, Nijmegen, no. 19 (Amsterdam: APA-Holland University Press, 1988), 260-261.

[171] Ibid., 363-364, 439-442. Laplanche gives the most complete description of Cappel's polemical battles in *L'Écriture*, 299-327, *passim*.

[172] Moshe Goshen-Gottstein, "The Textual Criticism of the Old Testament: Rise, Decline, Rebirth," *Journal of Biblical Literature* 102 (1983): 376.

versions as witnesses to the history of the Hebrew Bible text. Buxtorf's position on the Hebrew vowel points continued to be taught by many Lutheran and Reformed systematic theologians and even appeared as an article of faith in the Swiss *Formula Consensus* of 1678.[173] His views were rejected, however, by many scholars, Catholic and Protestant alike, as philologically incorrect. Their commitment to investigate the Hebrew Bible text critically, allowing for the possibility that it contained the kinds of transmission errors present in other ancient books, was one of the first steps toward the modern historical-critical study of the Bible.

---

[173] "In specie autem Hebraicus Vet. T. codex, quem ex traditione Ecclesiae Judaicae, cui olim (Rom. 3: 2) oracula Dei commissa sunt, accepimus hodieque retinemus, tum quoad consonans, tum quoad vocalia, sive puncta ipsa, sive punctorum saltem potestatem, et tum quoad res, tum quoad verba *theopneustos*, ut fidei et vitae nostrae ...." Canon 2 of the *Formula Consensus*, in *Die Bekenntnisschriften der reformierten Kirche*, ed. E. F. Karl Müller (Leipzig: A. Deichert (Georg Böhme), 1903), 862. On the circumstances surrounding the adoption of the Formula Consensus, see Martin I. Klauber, *Between Reformed Scholasticism and Pan-Protestantism: Jean-Alphonse Turretin (1671-1737) and Enlightened Orthodoxy at the Academy of Geneva* (Selinsgrove: Susquehanna University Press, 1994), 25-35.

CONCLUSION

Christian Hebraism in early modern Europe was a step-child of theology. Born of humanist ideals on the eve of the Reformation, it was nurtured and institutionally supported by both Protestants and Catholics throughout the Confessional age. Johannes Buxtorf wrote his books to enhance the role of Hebrew studies within Protestant schools and universities, but most of them continued to be used long after the great age of Christian Hebraism. The paradox of Buxtorf's enduring influence sheds light upon the place of Hebrew studies within the traditional academic world of the seventeenth and early eighteenth centuries, and also speaks to Buxtorf's place within the history of both biblical studies and Jewish studies.

Buxtorf's books fit well into the little world of seventeenth-century academia for three reasons. First and foremost, Buxtorf was theologically in tune not only with his Reformed contemporaries but also with Lutherans, as the numerous letters he received from Lutheran academics suggest. Buxtorf made a great deal of Jewish philological study readily accessible to Christian readers through his grammars, lexicons and other aids to the study of Hebrew. These works also simplified the task of learning post-biblical Hebrew, enabling Protestant theologians to utilize post-biblical Jewish literature, particularly medieval Jewish Bible commentaries and the Talmud, in their biblical research. By producing a new edition of the *Biblia rabbinica*, Buxtorf provided budding theologians not only with the a Hebrew Bible text but with an "improved" version of the Targums and masoras as well as a large selection of Jewish medieval Bible commentaries.

Buxtorf's works show that he was well aware of the theological implications of his philological research and writing. His book *Juden Schul* enjoyed the unique distinction of being considered both ethnographically true-to-life and theologically adept since it employed Polanus' argument that Scripture was the effective cause of true religion. By arguing for the integrity of the consonantal biblical text and the canonicity of the vowel points Buxtorf provided important philological underpinnings for the emerging high orthodox doctrine of Scripture. He sought to make the masoras a

Protestant weapon to use against Catholic polemicists when he published *Tiberias* in 1620. Buxtorf 's new edition of Isaac Nathan's Hebrew Bible concordance was intended not only to aid biblical scholars in their studies, but also to improve upon the Masora, a goal which had clear apologetic overtones. Buxtorf's works contained nothing that was inconsistent theologically with Reformed orthodoxy in Basel or elsewhere; he brought Hebrew philology fully and truly into the service of theology, the queen of sciences.

Apart from his theological commitments Buxtorf was also a pedagogue who followed the example of Latin and Greek teachers on liberal arts faculties. He encouraged students to learn not only biblical Hebrew, but also medieval Hebrew and Aramaic so that they could put the treasures of Jewish literature to use in much the same way that Greek and Latin teachers pressed classical literature into the service of Christian education. Buxtorf's array of grammars, dictionaries, and manuals enabled teachers and students to gain access to the world of Jewish literature without recourse to Jewish tutors. Johannes Buxtorf II acted completely in accord with his father's philosophy of Hebrew education when he translated Maimonides' *Guide to the Perplexed* into Latin.[1] In a world where the battle of the ancients and the moderns had not yet begun in earnest, Buxtorf's plan to recover a usable Hebrew heritage for humanist education seemed perfectly reasonable.

Finally, also in keeping with both humanist tradition and academic necessity, Buxtorf's manuals on Hebrew prose and poetry made it possible for Hebraists to participate in the public displays of learning which were so characteristic of early modern academic life. By providing instruction to Hebrew letter-writing and poetry Buxtorf enabled later scholars to compose occasional verse in Hebrew, and presumably Hebrew orations, to ornament solemn occasions in the way that his colleagues who taught Latin and Greek were frequently obliged to do. Buxtorf's guides to Hebrew literature and composition enabled his successors to contribute both substance to existing school curricula and style to academic festivals.

Buxtorf's works outlasted the demise of the traditional university with its curriculum based upon Aristotelian philosophy, logic,

---

[1] Pace Manuel's charactization of both Buxtorfs in *The Broken Staff*, 88.

and rhetoric. In a curious way Buxtorf contributed to the development of both academic biblical studies and Jewish studies in their modern forms. Buxtorf's grammars and lexicons of biblical Hebrew remained standard works until well into the nineteenth century, when they were finally superseded by the works of Gesenius and others who promoted the use of cognate Semitic languages for clarifying problems in Hebrew grammar and lexicography. Buxtorf's *Biblia rabbinica* continued to be used by both Jewish and Christian scholars throughout the nineteenth century, in part because the Targum was available in critical editions for only a few books of the Bible. Even *Tiberias* continued to be used as a masoretic manual by biblical scholars as late as the nineteenth century. Most of what Buxtorf wrote was designed to aid in the close study of the Hebrew Bible text, a pursuit which remained important to Protestant theologians long after the use of Jewish Bible commentaries and post-biblical Jewish literature to illuminate the Old and New Testaments had become less fashionable.

Buxtorf's role as a Christian predecessor to nineteenth-century *Jüdische Wissenschaft* is demonstrable but more problematic: the works of Buxtorf and other Christian Hebraists constituted the academic foundation upon which non-Jewish interpretations of Judaism, its history and its literature rested. Jewish scholars sought to revise and replace these works through the use of modern philological and historical tools as well as superior knowledge of the sources, thus reclaiming Jewish studies for Jews. In this revisionist climate Buxtorf's works fared comparatively well. His work on the Masora was not superseded until the mid-nineteenth century, when Bernhard Baer and Christian David Ginsberg took up where he had left off. Buxtorf's *Bibliotheca rabbinica* was a direct ancestor to Moritz Steinschneider's Bodleian catalogue by way of Johann Christoph Wolf's *Bibliotheca Hebraea* (1715-1733), although Steinschneider periodically used Buxtorf's descriptions directly. Buxtorf's talmudic lexicon was reprinted during the nineteenth century but eventually was superseded by Alexander Kohut's new edition of Nathan ben Yehiel's *Aruch Completum* (1878-92). While Buxtorf came in for his share of criticism from these ambitious scholars, they did not entirely repudiate his work either. To some degree they too were building upon his foundation.

Buxtorf's most widely read work, *Juden Schul*, was also the book least likely to attract a Jewish readership. Nonetheless, *Juden Schul* constitutes an important milestone in the study of Judaism since it was the standard work on Judaism for a century after Buxtorf's death, shaping subsequent Christian ethnographies of the Jews and later anti-Jewish polemics, including Johann Andreas Eisenmenger's *Entdecktes Judenthum* (1700). Jewish apologists such as Leon Modena did not have the luxury of presenting Judaism solely as they wished to portray it but were obliged to try and discredit Buxtorf's characterizations as well. Buxtorf's underlying theology of Judaism was common to Lutherans, Reformed, and Catholics alike during this period, but his efforts to present Judaism as Jews themselves understood it in *Juden Schul* places the book in a class by itself. He did not set out to create a caricature of Jewish life, but rather sought to portray Jewish halakic observance as it was described in Yiddish-language books of popular devotion. To undermine the credibility of the halakah Buxtorf used explicit comparisons of rabbinic injunction with biblical commands, and ironic or sarcastic comments, rather than conscious misrepresentation. Buxtorf's portrayal of Jewish life was frequently distorted both by omissions in what he discussed and by his own theological biases. Nevertheless, *Juden Schul* represented an important new departure in the Christian study of Judaism, one which was based upon an independent reading of Jewish sources.

Buxtorf and his successors sought to gain independent access to post-biblical Jewish literature, absorbing insights, translating individual passages and sometimes entire books to make them accessible to the Christian world. Jews played only a subordinate, supporting role in this process, serving as tutors, book sellers, and informants on their own tradition.[2] Johannes Buxtorf forged the philological key, derived from "the Jews' own books," which enabled several generations of successors to translate many important Jewish classics and to make much broader use of Jewish literature for Christian ends. John Lightfoot spoke for himself and for other Christian Hebraists of his generation when he wrote that the whole Christian world was "indebted to the great name of

---

[2] Hsia, "Ethnographies of Jews," 232.

Buxtorf."[3] This corpus of new literature, written by and for
Christians, helped to define in academic terms who the Jews were
and what Judaism was until university-trained Jewish scholars took
possession of their own tradition within the academy.

---

[3] John Lightfoot to Johannes Buxtorf II, Hereford, February 1, 1663, Basel
UB Ms G I 62: 11, printed in Lightfoot, *Works*, 1: 100 (English translation) and
13: 426 (Latin original).

SHORT TITLE LIST OF BUXTORF IMPRINTS

While searching for Buxtorf's correspondence, manuscripts and imprints I wrote to and received responses from over 400 libraries and archives in Europe; the first two appendices reflect the responses of these institutions. For this short title list I have also consulted the printed catalogues of the British Library, the Bibliothèque Nationale in Paris, the Klau Library of Hebrew Union College-Cincinnati, and the *National Union Catalogue*. With few exceptions I have included only those books I have examined, that Prijs or Fuks/Fuks-Mansfeld described, or for which I have photocopies of the title pages.

1. *De Abbreviaturis Hebraicis liber novus & copiosus.* Basel: Konrad Waldkirch, 1613. Prijs no. 212.

2. *De Abbreviaturis Hebraicis liber novus & copiosus.* Ed. Johannes Buxtorf II. Basel: Konrad Waldkirch, 1640. Prijs no. 239.

3. *De Abbreviaturis Hebraicis liber novus & copiosus.* Franeker: J. Horreus, 1696. FFM no. 132.

4. *De Abbreviaturis Hebraicis liber novus & copiosus.* Herborn: Andraeae, 1708.

5. *De Abbreviaturis Hebraicis liber novus & copiosus.* Herborn: Andraeae, 1708; reprint ed., Hildesheim: Georg Olms, 1985.

6. *ANASKEUE: Opinionibus a Petro de Aliaco, Cardinale Cameracensi, de Coena Dominica olim repetite: de qua in publica Disputatione 20. Iunij, Preside Iohanne Iacobo Grynaeo, respondebit Iohan. Bvxdorfivs,Westphalvs.* Basel: Oporinus, 1588. Basel UB Ki Ar H III 34, no. 20.

7. *Biblia Rabbinica.* Ed. Johannes Buxtorf. 4 Vols. Basel: Ludwig König, 1618-1619. Prijs no. 219.

8. *Concordantiae Bibliorum Hebraice et Chaldaice.* Basel: L. König, 1629. Copies of this imprint are preserved at HUC and at Darmstadt: Hessische Landesbibliothek V 1145.

9. *Concordantiae Bibliorum Hebraice et Chaldaice.* Basel: L. König, 1632. Prijs no. 235.

10. *Concordantiae Bibliorum Hebraice et Chaldaice Epitome.* Ed. Christian Ravius. Berlin & Frankfurt: Rupertus Völckerus, 1677. 8°. Luzern ZB KB. F.5.42.

11. *Concordantiae Bibliorum Hebraice et Chaldaice.* Ed. Bernhard Baer. Stettin: E. Schrentzelius, 1861. Hebrew Union College DL/B98/1861.

12. *Concordantiae Bibliorum Hebraice et Chaldaice.* Ed. Bernhard Baer. Berlin & Stettin: E. Schrentzelius, 1862. Princeton Theological Seminary.

13. *Concordantiae Bibliorum Hebraice et Chaldaice.* Ed. Bernhard Baer. Berlin & Stettin: E. Schrentzelius, 1867. Hebrew Union College DL/B98/1867.

14. *Epitome Grammaticae Hebraeae.* Basel: Konrad Waldkirch, 1613. Prijs no. 210.

15. *Epitome Grammaticae Hebraeae.* Basel: Ludwig König, 1617. Prijs no. 218.

16. *Epitome Grammaticae Hebraeae.* Basel: Ludwig König, 1620. Prijs no. 223.

17. *Epitome Grammaticae Hebraeae.* Basel(?): n. p., 1624. HAB 78.1 Gram. 2.

18. *Epitome Grammaticae Hebraeae.* Basel: Ludwig König, 1629. Prijs no. 228.

19. *Epitome Grammaticae Hebraeae.* Amsterdam: Janssonius, 1632. Münster: Priesterseminar Bibliothek, B N8 132.

20. *Epitome Grammaticae Hebraeae.* Goslar: Hallervordius, 1632. HAB 59.6 Gram (1).

21. *Epitome Grammaticae Hebraeae.* Basel: Ludwig König, 1640. Prijs no. 238.

22. *Epitome Grammaticae Hebraeae.* Amsterdam: Janssonius, 1645. Leiden UB.

23. *Epitome Grammaticae Hebraeae.* Cambridge: Roger Daniel, 1646.

24. *Epitome Grammaticae Hebraeae.* n. p.: n. p., 1647. Basel UB FA VIII 21.

25. *Epitome Grammaticae Hebraeae.* Amsterdam: Janssonius, 1652. FFM no. 298.

26. *Epitome Grammaticae Hebraeae.* London: Roger Daniel, 1653. Leiden UB 873 G 6.

27. *A Short Introduction to the Hebrew Tongue.* Trans. John Davis. London: R. Daniel, 1656.

28. *Epitome Grammaticae Hebraeae.* Basel: Georg Decker, 1658. Prijs no. 262.

29. *Epitome Grammaticae Hebraeae.* Ed. Johannes Terentus. Franeker: Johannes Wellens, 1665. FFM no. 127.

30. *Epitome Grammaticae Hebraeae.* London: John Redmayne, 1666.

31. *Epitome Grammaticae Hebraeae.* Basel: Johann Jacob Decker, 1669. Prijs no. 274.

32. *Epitome Grammaticae Hebraeae.* London: John Redmayne, 1669.

33. *Epitome Grammaticae Hebraeae.* Utrecht: Meinardum à Dreunen, 1672. Amsterdam UB OK 80-609.

34. *Epitome Grammaticae Hebraeae.* Utrecht: Meinardum à Dreunen, 1673. Amsterdam UB 1021 H54a.

35. *Epitome Grammaticae Hebraeae.* Utrecht: Balthasarum Lobé, 1691. Amsterdam UB 393 G61.

36. *Epitome Grammaticae Hebraeae.* Leiden: Jordanum Luchtmans, 1691. Munich: Bavarian State Library L. As. 103h.

37. *Epitome Grammaticae Hebraeae.* Leiden: Jordanum Luchtmans, 1701. Leiden UB 873 G7.

38. *Epitome Grammaticae Hebraeae.* Ed. Johannes Leusden. Bern: Daniel Tschiffelius, 1705. Munich UB.

39. *Epitome Grammaticae Hebraeae.* Basel: Johann Georg König, 1710. Prijs no. 286.

40. *Epitome Grammaticae Hebraeae.* Leiden: Samuel Luchtmans, 1716. Leiden UB.

41. *A Short Introduction to the Hebrew Tongue.* Trans. David Francis Lates. Oxford: J. Fletcher, 1760. The only extant copy of this book is held by the County Library of Glamorgan, Cardiff, Wales (B 728.05).

42. *Epitome Grammaticae Hebraeae.* Leiden: S. & J. Luchtmans, 1761. Durham Univ. Library R. XX. I. 3.

43. *Epitome Grammaticae Hebraeae.* Leiden: S. & J. Luchtmans, 1790. Cambridge: Trinity College Library.

44. ספר השרשים קצור. *Epitome Radicum Hebraicum.* Basel: Konrad Waldkirch, 1600. Prijs no. 171.

45. *Epitome Radicum Hebraicum et Chaldaicum.* Basel: Konrad Waldkirch, 1607. Prijs no. 193.

46. *Grammaticae Chaldaicae et Syriacae Libri III.* Basel: Konrad Waldkirch, 1615. Prijs no. 215.

248 APPENDIX ONE

47. *Grammaticae Chaldaicae et Syriacae Libri III*. Basel: Haered. Ludovici Regis, 1650. Prijs no. 254.

48. *Grammaticae Chaldaicae et Syriacae Libri III*. Basel: Ludovici & Emanuelis König, 1685. Prijs no. 279.

49. אגרות שלומים. *Sylvula Epistolarum Hebraicarum*. Ed. and Trans. Johannes Buxtorf. Basel: Konrad Waldkirch, 1603. Prijs no. 185B.

50. *Institutio Epistolaris Hebraica*. Basel: Konrad Waldkirch, 1610. Prijs no. 204.

51. *Institutio Epistolaris Hebraica*. Ed. Johannes Buxtorf II. Basel: Ludwig König, 1629. Prijs no. 230.

52. *Juden Schul*. Basel: Sebastian Henricpetri, 1603. Basel UB

53. *Synagoga Iudaica*. Trans. Hermann Germberg. Hanau: Guilielmum Antonium, 1604. 12°. Fribourg: Bibliothèque Cantonale et Universitaire, Rés. 22.

54. *Synagoga Iudaica*. Trans. Hermann Germberg. Hanau: Haeredum Guilielmi Antonii, 1614. 12°. Leiden UB 871 G16.

55. *Synagoga Iudaica*. Trans. Hermann Germberg. Hanau: Petri Antonii, 1622. 12°. Dortmund StB Ht 830.

56. *Excerptum e libro cui titulus est Synagoga iudaica ... Hanoviae edito anno 1614....* (Paris? 1617?). Excerpt from chap. 20. Only two extant copies are held by the Bibliotheque Nationale, Paris and the British Library, London.

57. *Synagoga Judaica*. Trans. David Le Clerc. Basel: Ludwig König, 1641. Prijs no. 231+.

58. *Juden Schul*. Basel: Ludwig Königs Erben, 1643.

59. *Schoole der Jooden*. Trans. from German by Jan Zoet. Amsterdam: Tymon Hovthaak, 1650. Bibliotheca Rosenthaliana (Amsterdam UB) 1868 G1.

60. *The Jewish Synagogue*. Trans. A. B. Mr A. of Q. Co. in Oxford. London: T. Roycroft, 1656. Only extant copy held by the National Library of Scotland, Edinburgh.

61. *The Jewish Synagogue*. Trans. A. B. Mr A. of Q. Co. in Oxford. London: T. Roycroft, 1657.

62. *Synagoga Judaica*. Ed. Johannes Buxtorf II. Basel: Johann Jacob Decker, 1661. Prijs no. 266*.

63. *Synagoga Judaica*. Ed. Johannes Buxtorf II. Basel: Emanuelis König, 1680. Prijs no. 277*.

64. *Schoole der Jooden.* Amsterdam: Willem de Coup, 1694. Bibliotheca Rosenthaliana (Amsterdam UB) 1889 H 52.

65. *Schoole der Jooden.* Leiden: Daniel Vanden Dalen en Hendrik van Damme, 1702. Leiden UB 181 G11.

66. *Synagoga Judaica.* Basel: Johann Georg König, 1712. Prijs no. 287*.

67. *Synagoga Judaica. Noviter Restaurata. Das ist Erneuerte Juedische Synagog.* Frankfurt and Leipzig: Johann Paul Kraussen, 1728.

68. *Synagoga Judaica. Noviter Restaurata. Das ist Erneuerte Juedische Synagog.* Frankfurt and Leipzig: Johann Paul Kraussen, 1729.

69. *Schoole der Jooden.* Rotterdam: Jan Daniel Berman, 1731.

70. *Synagoga Judaica. Noviter Restaurata. Das ist Erneuerte Juedische Synagog.* Frankfurt and Leipzig: Johann Paul Kraussen, 1737.

71. *Synagoga Judaica. Noviter Restaurata. Das ist Erneuerte Juedische Synagog.* Frankfurt and Leipzig: Johann Paul Kraussen, 1738.

72. *Synagoga Judaica.* Reprinted in Blasio Ugolino. *Thesaurus antiquitatum sacrum.* 34 Vols. Venice: H. G. Hertz, S. Coletti, 1744-1769. Vol. 4, pp. 729-1172.

73. *A Translation by Way of Abridgement of Buxtorff's Latin Account of the Religious Customs and Ceremonies of the Jews.* Printed in John P. Stehelin, *Rabbinical Literature.* 2 Vols. London: J. Robinson, 1748. Vol. 2, pp. 225-363.

74. *A 'zsikók nemzet történeti és ritka szokásai = The Jewish Nation, its Laws and Unusual Customs* [Hungarian translation]. Pest: Joseph Bimel, 1834. The first part of the book (pp. 1-84) concerns biblical history, but the second part has the same chapter divisions as *Juden Schul.* National Library of Hungary, Budapest.

75. *Lexicon Chaldaicum Talmudicum et Rabbinicum.* Ed. Johannes Buxtorf II. Basel: Ludwig König, 1639 or 1640. (Title pages with both dates exist). Prijs no. 237.

76. *Lexicon Chaldaicum Talmudicum et Rabbinicum.* Ed. Bernard Fischer. Leipzig: Mauritius Schaefer, 1869-1875.

77. *Lexicon Chaldaicum Talmudicum et Rabbinicum.* Ed. Johannes Buxtorf II. Basel: Ludwig König, 1639; reprint ed., Hildesheim: Georg Olms, 1977.

78. *Lexicon Hebraicum et Chaldaicum.* Basel: Konrad Waldkirch, 1615. Prijs no. 214.

79. *Lexicon Hebraicum et Chaldaicum.* Basel: Ludwig König, 1621. Prijs no. 225.

80. *Lexicon Hebraicum et Chaldaicum*. Basel: Ludwig König, 1631. Prijs no. 234.

81. *Lexicon Hebraicum et Chaldaicum*. Basel: Haered. Ludov. Regis, 1645. Prijs no. 246.

82. *Lexicon Hebraicum et Chaldaicum*. London: Jacob Junius & Joseph Bell, 1646.

83. *Lexicon Hebraicum et Chaldaicum*. Amsterdam: J. Janzonius Jun., 1655. FFM no. 199.

84. *Lexicon Hebraicum et Chaldaicum*. Basel: Johann König, 1655. Prijs no. 260.

85. *Lexicon Hebraicum et Chaldaicum*. Basel: Johann König, 1663. Prijs no. 269.

86. *Lexicon Hebraicum et Chaldaicum*. Basel: Johann König & Fil., 1676. Prijs no. 276.

87. *Lexicon Hebraicum et Chaldaicum*. Basel: Johann König, 1689. Prijs no. 280.

88. *Lexicon Hebraicum et Chaldaicum*. Basel: Franciscus Platter & Johann Phillip Richter, 1698. Prijs no. 282.

89. *Lexicon Hebraicum et Chaldaicum*. Basel: Haered. Johann Phillip Richter, 1710. Prijs no. 287.

90. *Lexicon Hebraicum et Chaldaicum*. Basel: Episcopiana, 1735. Prijs no. 290.

91. *Lexicon Hebraicum et Chaldaicum*. Ed. Josephus Montaldi. 4 Vols. Rome: Jo. Zempel, 1789.

92. *Lexicon Hebraicum et Chaldaicum*. Glasgow: John Duncan, 1824.

93. *Lexicon Hebraicum et Chaldaicum*. London: Whittaker, Treacher, 1833.

94. *Lexicon Hebraicum et Chaldaicum*. Rome: Joh. Ferretti, 1845.

95. *Manuale Hebraicum et Chaldaicum*. Basel: Konrad Waldkirch, 1613. Prijs no. 211.

96. *Manuale Hebraicum et Chaldaicum*. Basel: Ludwig König, 1619. Prijs no. 220.

97. *Manuale Hebraicum et Chaldaicum*. Basel: Ludwig König, 1631. Prijs no. 233.

98. *Manuale Hebraicum et Chaldaicum*. Basel (Rostock?): Ludwig König, 1634. Prijs no. 320*.

99. *Manuale Hebraicum et Chaldaicum.* Basel: Georg Decker, 1658. Prijs no. 261.

100. *Manuale Hebraicum et Chaldaicum.* Oxford: Clarendon, 1807.

101. *A Transcription of Buxtorf's Primitives; with the Leading signification to every word in English.* Carmarthen: S. P. C. K., 1812. Aberystwyth, Dyfed: The National Library of Wales (PJ 4831 B99).

102. *Praeceptiones de Grammaticae Lingua Hebraea.* Basel: Konrad Waldkirch, 1605. Prijs no. 189.

103. *Thesaurus Grammaticus Linguae Sanctae Hebraeae.* Basel: Konrad Waldkirch, 1609. Prijs no. 199.

104. *Thesaurus Grammaticus Linguae Sanctae Hebraeae.* Basel: Konrad Waldkirch, 1615. Prijs no. 216.

105. *Thesaurus Grammaticus Linguae Sanctae Hebraeae.* Basel: Ludwig König, 1620. Prijs no. 224.

106. *Thesaurus Grammaticus Linguae Sanctae Hebraeae.* Basel: Konrad Waldkirch, 1629. Prijs no. 229.

107. *Thesaurus Grammaticus Linguae Sanctae Hebraeae.* Basel: Haered. Ludovici Regis, 1651. Prijs no. 255.

108. *Thesaurus Grammaticus Linguae Sanctae Hebraeae.* Ed. Johannes Buxtorf II. Basel: Haered. Ludovici Regis, 1663. Prijs no. 270.

109. *Tractatus Brevis de Prosodia Metrica Hebraeorum.* Reprinted in Blasio Ugolino, *Thesaurus antiquitatum sacrum.* 34 Vols. Venice: H. G. Hertz, S. Coletti, 1744-1769. Vol. 31, pp. 953-974.

110. *Thesaurus Grammaticus Linguae Sanctae Hebraeae.* Basel: Haered. Ludovici Regis, 1651; reprint ed., Hildesheim: Georg Olms, 1981.

111. *Tiberias Sive Commentarius Masorethicus.* fol. Basel: Ludwig König, 1620. Prijs no. 222A.

112. *Tiberias Sive Commentarius Masorethicus.* 4°. Basel: Ludwig König, 1620. Prijs no. 222B.

113. *Masora. A Collection out of Commentarius Masorethicus.* Ed. Clement Barksdale. London: Matthias Thurston, 1665. The only extant copy of this book is preseved in Boston Public Library (**H.50a.28).

114. *Tiberias Sive Commentarius Masorethicus.* Ed. Johannes Buxtorf II. fol. Basel: Johann Jacob Decker, 1665. Prijs no. 272A.

115. *Tiberias Sive Commentarius Masorethicus.* 4°. Ed. Johannes Buxtorf II. Basel: Johann Jacob Decker, 1665. Prijs no. 272B.

APPENDIX TWO

CORRESPONDENCE OF JOHANNES BUXTORF

1593

Buxtorf to Pascallus Gallus and Jacob Zwinger. Basel. January 18, 1593. Basel UB Ms Fr Gr I 8: 83.

Buxtorf to Jacob Zwinger. Basel. August 4, 1593. Basel UB Ms Fr Gr II 9: 89. Roth & Schmidt, *Handschriftproben*, no. 30.

Buxtorf to Kaspar Waser. Basel. December 23, 1593. Zürich ZB Ms-S 149: 124, 1.

Buxtorf to Kaspar Waser. Basel. December 23, 1593 (Heb.). Zürich ZB Ms-S 149: 124, 6.

1594

Buxtorf to Kaspar Waser. Basel. April 29, 1594 (Heb.). Zürich ZB Ms-S 149: 124, 5.

Buxtorf to Kaspar Waser. Basel. April 29, 1594. (Heb.) Zürich ZB Ms S-149: 125, 4.

1595

Buxtorf to Kaspar Waser. Basel. January 28, 1595. Zürich ZB Ms S-150: 96.

Buxtorf to Kaspar Waser. Basel. October, [1595]. Zürich ZB Ms S-149: 124, 2.

1596

Buxtorf to Kaspar Waser. Basel. 1596. (Heb.) Zürich ZB Ms S-149: 125, 5.

Buxtorf to Kaspar Waser. Basel. January 28, [1596].[1] (Heb.) Zürich ZB Ms S-149: 125, 2.

Johann Drusius to Buxtorf. n. p. August 4, 1596. Basel UB Ms G I 59: 256.

Buxtorf to Kaspar Waser. Basel. December 15, 1596. Zürich ZB Ms S-151: 64.

---

[1] In this letter Buxtorf acknowledged the receipt of a book which he asked to borrow in his letter of October, 1595 (Ms S-149: 124, 2). In Zürich ZB Ms S 149: 125, 5 (dated 1596) Buxtorf mentioned that Waser had loaned him the book during the "previous year."

Buxtorf to Kaspar Waser. Basel. December 28, 1596. (Heb.) Zürich ZB Ms S-149: 125, 6.

1597

Buxtorf to Johann Drusius. Basel. August 29, 1597 (Heb.). Leeuwarden PB Ms 731: 71-75; Fuks, "Brievenboek," 13-14.

Graf Adolph von Bentheim to Buxtorf. Padua. December 22, 1597. Basel UB Ms G I 60: 2.

1599

Buxtorf to Kaspar Waser. Basel. May 1, 1599. Zürich ZB Ms S 150: 32.

Buxtorf to Kaspar Waser. Basel. September 1, 1599. Zürich ZB Ms S-154: 56.

Buxtorf to Kaspar Waser. Basel. October 16, 1599. Zürich ZB Ms S-154: 76.

Rabbi NN to Buxtorf. Nuremberg. November 18/19, 1599 (Heb.). Buxtorf, *Institutio*, 277-280 and Prijs, *Drücke*, 528.

1600

Buxtorf to Kaspar Waser. Basel. March 18, 1600. Zürich ZB Ms S-154: 113.

Buxtorf to Kaspar Waser. Basel. April 21, 1600. Zürich ZB Ms S-155: 8b.

Buxtorf to Kaspar Waser. Basel. May 30, 1600. Zürich ZB Ms S-155: 14,3.

Buxtorf to Kaspar Waser. Basel. June 13, 1600. Zürich ZB Ms S-155: 14,1.

Buxtorf to Kaspar Waser. Basel. July 11, 1600. Zürich ZB Ms S-155: 38.

Buxtorf to Kaspar Waser. Basel. August 6, 1600. Zürich ZB Ms S-155: 39.

Buxtorf to Kaspar Waser. Basel. September 7, 1600. Zürich ZB Ms S-155: 40.

Buxtorf to Kaspar Waser. Basel. November 23, 1600. Zürich ZB Ms S-155: 61.

1602

Bartholomaeus Keckermann to Buxtorf. Heidelberg. February 13, 1602. Basel UB Ms G I 60: 17.

1603

Buxtorf to Johann Drusius. August 1, 1603. Buxtorf, *Sylvula Epistolarum*, f. Ir.

Johann Molther to Buxtorf. Friedberg. October 1603. Basel UB Ms G I 60: 214-215.

1604

Johann Molther to Buxtorf. n. p. 1604. Basel UB Ms G I 60: 216.

Johann Drusius Jr to Buxtorf. n. p. February 12, 1604 (Heb.). Leeuwarden PB Ms 731: 83-84; Fuks, "Brievenboek," 16.

Hermann Germberg to J.J. Grynaeus, A. Polanus, J. Buxtorf and B. Heel. Heidelberg. May 24, 1604. Basel UB Ms G II 5: 236; Hamburg SB Ms Sup ep 54, 62 (copy).

Hermann Germberg to JJ Grynaeus, A. Polanus, J. Buxtorf and B. Heel. Heidelberg. August 1, 1604. Buxtorf, *Synagoga Iudaica* ,)(2r-)(5v.

1605

Johann Drusius to Buxtorf. n. p. February 21, 1605. Basel UB G I 59: 257; Buxtorf, *Institutio*, f.):(5r (partial copy).

Buxtorf to the Councillors and Senators of Hamm in Westphalia. Basel. May 4, 1605. Buxtorf, *Praeceptiones*, ff. (:)2r-(:)3v.

Johann Piscator to Buxtorf. Herborn. September 9, 1605. Basel UB Ms G I 60: 315.

1606

Jacob Amport to Buxtorf. Leiden. February 20, 1606. Basel UB Ms G I 63: 2.

Buxtorf to Joseph Scaliger. Basel. April 3, 1606. Utrecht UB Ms 987: 237-238; Burmann, *Syllologes*, 2: 362-364.

Joseph Scaliger to Buxtorf. Leiden. June 1, 1606. Basel UB Ms G I 59: 363; Scaliger, *Epistolae*, 521-524 (partial copy), and Buxtorf, *Institutio*, ff.):(5r-):(6r (partial copy).

Jacob Amport to Buxtorf. Leiden. June 8, 1606. Basel UB Ms G I 63: 3.

Buxtorf to Joseph Scaliger. Basel. September 4, 1606. Leiden UB BPL 246; Burmann, *Syllologes*, 2: 364-5.

Buxtorf to Matthias Martinius. Basel. September 4, 1606. Buxtorf, "Epistola," 598-603.

Joseph Scaliger to Buxtorf. n. p. October 13, 1606. Basel UB G I 59: 242. Printed in: Scaliger, *Epistolae*, 524-5; Buxtorf, *Institutio*, ff.):(6r-):(7r (partial copy).

Kaspar Waser to Buxtorf. Zürich. November 9, 1606. Zürich ZB Ms S-159: 68.

Jacob Amport to Buxtorf. Franeker. November 18, 1606. Basel UB G I 63: 4.

Johann Drusius to Buxtorf. n. p. November 20, 1606. Basel UB Ms G I 59: 258.

1607

Jacob Amport to Buxtorf. Franeker. March 9, 1607. Basel UB Ms G I 63: 5.

Buxtorf to Joseph Scaliger, Basel, March 17, 1607. London: British Library, Ms Add. 5158: 25; Burmann, *Syllolges,* 2: 366-367.

Johann Drusius Jr. to Buxtorf. n. p. March 17, 1607. (Heb.) Leeuwarden PB Ms 731: 125-128; Fuks, "Brievenboek," 35-36.

Jacob Amport to Buxtorf. Franeker. June 1, 1607. Basel UB Ms G I 63: 6.

Johann Friedrich Roede to Buxtorf. Berlin. July 7, 1607. Basel UB Ms G I 60: 333.

Johann Molther to Buxtorf. Marburg. July 7, 1607. Basel UB Ms G I 60: 219-220.

Johann Drusius to Buxtorf. n. p. August 10, 1607. Basel UB Ms G I 59: 259.

Buxtorf to Counts Adolph, Arnold-Justus and Wilhelm-Heinrich of Bentheim, Teckleburg, Steinfurt and Limburg. Basel. August 17, 1607. Buxtorf, *Epitome Radicum,* ff.):(2r-):(8v.

Buxtorf to Johann Drusius Jr. Basel. August 10, 1607. (Heb.). Leeuwarden PB Ms 731: 92-96; Fuks, "Brievenboek," 37-38.

Buxtorf to Johann Piscator. n. p. September 10, 1607. Gotha FB Ms Chart. A 130: 134; Cyprian, *Clarorum virorum,* 154-155.

Hugh Broughton to Buxtorf. Frankfurt/M. September 30, 1607. Basel UB Ms G I 62: 97 and Ms G 2 II 24: 2 (copy).

1608

Buxtorf to Kaspar Waser. Basel. February 7, 1608. Zürich ZB Ms S-160: 45.

Buxtorf to Michael Baldaeus. Basel. March 5, 1608. Leeuwarden PB Ms 731: 78-81; Fuks, "Brievenboek," 39-40.

Buxtorf to Johann Drusius Jr. n. p. March 5, 1608. (Heb.). Leeuwarden PB Ms 731: 89-92; Fuks, "Brievenboek," 41-42.

Johann Piscator to Buxtorf. Siegen. March 12, 1608. Basel UB Ms G I 60: 316.

Buxtorf to Konrad Vorstius. Basel. June 8, 1608. Bibliotheca Rosenthaliana (Amsterdam UB) Brieven, no. 110

Buxtorf to Kaspar Waser. n. p. August 29, 1608. Zürich ZB Ms S-160: 76.

1609

Johann Molther to Buxtorf. n. p. 1609. Basel UB G I 60: 209-210.

Buxtorf to the Estates General of the Republic of the United Netherlands. Basel. March, 1609. Buxtorf, *Thesaurus Grammaticus*, ff.):(2r-):(8r.

Buxtorf to Kaspar Waser. Basel. July 14, 1609. Zürich SA Ms E II 383: 853-4.

Johann Molther to Buxtorf. Marburg. September 1, 1609. Basel UB G I 60: 211.

Buxtorf to Isaac Casaubon. Basel. December 24, 1609. London: British Library, Burney Ms 363: 129.

1610

Buxtorf to Johann Drusius, Johann Uytenbogard and Daniel Heinsius. n. p. 1610. Buxtorf, *Institutio*, ff.):(2r-4v.

Kaspar Waser to Buxtorf. n. p. 1610. Buxtorf, *Institutio*, ff.):(7r-):(8v.

Isaac Casaubon to Buxtorf. Paris. February 12, 1610. Basel UB Ms G I 60: 99-100; Casaubon, *Epistolae*, 606-7 (# MXLII) and Buxtorf, *Catalecta*, 461-3; BF, 13.[2]

Buxtorf to Johann Wtenbogaert. Basel. March 15, 1610. Leiden UB Pap 2; *Praestantium ac eruditorum*, 244-5 (#137); BF, 15-16.

Daniel Heinsius to Buxtorf. Leiden. March 21, 1610. Basel UB G I 59: 244; Buxtorf, *Catalecta*, 464.

Karl Lombardius to Buxtorf. Kassel. November 10, 1610. Basel UB G I 62: 275.

Buxtorf to Isaac Casaubon. Basel. September, 1610. London: British Library, Burney Ms 363: 130.

1611

Buxtorf to Kaspar Waser. Basel. January 28, 1611. Zürich ZB Ms. A 49: 214, Ms S-162: 8 (copy).

Buxtorf to Kaspar Waser. Basel. January 28, 1611. Zürich ZB Ms S-162: 8.

Buxtorf to Kaspar Waser. Basel. March 10, 1611. Zürich ZB Ms S-162: 26.

Buxtorf to Kaspar Waser. n. p. April 8, 1611. Zürich ZB Ms S-162: 32.

---

[2] Karl Buxtorf-Falkeisen translated excerpts of some of Buxtorf's correspondence in his *Johannes Buxtorf*, abbreviated as BF.

Buxtorf to Johann Gosvini Bosmann of Dordrecht and Jakob Guilhelmi Hooft of Amsterdam. Basel. July 8, 1611. Buxtorf, *Manuale*, ff. a2r-a4v.

Robert Boyd to Buxtorf. Saumur. August 6, 1611. Basel UB Ms G I 62: 102-103; Buxtorf, *Catalecta*, 452-456; BF, 17-19.

Daniel Heinsius to Buxtorf. Leiden. July 20, 1611. Basel UB G I 59: 245; Buxtorf, *Catalecta*, 464-466.

Paschalis Le Coq to Buxtorf. Saumur. August 6, 1611. Basel UB Ms G I 62: 104-5.

Buxtorf to Robert Boyd. Basel. August 17, 1611. Buxtorf, *Catalecta*, 457-461; BF, 19-22.

Buxtorf to Kaspar Waser. Basel. September 8, 1611. Zürich ZB Ms S-162: 47.

1612

Buxtorf to Kaspar Waser. n. p. January 29, 1612. Zürich ZB Ms S-162: 87.

Jacob Amport to Buxtorf. Lausanne. April 22, 1612. Basel UB Ms G I 63: 8.

Buxtorf to Kaspar Waser. n. p. July 25, 1612. Zürich ZB Ms S-163: 5.

Buxtorf to Kaspar Waser. Basel. September 9, 1612. Zürich ZB Ms S-163: 33.

Kaspar Waser to Buxtorf. Zürich. September 10, 1612. Zürich ZB Ms S-163: 34.

Buxtorf to Kaspar Waser. Basel. September 28, 1612. Zürich ZB Ms S-163: 64.

Kaspar Waser to Buxtorf. Zürich. December 9, 1612. Zürich ZB Ms S-163: 99.

Buxtorf to Christoph Helvicus. Basel. December 24, 1612. Basel UB Ms Ki Ar 189: 8.

Buxtorf to Johann Molther. Basel. December 26, 1612. Basel UB Ms Ki Ar 189: 8.

1613

Johann Drusius to Buxtorf. n. p. February 8, 1613. Basel UB Ms G I 59: 260, Ms G 2 II 24: 16-18 (copy).

Walter Keuchen to Buxtorf. Hanau. May 20, 1613. Basel UB Ms G I 60: 317.

Buxtorf to Philippe du Plessis Mornay. Basel. August 8, 1613. Buxtorf, *De Abbreviaturis*, ff.):(2r-):(8v and BF, 23.

Buxtorf to C. Bauhin. n. p. August 9, 1613. Basel UB G/2 I 2: 100-101, 105; Basel UB Ms Ki Ar 189: 8 (draft).

Buxtorf to Johann Drusius. Basel. August 23, 1613. Basel UB Ms Ki Ar 189: 8.

Buxtorf to Philippe du Plessis Mornay. Basel. September 8, 1613. Basel UB Ms Slg Geigy-Hgb Nr 736, Ms Ki Ar 189: 8 (draft dated September 7, 1613).

Walter Keuchen to Buxtorf. Frankfurt/M. September 21, 1613. Basel UB Ms G I 60: 318.

1614

Franciscus Gomarus to Buxtorf. Frankfurt/M. 1614. Attached to the title page of Buxtorf's copy of the *Zohar* (Basel UB Sig. FA III 13).

Walter Keuchen to Buxtorf. Hanau. February 7, 1614. Basel UB G I 60: 319.

Thomas Erpenius to Buxtorf. Leiden. April 10, 1614. Basel UB G I 59: 273; BF, 27-28.

Buxtorf to Bartholomaeus Rülich. Basel. August 4, 1614. Magdeburg SA Abt. Kothen C18 31: 155.[3]

Theodor Ebert to Buxtorf. Frankfurt/O. December 24, 1614. Basel UB Ms G I 60: 334-335.

1615

Buxtorf to the Councillors and Senators of Bremen. Basel. March 27, 1615. Basel UB Ms Ki Ar 26b: 8. (German).

Buxtorf to the Councillors and Senators of Bremen. Basel. March 29, 1615. Buxtorf, *Grammaticae Chaldaicae*, ff.):(2r-):(8v.

Buxtorf to Thomas Erpenius. n. p. March 25, 1615. München BSB Clm 10359: 215.

Georg Pasor to Buxtorf. Siegen. March 29, 1615. Basel UB Ms Ki Ar 26b: 1.

Walter Keuchen to Buxtorf. Frankfurt/M. April 10, 1615. Basel UB Ms G I 60: 322.[4]

Philippe du Plessis Mornay to Buxtorf. Saumur. July 23, 1615. Basel UB Ms G I 62: 98; Buxtorf, *Catalecta*, 473-4; BF, 23-4.

Johann Molther to Buxtorf. Marburg. September 1, 1615. Basel UB Ms G I 60: 221-222.

---

[3] All Buxtorf letters with Magdeburg SA call numbers are actually housed at the Oranienbaum Landesarchiv, a smaller subunit of the Magdeburg archive.

[4] M. Kayserling incorrectly gave the year of this letter as 1625. Idem, "Richelieu," 79.

Abraham Braunschweig to Buxtorf. n. p. October 7, 1615. (Heb.).[5]

1616

Christoph Helvicus to Buxtorf. Giessen. January 12, 1616. Basel UB Ms A XII 19, no. 2.

Louis Cappel to Buxtorf. Saumur. January 18, 1616. Basel UB Ms G I 62: 106; Buxtorf, *Catalecta*, 474-476; BF, 24-25.

Johann G. Grob to Buxtorf. Kassel. September 27, 1616. Basel UB Ms G I 60: 223-224.

1617

Buxtorf to Wolfgang Ratich. Basel. January 3, 1617. Magdeburg SA Abt. Kothen C18 30: 179-180.

Wolfgang Ratich to Buxtorf. Frankfurt/M. January 7, 1617. Krause, *Ratichius*, 36 (partial).[6]

Buxtorf to Wolfgang Ratich. Basel. January 31, 1617. Magdeburg SA Abt. Kothen C18 30: 181-182.

Wolfgang Ratich to Buxtorf. n. p. March 3, 1617. Krause, *Ratichius*, 37 (partial).

Chistoph Helvicus to Buxtorf. Giessen. March 8, 1617. Magdeburg SA Abt Kothen C18 30: 183-184.

Buxtorf to Wolfgang Ratich. Basel. March 30, 1617. Magdeburg SA Abt Kothen C18 30: 185.

Peter Cunaeus to Buxtorf. Leiden. April 4, 1617. Basel UB Ms G I 59: 264.

Wolfgang Ratich to Buxtorf. Frankfurt/M. June 10, 1617. Krause, *Ratichius*, 37-38.

Buxtorf and Ludovicus Lucius to Wolfgang Ratich. Basel. June 27, 1617. Magdeburg SA Abt Kothen C18 34: 50.

Johann Molther to Buxtorf. Marburg. September 7, 1617. Basel UB Ms G I 60: 217-218.

Buxtorf to Kaspar Waser. Basel. September 30, 1617. Zürich ZB Ms F 167: 43.

---

[5] Ibid., 84. Kayserling incorrectly gave the date as November 13, 1617 and gave the call number for this letter as Basel UB Ms G I [62]: 350. The original Braunschweig letter has apparently been lost.

[6] Wolfgang Ratke, *Wolfgang Ratichius oder Ratke im Lichte seiner und der Zeitgenossischen Briefe und als Didacticus in Cöthen und Magdeburg*, ed. G. Krause (Leipzig: Dyk'ische Bachhandlung, 1872).

Kaspar Waser to Buxtorf. Zürich. October 5, 1617. Zürich ZB Ms S 166: 89a.

Kaspar Waser to Buxtorf. Zürich. October 12, 1617. Zürich ZB Ms S 166: 89b.

Kaspar Waser to Buxtorf. Zürich. December 6, 1617. Basel UB Ms G 2 II 6: 27.

1618

Franciscus Gomarus to Buxtorf. n. p. [January-March, 1618].[7] Basel UB Ms G I 59: 8; Itterzon, "Nog Twintig Brieven," 432.

Walter Keuchen to Buxtorf. n. p. January 19, 1618. Basel UB Ms G I 60: 320.

Buxtorf to Kaspar Waser. n. p. January 28, 1618. Zürich ZB Ms F 167: 45.

Buxtorf to Kaspar Waser. Basel. March 18, 1618. Zürich ZB Ms A 49: 216.

Buxtorf to Kaspar Waser. n. p. April 15, 1618. Zürich ZB Ms A 52: 57.

Georg Lingelsheim to Buxtorf. Heidelberg. June 9, 1618. Basel UB G I 60: 8; BF, 30.

Walter Keuchen to Buxtorf. Hanau. June 12, 1618. Basel UB Ms G I 60: 321.

Buxtorf to Benedict Turrettini. Basel. June 22, 1618. Geneva: Archives Turrettini, Fonds 1, Dd 4.1.

Buxtorf to Benedict Turrettini. Basel. July 9, 1618. Geneva: Archives Turrettini, Fonds 1, Dd 4.2.

Johann Molther to Buxtorf. Marburg. September 5, 1618. Basel UB Ms G I 60: 212-213.

Jacob Cappel to Buxtorf. Sedan. September 5, 1618. Basel UB G I 62: 121.

Georg Lingelsheim to Buxtorf. Heidelberg. October 13, 1618. Basel UB G I 60: 9; BF, 30-31.

1619

Heinrich von Diest to Buxtorf. Heidelberg. January 13, 1619. Basel UB Ms G I 59: 140.

Buxtorf to Kaspar Waser. Basel. February 3, 1619. Zürich ZB Ms F 167: 46.

Buxtorf to Kaspar Waser. Basel. June 15, 1619. Zürich ZB F 167: 47; Burnett, "Circumcision Incident," 143-144.

---

[7] This was a letter of introduction for a student named Philippe Vincent who matriculated at the Academy of Geneva on March 23, 1618, and at Basel University in August of 1618. Wackernagel, *Matrikel*, 3: 204.

Buxtorf to Benedict Turrettini. Basel. June 26, 1619. Geneva: Archives Turrettini, Fonds 1, Dd 4.3.

Jacob Cappel to Buxtorf. n. p. September 9, 1619. Basel UB Ms G I 62: 124.

Jacob Rolandus to Buxtorf. Amsterdam. September 12, 1619. (Heb) Basel UB Ms G I 59: 355.

Georg Lingelsheim to Buxtorf. Heidelberg. November 1, 1619. Basel UB Ms G I 60: 11-12; BF, 31-32.

Georg Lingelsheim to Buxtorf. Heidelberg. November 29, 1619. Basel UB Ms G I 60: 10; BF, 28, 33.

Janus Gruter to Buxtorf. Heidelberg. December 8, 1619. Basel UB G I 60: 7; BF, 28-29.

Samuel Hortin to Buxtorf. Sumiswald. December 17, 1619. Basel UB Ms G I 63: 9.

1620

Buxtorf to Marcus Rytemeyer. Basel. January 25, 1620. Bern SA Ms B III 33: 99.

Sixtius Amama to Buxtorf. Franeker. March 20, 1620. Basel UB Ms G I 59: 261.

Buxtorf to Peter Cunaeus. Basel. April 3, 1620. Leiden UB Ms Cun 2: 87; Cunaeus, *Epistolae*, 142.

Buxtorf to Kaspar Waser. Basel. April 9, 1620. Zürich ZB Ms F 167: 48.

Janus Gruter to Buxtorf. Frankfurt/M. April 18, 1620. Basel UB Ms G I 60: 6.

Buxtorf to the Estates General of the Netherlands. Basel. April 1, 1620. Buxtorf, *Tiberias*, ff. ***r-***4r.

Jacob Amport to Buxtorf. Lausanne. June 4, 1620. Basel UB Ms G I 63: 7.

Samuel Lagare to Buxtorf. Lausanne. June 22, 1620. Basel UB Ms G I 63: 96-97.

Buxtorf to Kaspar Waser. n. p. July 12, 1620. Zürich ZB Ms F 167: 49.

Franz Donatus to Buxtorf. Rome. August 5, 1620. Basel UB Ms G I 62: 259-260.

Buxtorf to Kaspar Waser. Basel. August 22, 1620. Zürich ZB Ms F 167: 54.

Buxtorf to Kaspar Waser. Basel. September 1, 1620. Zürich ZB Ms F 167: 52.

David Pareus to Buxtorf. Heidelberg. October 21, 1620. Basel UB Ms G I 60: 4.

Buxtorf to Kaspar Waser. Basel. December 5, 1620. Zürich ZB Ms F 167: 53.

1621

Buxtorf to Kaspar Waser. Basel. March 28, 1621. Zürich ZB Ms F 167: 55.

Buxtorf to Kaspar Waser. Basel. April 4, 1621. Zürich ZB Ms F 167: 56.

Buxtorf to Kaspar Waser. Basel. April 16, 1621. Zürich ZB Ms F 167: 57.

Buxtorf to Kaspar Waser. Basel. April 25, 1621. Zürich ZB Ms F 167: 58.

Buxtorf to Kaspar Waser. Basel. May 3, 1621. Zürich ZB Ms F 167: 59.

Buxtorf to Kaspar Waser. Basel. June 6, 1621. Zürich ZB Ms F 167: 60.

Buxtorf to Kaspar Waser. Basel. June 27, 1621. Zürich ZB Ms F 167: 61.

Buxtorf to Kaspar Waser. Basel. July 18, 1621. Zürich ZB Ms F 167: 50.

Buxtorf to Kaspar Waser. Basel. July 25, 1621. Zürich ZB Ms F 167: 62.

Buxtorf to Kaspar Waser. n. p. August 1, 1621. Zürich ZB Ms F 167: 63.

Buxtorf to Kaspar Waser. n. p. September 5, 1621. Zürich ZB Ms F 167: 64.

Franz Donatus to Buxtorf. Rome. October 10, 1621. Basel UB Ms G I 62: 261-261.

1622

Paul Ferry to Buxtorf. Metz. July 8, 1622. Basel UB Ms G I 62: 130; Paris: Bibliotheque de la Société de l'Histoire du Protestantisme Français (hereafter abbreviated BSHPF) réf Ms 761/2 (XII) (draft).

Louis Cappel to Buxtorf. Sedan. July 10, 1622. Basel UB Ms G I 62: 107-109; Buxtorf, *Catalecta*, 476-479.

Louis Cappel to Buxtorf. Sedan. July 26, 1622. Basel UB Ms G I 62: 110.

Louis Cappel to Buxtorf. Sedan. October 27, 1622. Basel UB Ms G I 62: 111.

Louis Cappel to Buxtorf. Sedan. December 9, 1622. Basel UB Ms G I 62: 112; Buxtorf, *Catalecta*, 479-480.

1623

Buxtorf to Louis Cappel. Basel. January 1, 1623. Zürich ZB Ms F 45: 246v-247v (copy).

Wilhelm Schickhard to Buxtorf. n. p. February 5, 1623. Basel UB Ms G I 61: 110.

Louis Cappel to Buxtorf. Sedan. March 1, 1623. Basel UB Ms G I 62: 113.

Paul Ferry to Buxtorf. Metz. March 5, 1623. Basel UB Ms G I 62: 131; Paris: BSHPF réf Ms 761/1 (draft).

Louis Cappel to Buxtorf. Sedan. April 3, 1623. Basel UB Ms G I 62: 114.

Jacob Cappel to Buxtorf. Sedan. June 23, 1623. Basel UB Ms G I 62: 122.

Paul Ferry to Buxtorf. Metz. July 3, 1623. Basel UB Ms G I 62: 132; Paris: BSHPF réf. Ms 761/2 (XII) (draft).

Buxtorf to Benedict Turrettini. Basel. July 6, 1623. Geneva: Archives Turrettini, Fonds 1, Dd 4.4.

Buxtorf to Theodor Tronchin. Basel. July 10, 1623. Geneva: BPU: Archiv Tronchin 29.

Buxtorf to Benedict Turrettini. Basel. August 21, 1623. Geneva: Archives Turrettini, Fonds 1, Dd 4.5.

Wilhelm Schickhard to Buxtorf. Tübingen. September 9, 1623. Basel UB Ms G I 61: 111.

Paul Ferry to Buxtorf. n. p. September 29, 1623. Paris: BSHPF réf. Ms 761/2 (XII) (draft).

Jacob Cappel to Buxtorf. Sedan. November 4, 1623. Basel UB Ms G I 62: 123.

Salomon Glassius to Buxtorf. Jena. December 23, 1623. Basel UB Ms G I 61: 271-272.

1624

Bartholomaeus Beck to Buxtorf. Leipzig. March 24, 1624. Basel UB Ms G I 61: 246.

Samuel Hortin to Buxtorf. n. p. May 12, 1624. Basel UB Ms G I 63: 11.

Nicolaus Girard to Buxtorf. Lausanne. May 21, 1624. Basel UB Ms G I 63: 95.

Paul Ferry to Buxtorf. Metz. August 18, 1624. Paris: BSHPF réf Ms 761/2 (XII) (draft).

Johann Nuber to Buxtorf. Marburg. September 20, 1624. Basel UB Ms G I 60: 175-176.

Wilhelm Schickhard to Buxtorf. Tübingen. September 24, 1624. Basel UB Ms G I 61: 112.

Bartholomaeus Beck to Buxtorf. Leipzig. October 15, 1624. Basel UB Ms G I
61: 248-249.

Paul Ferry to Buxtorf. Metz. December 26, 1624. Paris: BSHPF réf Ms 761/2
(XII) (draft).

1625

Peter Cunaeus to Buxtorf. Leiden. June 4, 1625. Basel UB Ms G I 59: 265-266;
BF, 37-39.

Buxtorf to Peter Cunaeus. Basel. June 24, 1625. Leiden UB Ms Cun 2: 89;
Cunaeus, *Epistolae*, 145-147.

Buxtorf to Peter Cunaeus. Basel. July 8, 1625. Leiden UB Ms Cun 2: 90;
Cunaeus, *Epistolae*, 147-8.

Buxtorf to Peter Cunaeus. Basel. July 22, 1625. Leiden UB Ms Cun 2: 92;
Cunaeus, *Epistolae*, 150-151.

Laurentius Fabricius to Buxtorf. Wittenberg. August 24, 1625. Basel UB Ms G I
61: 210; Buxtorf, *Catalecta*, 434-436.

Buxtorf to Peter Cunaeus. Basel. September 15, 1625. Leiden UB Ms Cun 2: 93;
Cunaeus, *Epistolae*, 151-2.

1626

Paul Ferry to Buxtorf. Metz. 1626. Paris: BSHPF réf. Ms 761/2 (XII) (draft).

Benedict Turrettini to Buxtorf. Geneva. February 27, 1626. Basel UB Ms G I
64: 100-101.

Paul Ferry to Buxtorf. Metz. March 24, 1626. Paris: BSHPF réf. Ms 761/2 (XII)
(draft).

Buxtorf to Hieronymus Avianus. Basel. July 3, 1626. Avianus, *Clavis*, ff. b5r-
c1r.

Gerardus Joannes Vossius to Buxtorf. n. p. July 11, 1626. Amsterdam UB Ms
III D 12b, part d, ff. 7-14.

Buxtorf to Wilhelm Schickhard. Basel. September 7, 1626. Stuttgart: WLB Cod.
hist. 2° 563.

Johann Philipp Pareus to Buxtorf. Hanau. September 25, 1626. Basel UB Ms G
I 60: 5; BF, 40-41.

Peter Cunaeus to Buxtorf. Leiden. September 26, 1626. Basel UB Ms G I 59:
267; Cunaeus, *Epistolae*, 152-153.

Peter Cunaeus to Buxtorf. Leiden. October 26, 1626. Basel UB Ms G I 59: 268; BF, 39.

1627

Buxtorf to Peter Cunaeus. Basel. March 8, 1627. Leiden UB Ms Cun 2: 98; Cunaeus, *Epistolae*, 153-154.

Buxtorf to Wilhelm Schickhard. Basel. August 12, 1627. Stuttgart: WLB Cod. hist. 2° 563.

Buxtorf to Wilhelm Schickhard. Basel. September 10, 1627. Stuttgart: WLB Cod. hist. 2° 563.

Buxtorf to Wilhelm Schickhard. Basel. October 10, 1627. Stuttgart: WLB Cod. hist. 2° 563.

Louis Cappel to Buxtorf. Saumur. October 27, 1627. Basel UB Ms G I 62: 115.

1628

David Le Clerc to Buxtorf (the elder?). Geneva. February 25, 1628. Basel UB Ms G I 64: 350-352.

Wilhelm Schickhard to Buxtorf. Tübingen. February 28, 1628. Basel UB Ms Ki Ar 26b: 4; Copenhagen: Royal Library Ms Th tt 481: 463 (partial copy).

André Rivet to Buxtorf. Leiden. March 27, 1628. Basel UB Ms G I 59: 38.

Buxtorf to Benedict Turrettini. Basel. April 20, 1628. Geneva: Archives Turrettini, Fonds 1, Dd. 4.6.

Buxtorf to André Rivet. Basel. April 24, 1628. Leiden UB Ms BPL 285 I, f. 99.

David Le Clerc to Buxtorf (the elder?). Geneva. May 27, 1628. Basel UB Ms G I 64: 353-354.

Louis Cappel to Buxtorf. Saumur. June 27, 1628. Basel UB Ms G I 62: 116; Buxtorf, *Catalecta*, 484-486; BF, 26.

David Le Clerc to Buxtorf (the elder?). Geneva. July 1, 1628. Basel UB Ms G I 64: 355-356.

Paul Ferry to Buxtorf. Metz. July 1. 1628. Paris: BSHPF réf. Ms 761/2 (XII) (draft).

David Le Clerc to Buxtorf (the elder?). Geneva. July 20, 1628. Basel UB Ms G I 64: 357-358.

Buxtorf to Wilhelm Schickhard. Basel. September 6, 1628. Stuttgart: WLB Ms Cod. hist. 2° 563.

Theological Faculty of Strasbourg Univ. to Buxtorf. Strasbourg. September 23, 1628. Basel UB Ms G I 61: 1-2; BF, 12.

Matthias Bernegger to Buxtorf. Strasbourg. September 28, 1628. Basel UB G I 61: 4; Hamburg SB Ms Sup. ep. 4° 31, 189 (draft); Buxtorf, *Catalecta*, 407-408.

Benedict Gros to Buxtorf. Strasbourg. October 1628. Basel UB Ms G I 61: 84-85.

Buxtorf to Wilhelm Schickhard. Basel. October 2, 1628. Stuttgart: WLB Cod. hist. 2° 563.

Hieronymus Avianus to Buxtorf. Leipzig. October 15, 1628. Basel UB Ms G I 61: 236.

André Rivet to Buxtorf. Leiden. November 1, 1628. Basel UB G I 59: 39.

Buxtorf to André Rivet. Basel. November 7, 1628. Leiden UB Ms BPL 285 I f. 100.

Benedict Gros to Buxtorf. n. p. November 29, 1628. Basel UB Ms G I 61: 86.

Theodor Ebert to Buxtorf. Frankfurt/O. December 5, 1628. Basel UB Ms G I 60: 329-332.

1629

Hieronymus Avianus to Buxtorf. n. p. January 12, 1629. Basel UB Ms G I 61: 235.

Benedict Gros to Buxtorf. Strasbourg. January 13, 1629. Basel UB Ms G I 61: 87.

Johann Georg Dorsch to Buxtorf. Strasbourg. January 13, 1629. Basel UB Ms G I 61: 49.

Constantijn L'Empereur to Buxtorf. Leiden. February 1, 1629. Basel UB Ms G I 59: 274.

Elias Diodati to Buxtorf. Geneva. February 6, 1629. Basel UB Ms G I 64: 28-31.

Conrad Schopp to Buxtorf. Bern. February 26, 1629. Basel UB Ms G I 63: 98.

Benedict Gros to Buxtorf. Strasbourg. March 5, 1629. Basel UB Ms Ki Ar 26b: 5.

Matthias Bernegger to Buxtorf. Strasbourg. March 8, 1629. Basel UB Ms G I 61: 5; Buxtorf, *Catalecta*, 408-411.

André Rivet to Buxtorf. Leiden. March 15, 1629. Basel UB Ms G I 59: 40.

Buxtorf to Wilhelm Schickhard. Basel. March 20, 1629. Stuttgart: WLB Cod. hist. 2° 563.

Buxtorf to André Rivet. Basel. March 21, 1629. Dortmund StB Ms. 3705.

David Le Clerc to Buxtorf (the elder?). n. p. March 25, 1629. Basel UB G I 64: 365-366.

Hieronymus Avianus to Buxtorf. Leipzig. May 6, 1629. Basel UB Ms G I 61: 237-238.

Conrad Schopp to Buxtorf. Bern. April 5, 1629. Basel UB Ms G I 63: 99.

Benedict Gros to Buxtorf. Strasbourg. June 12, 1629. Basel UB Ms G I 61: 88.

Johann Georg Dorsch to Buxtorf. Strasbourg. June 12, 1629. Basel UB Ms G I 61: 48.

Sixtius Amama to Buxtorf. n. p. June 16, 1629. Basel UB Ms G I 59: 262.

Samuel Hortin to Buxtorf. Bern. June 19, 1629. Basel UB Ms G I 63: 10.

Constantijn L'Empereur to Buxtorf. Leiden. August 29, 1629. Basel UB Ms G I 59: 275; BF, 42-44.

Gabriel Sionita to Buxtorf. Paris. September 15, 1629. Basel UB Ms G I 62: 308-309, Ms Ki Ar 189: 11, 1 (copy).

Martin Trost to Buxtorf. Wittenberg. October 1, 1629. Basel UB Ms G I 61: 120-121.

Bartholomaeus Beck to Buxtorf. Eisleben. October 29, 1629. Basel UB G I 61: 250.

Undated Letters

Jacob Amport to Buxtorf. n. p., n. d. Basel UB G I 63: 28.

Wilhelm Avianus to Buxtorf. Leipzig. October 8, 162--? Basel UB Ms G I 61: 239.

Abraham Braunschweig to Buxtorf. n. p, n. d. Moscow: Russian State Library of Moscow, Ginzburg Collection, Ms. 1213 , ff. 5b, 6a-6b, 10a, 13a. (4 letters, Heb.).[8]

Hugh Broughton to Buxtorf. Frankfurt/M. March 29, 1598? Basel UB Ms G I 62: 96 and Ms G 2 II 24: 1 (copy).

---

[8] I consulted a microfilm copy held by the Institute of Microfilmed Hebrew Manuscripts, JNUL Jerusalem. Eliakim Carmoly described the manuscript in "Varietes Critiques et Litteraires. IV. Sefer ha-Maaloth," *Revue orientale* (Brussels) 1 (1841): 345-348.

Buxtorf to Jacob Cappel. n. p., n. d. Basel UB Ms Ki Ar 189: 8.

Jacob Cappel to Buxtorf. Sedan. September 8, 16--. Basel UB Ms G I 62: 120.

Buxtorf to Johann Drusius. n. p., n. d. (Heb.). Leeuwarden PB Ms 731: 76-78. (partial).

Johann Drusius to Buxtorf. Before 1595. Johann Drusius, *De Quaesitis*, 153-154.

Johann Drusius Jr. to Buxtorf. n. p., n. d. (after January, 1609). (Heb.). Leeuwarden PB Ms 731: 96-98; Fuks, "Brievenboek ," 44-45.

Isaac Eckendorf to Buxtorf. n. p., n. d. (after 1599). Moscow: Russian State Library of Moscow, Ginzburg Collection, Ms. 1213, f. 8b (Heb.).

[Christian Gerson] to Buxtorf. (1611?). Moscow: Russian State Library of Moscow, Ginzburg Collection, Ms. 1213, f. 9a (partial copy, Heb.).

Mordecai Gumplin to Buxtorf. Moscow: Russian State Library of Moscow, Ginzburg Collection, Ms. 1213, ff. 6b-8b, 9b, 11b-12b (3 letters, Heb.).

Buxtorf to Georg Pasor. n. p. , n. d. Basel UB Ms Ki Ar 189: 8.

Buxtorf to Kaspar Waser. Basel. n. d. (1598-1600).[9] (Heb.). Zürich ZB Ms S-149: 125, 1.

Buxtorf to Kaspar Waser. Basel. n. d. (Heb.). Zürich ZB Ms S-149: 125, 3.

Lost or in Private Collections

Buxtorf to Wolfgang Ratich. Basel. January 13, 1614. (Privately owned).

Johann Buxtorf to Philippe du Plessis Mornay. 1615.[10]

---

[9] The year is probably 1598 or 1599 because Buxtorf dates it with the phrase "tenth year of our friendship" (שׁ עשׂר אהבה נפשׁ). He met Waser while attending the university of Basel, by 1590 at the very latest.

[10] Gustave Ponvert, "Livres et manuscrits provenant de la bibliothèque de Duplesses Mornay.--Que sont-ils devenus?" *Bulletin de la Société de l'Histoire du Protestantisme Français* 9 (1860): 203.

YIDDISH BOOKLIST OF 1609

The Yiddish Booklist is a list of titles that Buxtorf mentioned in his introduction to reading Yiddish.[1] He provided no imprint information (except for no. 16) but virtually every title can be indentified either with books in the 1705 sales list or with books described by Prijs in *Die Basler Hebräische Drucke*.[2] Although Buxtorf cited many of them in his works, particularly *Juden Schul*, he largely excluded Yiddish language works from *Bibliotheca rabbinica*.[3]

I. *Bibles*

1. חמשה חומשי תורה. f. Basel: Thomas Guarin, 1583. Basel UB FA III 21. StCB p. 178/1190. Prijs no. 137. *De Abbreviaturis*, 270.[4]

2. ספר שמות = Moses Schedel. מעשה יציאת מצרים. Prague: Jehudah Löb, 1604. Basel UB FA VI 13/1. StCB p. 177, no. 1184 and Cohn, 64-66.[5]

3. ספר יהושע. 4°. Cracow: Isaac b. Aaron Prostitz, 1594. Basel UB FA VI 13/2. StCB p. 183/1233. Cohn, 68-69.

4. ספר ירמיה. 4°. Prague: Salmon Setzer, 1602. Basel UB FA VI 26/1. StCB p. 186/1249.

---

[1] The Yiddish booklist was reprinted in Buxtorf, *Thesaurus Grammaticus*, 660-662. All references to the *Bibliotheca rabbinica* are taken from the first edition of *De Abbreviaturis* (1613).

[2] See also A. Cohn's discussion in "Ueber einige alte Drucke," *Festschrift zum Siebzigsten Geburtstage David Hoffmann's. Gewidmet von Freunden und Schülern*, 3 vols. ed. Simon Eppenstein, Meir Hildesheimer and Joseph Wohl-gemuth (Berlin: Louis Lamm, 1914; reprint ed., New York: Arno, 1980), 1, 46-70.

[3] The only Yiddish works from his title list that appear in *Bibliotheca rabbinica* are nos. 1, 9, 10, 17, 22, 23, 24, and 25. He may also have cited no. 18, but gave no information beyond the title.

[4] Buxtorf might also have referred here to the unaltered reprint of the Basel Yiddish Pentateuch of 1603 (Prijs 186), although the Buxtorf family library contains no copy of this imprint. He mentioned both imprints in *De Abbreviaturis*, 270.

[5] Steinschneider listed no Yiddish translation for Exodus that appeared in print during this period. On the basis of Cohn's description I think that this is the book Buxtorf had in mind.

270 APPENDIX THREE

5. ספר יחזקאל. Prague: Jehuda Löb, 1602. Basel UB FA VI 13/4. StCB p. 186/1251 and Cohn, 69.

6. ספר תהלים. Trans. Elias Levita. Cracow: Isaac b. Aaron Prostitz, 1598. Basel UB FA V 45.

7. שיר השירים. Trans. Isaac Sulkes. 4°. Cracow: Isaac b. Aaron Prostitz, 1600. Basel UB FA VI 13/3. StCB p. 181/1212 and Cohn, 66-67.

8. ספר דניאל. Basel: Jakob Kündig (=Parcus), 1557. Basel UB FA VI 34/2. Prijs no. 97 and Cohn, 60-61.

II. *Prayerbooks*

9. ברכות המזון. Basel: K. Waldkirch, 1600. Basel UB FA V 46. Prijs no. 169 and *De Abbreviaturis*, 283.

10. מחזור. f. Prague: Moses b. Jos. Bezalel Katz, 1600. Basel UB FA IV 1/1. StCB p. 390-391/2554 and *De Abbreviaturis*, 302.

11. סליחות. Trans. Josef b. Elia Levi von Töplitz. Prague: Mordecai b. Gerson, 1587. Basel UB FA IV 3. StCB p. 432/2838 and *De Abbreviaturis*, 313.

III. *Other Works*

12. מעשה בוך. Ed. Jacob b. Abraham of Miendzyrzecz, Lithuania. Basel: K. Waldkirch, 1602. Basel UB FA IX 113. Prijs no. 178. StCB p. 613/3893 and Cohn, 68.

13. Anshel. ספר ר אנשיל. Cracow: Isaac b. Aaron Prostitz, 1584. Basel UB FA VI 11b. StCB p. 738/4423/2.

14. Benjamin Aaron b. Abraham Slonik. פרואן בויכליין (איין שוין)). Basel: K. Waldkirch, 1602. Basel UB FA V 18/3. Prijs no. 177. StCB p. 787/4543/5 and Cohn, 70.

15. Isaac Akrish. מעשה בית דוד בימי פרס. Basel: K. Waldkirch, 1599. Basel UB FA VI 34/3. Prijs no. 159. StCB p. 1085/5305/4 and Cohn, 63-64.

16. Josippon. ספר יוסיפון. Trans. Michael Adam. Zürich: Froschover, 1546. Oxford: Bodleian: Opp. 1685Q. StCB p. 1551/6033/11.

17. Jonah Gerondi. ספר היראה. Zürich: n. p., 1546. Basel UB FA VI 24. StCB p. 1427/5859/28, Cohn, 69-70 and *De Abbreviaturis*, 297.

18. _____. ספר חיי עולם. Freiburg/Br.: Ambrosius Froben, 1583. Basel UB FA VI 24/2. Prijs no. 138. StCB p. 1427/5859/29, Cohn, 70 and *De Abbreviaturis*, 290?

19. Joseph b. Eliezer Halfan of Posen. אורח חיים. Basel: K. Waldkirch, 1602. Basel UB FA V 18/2. Prijs no. 176. StCB p. 518/3391.

20. Joseph b. Jacob Braunschw(e)ig. סוד הנשמה. Basel: K. Waldkirch, 1609. Oxford, Bodleian: Opp. 4° 893. Prijs no. 195. StCB p. 626/3973.

21. Moses Henochs. ברנט שפיגל. Basel: K. Waldkirch, 1602. Basel UB FA V 18/1. Prijs no. 175. StCB p. 1823/6473/1.

22. Moses Särtels. לקח טוב. Prague: Moses b. Jos. Berzalel Katz, 1605. Basel UB FA VI 11a/2. StCB p. 1994/6553/10 and *De Abbreviaturis*, 299.

23. Petahya of Regensburg. סיבוב. 4°. Prague: Moses b. Jos. Bezalel Katz, 1600. Basel UB FA VI 10a Cohn, 60-61 and *De Abbreviaturis*, 311.[6]

24. Simon Levi Günzburg. מנהגים. Venice: G. de Gara, 1601. Basel UB FA V 47/1. StCB p. 599/3821 and *De Abbreviaturis*, 304.

25. Solomon ibn Verga. שבט יהודה. Cracow: Isaac b. Aaron, 1591. Basel UB FA V 35/2. StCB p. 2396/6982/8 and *De Abbreviaturis*, 325-6.

---

[6] Steinschneider doubted this imprint's existence in StCB p. 2097/6728/3.

APPENDIX FOUR

BUXTORF FAMILY LIBRARY IN 1613:
HEBREW TITLE LIST

The *Bibliotheca Rabbinica* of 1613 and Yiddish book list of 1609 together provide valuable information for reconstructing Johannes Buxtorf I's personal library holdings. The city of Basel purchased the Buxtorf family collection in 1705 and the call numbers assigned these books on the handwritten inventory are closely related to their present day numbers.[1] I have assumed that if a book in the 1705 list corresponds to one described in the *Bibliotheca rabbinica*, or Buxtorf cited it in his works, then he owned it.[2] Buxtorf systematically excluded Basel Hebrew and Yiddish titles from his bibliography, and hence it provides no reliable information on how many of these works he owned. The Basel University Library also held some valuable Hebrew works in Buxtorf's day, including a copy of the Antwerp Polyglot which Buxtorf used extensively in the work on the Targums.[3] Some copies of books in the 1705 Buxtorf family library such as Isaac Aboab, מנורת המאור (no. 89) fit the description given in *Bibliotheca rabbinica*, but were purchased after 1613. Buxtorf II and Johann Jacob Buxtorf may also have traded or sold books acquired by Buxtorf I.[4] I have added whatever purchase information I could find for individual books, drawn largely from inscriptions on the title page or flyleaves.

---

[1] For example Buxtorf's copy of *Abodah Zara* (no. 29) has the call no. A. 1. 6. in Frey's catalog. See Johann Ludwig Frey, *Index Librorum Buxtorfianorum Bibliothecae Publiae*, Basel UB Ms AR I 31. A printed version of the Buxtorf library catalog also exists: [*Kleiner Katalog der Buxtorfschen Bibliothek*] (Basel: Johann Brandmüller, 1705), Basel UB Fr Gr D VII 109.

[2] In the few instances where Frey's *Index* lists two copies, I have given both of them (nos. 82-3, 104-7, 110-1, 121-2, and 124-5).

[3] Basel UB FG I 1-8. The polyglot is listed in the Basel library catalog of 1622, call no. FF 1.1-1.8. Basel UB Ms AR I 26.

[4] See Kayserling, "Richelieu," 74-95, and idem, "Les Correspondants Juifs de Jean Buxtorf," *Revue des études juives* 13 (1886): 261-276 for Buxtorf II's activities as a bookseller.

The spelling of authors' names have been established largely according to those used in the *National Union Catalog*, the Hebrew Union College Catalog of the Klau Library, and the Harvard College, *Catalog of Hebrew Books*. I have, in some cases, rearranged the order of the names so that personal names appear first followed by patronymic. For example, Elias Levita appears under "Elias." This is the current rule for establishing the correct form of Hebrew names and is reflected in the holdings of computerized union catalogs as OCLC and RLIN. Presenting authors' names in this way will be a greater help to future scholars than adhering to the inconsistent, outdated practices of older printed catalogs.[5] For the bibliographic descriptions I have used Steinschneider's Bodleian library catalog and Prijs' *Die Basler Hebräische Drucke*. Joseph Prijs' handwritten card file on Hebrew imprints held by Basel University Library and A. Cohn's description of several extremely rare Hebrew imprints held by Basel UB were also extremely useful.[6]

I. *Bibles*

A. Polyglot Bibles
1. *Biblia Polyglotta*. Alcalá de Henares: Arnaldi Guillelmi Brocario, 1514-17.Basel UB FA II 9a, 10,10a, b, c, d. StCB p. 5/26.

B. Rabbinical Bibles
2. מקרא גדולה. Ed. Felix Praetensis. Venice: Daniel Bomberg, 1517. Basel UB FG II 9-10. StCB p. 6/28

3. מקרא גדולה. Ed. Jacob b. Hayyim. Venice: Daniel Bomberg, 1525.Basel UB Fr Gr A I 16-17. StCB p. 11/52.

C. Hebrew Bibles
4. חמשה חומשי תורה. 4° with vowel points. Antwerp: C. Plantin, 1566. Basel UB FB VIII 3. StCB p. 33-34/190. Voet no. 649.

5. חמשה חומשי תורה. 16° with vowel points. Antwerp: C. Plantin, 1566. StCB p. 34/192. Voet no. 651.

---

[5] *Anglo-American Cataloging Rules*, 2d. ed, 1988 revision, ed. Michael Gorman and Paul W. Winkler (Chicago: American Library Association, 1988), pp. 403-4, rule 22.8B.
[6] A. Cohn, "Drucke," 46-70. Joseph Prijs' *Hebräisches Titelregister* is a special card catalog which is kept in the main reading room of Basel UB.

6. ‏תורה נביאים וכתובים‎. 8°. Paris: Robertus Stephanus, 1544. Basel UB FA IX 23-49. StCB p. 22/115.

7. ‏עשרים וארבעה‎. 8°. Basel: Konrad Waldkirch, 1611-12.[7] StCB p. 64/395. Prijs no. 207.

8. ‏יי מקדש‎. *En Tibi Lector Hebraica Biblia Latina.* f. Trans. Sebastian Münster. Basel: Michael Isingrinius & Henric Petri, 1546. Basel UB FA I 4. StCB p. 22/114. Prijs no. 73. Acquired in 1593.

D. Parts of Bibles

9. ‏חמשה חומשי תורה‎. 8°. Without vowel points. Antwerp: C. Plantin, 1573-74. Basel UB FA VIII 16/1 StCB p. 39/227. Voet no. 652. Gift in 1591-2.

10. ‏חומשי חמש‎. Venice: Giovanni di Gara, 1590-91. Basel UB FA VII 2a, 2b/1 StCB p. 50/295.

11. ‏חמשה חומשי תורה‎. f. Basel: Thomas Guarin, 1583. Basel UB FA III 21. StCB p. 178/1190. Prijs no. 137. Yiddish Booklist.

12. ‏חמשה חומשי תורה‎. f. Basel: Konrad Waldkirch, 1606-7. Basel UB FA III 1. StCB p. 60/361. Prijs no. 191. Acquired in 1610-11.

13. ‏ספר יהושע‎. 4°. Cracow: Isaac b. Aaron Prostitz,1594. Basel UB FA VI 13/2. StCB p. 183/1233. Cohn, 68-69. Yiddish Booklist.

14. ‏ספר ירמיה‎. 4°. Prague: Salmon Setzer, 1602. Basel UB FA VI 26/1. StCB p. 186/1249. Yiddish Booklist.

15. ‏ספר יחזקאל‎. Prague: Jehuda Löb, 1602. Basel UB FA VI 13/4. StCB p. 186/1251; Cohn, 69. Yiddish Booklist.

16. ‏ספר תחלים‎. (With Kimhi's commentary). Ed. Paul Fagius. f. Isny: Paul Fagius, 1541-2. Basel UB FA III 23. StCB p. 17-18/91. Acquired 1592.

17. ‏ספר תהלים‎. (With Kimhi's commentary). 16°. Venice: n. p., 1565. Basel UB FA IX 14. StCB p. 54/315 and p. 35/198.

18. ‏ספר תחלים‎. 32° with Prayerbook. Venice: n. p., 1586. Perhaps StCB p. 51/299 and p. 314/2100 (1591)?[8]

19. ‏ספר תחלים‎. Trans. Elias Levita. Cracow: Isaac b. Aaron Prostitz, 1598. Basel UB FA V 45. Yiddish Booklist.

20. ‏שיר השירים‎. Trans. Isaac Sulkes. 4°. Cracow: Isaac b. Aaron Prostitz, 1600. Basel UB FA VI 13/3. Cohn, 66-67. Yiddish Booklist.

---

[7] Buxtorf gave the year as 1610 in *De Abbreviaturis*, 269. Basel UB had a copy of the work in 1622 (Basel UB Ms AR I 26, call no. E 2 33).

[8] The book was missing in the 1705 inventory.

21. ספר דניאל. Basel: Jakob Kündig (=Parcus), 1557. Basel UB FA VI 34/2. Prijs no. 97. Cohn, 60-61. Yiddish Booklist.

E. Apocrypha
22. *Ben Sira.* בן סירא. 4°. Constantinople: n. p., 1519. Basel UB FA VI 10. StCB p. 203/1363. Cited in *Juden Schul*, 99-100.

23. *Ben Sira.* בן סירא. 4°. Trans. Paul Fagius. Isny: Paul Fagius, 1542. Basel UB FB III 10/2. StCB p. 204/1366.

F. New Testament
24. תורת המשיח. *Evangelium Secundum Matthaeum*. Trans. Sebastian Münster. 8°. Basel: Sebastian Henric-Petri, 1582. Basel UB FA VII 17/1 StCB p. 2016/6591/28. Prijs no. 135. Acquired 1590.

II. *Mishnah and Talmud*

25. משנה. f. Venice: Giovanni Zanetti, 1606. Basel UB FA III 15. StCB p. 281/1988.

26. משניות. 8°. Venice: Giovanni di Gara, 1609. Basel UB Fr Gr A V 42b. StCB p. 281/1989.

27. פרקי אבות. Trans. Paul Fagius. Isny: Paul Fagius, 1541. Basel UB FB III 10/3. StCB p. 229/1435.

28. תלמוד בבלי. Ed. Israel Sifroni. Censored by Marcus Marinus. Basel: Ambrosius Froben, 1578-80. Basel UB FA I 5, 5a-e. StCB p. 220/1407. Prijs no. 124.

29. תלמוד בבלי. Cracow: n. p., ca. 1580. Basel UB FA I 6 (Only tractate *Abodah Zarah*). StCB p. 228/1427.

30. תלמוד ירושלמי. Cracow: Isaac b. Aaron Prostitz, 1609. Basel UB FA I 7. StCB p. 291/2040.

III. *Prayerbooks*

31. ברכת המזון. 4°. Basel: Konrad Waldkirch, 1600. Basel UB FA V 46. Prijs no. 169. Yiddish Booklist.

32. מחזור. Sabionetta: Vincent Conti, 1556-1560. Basel UB FA V 15. StCB p. 370/2452

33. מחזור. f. Prague: Moses b. Joseph Bezalel Katz, 1600. Basel UB FA IV 1/1. Yiddish Booklist.

34. מעמדות. 8°. Venice: Saul Belgrad, 1606.[9] Basel UB FA VIII 49/2. StCB p. 428/2811.

35. מעמדות. Verona: n. p., 1598. Basel UB FA VIII 54a. Cohn, 53-54.

36. סליחות. Trans. Josef b. Elia Levi von Töplitz. f. Prague: Mordecai b. Gerson, 1587. Basel UB FA IV 3. StCB p. 432/2838. Yiddish Booklist.

37. סליחות. f. Prague: Moses b. Joseph Bezalel Katz, 1602. Basel UB FA IV 1/2. StCB p. 442/2911. Yiddish Booklist.

38. [תפלות]. (Title page missing). 16°. Augsburg: Hayyim Schwarz, 1534. Basel UB FA VIII 57.[10] StCB p. 306/2072. *Juden Schul*, 226-228.

39. תפלה מכל השנה. (Title page missing). 4°. Cracow: Isaac b. Aaron Prostitz, 1597. Basel UB FA VI 29/1. StCB p. 316/2103.

40. Akiba Frankfurt ben Joseph of Neuss. זמירות ותושבחות. 8°. Ed. Elijah Loanz. Basel: Konrad Waldkirch, 1599. Basel UB FA VIII 49/3. StCB p. 943/4961/4. Prijs no. 163a.

IV. *Anonymous Works*

41. ספר אמנה. Ed. and Trans. Paul Fagius. 4°. Isny: Paul Fagius, 1542. Basel UB FA V 6/3. StCB p. 521/3406.

42. זוהר חדש. 4°. Cracow: Isaac b. Aaron Prostitz, 1603. Basel UB FA VI 12. StCB p. 542/3498.

43. כל בו. f. Venice: Zorzo dei Cavalli, 1567. Basel UB FA IV 19/3. StCB p. 556/3593. *Juden Schul*, 352, 354, 361.

44. מגלת ספר. 8°. Cremona: n. p., 1566. StCB p. 579/3716. Buxtorf owned the book in 1603.[11]

45. מגלת ספר. *Institutio epistolaris Hebraica*. 8°. Basel: Konrad Waldkirch, 1610. StCB p. 810/4637/4. Prijs no. 204.[12]

46. מדרש רבות. f. Cracow: Isaac b. Aaron Prostitz, 1608-9. Basel UB FA III 12. StCB p. 591/3761. *Juden Schul*, 173-174.[13]

---

[9] The actual date for this entry is 1506 in *De Abbreviaturis*, 306.

[10] Moshe N. Rosenfeld described this book in *Der Jüdische Buchdruck in Augsburg in der ersten Hälfte des 16. Jahrhunderts*, (London: By the Author, 1985), no. 48 (cf. also no. 37).

[11] *Syvula Epistolarum*, 1. See Prijs, *Drucke*, 524.

[12] This book presumably served as the *Vorlage* for the Basel, 1629 reprint (Prijs no. 230).

[13] Buxtorf apparently described the Venice, 1545 edition (StCB p. 590/3756) in *De Abbreviaturis*, 323, since Giustiniani was at least notionally working for Bomberg at this time.

47. מעשה בוך. Ed. Jacob b. Abraham of Miendzyrzecz Basel: Konrad Waldkirch, 1602. StCB p. 613/3893. Prijs no. 178. Yiddish Booklist. *Juden Schul*, 112.

48. ספרא. f. Venice: Daniel Bomberg, 1545. Basel UB FA IV 20 StCB p. 627/3979.
Juden Schul, 184.

49. עברונות. 4°. Riva de Trento: n. p., 1560. Basel UB FA V 35b/2. StCB p. 628/3989.

50. פרקי אליעזר. 4°. Venice: Giovanni di Farri, 1544. Basel UB FA V 6/2. StCB p. 634/4009. *Juden Schul*, 61, 553, 577.

51. קנה בינה. Ed. Eliezer Perles Altschüler b. Abraham. Prague: Moses b. Joseph Bezalel Katz, 1610. Basel UB FA V 37/1. StCB p. 637/4032.

52. תנחומא. f. Verona: Francesco delle Donne, 1595. Basel UB FA IV 14/2. StCB p. 596/3799. *Juden Schul*, 38, 75.

V. *Works whose Authors are known*

53. Abraham bar Hiyya. ספר צורת הארץ. *Sphaera Mundi*. 4°. Ed. Sebastian Münster. Trans. Erasmus O. Schreckenfuchs. Basel: Henric Petri, 1546. Basel UB Fr Gr A VI 72.[14] StCB p. 673/4206/3. Prijs no. 75.

54. Abraham ben David ha-Levi. ספר הקבלה. 8°. Venice: Marco Antonio Giustiniani, 1545. Basel UB FA V 6/4. StCB p. 1434/5873/3.

55. Abraham ben Meir de Balmes. מקנה אברהם. 4°. Venice: Daniel Bomberg, 1523. StCB p. 667/4188/1.

56. Abraham ben Samuel Zacuto. יוחסין 4°. Cracow: n. p., 1580. Basel UB FA V 12/2. StCB p. 707/4303/1.

57. Abraham Saba. צרור המור. f. Venice: Daniel Bomberg, 1523. StCB p. 706/4301/1.[15] *Juden Schul*, 122, 364.

58. Abraham Shalom ben Isaac. נוה שלום. Venice: Giovanni di Gara, 1574. Basel UB FA VI 4/1. StCB p. 709/4311/1. Gift of Thomas Erpenius.

59. Abraham Yagel. אשת חיל. 8°. Venice: Daniel Zanetti, 1611. Basel UB FA VIII 28/2. StCB p. 694/4241/1.

60. Anshel. ספר ר אנשיל. Cracow: Isaac b. Aaron Prostitz, 1584. Basel UB FA VI 11b. StCB p. 738/4423/2. Yiddish Booklist.

---

[14] Buxtorf probably owned two copies; the copy listed in the 1705 inventory; copy FA VI 16, was exchanged in 1972 (notation on Shelflist).
[15] This is the edition mentioned in *Bibliotheca rabbinica*, but no copy of the book was sold to Basel UB in 1705.

61. Azariah de Rossi. מאור עינים. Mantua: n. p., 1574-5. Basel UB FA V 4.[16] StCB p. 747/4448/1. *Aus was Ursachen*, ff. 13-14, 17, 33, 45.

62. Bahya ben Asher. בחיי על התורה. f. Venice: Daniel Bomberg, 1546. Basel UB FA III 10a. StCB p. 779/4525/7. *Juden Schul*, 61, 88, 125.

63. ____. כד הקמח. Venice: n. p., 1545.[17] StCB p. 779/4525/14. *Juden Schul*, 31, 78, 222, 458, 470.

64. Baruch ben Isaac of Worms. תרומה. Large 4°. Venice: Daniel Bomberg, 1523.[18] Basel UB FA IV 27. StCB p. 774/4508/1.

65. Benjamin Aaron Slonik. (איין שוין) פרואן בויכליין. Basel: Konrad Waldkirch, 1602. Basel UB FA V 18/3. StCB p. 787/4543/5. Prijs no. 177. Cohn, 70. Yiddish Booklist. *Juden Schul*, 245, 595.

66. Benjamin ben Jonah of Tudela. מסעות ר בנימין. 8°. Trans. Benedict Arias Montano. Antwerp: C. Plantin, 1575. Basel UB FA VII 11/3. StCB p. 794/4570/12.

67. ____. מסעות ר בנימין. 8°. Basel: Ambrosius Froben, 1583 Basel UB FA VIII 48a/1. StCB p. 793/4570/3. Prijs no. 139.

68. David de Pomi. צמח דוד. f. Venice: Giovanni di Gara, 1587. Basel UB FA IV 23. StCB p. 885/4841/1. Given to Buxtorf in 1593.

69. David Gans. צמח דוד. 4°. Prague: n. p., 1592. Basel UB FA V 12/1. StCB p. 862/4805/3.

70. David Kimhi. מכלול. 8°. Venice: n. p., 1550. Basel UB FA VIII 20. Perhaps StCB p. 873/4821/41.

71. ____. שורשים. Ed. Elias Levita. Venice: Marco Antonio Giustiniani, 1552. Basel UB FA III 6/2. Perhaps StCB p. 874-5/4821/50.

72. Elijah Loanz. רנת דודים. 4°. Basel: Konrad Waldkirch, 1600. Basel UB FA V 42/3. StCB p. 56/335. Prijs no. 166.

---

[16] Buxtorf wrote concerning this book, "Videtur historicus esse: nam saepe in Tzemech citatur." Buxtorf's description of the book in *De Abbreviaturis*, 300 is curious, since he quoted it in *Aus was Ursachen*, Basel UB Ms A IX 78, f. 44r, which was completed about 1606. He may not have owned it, however, since he sought a copy in 1615. See M. Kayserling, "Richelieu," 79, quoting Walter Keuchen to Johannes Buxtorf, Frankfurt/M, April 10, 1615, Basel UB Ms G I 60: 322.

[17] The Buxtorf family library copy is the Lublin 1596 printing, presumably purchased after 1613. Basel UB FA III 10/1.

[18] Buxtorf said that it was a folio and was printed in 1528. *De Abbreviaturis*, 335.

73. Elijah Mizrahi. מלאכת המספר. *Arithmetica*. Trans. Sebastian Münster and Erasmus O. Schreckenfuchs. Basel: Henric-Petri, 1546. Basel UB Fr Gr A VI 72.StCB p. 946/4965/3. Prijs no. 75.

74. Elias Levita. ספר הדקוק. *Grammatica Hebraea*. Ed. and trans. Sebastian Münster. Basel: Hieronymus Froben & Nicolaus Episcopius, 1552. Basel UB FA VIII 41. StCB p. CIX, addition to page 2013/4. Prijs no. 87.

75. ____. הרכבה. *Composita Verborum & Nominum Hebraicorum*. Ed. and trans. Sebastian Münster. 8°. Basel: Johann Froben, 1525. Basel UB FA VIII 29/2. StCB p. 937/4960/14. Prijs no. 21.

76. ____. ספר טוב טעם. Ed. Sebastian Münster. 8°. Basel: Henricus Petri, 1539. Basel UB FA VIII 34. StCB p. 937/4960/18. Prijs no. 58.

77. ____. מסורת המסורת. Ed. Sebastian Münster. 8°. Basel: Henricus Petri, 1539. Basel UB FA VIII 34. StCB p. 938/4960/22. Prijs no. 58.

78. ____. מתורגמן. Cologne: Birckmannum, 1560. Basel UB FA III 20. See StCB p. 939/4960/27.

79. ____. פרקי אליהו. *Capitula Cantici*. Ed. Sebastian Münster. Basel: Johann Froben, 1527. Basel UB FA VIII 29/1. StCB p. 940/4960/37. Prijs no. 27.

80. ____. תשבי. 4°. (Hebrew text only). Isny: Paul Fagius, 1541. Basel UB FB III 10/6. StCB p. 942/4960/46. *Juden Schul*, 615, 650.

81. ____. תשבי. 4°. (Hebrew and Latin). Isny: Paul Fagius, 1541. Basel UB FB III 10/1. StCB p. 942/4960/46.

82. Gedaliah Ibn Yahya. שלשלת הקבלה. 4°. Cracow: Isaac b. Aaron Prostitz, 1596. Basel UB FA VI 28/2. StCB p. 1002/5120/1.

83. Hai ben Sherira Gaon. שירי מוסר השכל. Frankfurt a. O.: n. p., 1597. Basel UB FA VIII 13/3. StCB p. 1029/5183/9. *Thesaurus Grammaticus* (1609).

84. Hezekiah ben Abraham. מלכיאל. 4°. Tiengen: n. p., 1560. Basel UB FA VI 39/1. StCB p. 843/4743/1.

85. Isaac Aboab. מנורת המאור.[19] Exact edition uncertain, since Buxtorf gave no description in *De Abbreviaturis*. StCB p. 1071/5294/4-7. *Juden Schul*, 81, 91.

86. Isaac Abravanel. עטרת זקנים. 4°. Sabionetta: Tobias b. Eliezer Foa, 1557. Basel UB FA VI 35. StCB p. 1081/5302/40.

87. ____. נחלת אבות. 4°. Venice: Marco Antonio Giustiniani, 1545. Basel UB FA V 3/2. StCB p. 1081/5302/39, and p. 229/1435A. *De Abbreviaturis*, 314.

---

[19] The Buxtorf family library copy, FA III 26, was purchased in 1642.

88. Isaac Akrish. מעשה בית דוד בימי פרס. Basel: Konrad Waldkirch, 1599. Basel UB FA VI 34/3 (unicum). StCB p. 1085/5305/4. Prijs no. 159. Cohn, 63-64. Yiddish Booklist.

89. Isaac Arama. עקדת יצחק. f. Venice: Daniel Bomberg, 1573. Basel UB FA III 4. StCB p. 1093/5812.

90. Isaac ben Jacob Alfasi. ספר ר אלפסי. Cracow: Isaac b. Aaron Prostitz, 1597-1598. Basel UB FA III 3a, b, c. StCB p. 1090/5310/6. *Juden Schul*, 218, 286, 288, *passim*.

91. Isaac ben Joseph of Corbiel. עמודי גולה. Cracow: Isaac b. Aaron Prostitz, 1596. Basel UB FA V 32/2. StCB p. 1103/5337/4.

92. Isaac ben Meir of Düren. שערי דורא /איסור והיתר. 4°. Ed. Elijah Loanz. Basel: Konrad Waldkirch, 1599. Basel UB FA V 42/2. StCB p. 1106/5341/7. Prijs no. 164.

93. Isaac Nathan ben Kalonymos. מאיר נתיב. f. Basel: Ambrosius Froben, 1581. Basel UB FA III 29/1. StCB p. 1142/5399/4-5. Prijs no. 133.

94. Isaac Tyrnau. מנהגים. Cracow: n. p.,1597. Basel UB FA VI 29/3. StCB p. 316/2103. *Juden Schul*, 548.

95. Issachar Baer ben Moses Pethahiah. אמרי בינה. Prague: Moses b. Joseph Bezalel Katz, 1610. Basel UB FA V 37/1. StCB p. 1064/5286/1.

96. _____ . יש שכר. Prague: Moses b. Joseph Bezalel Katz, 1610. Basel UB FA V 37/1. StCB p. 1064/5286/3.

97. _____ . מקור בער. Prague: Moses b. Joseph Bezalel Katz, 1610. Basel UB FA V 37/1. StCB p. 1064/5286/4.

98. _____ . פתחי יה. Prague: Moses b. Joseph Bezalel Katz, 1610. Basel UB FA V 37/1. StCB p. 1065/5286/6.

99. Jacob ben Mordecai Pogetti. קיצור ראשית חכמה. Basel: Konrad Waldkirch, 1603. Basel UB FA VIII 28/1. StCB p. 1239/5577/2. Prijs no. 187. *Juden Schul*, 164, 279, 289, 556, 600.

100. Jacob Ibn Habib. בית יעקב. Venice: Marco Antonio Giustiniani, 1546-7. Basel UB FA IV 15. StCB p. 1199/5518/2. *Juden Schul*, 32, 91.

101. Jacob Luzzatto. כפתור ופרח. 4°. Basel: Ambrosius Froben, 1580. Basel UB FA V 1/1. StCB p. 1230/5571/1. Prijs no. 131. *Juden Schul*, 351, 481, 534.

102. Jacob Weil. שחיטות ובדיקות. 4°. Venice: n. p., 1605. Basel UB FA VIII 31/8.[20]

---

[20] Buxtorf presumably used the Basel, 1601 edition (Prijs no. 173) when he quoted from the book in *Juden Schul*, 565-573.

103. _____. שחיטות ובדיקות. 4°. Basel: Konrad Waldkirch, 1610. Basel UB FA V 47/2. StCB p. 1261/5631/20. Prijs no. 202.

104. Jediah Happenini ben Abraham Bedershi. בחינת עולם. 8°. Cracow : Isaac b. Aaron Prostitz, 1591. Basel UB FA VIII 25/1. StCB p. 1285/5670/6.

105. _____. בחינת עולם. Prague: n. p., 1598. Basel UB FA VI 17. StCB p. 1285/5670/7.

106. Jehiel Ashkenazi. היכל הי. 4°. Venice: Daniel Zanetti, (n. d., probably 1596-1606). Basel UB FA VI 4/2. StCB p. 1273/5654/1.

107. Jonah Gerundi. ספר חיי עולם. Freiburg/Br: Ambrosius Froben, 1583. Basel UB FA VI 24/2. StCB p. 1427/5859/29. Prijs no. 138. Cohn, 70. Yiddish Booklist.

108. _____. ספר יראה. 4°. Venice: [Giovanni di Farri?], 1544. Basel UB FA V 6/1. StCB p. 1425/5859/15 and 38.

109. _____. ספר היראה. Zürich: n. p., 1546. Basel UB FA VI 24. StCB p. 1427/5859/28. Cohn, 69-70. Yiddish Booklist.

110. _____. שערי תשובה. Venice: [Giovanni di Farri?], 1544. Basel UB FA V 6/1. StCB p. 1429/5859/38.

111. Joseph Albo. עקרים. Lublin: Kalonymos Jafe, 1597. Basel UB FA VI 18/1. StCB p. 1444/5882/6. *Juden Schul*, 23.

112. Joseph ben Eliezer Halfan of Posen. אורח חיים. Basel: Konrad Waldkirch, 1602. Basel UB FA V 18/2. StCB p. 518/3391. Prijs no. 176. Yiddish Booklist. *Juden Schul*, 260.

113. Joseph ben Gikatilla. שערי אורה. 4°. Cracow : Isaac b. Aaron Prostitz, 1600. Basel UB FA V 32/1. StCB p. 1466/5923/12.

114. Judah ben Kalas. ספר מוסר. 4°. Cracow: Isaac b. Aaron Prostitz, 1597-8. Basel UB FA VI 28. StCB p. 1300/5693/3.

115. Joseph Karo שלחן ערוך. Cracow: Naphtali b. Tobias Altschul of Lublin, 1593-4. Basel UB FA IV 13. StCB p. 1482/5940/10.

116. Judah ben Samuel he-Hasid of Regensburg. חסידים. Basel: Ambrosius Froben, 1581. Basel UB FA V 1/2. StCB p. 1322/5701/2. Prijs no. 132. *Juden Schul*, 600.

117. _____. שיר היחוד. Tiengen: n. p., 1560.[21] Basel UB FA VI 39/3. StCB p. 503-4/3313.

---

[21] Buxtorf thought that it was printed in Freiburg/Br. *De Abbreviaturis*, 326.

118. Judah de Modena. סור מר. 8°. Venice: Giovanni di Gara, 1595. StCB 1351/5745/22.[22]

119. Judah Ha-Levi. כוזרי. 4°. Venice: n. p., 1547. Basel UB FA VI 37. StCB p. 1340/5738/2.

120. _____. כוזרי. 4°. Venice: Giovanni di Gara, 1594. Basel UB FA V 11. StCB p. 1340/5738/3.

121. Judah Ibn Tibbon. רוח חן. Trans. Johannes Isaac Levita. Cologne: Maternum Colinum, 1555. Basel UB FA VIII 46/1. StCB p. 639/4038.

122. Kalonymus ben Kalonymus. אגרת בעלי חיים. 8°. Mantua: Vintorin Rufinelli, 1557. Basel UB FA VIII 25/2. StCB p. 1579/6068/5.

123. Machir of Toledo. אבקת רוכל. 8°. Venice: Giorgio de Cavalli, 1566. Basel UB FA VIII 28/4. StCB p. 1641/6196/3. *Juden Schul*, 625-646.

124. Machir of Toledo. אוקת רוכל. 8°. Basel UB Ms R III 3.

125. Meir Aldabi. שבילי אמונה. 4°. Riva de Trento: Joseph Ottolenghi, 1558. StCB p. 1690/6288/1. *De Abbreviaturis*, p. 314.

126. Meir Arama. אורים ותומים. Venice: n. p., 1608.[23] Basel UB FA V 14/2. StCB p. 1694/6291/1.

127. Menahem ben Benjamin Recanati. טעמי מצות. 4°. Basel : Ambrosius Froben, 1581. Basel UB FA V 1/3. StCB p. 1736/6363/2. Prijs no. 134.

128. _____. (רקנטי) פרוש על תורה. StCB p. 1736-7/6363/1-5?[24] *Juden Schul*, 462.

129. Mordecai Jaffe. לבוש מלכות. Prague: Moses b. Joseph Bezalel, 1609. Basel UB FA IV 10a, b, c. StCB p. 1664/6229/6.

130. Moses Alfalas. הואיל משה. Venice: Daniel Zanetti, 1597. Basel UB FA VI 8/1 (T. 1-2). StCB p. 1769/6428/1.

131. Moses Alsheikh. חלקת מחוקק. 4°. Venice: Giovanni di Gara, 1603. Basel UB FA V 20/2. StCB p. 1777/6431/16 and p. 59/353.

132. Moses Ibn Habib. מרפא לשון. 8°. Venice: Daniel Bomberg, 1546. Basel UB FA VIII 28/3. StCB p. 1786/6445/2. *Thesaurus Grammaticus*, 628-629.

133. Moses ben Jacob of Coucy. ספר מצות גדול. f. Venice: Daniel Bomberg, 1547. Basel UB FA IV 12. StCB p. 1797/6453/4. *Juden Schul*, 56.

---

[22] The book was missing in the 1705 inventory.
[23] Steinschneider wrote, "... male 1 6 0 8 ap. Sabb., W[1.3] 1386 = 1366c, Catal. Bibl. Bodl. I, 106a et Ros., Diz. -- Liber non frequens."
[24] The exact imprint is uncertain since no copy was sold to Basel UB.

134. Moses ben Maimon. אגרת ר משה בן מימון על גזרת משעטי הכוכבים. Trans. Johannes Isaac Levita. Cologne: Maternum Colinum, 1555. Basel UB FA VIII 46/2. StCB p. 1059/5273/4.

135. Moses ben Maimon. יד חזקה. f. Venice: Aloys Bragadini, 1574-5. Basel UB FA IV 16, 16a, b, c. StCB p. 1871-2/6513/7.

136. _____. הגיון. Trans. Sebastian Münster. Basel: Froben, 1527. Basel UB FA VIII 33. StCB p. 1893/6513/96. Prijs no. 28.

137. Moses ben Nahman. אגרת הקדש. Basel: Ambrosius Froben, 1580. Basel UB FA VIII 25/4. StCB p. 1953/6532/10. Prijs no. 127.

138. _____. פירוש על התורה. f. Venice: Marco Antonio Giustiniani, 1545. Basel FA III 16. StCB p. 1961/6532/52. *Juden Schul*, 88.

139. Moses Cordovero. פרדס רמונים. Cracow: Isaac b. Aaron, 1592. Basel UB FA IV 4/1. StCB p. 1794/6452/8. *De Abbreviaturis*, 322.

140. Moses de Leon. נפש חכמה. 4°. Basel: Konrad Waldkirch, 1608. Basel UB FA V 29/3. StCB p. 1852/6505/1. Prijs no. 194.

141. Moses Henochs. ברנט שפיגל. Basel: Konrad Waldkirch, 1602. Basel UB FA V 18/1. StCB p. 1283/6473/1. Prijs no. 175. Yiddish Booklist.

142. Moses Kimhi. מהלך שבילי הדעת. Ed. Sebastian Münster. 8°. Basel: Andreas Cratander (=Hartmann), 1531. Basel UB FA VIII 19/1. StCB p. 1842/6498/7. Prijs no. 33. Acquired in 1610/1611 from library of Polanus.

143. Moses Shedel. מעשה יציאת מצרים. Prague: Judah Löb, 1604. Basel UB FA VI 13/1. Cohn, 64-66. See StCB p. 177, no. 1184. Yiddish Booklist.

144. Nathan ben Yehiel. ערוך. Basel: Konrad Waldkirch, 1599. Basel UB FA III 24. StCB p. 2042/6632/5. Prijs no. 158.

145. _____. ערוך הקצור. Cracow: Isaac b. Aaron Prostitz, 1591. Basel UB FA VI 2. StCB p. 2042/6632/9.

146. Pethahiah ben Jacob. סיבוב. 4°. Prague: Moses b. Joseph Bezalel Katz, 1600. Basel UB FA VI 10a. Cohn, 60-61. Yiddish Booklist.[25]

147. Shabbethai Sheftel Horowitz of Prague. שפע טל. Hanau: [Hans Jacob Henne], 1612. Basel UB FA IV 4/2. StCB p. 2241/6865/2.

148. Samuel ben Isaac ha-Sardi. תרומות. f. Prague: Moses b. Joseph Bezalel Katz, 1605. Basel UB FA III 17. StCB p. 2476/7069/1.

149. Samuel Valerio. חזון למועד. Venice: Giovanni di Gara, 1586. Basel UB FA V 2/1. StCB p. 2494/7080/1 and p. 46/274.

---

[25] StCB p. 2097/6728/3 doubted this imprint's existence.

150. Simeon ben Samuel. אדם שכלי. Tiengen: n. p., 1560.[26] Basel UB FA VI 26/2, FA VI 39/2. StCB p. 2629/7224/1.

151. Simeon Kara. ילקוט. Cracow: Isaac b. Aaron Prostitz, 1595-6. Basel UB FA III 14a. StCB p. 2602/7197/3.

152. Simon Levi Günzburg. מנהגים. 4°. Venice: Giovanni di Gara, 1601. Basel UB FA V 47/1. StCB p. 599/3821. Cohn, 56. Yiddish Booklist.

153. Solomon ben Abraham Ibn Adret. עבודת הקודש. 4°. Venice: Daniel Zanetti, 1601-2. StCB p. 2272/6891/22. De Abbreviaturis, 322.

154. Solomon ben Abraham of Urbino. אהל מועד. 4°. Venice: Marco Antonio Giustiniani, 1548. Basel UB FA VI 34/1. StCB p. 2391/6980/1.

155. Solomon ben Jehiel Luria. יריעות שלמה. 4°. Prague: Moses b. Joseph Bezalel Katz, 1609. Basel UB FA V 37/3. StCB p. 2368/6950/18.

156. Solomon ben Judah Ibn Gabirol. מבחר הפנינים. 4°. Cremona: Vincent Conti, 1558. Basel UB FA V 37a/2. StCB p. 2323/6916/3.

157. Solomon ben Mordecai of Miendzyrecz. מזבח הזהב. Basel: Konrad Waldkirch, 1602. Basel UB FA V 29/2. StCB p. 2371/6952.

158. Solomon Ibn Verga. שבט יהודה. 4°. Cracow: Isaac b. Aaron Prostitz, 1591. Basel UB FA V 35/2. StCB p. 2396/6982/8. Yiddish Booklist. *Juden Schul*, 511-514, 614, 623.

159. Yeshua ben Joseph ha-Levi. הליכות עולם. 4°. Mantua: Tommas Rufinelli, 1593. Basel UB FA V 32/3. StCB p. 1393/5817/5.

VI. *Marginal Commentaries*

1*. Hezekiah ben Manoah. חזקוני. Biblical commentary. StCB p. 844/4746/1.

2*. Isaac Ibn Gabbai. כף נחת. Commentary on the Mishnah. StCB p. 1110/5348.

3*. Issachar ben Naphtali. מתנות כהומה. Commentary on *Midrash rabba*. StCB p. 1063/5283/4.

4*. Joseph Qaro. כסף משנה. StCB p. 1495/5940/109. Commentary on Maimonides, *Mishneh Torah*.

5*. Levi Ibn Habib. פירוש. StCB p. 1606/6136/1. Commentary on Maimonides, *Mishneh Torah*.

---

[26] Buxtorf thought that it was printed in Freiburg/Br. *De Abbreviaturis*, 272.

BIBLIOGRAPHY

Unpublished Sources

Amsterdam: Universiteitsbibliotheek (Bibliotheca Rosenthaliana)
Brieven-collectie van de Bibliotheca Rosenthaliana, Ms. 110

Basel: Staatsarchiv
Erziehungsakten CC 8; Handel und Gewerbe JJJ 4; Kirchenarchiv W 12, 2;
Klosterarchiv 001: Domstift; Protokolle, Kleiner Rat, vols. 9, 15, 16; Ratsbücher
A6; Universitätsarchiv B 1, C 1, C 6, R III 1, VII, VIII 5, 1

Basel: Universitätsbibliothek
Mss. A III 1; A IX 78, A XII 3, 7, 9-11, 16, 19, 20; AN VI 26z; AN IX 1; AR I
26, 31; C VIa 31; EL I; F IX 41; FA II 42; Fr Gr G V 16/3; Fr Gr II 8: 257; Fr
Gr II 9: 89; Fr Gr III 22a-b; G I 59-63, 66; G II 9; G2 II 24; Ki Ar 26b, 56, 189,
190a; R III 3; R III 7; Slg Geigy Hgb no. 736; VB O 11b, O 11g, Q 73

Bernoulli, Rudolf. *Basler Akademiker Katalog*. (Handschriftenabteilung)
Prijs, Joseph. *Hebräisches Titelregister*. (Lesesaal)

Bern: Burgerbibliothek
Ms. Cod. 200, 3

Copenhagen: Royal Library
Ms. E dan var. 13, 8°

Geneva: Archives Turrettini (Private Collection)
Ms. Fonds 1: Dd 4.1, 4.3, 5.1, 5.6, 5.7

Gotha: Forschungsbibliothek
Ms. Chart. A 130: 134

Leeuwarden: Friesland Provincial Library
Ms. 731

Leiden: Universiteitsbibliotheek
Mss. BPL 285 I; Cun 2; Pap 2

London: British Library
Mss. Add 5158; Add 22 905; Burney Ms 363; OR. 5395

Magdeburg: Staatsarchiv
Abt. Kothen C 18, 30, 31

Oxford: Bodleian Library
Ms. Rawlinson 76 (b): 91

Stuttgart: Württembergische Landesbibliothek
Ms. Cod hist. 2° 563

Utrecht: Universiteitsbibliotheek
Ms 987

Wiesbaden: Hessisches Staatsarchiv
Abt. 171 H 322C, R 1334b, Z 1931

Zürich: Staatsarchiv
Ms. E II 383

Zürich: Zentralbibliothek
Mss. Car I 96; F-45; F-51; F-167; F-169; S-149-151, 154-155, 160, 162

Published Primary Sources

I. Anonymous Hebrew Works

אגרות שלומים. Augsburg: Hayyim Schwarz, 1534.

אגרות שלומים. *Sylvula Epistolarum Hebraicarum.* Ed. and Trans. Johannes Buxtorf. Basel: Konrad Waldkirch, 1603.

מגלת ספר. Cremona: n. p., 1566.

מגלת ספר. Basel: Konrad Waldkirch, 1610.

II. Bibles

מקרא גדולה. 4 Vols. Venice: Daniel Bomberg, 1524-25; reprint ed., Jerusalem: Makor, 1972.

מקרא גדולה. 4 Vols. Venice: Daniel Bomberg, 1546-1548.

Biblia Rabbinica. Ed. Johannes Buxtorf. 4 Vols. Basel: Ludwig König, 1618-1619.

Biblia sacra Polyglotta. Ed. Brian Walton. 6 Vols. London: Thomas Roycroft, 1657.

חומש תורה. 3 parts. Venice: Aaron Pesaro, 1590-91.

III. Other Published Sources

Avianus, Hieronymus. *Clavis Poeseso Sacrae.* Leipzig: Gottfried Gros, 1627.

The Babylonian Talmud. Ed. I. Epstein. 18 Vols. London: Soncino, [1961].

Bahya ben Asher. ביאור על התורה. Ed. Charles Chavel. 3 Vols. Jerusalem: Mossad Ha-Rav Kook, 1966-1968.

_____. כד הקמח *Encyclopedia of Torah Thoughts*. Ed. and Trans. Charles B. Chavel. New York: Shilo, 1980.

_____. כתבי רבינו בחיי. Ed. Haim Dov Shevel. Jerusalem: Mossad Ha-Rav Kook, 1970.

Bellarmine, Robert. *Opera omnia*. 12 Vols. Paris: Louis Vives, 1870-1874; reprint: Frankfurt a. M.: Minerva GMBH, 1965.

Burman, Pieter. *Sylloges epistolarum a viris illustribus scriptarum*. 5 Vols. Leiden: S. Luchtmans, 1727.

Buxtorf, Johannes. *De Abbreviaturis Hebraicis liber novus & copiosus*. Basel: Konrad Waldkirch, 1613.

_____. *De Abbreviaturis Hebraicis liber novus & copiosus*. Ed. Johannes Buxtorf II. Basel: Konrad Waldkirch, 1640.

_____. *De Abbreviaturis Hebraicis liber novus & copiosus*. Herborn: Johann Nicholai Andraeae, 1708; reprint ed., Hildesheim: Georg Olms, 1985.

_____. *Concordantiae Bibliorum Hebraice et Chaldaice*. Ed. Bernhard Baer. Stettin: E. Schrentzelius, 1861.

_____. "Epistola Johannis Buxtorfii, P. ad Matthiam Martinium." *Bibliotheca historico-philologico-theologica* classis 4, fascicle 3 (1721): 598-603.

_____. *Epitome Grammaticae Hebraeae*. Basel: Konrad Waldkirch, 1613.

_____. *Epitome Grammaticae Hebraeae*. Basel: Konrad Waldkirch, 1617.

_____. ספר השרשים קצור. *Epitome Radicum Hebraicum*. Basel: Konrad Waldkirch, 1600.

_____. *Epitome Radicum Hebraicum et Chaldaicum*. Basel: Konrad Waldkirch, 1607.

_____. *Grammaticae Chaldaicae et Syriacae Libri III*. Basel: Konrad Waldkirch, 1615.

_____. *Institutio Epistolaris Hebraica*. Ed. Johannes Buxtorf II. Basel: Ludwig König, 1629.

_____. *Juden Schul*. Basel: Sebastian Henricpetri, 1603.

_____. *Lexicon Chaldaicum Talmudicum et Rabbinicum*. Ed. Johannes Buxtorf II. Basel: Ludwig König, 1639; reprint ed., Hildesheim: Georg Olms, 1977.

_____. *Lexicon Hebraicum et Chaldaicum*. Basel: Konrad Waldkirch, 1615.

_____. *Manuale Hebraicum et Chaldaicum*. Basel: Konrad Waldkirch, 1613.

_____. *Praeceptiones de Grammaticae Lingua Hebraea*. Basel: Konrad Waldkirch, 1605.

_____. *Synagoga Iudaica*. Ed. Johannes Buxtorf II. Basel: L. König, 1640.

_____. *Thesaurus Grammaticus Linguae Sanctae Hebraeae*. 1st Ed. Basel: Konrad Waldkirch, 1609.

_____. *Thesaurus Grammaticus Linguae Sanctae Hebraeae*. Basel: Haered. Ludovici Regis, 1651; reprint ed., Hildesheim: Georg Olms, 1981.

_____. *Tiberias Sive Commentarius Masorethicus*. 4°. Basel: Ludwig König, 1620.

_____. *Tiberias Sive Commentarius Masorethicus*. fol. Basel: Ludwig König, 1620.

Buxtorf III, Johannes. ספר קבוצים *sive Catalecta Philologico-Theologica*. Basel: Johann Ludwig König, 1707.

Buxtorf-Falkeisen, Karl. *Johannes Buxtorf Vater, Prof. ling. hebr., 1564-1629, erkannt aus seinem Briefwechsel*. Basel: Bahnmaier's Buchhandlung (C. Detloff), 1860.

Cappel, Louis. *Commentarii et notae criticae in Vetus Testamentum ... Vindiciae hactenus ineditae*. Ed. Jacques Cappel. Amsterdam: P. & J. Blaeu, 1689.

_____. סוד הניקוד נגלה *Hoc est Arcanum Punctationis Revelatum. Sive De Punctorum Vocalium & Accentuum apud Hebraeos vero & germana Antiquitate, Diatriba*. Leiden: Johannes Maire, 1624.

Carmina Gratulatoria ab amicis scripta, in Honorem Ornatiss. Viri D. M. Balthasiris Crosnievvicii, Lituani cum ei in Illustri Academic Basiliensi Gradus Docturae Theologicae 8. Septembr. conferretur à Clariß. & excellentiß. viro, Dn. Amando Polano à Polansdorf, SS. Theo. D. & Professore, Decano Facultatis Theologicae. Basel: Conrad Waldkirch, 1601.

Chevallier, Antoine. *Rudimenta Hebraicae Linguae, Accurata methodo & brevitate conscripta*. Ed. Pierre Chevallier. Geneva: Fransiscus Le Preux, 1590.

Christliche Leich=und Trost-Predigten Darinn allerhand außerlesene Text heiliger Schrifft/ auß dem Alten und Newen Testament/ grundlich erkläret/ nutzlich appliciert, auff läidige Trawr=und Todes-fähl gerichtet/ beneben auch Christlicher Ehren-leuthen seliges Absterben beschreiben wird. Basel: Georg Decker, 1657.

Coton, Pierre. *Genève Plagiaire*. Paris: Sebastien Chappelet, 1618. (St. Paul MN: Lutheran Brotherhood Foundation Reformation Library, text-fiche).

Cunaeus, Petrus. *Petri Cunaei & Doctorum Virorum ad Eumdem Epistolae. Quibus accedit Oratio in obitum Bonaventurae Vulcanii.* Ed. Pieter Burmann. Leiden: Peter Vander Aa, 1725.

Cyprian, Ernst Salomon. *Clarorum virorum epistolae CXVII e Bibliothek Gothanae Autographis.* Leipzig: Jo. Frider. Gleditsch & Filium, 1714.

Drusius, Johannes. *Proverbiorum Classes duae, in quibus explicatur proverbia sacra, & ex sacris litteris orta: Item Sententiae Salomonis et allegoriae, & etc.* Franeker: Aegidius Radaeus, 1590

_____. *De Quaesitis per Epistolam.* Franeker: Aegidium Radaeum, 1595.

Flacius Illyricus, Matthias. *Clavis Scripturae Sacrae. De Sermone Sacrarum Literarum, in duas partes divisae.* Ed. Theodor Suicerius. Frankfurt and Leipzig: Hieronymus Christian Paulus, 1719.

Fuks, L. "Het Hebreeuwse Brievenboek van Johannes Drusius Jr. Hebreeuws en Hebraisten in Nederland Rondom 1600." *Studia Rosenthaliana* 3 (1969): 1-52.

Gans, David. צמח דוד. Prague: n. p., 1592.

Génébrard, Gilbert. *Chronographia in Duos Libros Distincta.* Louvain: Johann Foulerum, 1572.

_____. *EISAGOGE: Ad Legenda et Intelligenda Hebraeae et Orientalium sine Punctis Scripta.* Paris: Aegidius Corbinus, 1587.

Gordon, James. *Controversarum Epitomen.* Cologne: Johannes Kinchium, 1620. (St. Paul MN: Lutheran Brotherhood Foundation Reformation Library, text-fiche).

Hai Gaon b. Sherira. שירי מוסר השכל. Ed. Jacob Ebert. Frankfurt/O: n. p., 1596.

Herzog, Johann W. *Athenae Rauricae sive Catalolgus Professorum Academicae Basileensis ab anno MCCCCLX ad annum MDCCLXXVIII.* 2 Vols. Basel: Car. Aug. Serini, 1778-1780.

Hess, Ernst Friedrich. *Flagellum Iudaeorum. Juden Geissel.* Erfurt: Martin Wittel, 1599.

Isaac Nathan b. Kalonymus. ספר יאיר נתיב *Concordantiae Bibliorum Hebraeorum.* Basel: Ambrosius Froben, 1581.

Itterzon, G. P. "Nog Twintig Brieven van Gomarus." *Nederlands Archief voor Kerkgeschiedenis* 56 (1975-76): 412-449.

Jacob b. Hayyim ibn Adoniyah. *Introduction to the Rabbinical Bible, Hebrew and English.* Ed. Christian D. Ginsburg. 2d Ed. London: Longmans, Green, Reader & Dyer, 1867.

Junius, Franciscus. *Animadversiones ad controversiam secundam Christianae fidei*. Leiden: C. Plantin, 1600.

Kimhi, David. *The Commentary of David Kimhi on Isaiah*. Ed. Louis Finkelstein. Columbia University Oriental Studies, Vol. 19. New York: Columbia Univ. Press, 1926.

———. ספר השרשים. *Radicum Liber sive Hebraeum Bibliorum Lexicon*. Ed. J. H. R. Biesenthal and F. Lebrecht. Berlin: G. Bethge, 1847; reprint ed, Jerusalem: n. p., 1967.

Leges Scholae Herbornensis: Quam nuper Illustris ac Generosis Dominus Iohannes Comes a Nassovv Catzenelnbogen, Dietz, Vianden: Dominus in Bielstein & c. in oppido Herborna feliciter aperuit. [Neustadt a. d. Weinstraße: Matthaeus Harnisch], 1585.

Leucht, Johann Jacob. *Geistlicher Kauffmann/Christliche Leich-predigt anzeigend/Welches das edelste perle und wahrhaftes Keinot seye der Kinder Gottes ... Bey Christlicher Leich-Bestattung der Ehren=und Tugendreichen Frawen/Margaretha Curionin ...*. Basel: Georg Decker, 1659.

Leusden, Johannes. *Philologus Hebraeo-Mixtus*. Utrecht: Franciscus Halma, 1682.

Levita, Elias. *The Massoreth Ha-Massoreth of Elias Levita, Being an Explanation of the Massoretic Notes of the Hebrew Bible*. Trans. Christian D. Ginsburg. London: Longmans, Green, Reader & Dyer, 1867; reprint ed., New York: KTAV, 1968.

———. מתורגמן. Cologne: Birckmannum, 1560.

———. פרקי אליהו *Capitula Cantici*. Basel: Johann Froben, 1527.

Levita, Johannes Isaac. *Defensio Veritatis Hebraicae Sacrarum Scripturam, adversus Libros tres Reverend. D. Wilhelmi Lindani S. T. Doctoris, quos de optimo Scripturas interpretandi genere inscripsit*. Cologne: Jacob Soterem, 1559.

Lightfoot, John. *The Whole Works of the Rev. John Lightfoot*. Ed. John Rogers Pittman. 13 Vols. London: J. F. Dove, 1822-25.

Margaritha, Antonius. *Der Gantz Jüdisch Glaub*. Augsburg: Heynrich Steyer, 1530.

Martini, Raymond. *Pugio fidei Adversus Mauros et Judaeos, cum Observationibus Josephi de Voisin, et Introductione Jo. Benedicti Carpzovii*. Leipzig: Haeredum Friedrich Lanckisius, 1687; reprint ed., Farnborough Hants: Gregg International, 1969.

Martinius, Petrus. *Grammaticae Hebraeae Technologia*. Rupellae: Hieronymus Haultinus, 1590.

Mercier, Jean. *Tabulae in Grammaticen Linguae Chaldaeae, quae & Syriaca Dicitur.* Paris: Guillaume Morelium, 1560.

Merx, Adalbert, ed. "Johannes Buxtorf's des Vaters Targumcommentar Babylonia." *Zeitschrift für wissenschaftliche Theologie* 30 (1887): 280-299, 462-471; 31 (1888): 42-48.

Modena, Leon. *The Autobiography of a Seventeenth Century Venetian Rabbi: Leon Modena's Life of Judah.* Ed. and Trans. Mark R. Cohen. Princeton: Princeton Univ. Press, 1988.

_____. *The History of the Rites, Customes and Manner of Life of the Present Jews, throughout the World.* Trans. Edmund Chilmead. London: John Martin and John Ridley, 1650.

Moses b. Enoch Altschuler. שפיטל ברנט. Basel: Conrad Waldkirch, 1602.

Moses b. Jacob of Coucy. ספר מצות הגדול. 2 Vols. Toronto: Yeshivah Torath Chaim, 1972-1978.

Münster, Sebastian. *Briefe Latein und Deutsch.* Ed. and Trans. Karl Heinz Burmeister. Ingelheim/Rhein: Insel, 1964.

_____. *Chaldaica Grammatica.* Basel: Johann Froben, 1526.

_____. ספר הדקוק *Grammatica Hebraea Eliae Levitae Germani, per Seb. Munsterum versa & scholijs illustrata.* Basel: Johann Froben, 1552.

_____. ערוך *Dictionarium Chaldaicum.* Basel: Johann Froben, 1527.

Nathan ben Yehiel, ערך השלם *Aruch Completum.* Ed. Alexander Kohut. 8 Vols. in 4. Vienna: Georg Brög, 1878-92.

Neander, Michael. *Sanctae linguae Hebraeae Erotemata.* Basel: Bartholomäeus Franco, 1567.

Pagninus, Sanctes. *Epitome Thesaurus Linguae Sanctae Hebraeae.* Ed. F. Raphalengius. Antwerp: C. Plantin, 1588.

Platter, Felix. *Beschreibung der Stadt Basel 1610 und Pestbericht 1610/1611.* Ed. Valentin Lötscher. Basler Chroniken, Band 11. Basel and Stuttgart: Schwabe Verlag, 1987.

_____. *Tagebuch (Lebensbeschreibung) 1536-1567.* Ed. Valentin Lötscher. Basler Chroniken, no. 10. Basel: Schwabe, 1976.

Platter, Thomas the Younger. *Beschreibung der Reisen durch Frankreich, Spanien, England und die Niederlande 1595-1600.* Ed. Rut Keiser. 2 Vols. Basler Chroniken, no. 9. Basel and Stuttgart: Schwabe Verlag, 1968.

Polanus von Polansdorf, Amandus. *Syntagma Theologiae Christianae.* Geneva: Jacob Stoër, 1617.

Pomis, David de. צמח דוד. Venice: G. di Gara, 1587.

Praestantium ac Eruditorum virorum Epistolae Ecclesiasticae et Theologicae. Amsterdam: Henricum Dendrinum, 1660.

Quinquarboreus (=Cinqarbres), Johann. *De Notis Hebraeorum Liber, Hoc des De Literis Multarum Literarum vim habentibus, quae hactenus a viris doctissimis ex variis Hebraeorum authoribus sunt excerptae.* Paris: Martinum Juvenem, 1582.

Rivet, Andre. *Correspondence intégrale d'André Rivet et de Claude Sarrau.* Ed. Hans Bot and Pierre Leroy. 3 Vols. Amsterdam: APA-Holland University Press, 1978-1983.

_____. *Isagoge, Seu Introductio generalis, ad Scripturam Sacram Veteris & Novi Testamenti.* Leiden: Isaac Commelinius, 1627.

Rossi, Azariah de. מאור עינים. 2 Vols. Vilna: R. Romm, 1864-66.

Scaliger, Joseph J. *Epistolae omnes quae reperiri, potuerunt, nunc primum collectae ac editae.* Ed. Daniel Heinsius. Leiden: B. & A. Elzevir, 1627.

_____. *Scaligerana.* Cologne: Gerbrandum Scagen, 1667.

Schadaeus, Elias. *Oratio de Linguae Sanctae Origine Progressu, & Varia Fortuna, ad Nostrum usque Saeculum.* Strasbourg: Jodocus Martinus, 1591.

Schickhard, Wilhelm. בחינת הפרושים *Bechinath Happeruschim Hoc est Examinis Commentationum Rabbinicarum in Mosen Prodromus.* Tübingen: Johann-Alexander Cellius, 1624.

Seck, F. *Wilhelm Schickhard Briefwechsel.* 4 Vols. Tübingen: Typescript, 1975.

Simon, Richard. *Disquisitiones criticae de variis per diversa loca & Tempora Bibliorum Editionibus.* London: Richard Chiswel, 1684.

_____. *Histoire critique du Vieux Testament.* Rotterdam: R. Leers, 1685; reprint ed., Frankfurt/M: Minerva G. M. B. H, 1967.

_____. *Lettres Choisies de M. Simon, ou L'on Trouve un Grand nombre de faits anecdotes de Literature.* 2d Ed. 4 Vols. Rotterdam: R. Leers, 1702-1705; reprint ed., Frankfurt a. M.: Minerva, 1967.

Simon Levi Günzburg. מנהגים. Venice: Johannes di Gara, 1601.

Solomon ibn Verga. שבט יהודה. Ed. Azriel Shochet. Jerusalem: Mossad Bialik, 1946-1947.

Tossanus, Daniel. *Johannis Buxtorfii, Senioris, Linguae Sanctae in Academia Basileensi Professoris Publici, Vita et Mors, Quam Oratione Parentali, in frequenti Theologorum Auditorio, Basil, d. 22. Octobr. Anno M. DC. XXIX.* Basel: Ludwig König, 1630.

Turrettini, Benedict. *Défense de la fidélité des traductions de la S. Bible faties à Genève opposée au livre de Pierre Coton jésuite intitulé Genève plagiare.* Geneva: P. et J. Chouet, 1618. (St. Paul MN: Lutheran Brotherhood Foundation Reformation Library, text-fiche).

Ulrich, Johann Caspar. *Sammlung Jüdischer Geschichten, welche sich mit diesem Volk in dem XIII. und folgenden Jahrhunderten bis auf M DCC LX in der Schweiz von Zeit zu Zeit zugetragen. Zur Beleuchtung der allgemeinen Historie dieser Nation herausgetragen.* Basel: n. p.,1768; reprint ed., Farnborough Hants: Gregg International, 1969.

Urkundenbuch der Stadt Basel. Bd. 11: 1602-1797. Ed. Historischen und Antiquarischen Gesellschaft zu Basel. Basel: Helbing & Lichtenhahn, 1910.

Ussher, James. *The Whole Works of the Most Rev. James Ussher, D. D., Lord Archbishop of Armagh, and Primate of All Ireland.* 17 Vols. Dublin: Hodges, Smith, 1864.

Wackernagel, Hans Georg. *Die Matrikel der Universität Basel: 1460-1818.* 5 Vols. Basel: Verlag der Universitätsbibliothek, 1951-1980.

Walton, Brian. *Biblicus Apparatus Chronologico-Typographico-Philologus.* Zürich: Bodmerianus, 1673.

Published Secondary Works

Adelmann, Howard E. "Custom, Law, and Gender: Levirate Union among Ashkenazim and Sephardim in Italy after the Expulsion from Spain," 107-125. In: *The Expulsion of the Jews: 1492 and After.* Ed. Raymond B. Waddington and Arthur H. Williamson. Garland Studies in the Renaissance, Vol. 2. New York: Garland, 1994.

_____. "Rabbis and Reality: Public Activities of Jewish Women in Italy during the Renaissance and Catholic Restoration." *Jewish History* 5 (1991): 27-40.

Armbruster, Thomas. " Die jüdische Dörfer von Lengnau und Endingen," 38-86. In *Landjudentum im Süddeutschen- und Bodenseeraum. Wissenschaftliche Tagung zur Eröffnung des Jüdischen Museums Hohenems vom 9. bis 11. April 1991,* Forschungen zur Geschichte Vorarlbergs. Vol. 11. Dornbirn: Vorarlberger Verlagsanstalt, 1992.

Bacher, Wilhelm. "Kritische Untersuchungen zum Prophetentargum. Nebst einem Anhange über das gegenseitige Verhältnis der pentateuchischen Targumim." *Zeitschrift der deutschen Morgenländischen Gesellschaft* 28 (1874): 1-72.

Battenberg, J. Friedrich. "Reformation, Judentum und Landesherrliche Gesetzgebung. Ein Beitrag zum Verhältnis des protestantischen Landeskirchentums zu den Juden," 315-346. In *Reformatio et Reformationes. Festschrift für Lothar Graf zu Dohna zum 65. Geburtstag.*

Ed. Andreas Mehl und Wolfgang Christian Schneider. Darmstadt: Lehrdruckerei der Technische Hochschule Darmstadt, 1989.

Berner, Hans. *"Die Gute Correspondence." Die Politik der Stadt Basel gegenüber dem Fürstbistum Basel in den Jahren 1525-1585.* Basler Beiträge zur Geschichtswissenschaft, no. 158. Basel: Helbing & Lichtenhahn, 1989.

Bindseil, Heinrich Ernst, *Concordantiarum Homericarum Specimen cum Prolegomenis in quibus Praesertim Concordantiae Biblicae Recensentur earumque Origo et Progressus Declarantur.* Halle: Hendeliis, 1867.

Blau, Ludwig. Introduction to Leon Modena, *Leo Modenas Briefe und Schriftstücke: Ein Beitrag zur Geschichte des hebräischen Privatstils.* Ed. Ludwig Blau. Strasbourg: Karl J. Trübner, 1907.

Bos, Frans Lukas. *Johannes Piscator; ein Beitrag zur Geschichte der reformierten Theologie.* Kampen: Kok, [1932].

Brisman, Shimeon. *A History and Guide to Judaic Bibliography.* Vol. 1: *Jewish Research Literature.* Cincinnati and New York: Hebrew Union College Press and KTAV, 1977.

Brugman, J. "Arabic Scholarship," 203-215. In: *Leiden University in the Seventeenth Century: An Exchange of Learning.* Ed. Th. H. Linsingh Scheurleer and G. H. M. Posthumus Meyjes. Leiden: E. J. Brill, 1975.

Buri, Fritz. "Johann Jacob Grynaeus," 55-58. In: *Der Reformation Verpflichtet: Gestalten und Gestalter in Stadt und Landschaft Basel aus fünf Jahrhunderten.* Basel: Christoph Merian, 1979.

Burmeister, Karl Heinz. "Die jüdische Landgemeinde in Rheineck im 17. Jahrhundert," 22-37. In *Landjudentum im Süddeutschen- und Bodenseeraum. Wissenschaftliche Tagung zur Eröffnung des Jüdischen Museums Hohenems vom 9. bis 11. April 1991,* Forschungen zur Geschichte Vorarlbergs. Vol. 11. Dornbirn: Vorarlberger Verlagsanstalt, 1992.

_____. *Sebastian Münster: Versuch eines biographischen Gesamtbildes.* Basler Beiträge zur Geschichtswissenschaft, no. 91. Basel: Helbing & Lichtenhahn, 1963.

Burnett, Stephen G. "Buxtorf Family Papers," 71-88. In: Joseph Prijs, *Die Handschriften der Universität Basel: Die hebräische Handschriften.* Ed. Bernhard and David Prijs. Basel: Verlag der Universitätsbibliothek, 1994.

_____. "Calvin's Jewish Interlocutor: Christian Hebraism and Anti-Jewish Polemics during the Reformation." *Bibliothèque d'Humanisme et Renaissance* 55 (1993): 113-123.

_____. "Distorted Mirrors: Antonius Margaritha, Johann Buxtorf and Christian Ethnographies of the Jews." *Sixteenth Century Journal* 25 (1994): 275-287.

_____. "Hebrew Censorship in Hanau: A Mirror of Jewish-Christian Coexistence in Seventeenth Century Germany," 199-222. In: *The Expulsion of the Jews: 1492 and After*. Ed. Raymond B. Waddington and Arthur H. Williamson. Garland Studies in the Renaissance, Vol. 2. New York: Garland, 1994.

_____. "Johannes Buxtorf and the Circumcision Incident of 1619," *Basler Zeitschrift für Geschichte und Altertumskunde* 89 (1989): 135-144.

_____. "The Regulation of Hebrew Printing in Germany, 1555-1630: Confessional Politics and the Limits of Jewish Toleration." In: *Infinite Boundaries: Order, Re-Order, and Dis-Order in Early Modern German Culture*. Ed. Max Reinhart and Thomas Robisheaux. Sixteenth Century Essays and Studies. Kirksville: Sixteenth Century Journal Publishers, forthcoming.

Buschmann, Friedrich. "Geschichte der Stadt Camen," *Zeitschrift für vaterländische Geschichte und Altertumskunde* (Münster) 4 (1841): 177-288.

Bursill-Hall, G. L. "Mediaeval Grammatical Theories." *Canadian Journal of Linguistics* 9 (1963): 40-54.

_____. *Speculative Grammars of the Middle Ages. The Doctrine of Partes Orationis of the Modistae*. Approaches to Semiotics, no. 11. The Hague: Mouton, 1971.

Carmoly, Eliakim. "Varietes Critiques et Litteraires." *Revue orientale* (Brussels) 1 (1841): 344-348.

Centi, Timoteo M. "L'Attivita Letteraria di Santi Pagnini (1470-1536) Nel Campo delle Scienze Bibliche." *Archivum Fratrem Praedicatorum* 15 (1945): 5-51.

Chazan, Robert. *Daggers of Faith: Thirteenth Century Christian Missionizing and Jewish Response*. Berkeley: Univ. of California Press, 1989.

Cohen, Jeremy. *The Friars and the Jews: The Evolution of Medieval Anti-Judaism* (Ithaca: Cornell University Press, 1982.

Cohen, Mark R. "Leone da Modena's *Riti*: a Seventeenth Century Plea for Social Toleration of the Jews." *Jewish Social Studies* 34 (1972): 287-319.

Cohen, Menachem. "Systems of Light *Gayot* in Medieval Biblical Manuscripts and their Importance for the History of the Tiberian System of Notation." *Textus* 10 (1982): 44-83.

Cohn, A. "Ueber einige alte Drucke." In: *Festschrift zum Siebzigsten Geburtstage David Hoffmann's. Gewidmet von Freunden und Schülern*. 3 Vols. Ed. Simon Eppenstein, Meir Hildesheimer and Joseph Wohlgemuth, 1: 46-70. Berlin: Louis Lamm, 1914; reprint ed., New York: Arno, 1980.

Derenbourg, Joseph. "L'Édition de la Bible Rabbinique de Jean Buxtorf." *Revue des études juives* 30 (1895): 70-78.

Diest, F. E. *Towards the Text of the Old Testament.* Trans. W. K. Winckler. Pretoria: N. G. Kerkboekhandel Transvaal, 1987.

Dunn, E. Catherine. "Lipsius and the Art of Letter-Writing." *Studies in the Renaissance* 3 (1956): 145-156.

Epstein, Morris. "Simon Levi Ginzburg's Illustrated Custumnal (Minhagim-Book) of Venice, 1593, and its Travels." *Proceedings of the Fifth World Congress of Jewish Studies, Jerusalem, 3-11, August 1969.* Vol. 4: 197-218.

Ettinger, S. "The Beginnings of the Change in the Attitude of European Society Towards the Jews." *Scripta Hierosolymitana* 7 (1961): 193-219.

Faulenbach, Heiner. *Die Struktur der Theologie des Amandus Polanus von Polansdorf.* Basler Studien zur historischen und systematischen Theologie, Bd. 9. Zürich: EVZ-Verlag, 1967.

Fox, Marvin. "Nahmanides on the Status of the Aggadot: Perspectives on the Disputation at Barcelona, 1263." *Journal of Jewish Studies* 40 (1989): 95-109.

Freedman, Joseph S. "Cicero in Sixteenth- and Seventeenth-Century Rhetorical Instruction." *Rhetorica* 4 (1986): 227-254.

———. "Philosophy Instruction within the Institutional Framework of Central European Schools and Universities during the Reformation Era." *History of Universities* 5 (1985): 117-166.

Friedenwald, Harry. "Apologetic Works of Jewish Physicians," 31-68. In: Idem. *The Jews and Medicine: Essays.* Vol. 1. Baltimore: The Johns Hopkins Press, 1944.

Friedman, Jerome. *The Most Ancient Testimony: Christian Hebraica in the Age of Renaissance Nostalgia.* Athens, OH: Ohio Univ. Press, 1983.

Friedrich, Martin. *Zwischen Abwehr und Bekehrung. Die Stellung der deutschen evangelischen Theologie zum Judentum im 17. Jahrhundert.* Beiträge zur historischen Theologie, no. 72. Tübingen: J. C. B. Mohr (Paul Siebeck), 1988.

Geiger, Ludwig. *Das Studium der Hebräischen Sprache in Deutschland vom Ende des XV. bis zur Mitte des XVI Jahrhunderts.* Breslau: Schletter'sche Buchhandlung, 1870.

Geiger, Max. *Die Basler Kirche und Theologie im Zeitalter der Hochorthodoxie.* Zürich: Evangelischer Verlag, 1952.

Gesenius, Wilhelm. *Geschichte der hebräischen Sprache und Schrift: Eine philologisch-historische Einleitung in die Sprachlehren und Worterbücher der hebräischen Sprache.* Leipzig: Friedrich Christian Vogel, 1815; reprint ed., Hildesheim: Georg Olms, 1973.

_____. *Gesenius' Hebrew Grammar*. Ed. Emil Kautzsch and A. E. Cowley. 2d English Ed. Oxford: Clarendon, 1910; reprint ed., Oxford: Clarendon, 1983.

Gildersleeve, B. L. and Gonzalez Lodge. *Gildersleeve's Latin Grammar*. 3d Ed. New York: University Publishing Co., 1898.

Gilly, Carlos. "Quelques additions à la Bibliographie des manuscrits de Guillaume Postel," 41-77. In: *Guillaume Postel 1581-1981, Actes du Colloque International d'Avranches 5-9 septembre 1981*. Paris: Éditions de la Maisnie, 1985.

_____. *Spanien und der Basler Buchdruck bis 1600*. Basler Beiträge zur Geschichtswissenschaft, no. 151. Basel: Helbing & Lichtenhahn, 1985.

Goshen-Gottstein, Moshe. "Foundations of Biblical Philology in the Seventeenth Century: Christian and Jewish Dimensions," 77-94. In: *Jewish Thought in the Seventeenth Century*. Ed. Isadore Twersky and Bernard Septimus. Cambridge, MA: Harvard Univ. Press, 1987.

_____. Introduction to *Biblia Rabbinica: A Reprint of the 1525 Venice Edition Edited by Jacob ben Hayim ibn Adoniya*, 4 vols. and separate introduction fascicle. Jerusalem: Makor, 1972.

_____. "The Textual Criticism of the Old Testament: Rise, Decline, Rebirth." *Journal of Biblical Literature* 102 (1983): 365-399.

_____. "The "Third Targum" on Esther and Ms. Neofiti 1." *Biblica* 56 (1975): 301-329.

_____. "The Thirteen Principles of Rambam according to al-Harizi's Translation." (Hebrew) *Tarbiz* 26 (1957): 185-196.

Grafton , Anthony. "Close Encounters of the Learned Kind. Joseph Scaliger's Table Talk." *The American Scholar* 57 (1988): 581-588.

_____. "Joseph Scaliger and Historical Chronology: The Rise and Fall of a Discipline." *History and Theory* 14 (1975): 156-185.

_____. and Lisa Jardine. *From Humanism to the Humanities. Education and the Liberal Arts in Fifteenth- and Sixteenth-Century Europe*. Cambridge: Harvard Univ. Press, 1986.

Grieve, Hermann. "Die hebräische Grammatik Johannes Reuchlins De rudimentis hebraicis." *Zeitschrift für die alttestamentlichen Wissenschaft* 90 (1978): 395-409.

Guggisberg, Hans R. "Reformierter Stadtstaat und Zentrum der Spätrenaissance: Basel in der zweiten Hälfte des 16. Jahrhunderts," 197-216. In: *Renaissance/Reformation: Gegensätze und Gemeinsamkeiten*. Ed. August Buck. Wolfenbütteler Abhandlungen zur Renaissanceforschung, no. 5. Wiesbaden: O. Harrassowitz, 1984.

Habermann, A. M. "Fragments of Letters from the Archives of Israel Zifroni in Basel," 272-289. (Hebrew) In A. M. Habermann, *Studies in the History of Hebrew Printers and Books*. Jerusalem: Rubin Mass, 1978.

Hamilton, Alastair. *William Bedwell the Arabist 1563-1632*. Publications of the Thomas Browne Institute of Leiden, n. s., no. 5. Leiden: E. J. Brill, 1985.

Heider, Hedwig. "Die Rechtsgeschichte des Deutschen Judentums bis zum Ausgang des Absolutismus und die Judenordnungen in den Rheinischen Territorialstaaten." Doctor of Legal Sciences, Universität Bielefeld, 1973.

Henderson, Judith Rice. "Erasmus on the Art of Letter-Writing," 331-355. In: *Renaissance Eloquence: Studies in the Theory and Practice of Renaissance Rhetoric*. Ed. James J. Murphy. Berkeley: Univ. of California Press, 1983.

Horowitz, Elliott. "'A Different Mode of Civility': Lancelot Addison on the Jews of Barbary." *Studies in Church History* 29 (1992): 309-325.

_____. "The Eve of the Circumcision: a chapter in the History of Jewish Night Life." *Journal of Social History* 23 (1989): 45-69.

Hsia, R. Po-Chia. "Christian Ethnographies of Jews in Early Modern Germany," 223-235. In: *The Expulsion of the Jews: 1492 and After*. Ed. Raymond B. Waddington and Arthur H. Williamson. Garland Studies in the Renaissance, Vol. 2. New York: Garland, 1994.

_____. *The Myth of Ritual Murder: Jews and Magic in Reformation Germany*. New Haven: Yale Univ. Press, 1988.

_____. "Printing, Censorship, and Antisemitism in Reformation Germany," 135-148. In: *The Process of Change in Early Modern Europe. Essays in Honor of Miriam Usher Chrisman*. Eds. Phillip N. Bebb and Sherrin Marshall. Athens OH: Ohio Univ. Press, 1988.

_____. *Society and Religion in Münster, 1535-1618*. Yale Historical Publications, Miscellany, no. 131. New Haven: Yale Univ. Press, 1984.

Hundsnurscher, Franz and Gerhard Taddey. *Die jüdischen Gemeinden in Baden. Denkmale, Geschichte, Schicksale*. Veröffentlichungen der Staatliche Archivverwaltung Baden-Württemberg, Bd. 19. Stuttgart: Kohlhammer, 1968.

Israel, Jonathan. *European Jewry in the Ages of Mercantilism*. Oxford: Clarendon, 1985.

Kalir, Joseph. "The Jewish Service in the Eyes of Christian and Baptized Jews in the 17th and 18th Centuries." *Jewish Quarterly Review* 56 (1966): 51-80.

Katchen, Aaron L. *Christian Hebraists and Dutch Rabbis: Seventeenth Century Apologetics and the Study of Maimonides' Mishneh Torah*. Harvard Judaic Texts and Studies, no. 3. Cambridge, MA: Harvard Univ. Press, 1984.

Katz, David S. "The Abendana Brothers and the Christian Hebraists of Seventeenth Century England." *Journal of Ecclesiastical History* 40 (1989): 28-52.

_____. *Philo-Semitism and the Readmission of the Jews to England, 1603-1655.* Oxford: Clarendon, 1982.

Katz, Jacob. "The Sources of Modern Anti-Semitism--Eisenmenger's Method of Presenting Evidence from Talmudic Sources," 210-216 (Hebrew); English summary, 227-228. In: *Proceedings of the Fifth World Congress of Jewish Studies,* Jerusalem, 3-11 August, 1969, Vol. 2. Jerusalem: World Union of Jewish Studies, 1969.

_____. *Exclusiveness and Tolerance: Studies in Jewish-Gentile Relations in Medieval and Modern Times.* Scripta Judaica, no. 3. Oxford: Oxford Univ. Press, 1961.

Kaufmann, David. "Lazarus de Viterbo's Epistle to Cardinal Sirleto Concerning the Integrity of the Text of the Hebrew Bible." *Jewish Quarterly Review* o. s. 7 (1894-95): 278-296.

_____. "Buxtorf's Aruchhandschrift, wiederaufgefunden." *Monatsschrift für Geschichte und Wissenschaft des Judentums* 34 (1885): 185-192, 225-233.

Kautzsch, Emil. *Johannes Buxtorf der Ältere.* Basel: C. Detloff, 1879.

Kayserling, M. "Richelieu Pére et Fils, Jacob Roman. Documents pour servir à l'histoire du commerce de la librairie juive au XVIIe siècle." *Revue des études juives* 8 (1884): 74-95.

Kirn, Hans-Martin. *Das Bild vom Juden im Deutschland des frühen 16. Jahrhunderts dargestellt an den Schriften Johannes Pfefferkorns.* Texts and Studies in Medieval and Early Modern Judaism, no. 3. Tübingen: J. C. B. Mohr (Paul Siebeck), 1989.

Kisch, Guido. "Die Zensur jüdischer Bücher in Böhmen. Beiträge zu ihrer Geschichte, 326-360. In: Idem. *Forschungen zur Rechts-, Wirtschafts- und Sozialgeschichte der Juden.* Sigmaringen: Jan Thorbecke, 1979.

Klauber, Martin I. *Between Reformed Scholasticism and Pan-Protestantism: Jean-Alphonse Turretin (1671-1737) and Enlightened Orthodoxy at the Academy of Geneva.* Selinsgrove: Susquehanna University Press, 1994.

Kohn, Samuel. Review of Johannes Buxtorf, *Lexicon Chaldaicum, Talmudicum et Rabbinicum, Monatsschrift für Geschichte und Wissenschaft des Judentums* 15 (1866): 233-236.

Kohut, George A. "The Hebrew Letters of Jacob Alting," 70-76. In: *Festschrift für Aron Freimann zum 60. Geburtstage.* Soncino-Blätter, Bd. 4. Ed. Alexander Marx and Herrmann Meyer. Berlin: Soncino-Gesellschaft, 1935.

Könnecke, Gustav. *Hessisches Buchdruckerbuch enthaltend Nachweis aller bisher bekannt gewordenen Buchdruckereien des jetzigen Regierungsbezirks Cassel und des Kreises Biedenkopf.* Marburg: N. G. Elwert, 1894.

Kugel, James L. *The Idea of Biblical Poetry: Parallelism and its History.* New Haven: Yale Univ. Press, 1981.

_____. "The Influence of Moses ibn Habib's *Darkhei Noam*," 308-325. In: *Jewish Thought in the Sixteenth Century.* Ed. Bernard Dov Cooperman. Harvard University Center for Jewish Studies: Texts and Studies, no. 2. Cambridge MA: Harvard Univ. Press, 1983.

Kukenheim, Louis. *Contributions à L'Histoire de la Grammaire Grecque, Latine et Hébraïque à L'Époque de la Renaissance.* Leiden: E. J. Brill, 1951.

Laplanche, François *L'Écriture, Le Sacré et L'Histoire: Érudits et Politiques Protestants devant la Bible en France au XVIIe siècle.* Studies of the Institute of Intellectual Relations Between the West-European Countries in the Seventeenth Century, Vol. 12. Amsterdam: APA-Holland Univ. Press, 1986.

_____. *L'Evidence du Dieu Chrétien. Religion, culture et société dans l'apologétique protestante de la France classique (1576-1670).* Strasbourg: Associon des Publications de la Faculté de Théologie Protestante de Strasbourg, 1983.

Lebram, J. C. H. "De Hasidaeis: Over Joodse studiën in het oude Leiden." *Voordrachten Faculteitendag 1980* (Leiden, 1981): 21-31.

_____. "Ein Streit um die hebräischen Bibel und die Septuaginta," 21-63. In: *Leiden University in the Seventeenth Century: An Exchange of Learning.* Ed. Th. H. Linsingh Scheurleer and G. H. M. Postumus Meyjes. Leiden: E. J. Brill, 1975.

_____. "Hebräische Studien zwischen Ideal und Wirklichkeit an der Universität Leiden in den Jahren zwischen 1575-1619." *Nederlandsch Archief voor Kerkgeschiedenis* 56 (1975-76): 317-357.

Lesley, Arthur M. "Jewish Adaptations of Humanist Concepts in Fifteenth- and Sixteenth Century Italy," 51-66. In: *Renaissance Rereadings: Intertext and Context.* Ed. Maryanne Cline Horowitz, Anne J. Cruz and Wenday A. Furman. Urbana: Univ. of Illinois Press, 1988.

Lloyd Jones, G. *The Discovery of Hebrew in Tudor England: A Third Language.* Manchester: Manchester Univ. Press, 1983.

Menk, Gerhard. "Caspar Olevian während der Berleburger und Herborner Zeit (1577-1587). Ein Beitrag zum Selbstverständnis des frühen deutschen Kalvinismus." *Monatshefte für Evangelische Kirchengeschichte des Rheinlandes* 37/38 (1988-1989): 139-204

_____. *Die Hohe Schule Herborn in ihrer Frühzeit (1584-1660): Ein Beitrag zum Hochschulwesen des deutschen Kalvinismus im Zeitalter der*

Gegenreformation. Veröffentlichungen der Historischen Kommission für Nassau, no. 30. Wiesbaden: Historischen Kommission für Nassau, 1981.

Merx, Adalbert. "Bemerkungen über die Vocalisation der Targume." *Verhandlungen des fünften internationalen Orientalisten-Congresses* 2, 1 (Abhandlungen und Vorträge der semitischen und afrikanischen Section, 1) (1882): 145-225.

Muller, Richard A. "The Debate over the Vowel Points and the Crisis in Orthodox Hermeneutics." *Journal of Medieval and Renaissance Studies* 10 (1980): 53-72.

_____. *Post-Reformation Reformed Dogmatics*. Vol. 1: *Prolegommena to Theology*; Vol. 2: *Holy Scripture: The Cognitive Foundation of Theology*. Grand Rapids: Baker, 1987-1993.

Nordmann, Achilles. "Geschichte der Juden in Basel seit dem Ende der zweiten Gemeinde bis zur Einführung der Glaubens und Gewissensfreihiet. 1375-1875." *Basler Zeitschrift für Geschichte und Altertumskunde* 13 (1914): 1-190.

_____. "Über den Judenfriedhof in Zwingen und Judenniederlassungen im Fürstbistum Basel." *Basler Zeitschrift für Geschichte und Altertumskunde* 6 (1907): 120-151.

Ong, Walter J. *Ramus, Method and the Decay of Dialogue*. Cambridge, MA: Harvard Univ. Press, 1958.

Padley, G. A. *Grammatical Theory in Western Europe 1500-1700: The Latin Tradition*. Cambridge: Cambridge Univ. Press, 1976.

_____. *Grammatical Theory in Western Europe 1500-1700: Trends in Vernacular Grammar*. Cambridge: Cambridge Univ. Press, 1985.

Pagis, Dan. "Hebrew Metrics in Italy and the Invention of Hebrew Accentual Iambs." *ha-Sifrut* 4 (1973): 651-712 (Hebrew); English summary, xxxii-xl.

Pattison, Mark. *Isaac Casaubon 1559-1614*. 2d Ed. Oxford: Clarendon, 1892; reprint ed., Geneva: Slatkine Reprints, 1970.

Penkower, Jordan S. "Jacob Ben Hayyim and the Rise of the Biblia Rabbinica." 2 Vols. Ph.D. diss., Hebrew University, 1982 (Hebrew).

Percival, W. Keith . "Deep and Surface Structure Concepts in Renaissance and Medieval Syntactic Theory," 238-253. In: *History of Linguistic Thought and Contemporary Linguistics*. Ed. Herman Parret. Foundations of Communication. Berlin and New York: Walter de Gruyter, 1976.

_____. "Grammar and Rhetoric in the Renaissance," 303-330. In: *Renaissance Eloquence: Studies in the Theory and Practice of Renaissance Rhetoric*. Ed. James J. Murphy. Berkeley: Univ. of California Press, 1983.

Platt, J. E. "Sixtinus Amama (1593-1629): Franeker Professor and citizen of the Republic of Letters," 236-248. In: *Universiteit te Franeker: 1585-1811. Bijdragen tot de geschiedenis von de Friese hogeschool.* Ed. G. Th. Jensma, F. R. H. Smit and F. Westra. Leeuworden: Fryske Akademy, 1985.

Pollack, Herman. "An Historical Explanation of the Origin and Development of Jewish Books of Customs (*Sifre Minhagim*): 1100-1300." *Jewish Social Studies* 49 (1987): 195-216.

Popper, William. *The Censorship of Hebrew Books.* New York: The Knickerbocker Press, 1899.

Porges, N. "Der hebräische Index expurgatorius ספר הזיקוק." Vol. 2, part 2, 273-295. In: *Festschrift zum Siebzigsten Geburtstage A. Berliner's.* Ed. A. Freimann and M. Hildesheimer. 3 Vols. Frankfurt a. M.: J. Kauffmann, 1903.

Preus, Robert D. *The Inspiration of Scripture: A Study of the Theology of the Seventeenth Century Lutheran Dogmaticians.* 2d Ed. Edinburgh: Oliver and Boyd, 1957.

_____. *The Theology of Post-Reformation Lutheranism: A Study of Theological Prolegomena.* St. Louis: Concordia Publishing House, 1970.

Prijs, Joseph. *Die Basler Hebräischen Drucke (1492-1866).* Ed. Bernhard Prijs. Olten and Freiburg i. Br.: Urs Graf, 1964.

_____. *Die Handschriften der Universität Basel: Die hebräische Handschriften.* Ed. Bernhard and David Prijs. Basel: Verlag der Universitätsbibliothek, 1994.

Reinhard, Wolfgang. "Konfession und Konfessionalizierung in Europe," 165-189. In: *Bekenntnis und Geschichte. Die Confessio Augustana im historischen Zusammenhang.* Ed. Wolfgang Reinhard. Schriften der Philosophischen Fakultäten der Universität Augsburg, no. 20. München: Ernst Vögel, 1981.

Reis, Rotraud. "Zum Zusammenhang von Reformation und Judenvertreibung: Das Beispiel Braunschweig," 630-654. In: *Civitatum Communitas. Studien zum europäischen Städtewesen. Festschrift Hans Stoob zum 65. Geburtstag.* Eds. Helmut Jäger, Franz Petri, and Heinz Quirin. Part 2. Köln: Böhlau, 1984.

Rekers, B. *Benito Arias Montano (1527-1598).* Studies of the Warburg Institute, Vol. 33. London and Leiden: The Warburg Institute and E. J. Brill, 1972.

Rice, Eugene F. Jr. *Saint Jerome in the Renaissance.* Baltimore: Johns Hopkins Univ. Press, 1985.

Robinson, John F. "The Doctrine of Holy Scripture in Seventeenth Century Reformed Theology." Thèse de Doctorat ès Sciences Religièses, Université de Strasbourg, 1971.

Rosenfeld, Moshe N. "The Development of Hebrew Printing in the Sixteenth and Seventeenth Centuries," 92-100. In: *A Sign and a Witness: 2,000 Years of Hebrew Books and Illuminated Manuscripts*. Ed. Leonard Singer Gold. New York: Oxford Univ. Press, 1988.

_____. "Jüdischer Buchdruck am Beispiel der Sulzbacher Druckerei," 237-243. In: *Geschichte und Kultur der Juden in Bayern. Aufsätze*. Eds. Manfred Treml, Josef Kirmeier, and Evamaria Brockhoff. Veröffentlichungen zur Bayerischen Geschichte und Kultur, Nr. 17/88. München: Haus der Bayerischen Geschichte, 1988.

_____. *Der Jüdische Buchdruck in Augsburg in der ersten Hälfte des 16. Jahrhunderts*. London: By the Author, 1985.

Roth, Carl. "Die Bücherzensur im alten Basel." *Zentralblatt für Bibliothekswesen* 31 (1914): 49-67.

_____. "Stammtafeln einiger ausgestorbener Basler Gelehrtenfamilien. *Basler Zeitschrift für Geschichte und Altertumskunde* 16 (1917): 396-403.

Roth, Carl and Th. Schmidt. *Handschriftsproben zur Basler Geistesgeschichte*. Basel: R. Geering, 1926.

Roth, Cecil. "Immanuel Aboab's Proselytization of Marranos." *Jewish Quarterly Review* 23 (1932-33): 121-162.

_____. "The Strange Case of Hector Mendes Bravo." *Hebrew Union College Annual* 18 (1944): 221-243.

Roth, Cecil and Geoffrey Wigoder, eds. *Encyclopaedia Judaica*. Jerusalem: Macmillan, 1971-72. S. v. "Acrostics," by Nahum Sarna and Yehudah Klausner.

_____. *Encyclopaedia Judaica*. Jerusalem: Macmillan, 1971-72. S. v. "Sukkot," by Louis Jacobs and Abram Kanof.

Roth, Norman. "Forgery and Abrogation of the Torah: A Theme in Muslim and Christian Polemic in Spain." *Proceedings of the American Academy for Jewish Research* 54 (1987): 203-236.

Roussel, Bernard. "Un "École Rhénane d'Exégèse" (ca. 1525-1540)," 215-240. In: *Le Temps des Réformes et la Bible*. Ed. Guy Bedouelle and Bernard Roussel. Bible de Tous les Temps, no. 5. Paris: Beasuchesne, 1989.

Ruderman, David B. *The World of A Renaissance Jew: The Life and Thought of Abraham ben Mordecai Farissol*. Monographs of the Hebrew Union College Press, no. 6. Cincinnati: Hebrew Union College, 1981.

Sacerdote, Gustave. "Deux Index Expurgatoires de Livres Hébreux." *Revue des études juives* 30 (1895): 257-283.

Schertz, Chaim E. "Christian Hebraism in 17th Century England as Reflected in the Works of John Lightfoot." Ph.D. diss., New York University, 1977.

Schilling, Heinz. *Religion, Political Culture and the Emergence of Early Modern Society. Essays in German and Dutch History.* Trans. Stephen G. Burnett. Studies in Medieval and Renaissance Thought, no. 50. Leiden: E. J. Brill, 1992.

Schmuki, Karl. "Wann wurde in Schaffhausen die erste Druckerei eingerichtet? Zur Niederlassung des Buchdruckers Hans Conrad von Waldkirch in Schaffhausen." *Schaffhauser Beiträge zur Geschichte* 61 (1984): 29-42.

Schnederman, Georg. *Die Controverse des Ludovicus Cappellus mit den Buxtorfen über das Alter der hebräischen Punctation.* Leipzig: Hundertstund & Preis, 1878.

Schoeps, Hans Joachim. *Philosemitismus im Barock: Religions- und geistesgeschichtliche Untersuchungen.* Tübingen: J. C. B. Mohr, 1952.

Schreckenberg, Heinz. *Die christlichen Adversus-Judaeos-Texte und ihr literarisches und historisches Umfeld (1.-11. Jh.).* Europäische Hochschulschriften, Ser. 23: Theologie, Vol. 172. 2d Rev. Ed. Frankfurt a. M.: Peter Lang, 1990.

Schulze-Marmeling, Wilhelm. "Johannes Buxtorf der Ältere: Ein Leben für die Wissenschaft," 102-111. In: *100 Jahre Stätische Höhere Lehranstalt Kamen: Festschrift.* Ed. Theo Simon. Hemer=Sundwig: Schälter, n. d.

Schwab, Moïse. "Manuscrits Hébreux de Bâle." *Revue des études juives* 5 (1882): 253-257.

Secret, Francois. "Notes pour une histoire du Pugio Fidei a la Renaissance." *Sefarad* 20 (1960): 401-407.

Shulman, Nisson. *Authority and Community: Polish Jewry in the Sixteenth Century.* Hoboken, NJ and New York: KTAV Publishing House/Yeshiva Univ. Press, 1986.

Slatkine, Menahem M. *Origins of the Earliest Hebrew Bibliography.* Tel Aviv: n. p., 1958 (Hebrew).

Sonne, Isaiah. *Expurgation of Hebrew Books--the Work of Jewish Scholars. A Contribution to the History of Censorship of Hebrew Books in Italy During the Sixteenth Century.* New York: New York Public Library, 1943.

Staehelin, Andreas. *Geschichte der Universität Basel 1632-1818.* 2 Vols. Studien zur Geschichte der Wissenschaften in Basel, nos. 4-5. Basel: Helbing & Lichtenhahn, 1957.

_____. "Die Universität Basel und Ihre Deutschen Besucher von 1580 bis 1620," 77-99. In: *Das Reich und die Eidgenossenschaft 1580-1650. Kulturelle*

Wechselwirkungen im konfessionellen Zeitalter. Ed. Ulrich Im Hof and Suzanne Stehelin. Freiburg/U: Universitätsverlag, 1986.

Staehelin, Ernst. *Amandus Polanus von Polansdorf.* Studien zur Geschichte der Wissenschaften in Basel, Vol. 1. Basel: Helbing & Lichtenhahn, 1955.

_____. "Des Basler Buchdruckers Ambrosius Forben Talmudausgabe und Handel mit Rom." *Basler Zeitschrift für Geschichte und Altertumskunde* 30 (1931): 7-37.

Steiman, Sidney. *Custom and Survival. A Study of the Life and Work of Rabbi Jacob Molin (Moelln) known as Maharil (c. 1360 -1427) and his influence in establishing the Ashkenazic Minhag (customs of German Jewry).* New York: Bloch, 1963.

Steinschneider, Moritz. *Bibliographisches Handbuch über die theoretische und praktische Literatur für hebräische Sprachkunde. Mit Zusätzen und Berichtigungen von A. Freimann, M. Grunwald, E. Nestle, N. Porges, M. Steinschneider.* Hildesheim: Georg Olms Verlag, 1976.

_____. *Catalogus Codicum Hebraeorum Bibliothecae Academiae Lugduno-Batavae.* Leiden: E. J. Brill, 1858.

Steubing, Hermann. "Lebensnachrichten von den Herborner Theologen. Aus dem literarischen Nachlasse des D. Johann Hermann Steubing. Erste Lieferung. Caspar Olevian und Johannes Piscator." *Zeitschrift für historische Theologie* (Leipzig) 11/3 (1841): 74-138.

Steubing, Johann Herman. *Geschichte der hohen Schule Herborn.* Hadamer: Gelehrten Buchhandlung, 1823.

Tavard, George H. *Holy Writ or Holy Church? The Crisis of the Protestant Reformation.* New York: Harper, 1959.

Thommen, Rudolf. *Geschichte der Universität Basel, 1532-1632.* Basel: C. Detloff, 1889.

Trachtenberg, Joshua. *Jewish Magic and Superstition: A Study in Folk Religion.* New York: Atheneum, 1974.

Trunz, Erich. "Der deutsche Späthumanismus als Standeskultur," 147-181. In: *Deutsche Barockforschung: Dokumentation einer Epoche.* Ed. Richard Alewyn. Neue Wissenschaftliche Bibliothek, no. 7. Cologne: Kiepenheuer & Witsch, 1966.

Van Rooden, Peter T. "Conceptions of Judaism as a Religion in the Seventeenth Century Dutch Republic," *Studies in Church History* 29 (1992): 299-308.

_____. *Theology, Biblical Scholarship and Rabbinical Studies in the Seventeenth Century: Constantijn L'Empereur (1591-1648) Professor of Hebrew and Theology at Leiden.* Trans. J. C. Grayson. Studies in the History of Leiden University, Vol. 6. Leiden: E. J. Brill, 1989.

_____. and J. W. Wesselius. "The Early Enlightenment and Judaism: The "Civil Dispute" between Philippus van Limborch and Isaac Orobio de Castro (1687)." *Studia Rosenthaliana* 21 (1987): 140-153.

Van Stam, Frans Pieter. *The Controversy over the Theology of Saumur, 1635-1650. Disrupting Debates among the Huguenots in Complicated Circumstances.* Studies of the Institute Pierre Bayle, Nijmegen, no. 19. Amsterdam: APA-Holland University Press, 1988.

Vischer, Eberhard. "Die Lehrstuhle und der Unterricht an der theologischen Fakultät Basels seit der Reformation," 115-132. In: *Festschrift zur Feier des 450. Jährigen Bestehens der Universität Basel.* Ed. Rektor und Regenz der Universität Basel. Basel: Helbing & Lichtenhahn, 1910.

Voet, Leon. *The Golden Compasses: A History and Evaluation of the Printing and Publishing Activities of the Officina Plantiniana at Antwerp.* Vol. 2: *The Management of a Printing and Publishing House in Renaissance and Baroque.* Amsterdam:P Vangendt & Co., 1972.

_____. and Jenny Voet-Grisolle. *The Plantin Press (1555-1589): A Bibliography of the Works Printed and Published by Christopher Plantin at Antwerp and Leiden.* 6 Vols. Amsterdam: Van Hoeve, 1980-1983.

Wackernagel, Rudolf. *Geschichte der Stadt Basel.* 3 Vols. Basel: Helbing & Lichtenhahn, 1907-1924.

Weil, Gérard. *Élie Lévita Humaniste et Massoréte (1469-1549).* Studia Post-Biblica, Vol. 7. Leiden: E. J. Brill, 1963.

Weill, Georges. "Recherches sur la Démographie des Juifs d'Alsace du XVIe au XVIIIe Siècle." *Revue des études Juives* 130 (1971): 52-89.

Weissler, Chava. "The Religion of Traditional Ashkenazic Women: Some Methodological Issues." *AJS Review* 12 (1987): 73-94.

Weldler-Steinberg. Augusta. *Geschichte der Juden in der Schweiz vom 16. Jahrhundert bis nach der Emanzipation.* Ed. Florence Guggenheim-Grünberg. 2 Vols. Goldach: Schweizerischen Israelitischen Gemeindebund, 1966-1970.

Wesselius, J. W. "Johannes Drusius the Younger's Last Journey to England and his Hebrew Letter-Book." *Lias* 16 (1989): 159-175.

_____. Review of *Theology, Biblical Scholarship and Rabbinical Studies in the Seventeenth Century* by Peter T. Van Rooden, *Studia Rosenthaliana* 23 (1989): 214-216.

Whaley, Joachim. *Religious Toleration and Social Change in Hamburg, 1529-1819.* Cambridge: Cambridge University Press, 1985.

Willi, Thomas. "Übersicht über den Inhalt der Kollektaneen von Johann Buxtorf I," 89-98. In: Joseph Prijs, *Die Handschriften der Universität Basel: Die hebräische Handschriften*. Ed. Bernhard and David Prijs. Basel: Verlag der Universitätsbibliothek, 1994.

Yaari, Abraham. "Complaints of Proofreaders about Printing by Gentiles on the Sabbath," 170-178 (Hebrew). In: Idem. *Studies in Hebrew Booklore*. Jerusalem: Talmudic Research Institute--Mossad Harav Kook, 1958.

Yardeni, Myriam. "The View of Jews and Judaism in the Works of Richard Simon," 179-203. In: Idem. *Anti-Jewish Mentalities in Early Modern Europe*. Studies in Judaism. Lanham, MD: University Press of America, 1990.

Zafren, Herbert C. "Variety in the Typography of Yiddish: 1535-1635." *Hebrew Union College Annual* 53 (1983): 137-163.

Zimmer, Eric. "Jewish and Christian Collaboration in Sixteenth Century Germany." *Jewish Quarterly Review* 71 (1980): 69-78.

_____. *Jewish Synods in Germany during the Late Middle Ages (1286-1603)*. New York: Yeshiva University Press, 1978.

Zürcher, Christoph. *Konrad Pellikans Wirken in Zürich, 1526-1556*. Zürcher Beiträge zur Reformationsgeschichte, Band 4. Zürich: Theologischer Verlag, 1975.

INDEX OF NAMES AND PLACES

SUBJECT INDEX

"superstitions," 77, 78; Talmud, role of, 58, 59, 61, 62, 63, 64, 68, 69, 75, 76, 78, 83, 85; theology of, 72, 91, 92, 98, 243

Kabbalah, 208

Latin Schools, 1, 4

Leipzig Book Fair, 198

Letter-writing, Hebrew, 136, 138-141, 143-145, 241; Latin, 135, 141, 143

Lutheran Theology, doctrine of Scripture, 237, 239

Masora, 122, 153, 168, 170, 171, 174, 193, 196, 201, 202, 217, 218, 221, 227, 228, 233, 240, 241, 242; mentioned in the Talmud, 221; printing and editing, 173, 190-193; schools of masoretes, 219, 220, 223, 232, 233; theories of origin, 225, 226, 230; witness to biblical text, 221, 222, 227

Midrash, 65, 70

Mishnah, 166, 208

New Testament Studies, 132

Persian Language, 208

Peshitta, 117

Philo, 146

Poetry, Greek and Latin meters, 146, 147; Hebrew, 135; Hebrew meters, 146-51; Hebrew occasional verse, 149, 151, 167, 241; Hebrew rhyme, 146, 149, 150, 151; neo-Latin verse, 135

Polemics, against Jews, 3, 57, 58, 61, 62, 73, 77, 79, 80-85, 89, 91, 95, 101, 131, 169, 206,

240, 243; between Christian confessions, 3, 34, 61, 62, 83, 169, 206, 209, 226, 230, 231, 236, 241

Polyglot Bibles, Antwerp polyglot, 129, 170, 175; London polyglot, 194, 238; Paris polyglot, 194, 238

Rabbinical Bibles, Basel edition, 28, 46, 48, 51, 97, 98, 130, 165, 171-176, 191, 194, 217, 242; Bomberg editions, 5, 123, 149, 156, 168, 169, 172, 174, 176, 188, 190, 233

Ramism, 8, 108-111, 132

Reformed Theology, doctrine of Scripture, 5, 168, 169, 202, 209, 214, 222, 239, 240; Formula of Consensus, 239; Heidelberg Catechism, 11 religious authority, 61, 62, 76, 100; Saumur theology, 238; Second Helvetian Confession, 62; Synod of Dordrecht, 21; vowel points, 203, 236-239

Regius professorships of Hebrew, 104

Republic of Letters, 3, 7, 27, 33

Samaritans, 211

Septuagint, 205, 211, 213, 222, 224, 226, 233, 234

Synod of Dordrecht, 21

Syriac, 116, 208

Talmud, Babylonian, 12, 47, 125, 131, 132, 212, 221-223, 240; Basel printing, 137, 142, 154; historical source, 211, 219; philological resource, 127,

Studies in the History
of Christian Thought

EDITED BY HEIKO A. OBERMAN

50. HOENEN, M. J. F. M. *Marsilius of Inghen*. Divine Knowledge in Late Medieval Thought. 1993
51. O'MALLEY, J. W., IZBICKI, T. M. and CHRISTIANSON, G. (eds.) *Humanity and Divinity in Renaissance and Reformation*. Essays in Honor of Charles Trinkaus. 1993
52. REEVE, A. (ed.) and SCREECH, M. A. (introd.) *Erasmus' Annotations on the New Testament*. Galatians to the Apocalypse. 1993
53. STUMP, Ph. H. *The Reforms of the Council of Constance (1414-1418)*. 1994
54. GIAKALIS, A. *Images of the Divine*. The Theology of Icons at the Seventh Ecumenical Council. With a Foreword by Henry Chadwick. 1994
55. NELLEN, H. J. M. and RABBIE, E. (eds.). *Hugo Grotius – Theologian*. Essays in Honour of G. H. M. Posthumus Meyjes. 1994
56. TRIGG, J. D. *Baptism in the Theology of Martin Luther*. 1994
57. JANSE, W. *Albert Hardenberg als Theologe*. Profil eines Bucer-Schülers. 1994
58. ASSELT, W.J. VAN. *The Covenant Theology of Johannes Cocceius (1603-1669)*. An Examination of its Structure. *In preparation*
59. SCHOOR, R.J.M. VAN DE. *The Irenical Theology of Théophile Brachet de La Milletière (1588-1665)*. 1995
60. STREHLE, S. *The Catholic Roots of the Protestant Gospel*. Encounter between the Middle Ages and the Reformation. 1995
61. BROWN, M.L. *Donne and the Politics of Conscience in Early Modern England*. 1995
62. SCREECH, M.A. (ed.). *Richard Mocket, Warden of All Souls College, Oxford, Doctrina et Politia Ecclesiae Anglicanae*. An Anglican Summa. Facsimile with Variants of the Text of 1617. Edited with an Introduction. 1995
63. SNOEK, G.J.C. *Medieval Piety from Relics to the Eucharist*. A Process of Mutual Interaction. 1995
64. PIXTON, P.B. *The German Episcopacy and the Implementation of the Decrees of the Fourth Lateran Council, 1216-1245*. Watchmen on the Tower. 1995
65. DOLNIKOWSKI, E.W. *Thomas Bradwardine: A View of Time and a Vision of Eternity in Fourteenth-Century Thought*. 1995
66. RABBIE, E. (ed.). *Hugo Grotius, Ordinum Hollandiae ac Westfrisiae Pietas (1613)*. Critical Edition with Translation and Commentary. 1995
67. HIRSH, J.C. *The Boundaries of Faith*. The Development and Transmission of Medieval Spirituality. 1996
68. BURNETT, S.G. *From Christian Hebraism to Jewish Studies*. Johannes Buxtorf (1564-1629) and Hebrew Learning in the Seventeenth Century. 1996
69. BOLAND O.P., V. *Ideas in God according to Saint Thomas Aquinas*. Sources and Synthesis. 1996
70. LANGE, M.E. *Telling Tears in the English Renaissance*. 1996
71. CHRISTIANSON, G. and T.M. IZBICKI (eds.) *Nicholas of Cusa on Christ and the Church*. Essays in Memory of Chandler McCuskey Brooks for the American Cusanus Scoiety. 1996

Prospectus available on request

E. J. BRILL — P.O.B. 9000 — 2300 PA LEIDEN — THE NETHERLANDS